The Basic Theory of Chinese Economy

Yanan Wang

The Basic Theory of Chinese Economy

商務印書館
SINCE 1897
The Commercial Press

Springer

Yanan Wang
Xiamen University
Xiamen, China

ISBN 978-981-95-6329-6 ISBN 978-981-95-6330-2 (eBook)
https://doi.org/10.1007/978-981-95-6330-2

Jointly published with The Commercial Press, Ltd.
The printed edition is not for sale in Mainland China. Customers from Mainland China please order the print book from The Commercial Press, Ltd.

This book is published with financial support from the Chinese Fund for the Humanities and Social Sciences.

This Springer imprint is published by the registered company Springer Nature Singapore Pte Ltd.
The registered company address is: 152 Beach Road, #21-01/04 Gateway East, Singapore 189721, Singapore

Contents

Part I
A General Introduction to the Study of the Chinese Economy

Abstract This chapter dissects the unique characteristics of China's commodity economy. While commodity exchange existed, production remained largely subordinate to pre-capitalist modes. The dominant economic form was a small-scale peasant economy integrated with household handicrafts, primarily producing for use-value rather than exchange-value. This defined its nature as "simple commodity" production. This constrained development manifested in a commodification process largely limited to the surplus extracted by landlords as rent, rather than widespread producer participation. Although a monetary economy emerged, it failed to fully dismantle the natural economy. Market relations were severely hampered by feudal localism, guild monopolies, and exorbitant transport costs. Consequently, commodity circulation remained limited, preventing the formation of a unified national market. Crucially, the development of China's commodity economy served to reinforce, rather than dissolve, the underlying feudal economic structure. This foundational difference is key to understanding why capital in China developed differently from the European model.

Chapter 1
Three Stages of Chinese Economic Research

It is only about a decade since the study of the Chinese economy was officially proposed and taken as a dedicated research object. While the achievements are still inadequate, they are commendable given the short time frame. Objectively speaking, the progress of this research has benefited from two key factors: the urgent demands of practice, and the clear picture of global social development history provided by the modern world. In fact, this latter factor—the general trend of world development—has tended to drive the former, both directly and indirectly.

Based on these core factors, Chinese economic research can be divided into three stages: the first covers the years around the Mukden Incident (September 18, 1931); the second spans the period before the Lugouqiao Incident (July 7, 1937); and the third began with the Chinese People's War of Resistance against Japanese Aggression(1937–1945) and continues to the present—it's the current phase of Chinese economic research. Let me share my observations on the characteristics and dynamics of each stage.

The first stage roughly covers the years around the Mukden Incident in September 1931. Why are these years significant for Chinese economic research? Well, it all ties back to the social and political upheaval of the era. Before the Northern Expedition(1926–1927), there were occasional discussions about the Chinese economy in academic circles, but the research was fragmented and scattered. Admittedly, the Manifesto of the First National Congress of the Kuomintang was the first document to outline the general characteristics of the Chinese economy. However, its theoretical basis—the Principle of People's Livelihood—focused more on positive aspirations and barely delved into the realistic economic foundations that this principle had to rely on.

Major changes occurred after the National Revolutionary Army (founded in August 1925 through the cooperation of the Kuomintang and the Communist Party to overthrow the reactionary rule of the Northern Warlords backed by capitalist powers) reached Wuhan and Nanjing. These changes demanded a theoretical re-examination of the direction of practice. Thanks to the ideological emancipation of

Y. Wang, *The Basic Theory of Chinese Economy*,
https://doi.org/10.1007/978-981-95-6330-2_1

the May fourth Movement(1919) and the limited but valuable knowledge of new social sciences gained in the early years of the Northern Expedition, these demands became increasingly clear.

Thus, questions about the nature of Chinese society and the study of the Chinese economy were formally raised. Many papers on the topic were published collectively in journals like New Thought and Reading Magazine. Examples include Wang Xuewen's Position of Capitalism in Chinese Economy—Its Development and Prospect, Pan Dongzhou's Nature of the Chinese Economy, Yan Lingfeng's Research on Chinese Economic Issues (mainly critiquing Wang and Pan's viewpoints), Ren Shu's Introduction to Chinese Economic Research, Liu Mengyun's Research on the Nature of the Chinese Economy (commenting on Yan and Ren's positions), Bo Hu's Nature of the Chinese Economy, and Liu Jingyuan's Reviews of Two Works on the Chinese Economy and Analysis of the Chinese Economy and Prediction of the Future. Nearly all these papers came out between 1929 and 1932, with their core focus on exploring the nature of the Chinese economy.

Wang and Pan argued that China's economy was semi-colonial and feudal, shaped by imperialist aggression—semi-feudal economic elements dominated, while Chinese capitalism and national industry were still in the early stage of capitalist light industry. Yan and Ren, however, held the opposite view. They insisted that China's economy was already capitalist—a prerequisite for their theoretical framework. They equated small-scale commodity production with capitalist commodity production, and foreign capital in China with Chinese national capital. For Yan, small Chinese enterprises and large foreign enterprises differed only in quantity, not quality—both represented capitalist forces. Ren believed that combining foreign capitalism (banks, factories, shops, mines, shipping, railways) and domestic capitalist elements was sufficient to crush feudalism and dominate national life.

Based on these assumptions, Yan and Ren claimed China had achieved an economic foundation comparable to Russia's before its revolution. Liu Jingyuan generally sided with them but questioned whether" capitalism" was the right term. He proposed a more moderate label:" backward capitalism." While the debate on China's economic nature didn't reach a final conclusion, it temporarily subsided—marking the end of what I call the first research stage.

Looking back, the most significant achievement of this stage wasn't solving problems, but raising them. It marked the starting point of scientific research on the nature of the Chinese economy. Today, rereading those papers, we can find many immature and superficial discussions, even though some sound propositions emerged. For example, the so-called"New Thought School"(as He Ganzhi labeled Wang Xuewen and others in his Debate on the Nature of Chinese Society) proposed that China's economy was"semi-colonial feudal under imperialist aggression"—a notion very close to the modern term"semi-colonial and semi-feudal economy,"differing only slightly in wording.

But from a theoretical perspective, their methodological flaws are noticeable. Both sides overly focused on footnote-style interpretations of terms like" capitalism,"" national capital,""semi-colony," and" feudal economy," often drawing shallow comparisons to surface-level phenomena of the Chinese economy. As a result, while they sought to grasp the essence of China's economy, their arguments only revealed fragmented and ambiguous insights. Moreover, their research was largely limited to urban industry—either criticizing it as an early capitalist stage dominated by feudalism or claiming it had developed into a capitalist phase controlling the entire economy. The vast rural economy, which underpins urban industry, received little attention—mainly because their interpretive methods couldn't support in-depth exploration in this area.

The second stage of research covers 1933 to 1937. This stage mainly built on or further explored the issues raised in the previous phase. As I noted earlier, research in the first stage was generally confined to the urban economy; now, the focus has largely shifted to the rural economy. Additionally, while the first stage centered on prominent aspects of the Chinese economy and the social science terminology needed to explain them, this stage dug deeper into China's economic nature and the methodologies for studying it.

How did research advance so rapidly in such a short time? On one hand, emerging social sciences spread quickly in Chinese academic circles around the Mukden Incident. On the other hand, research by Soviet and Japanese social scientists on China's economic and social nature, along with rural economic surveys conducted by domestic and international institutions (such as the Academia Sinica, the Peiping Social Survey Institute, University of Nanking, and the China International Famine Relief Commission), laid the groundwork for more in-depth studies.

For instance, the full agricultural survey report of Guangdong Province wasn't published until 1929; L. Madjar's The Agricultural Economy in China was drafted the same year and translated into Chinese in 1931; the Academia Sinica and the Peiping Social Survey Institute launched their survey work in 1930, with findings published continuously in subsequent years;J.L.Buck's Chinese Farm Economy also came out in 1930. These surveys, studies, and translated works were just preliminary steps—we need to further elaborate on the objective conditions of the time.

After the 1929 global Great Depression, China became an ideal target for capitalist powers to implement dumping policies. Domestic political turmoil, frequent wars, and natural disasters worsened the situation. Consequently, the fledgling national industries that had emerged during World War I—such as textiles, flour, and matches—were pushed to the brink of collapse one after another.

During this period, banking capital—which had flourished amid rural unrest and the concentration of financial resources in major cities—began to shift its focus from urban to rural areas. This gave rise to the slogan"Revival of the countryside."Funds that had been concentrated in cities through primitive accumulation were now poised to flow back to rural areas in the form of rural credit—a process known as the" Capital to the Countryside" movement, which began in 1933 (the 22nd year of the Republic of China). When the countryside gained special attention in practice, it inevitably became a topic of theoretical study.

At that time, rural economic research was mainly published in two journals: Chinese Economy, edited by Deng Feihuang, featuring discussions by Wang Yichang, Wang Yinjin, Wang Jingbo, Zhang Zhicheng, and others; and Rural Areas in China, published by the China Rural Economic Research Association, with contributions from Sun Yefang, Qian Junrui, Xue Muqiao, Tao Zhifu, and others. Chen Hansheng—who put forward insightful viewpoints on rural economic research—and Qian Jiaju—who later joined the economic debate—also belonged to this research community. Due to space constraints, I won't list their specific topics and arguments here.

In general, these two groups had certain connections to the opposing factions of the previous stage. The first group (represented by Wang Yichang) believed that China's rural economy was highly commercialized—both agricultural products and rural labor were significantly commercialized, and the rural economy was largely capitalist. The second group (represented by Sun Yefang) revised and accepted Wang and Pan's assertion that feudalism still dominated China.

Their debates expanded beyond core propositions to include research methodologies and the study of productive forces and relations of production (which define social nature). They also delved into specific economic categories like small-scale peasant economy, commodities, wage labor, and primitive markets. Setting aside the right and wrong of their arguments, it's clear that the content and methods of the debate made significant progress.

However, there were shortcomings: their methodological critiques seemed disconnected from the actual context of the Chinese economy (and rural economy in particular), and the various agricultural economic categories they discussed appeared isolated, lacking a coherent and comprehensive system. Therefore, our research on the Chinese economy needed to go further. We needed to adopt a rigorous methodology that integrates all economic phenomena—from urban to rural areas—into a unified system, thereby revealing the fundamental laws of motion and development trends. This was the mission we set out to accomplish in the third stage of Chinese economic research.

The third stage began with the July seventh Incident in 1937 and has lasted for seven to eight years—much longer than the previous two stages. Up to now, both subjective and objective conditions for research have been quite favorable. Subjectively, the achievements of the first two stages provide a solid foundation. Objectively, as the war progressed, the weak foundations of China's nascent industries could hardly be sustained.

Furthermore, the" Interior" under Kuomintang rule—once deemed capitalist by coastal urban experts—has now been fully exposed for what it truly is. Backward economic activities that have long plagued Chinese society—such as the operations of commercial capital, usurious capital, and land capital—force us to abandon any denial of feudal economic elements'dominant position. Reality clarifies human knowledge: unlike the previous two stages, there were no similar large-scale debates on Chinese economic research during the war.

But unfavorable factors for research still played a major role during the war. For instance, due to shortages of human and material resources, conducting studies was extremely difficult. Many long-standing journals—such as Rural Areas in China, Chinese Economy, and Food and Goods—gradually ceased publication. On the other hand, some journals thrived as if unaffected by these constraints. Economic research journals sprang up like mushrooms: almost all economic sectors—banking, finance, cooperatives, taxation, franchises, industrial mining, water conservancy, agriculture and forestry, and commerce—had their own representative publications.

Most of the discontinued journals (including authoritative ones like Review of Finance, Economic Report, and Financial Knowledge) shared a common flaw: articles discussing Chinese finance and economy treated China's weak economy equally with those of advanced modern societies, without restraint. Sometimes, writers would emphasize China's backward social and technological conditions; other times, they would recklessly ignore them. As a result, this research style never fully explored the true nature of the Chinese economy.

It is also worth noting that while these researchers never adequately grasped China's economic nature, they unconsciously regarded it as a capitalist commodity economy. This surrealistic research approach didn't originate during the war—though it prevailed then—just like the corrosive effects of commercial capital in China. We don't need to investigate how this style formed, but we should point out two key points.

Ninety percent of the economic theories applied to Chinese economic research originated from the Austrian School of Economics, which lacks a genuine historical context and thus treats all economic structures uniformly. (For detailed analysis, see Supplementary Theory 5: The Austrian School of Economics in Chinese Economic Circles.) Neither side in the earlier debate on China's economic nature paid much attention to the arguments of British-American School scholars (a later variant of the Austrian School born in Britain and America). This is partly because these scholars only focused on topics like currency and finance, with little understanding of China's real economic nature (e.g., Ma Yingchu's masterpiece Reconstruction of the Chinese economy). Additionally, those studying China's economic nature felt disconnected from the economies that British-American scholars based their theories on, so they could rarely engage with their discussions on China's economy.

As for why these scholars still play a leading role in today's economic research, the answer largely lies in realpolitik. We should also recognize a major reason: they too easily abandoned their research methods and superficial understanding of the Chinese economy from the debate era. On the one hand, they advocated the Principle of People's Livelihood as a guideline and national policy for regulating China's economic activities; on the other hand, they allowed this economic ideology—lacking historical and revolutionary character—to play a dominant role. In other words, the Austrian School, as a representative ideology of late capitalism, exerted a reactionary influence on countries needing to reform their socioeconomic organizations. This is rather strange—and even stranger is that no one ever pointed out this long-standing truth. (The aforementioned The Austrian School of Economics in Chinese Economic Circles includes a section specifically addressing how the Austrian School deviates from the Principle of People's Livelihood, from theory to practice.)

Based on the above explanation, we know there are two major tasks to accomplish in the current stage of Chinese economic research. In the negative respect, we must critique various theories that hinder understanding of the Chinese economy—especially the rampant merchant mentalities that parallel the excesses of commercial capital today. In the positive respect, we must rely on correct economic theories to adopt a progressive, comprehensive, and comparative approach, so as to discern the fundamental trends and rules of China's transitional economic nature.

Clearly, these two missions won't be easily accomplished. However, to arouse people's dedication to these goals, I'd like to propose a new concept:" Chinese Economics." I don't mean to establish a new school of thought—schools aren't created by merely coining a term. The" Chinese Economics" I propose is quite different from the" Chinese National Economics" that some economic theorists have emphasized recently. From a scientific research perspective, inserting" national" between" Chinese" and" economics" is too vague; it's hard to clearly define the research object of" Chinese National Economics." If it focuses on" techniques,""policies," and" economic guiding principles" rather than" science," it deviates from the starting point and procedures of the scientific research on the Chinese economy that I uphold.

Chapter 2
The Need for Scientific Chinese Economic Research in both Theory and Practice

Therefore, based on these factors, it is clear that deeper research on the Chinese economy leads to a better understanding of it. In the research process, knowledge of the positive aspects becomes clearer, while views on the negative aspects, whether consciously or unconsciously, often become more entrenched and misleading. This, in turn, complicates practical application. That is to say, with the advancement of knowledge, the broadening of perspectives, and enhanced research capacity, the task of researching the Chinese economy appears to become proportionally larger and more demanding.

In this chapter, I will explain why deeper and more systematic research on the Chinese economy is necessary, both in theory and in practice.

Theoretical discussion comes first.

Since the end of the nineteenth century, the scope of economic research has significantly expanded, evolving from a narrow to a broad sense. Economics in the narrow sense—as discussed in the previous chapter—focused on the commodity-money economy of modern capitalist society. In contrast, economics in the broad sense examines the economic forms of all societies, including capitalist ones. Over more than half a century, considerable achievements have been made in broad-sense economics. However, these findings have only laid the foundation for establishing broad-sense economics as an emerging science. Clearly, a long and complex journey remains before this field can be considered complete.

It is well-established that human society has progressed through a series of distinct historical periods, each characterized by unique socioeconomic foundations. In other words, these periods can be distinguished by their socioeconomic systems or structures. The commonly acknowledged historical periods are no longer described using vague and general terms like "ancient," "medieval," and "modern." Instead, they are now referred to as the eras of primitive, slave, feudal, capitalist, and socialist societies. While some scholars have reservations regarding the initial primitive era and the relationship between slavery and feudal serfdom, this classification is widely accepted by the majority.

Y. Wang, *The Basic Theory of Chinese Economy*,
https://doi.org/10.1007/978-981-95-6330-2_2

Given that human social development encompasses these five stages, and broad-sense economics aims to study all socioeconomic forms across these periods, it is incumbent upon economists to investigate the fundamental laws of change governing each. At this stage, I do not intend to elaborate on these fundamental laws; rather, I wish to highlight a key fact relevant to my research: the general tendency of historical development from simplicity to complexity. This trend is evident, but we must also find a scientific argument to illustrate it—namely, that earlier societies exhibited weaker social productive power used to sustain existence and overcome nature. If this holds true, we can posit that earlier stages of social development were more constrained by natural conditions. Even within the same historical period, societies exhibited notable differences.

Conversely, as society progresses, social productivity increases, and social structures become better at overcoming constraints like climate, terrain, and race. From this, we can infer that the gap between capitalist societies (A and B) with high productivity is narrower than that between feudal societies (C and D) with lower productivity. In other words, two capitalist societies display a greater degree of homogeneity than two feudal societies. For instance, the discrepancies between the capitalist systems of the United States, Britain, and Japan are less pronounced than the divergences between European and Asian feudal systems. Meanwhile, the economic structures of slavery in ancient Greece/Rome and the East appear more divergent than feudal economic forms in the West and East. Ultimately, advances in productivity have narrowed the gaps between different societies. Increased productivity has amplified mutual influence among countries and fostered a degree of global uniformity.

These observations may seem novel, but they are not my invention. This study aims to integrate and systematize fragmented arguments concerning modern economic history. (For specifics, see my book, Natural Forces and Social Productivity).

The connection between these ideas and our topic may not be immediately clear. First, we must recognize that the challenge in understanding broad-sense economics stems from its vast scope, which includes not only capitalist economies but also the diverse systems that preceded and may succeed it. Setting aside post-capitalist societies, we see that in pre-capitalist periods, the further back we go, the greater the differences between nations at the same developmental stage. Although the economic phenomena of these earlier societies become simpler further back in time, deriving general laws becomes increasingly difficult due to the significant variations these societies exhibited under different geographical and natural conditions, even within the same historical stage.

For example, while the basic tenets of feudalism have been largely delineated globally, they are insufficient for a comprehensive socio-economic explanation of this historical era within a broad-sense economics framework. China's feudal economic model is highly specific within the global context. Moreover, it endured over a vast territory for an exceptionally long time. A detailed examination of the original form of China's feudal system, including its modern elements, would significantly contribute to and enhance broad-sense economics.

What were the objective social conditions in a semi-feudal China with backward agriculture? While feudalism is typically characterized by a focus on agricultural life and a natural economy, the reasons why Chinese peasants were subjected to feudal pressures are complex and multifaceted. The following passage provides some enlightening explanations for understanding this complicated issue.

"Due to different historical conditions, the developmental sectors in the countries with underdeveloped commodity economies are quite different. In these still united feudal domains, which once got connected with advanced capitalist countries, marketing relationships immediately came into being. Therefore, the production with the purpose of marketing grew up in the resurrection of hard labor and the reestablishment of serfdom. The combination of feudal domains adopting serfdom with early capitalist relations is not a sign of progress. This combination merely indicates the stagnation and backwardness of the economic production in countries where capitalism is underdeveloped and serfdom has been reestablished. (Such as Russia, Germany, Poland and Romania)." This is what Ivan Mikhailovich Leher, a Soviet scholar, wrote in his book *A History of Pre-capitalist Society,* about the complex economic conditions in Russia, Germany, Poland, and Romania after they connected themselves with capitalism in the 18th and 19th centuries. Although this kind of explanation can help people to understand the nature of the Chinese economy, it is far from being adequate. It may greatly contribute to the establishment of the so-called "broad-sense economics," but, if it conducts a systematic and scientific study into the Chinese economy, then not only the broad-sense economics but also the history of economics will embark upon a new chapter.

However, each new academic achievement, while significant in theory, must be scrutinized for its practical implications for economic reform. The case of China is particularly instructive. Soon after contact with Western European capitalist powers, China began advocating "renewal," "reform," and "construction." For instance, following the upheavals like the Taiping Rebellion (1851–1864), influential figures such as Zeng Guofan and Li Hongzhang initiated efforts to emulate foreign methods, establishing manufacturers for military supplies—a policy later championed by Zhang Zhidong and broader circles.

Over approximately three-quarters of a century, Chinese society underwent certain changes, yet these transformations often bore little relation to, and sometimes even contradicted, the professed goals of fundamental "renewal" and "reform." Society remained deeply entrenched in traditions perpetuated over millennia.

How should we interpret this phenomenon? While external pressures certainly played a role, this explanation is insufficient. A glance at modern history reveals that other late-developing nations, such as Germany, the United States, Japan, and Russia, also faced external constraints during their modernization, yet achieved significant reforms.

Attributing China's stalled modernization solely to external forces, though partially valid regarding the oppression suffered, risks obscuring other critical, internal factors that hindered progress. After nearly a century of reform efforts, it appears that our compatriots, across the political and academic spectrum, have often lacked a clear grasp of the essential paths for national transformation.

In this context, Dr. Sun Yat-sen's Principle of People's Livelihood provided a crucial theoretical direction for economic reform. Its introduction highlighted that earlier measures—establishing factories, building railways and ships—had failed to address the fundamental issues requiring societal renewal.

A pressing question arises: why has Sun Yat-sen's principle long remained largely theoretical? Among many reasons, one pertinent to our research is the enduring influence of China's specific socioeconomic forms. The same feudal economic structure that constrained the reform consciousness of figures like Li Hongzhang and Zhang Zhidong likely continued to impede later political and economic theorists, even after the Principle of People's Livelihood was advanced.

China's feudal economy possessed a unique characteristic that often led to theoretical confusion. Unlike the feudal lord economy prevalent elsewhere, where land was hereditary and labor bound, China developed a landlord economy where land could generally be bought and sold, and labor was relatively free to transfer.

These conditions—free transfer of land and labor—are, in theory, the fundamental prerequisites for a capitalist commodity economy. In a typical capitalist society, the commodification of factors of production is essential for capital accumulation, profit calculation, and the establishment of modern economic relations like rent and wages. Normally, transitioning to capitalism requires land reform to liberate these very factors from feudal restraints.

Paradoxically, China's feudal system, with its apparent preconditions of free land and labor transfer, seemed theoretically predisposed to capitalism, potentially obviating the need for extensive land reform.

This superficial modernity misled early reformers. Figures like Li Hongzhang and Zhang Zhidong attempted to implant modern economic structures without altering the underlying social system. Even later proponents of the People's Livelihood principle, when faced with practical challenges, often prioritized short-term "convenience and cheapness," effectively setting aside fundamental socioeconomic transformation. This cannot be simply attributed to a lack of belief in the principle. Rather, the deceptive nature of China's feudal system was a significant obstacle. It appeared feudal yet exhibited features resembling capitalist prerequisites. This misleading outward appearance likely contributed to a lack of profound, scientific analysis of the Chinese economy's essence.

Critically, the "freedom" of land and labor under Chinese feudalism was distinct from that required by capitalism. It was a feudal-level freedom, not the institutionalized, capitalist freedom necessary for robust and sustained capitalist development. Despite its superficial progressiveness, the system remained fundamentally feudal, and beneath the guise of this "freedom," numerous elements actively obstructed the emergence and maturation of capitalism.

Many past reform efforts faltered because they were based on an intuitive grasp of the Chinese economy's surface phenomena rather than a scientific analysis of its essence. This deep-seated habit of isolating reforms from the underlying socioeconomic reality led to confused and chaotic practical steps. Therefore, strengthening the scientific study of the Chinese economy is not just an academic exercise but a necessary corrective to the missteps born of an unclear understanding.

Chapter 3
Scientific Foundations and Methods of Research on Chinese Economy

3.1 Scientific Foundations

The above discussion may be seen as having outlined the scientific foundations for research on the Chinese economy. In reality, whatever aspect of the Chinese economy we focus on, scientific inquiry is bound to involve—directly or indirectly—a multitude of disciplines. Yet if my aim in raising this issue were only to emphasize such an obvious point, the discussion would become unnecessarily verbose.

At the present stage, inspired by emerging scientific developments and driven by the practical needs of society, research on the Chinese economy is certain to yield substantial results. It will undoubtedly help remove obstacles that have long obscured a clear understanding of the economy's true nature. Still, in many domains and on many occasions, Chinese academic inquiry lags far behind real-world practice. Besides the influence of material interests, this gap also stems from a general underestimation of the preparatory work required for the study of the Chinese economy.

I shall refrain for now from elaborating on what exactly such preparation entails or how it should be carried out. Instead, I will first discuss three academic disciplines that must be thoroughly understood in order to conduct meaningful research on the Chinese economy.

3.1.1 Economics

It is evident that the study of the Chinese economy must be grounded in economics—including its general principles and various established conclusions. In practice, learning economics often means using economic theory to indirectly comprehend the real-world phenomena it reflects. When we examine the theories of Adam Smith

Y. Wang, *The Basic Theory of Chinese Economy*,
https://doi.org/10.1007/978-981-95-6330-2_3

or David Ricardo, for example, we are also examining the British economic reality at the turn of the 18th and 19th centuries on which their theories were based.

Yet while economic theories generalize concrete phenomena and reflect economic realities, it is their conclusions and core concepts that people primarily use to identify and make sense of corresponding economic situations.

Naturally, it is reasonable to use British—or more broadly, Western—capitalist principles to interpret or validate general capitalist economies. But a problem arises when such rules are applied to China's transitional economic forms, which are neither fully capitalist nor free of pre-capitalist elements. Strictly speaking, capitalist economics is not entirely applicable to the Chinese economy. Still, it ought to apply at least to that part of the Chinese economy that is already capitalist in nature. Even if we cannot affirm in positive terms what that part is, we can at least clarify what it is not. In this limited sense, capitalist economics does help us understand the Chinese economy to some extent.

But we cannot rely solely on such a mechanical approach.

Capitalist economics itself is not a unified system. The type of economics that offers even partial insight into China is largely confined to early capitalist ideology—from a period when the bourgeoisie still sided with producers and innovators seeking liberation from feudal constraints. The economic theories of that era reflected the basic dynamics of capitalism and can partly explain China's economy during its own incipient capitalist phase.

By contrast, the mainstream capitalist economics of later periods struggles to illuminate the complex economic forms of Chinese society. Rather than reflecting China's socio-economic reality, it often obscures its true nature, as economists of that stage were not encouraged by capital to expose the fundamental crises of capitalist society.

Take the Austrian School, often regarded as the pinnacle of mainstream economics. Interestingly, as the world economy sinks deeper into crisis, this school's theories appear ever more vibrant and prosperous. In capitalist countries, such theories—tailored to the consumption habits of the leisure class—help mask harsh realities. They are especially influential in underdeveloped regions where capitalism thrives parasitically, preventing people from seeing beyond a veneer of prosperity to the real causes of their economic hardship.

We might say that the export of classical enlightened ideology reflected the naivety of advanced capitalist societies in the era of commodity export, while the export of rebellious yet ultra-conservative ideology reveals the pretentiousness of the capital-export era. Meanwhile, China's comprador economy, increasingly detached from any thirst for political reform and prosperity, now and then contents itself with idle talk and muddling through. All this shows how deeply the theories of a consumer economy have poisoned public understanding, shrouding the real nature of our national economy.

Yet amid this fog, another perspective within Chinese academic circles is steadily gaining clarity. In economics, more people have come to recognize that progressive and critical economics should replace the conservative, ahistorical economics of the wealthy leisure class.

Why is critical economics especially valuable for studying the Chinese economy? I see three main reasons.

First, critical economics inherits the legacy of classical economic theory, which helps us understand not only the capitalist economy itself and its operating rules, but also the historical development and inherent sufferings of capitalism, since these theories emerged in capitalism's early years.

Second, critical economics takes the whole of history and existing capitalist economic theories as its objects of research and critique. Its most vital insight—serving also as a warning—is its revelation that as capitalism approaches a transitional period, it is bound to intensify imperialist policies, with people in underdeveloped areas becoming the primary victims. Applying critical economics to the study of the Chinese economy can help prevent us from being trapped in the maze of cultural aggression consciousness.

Finally, it embodies the essence of new logical theories, emphasizing qualitative change and the role of negation in social development. In other words, this type of economics, imbued with a philosophical spirit, teaches us that no matter how many revolutionary or progressive economic or technological elements are introduced, they can hardly take root until a society's old fundamental production relations have undergone qualitative change or have been negated.

That said, simply knowing a few formulas or terms of critical economics will not help nearly as much as some imagine. Mechanical formalists keep people just as isolated from a real understanding of the Chinese economy as do scholars who specialize in popular economics. It is both ironic and troubling that, on the one hand, some users of critical economics still simplistically treat the Chinese economy as a capitalist commodity economy, while on the other hand, popular economics cites classical texts to claim that China is already a capitalist society with a full-fledged commodity economy.

As a more developed science than conventional capitalist economics, critical economics must be thoroughly understood, critically digested, and then applied in light of China's actual conditions.

3.1.2 The History of Economic Study

The modern study of economic history emerged long after economics was established as a discipline. Strictly speaking, its development was spurred by—or intellectually imported from—critical economics. Since the capitalist economy, as the primary object of economic inquiry, represents a more developed form of economic organization, scholars began to identify general economic laws and also came to recognize that earlier socioeconomic formations equally possessed their own internal rules. Moreover, it became accepted that there exist principles governing the transition from one socioeconomic form to another.

Today, the distinction between the study of economic history and broad-sense economics is often overlooked or poorly articulated. In simple terms, broad-sense economics emphasizes the general principles and economic rules governing each historical society, whereas economic history focuses on historical realities and the concrete economic dynamics underlying successive societal transitions.

In their early stages, the two fields were closely intertwined. For the purpose of studying the economic formations of less developed societies, it suffices to acknowledge that both disciplines offer valuable insights. That said, economic history has since established itself as a relatively autonomous and methodologically mature science.

Originally, critical economics was designed to expose the inner laws of capitalist economics in line with a historical vision. It tends to focus more on where capitalism is headed than on its historical origins. Yet, for researching a transitional economy like China's—and understanding the historical trajectory of its predecessor, Chinese feudal society—precisely this historical dimension demands special attention. Under such requirements, our research must learn from or directly draw upon the strengths of economic history from the very outset.

First, economic history, by drawing on information from inevitable stages of historical development, helps identify the specific stage of historical development the Chinese economy has reached and the nature of its current foundations.

Second, through the general historical principles it has substantiated, this field shows what economic laws should govern China's present stage of development—in other words, the inevitable direction in which its economy is bound to evolve.

Third, it also reveals that historical principles are not as convoluted and manifold as historical realities themselves; it confirms that societies sharing the same economic base and level of development can exhibit vastly different empirical phenomena.

Furthermore, economic history demonstrates that there is no uniform path for the transition from feudalism to capitalism, given the diverse social conditions different societies face.

However, its greatest "kindness" to subjective human effort lies only in indicating that the time and suffering associated with necessary historical stages may be shortened—not wholly overcome or avoided. It firmly rejects the view that the old society can be negated or abandoned before a new one is fully constituted.

For those engaged in studying the Chinese economy, these insights are initially derived from a general engagement with economic history. It is through the accumulation of such diverse historical understanding that they can avoid the fallacy of treating the Chinese economy as a malleable entity that can be arbitrarily shaped, disguised, or manipulated to fit preconceived outcomes.

3.1.3 The History of the Chinese Economy

It is evident that the study of Chinese economic history has been profoundly shaped by, and has actively drawn upon, the theories and methodologies of modern economic history as a discipline. Although research on China's economic history remains a relatively young field, scholarly efforts over the past two decades—both within China and internationally—have substantially advanced our understanding of the Chinese economy. Early inquiries into China's socioeconomic history primarily sought to answer foundational questions regarding the nature of modern Chinese society. As previously discussed, the subsequent debate on the character of Chinese society naturally stimulated a parallel discourse on the nature of Chinese social history. It was within the context of these scholarly exchanges, and aided by the broader study of economic history, that the field of Chinese economic history gradually emerged and developed.

Research grounded in the factual record of China's socioeconomic development and the principles of historical analysis has since provided explanations for many economic phenomena that were once elusive or misunderstood. For instance, various economic forms—such as the landlord economy, wage labor relationships, and merchant capital—which often bore a deceptive resemblance to capitalist institutions, as well as state and bureaucratic enterprises that presented an appearance of a regulated economy, have become more intelligible. These "public" economic forms, as they were termed, previously caused significant misunderstandings and obstacles in comprehending the true nature of the Chinese economy.

By applying the fundamental principles and conceptual frameworks derived from the general study of economic history, scholars have increasingly identified these phenomena as specific manifestations of the unique character of China's feudal economy. Some represented intensified forms influenced by the modern capitalist economy, while others were illusions pervasive in earlier interpretations of China's economy.

Consequently, it is imperative that research on the Chinese economy duly acknowledges the direct and indirect assistance offered by Chinese economic history, a discipline that is still evolving but already indispensable.

3.2 Methods Adopted

As a matter of fact, the several sciences upon which the research on Chinese economy should be based have implied or regulated the methods people should adopt for the research. To be lucid and specific, this book would like to briefly explain the following three methods.

3.2.1 Comparative Research Method

It is generally acknowledged that research on the Chinese economy often applies methods developed for the study of general economic principles—though such approaches carry even greater significance when tailored specifically to China's context.

What may seem puzzling, however, is that when studying the Chinese economy or its particular forms, many researchers choose to begin by examining economic systems that are either opposite to or more advanced than China's, rather than addressing the Chinese case directly. At first glance, this preference might be attributed to explanatory convenience. Yet on closer inspection, it stems largely from the fact that we still lack the conceptual tools to define the Chinese economy in its own terms.

Why is this the case?

It is well understood that analyzing real-world economies requires the use of established economic principles or foundational concepts. When such principles have not yet been clearly articulated for a specific economic reality—or when reliable theoretical foundations are absent—we often have no choice but to resort to metaphor or comparison.

This explains why researchers frequently turn to economic forms that historically coexisted with or preceded the economy under study, and whose operating rules are already well-documented. These can serve as a baseline for statistical or conceptual comparison.

Take, for example, the economic system of the Soviet Union, which stood in clear opposition to capitalism. If one were to explain or define specific phenomena in the Soviet economy—such as its concepts of currency, wages, or credit—using laws or categories derived from capitalist economics, the result would be deeply misleading. Despite this inherent limitation, examining comparable concepts or rules under capitalism offers a practical, if imperfect, way to highlight differences and clarify the unique logic of the Soviet system. This is why comparative methods have so often been used in studies of Soviet monetary policy, credit mechanisms, and wage structures.

The same logical constraint applies to the study of the Chinese economy. Just as the Soviet economy could not be adequately interpreted through the lens of more developed capitalist principles, the Chinese economy—which historically lagged behind capitalist systems—cannot be fully grasped using the same external framework. In the case of the Soviet Union, even as it was developing its own economic laws, it still required comparative reference to capitalist principles in order to illuminate its unique structure and dynamics. Similarly, in the case of China, sub-disciplines such as broad-sense economics and economic history remain relatively underdeveloped. Therefore, to identify and verify the specific principles governing the Chinese economy, scholars still need to engage in comparative observation of capitalist economic laws.

Moreover, while capitalist elements in the Soviet economy were progressively negated and abandoned—though never completely eradicated—in China, such factors have continued to exert a growing influence, even as they undergo qualitative transformation. Given these parallel yet divergent trajectories, it remains intellectually necessary to use the capitalist economy as a key reference point in comparative study.

3.2.2 Comprehensive Research Method

It is evident that a comprehensive research method, such as the comparative approach previously discussed, should not be applied merely in its intuitive or commonly understood sense—that is, as a simple shift from an isolated to a holistic perspective, which in itself requires little elaboration. Indeed, many scholars in the field of economic studies claim to examine the Chinese economy within the global context and to analyze its various sectors as integral parts of an organic whole. Yet, despite such methodological posturing, their discussions and research outcomes often remain superficial, failing to grasp the essential nature of the Chinese economy. The root of this shortcoming may lie in their ability to distinguish only between partial and comprehensive representations of the economy, without possessing the means to decipher the underlying essence. To achieve genuine understanding, it is necessary to genuinely adopt not only the comparative method but also a progressive research approach—to which we shall return later—in order to meaningfully compare and interpret the Chinese economy.

No one can reasonably deny that the Chinese economy is continuously influenced by global economic dynamics, particularly those of the capitalist world. Likewise, it is indisputable that the world economy is, directly or indirectly, affected by changes within China. However, to prevent analysis from becoming generalized, ambiguous, or marginal, and to accurately capture the actual interactions at play, researchers must employ a comprehensive research method to investigate issues in their entirety rather than in fragments. This entails probing into the complete system of interactions to uncover the specific mechanisms that generate differential effects. For example, to understand the global capitalist economy that impinges on China, we must study it as an integrated system. Only by grasping its periodic crises, its law of uneven development, its inevitable tendency from free competition to monopoly, its shift from commodity export to capital export, and the evolution of its expansionist colonial policies into more subtle forms of containment, can we comprehend how it concretely impacts China's national economy.

At the same time, different sectors or fields within the Chinese economy—which together constitute the whole—exhibit varying degrees of capitalization and modernization in response to international influences. This variation stems from their divergent levels of dependence on international capital, their extent of integration into global commodity and financial markets, and the resilience of their underlying traditional social organizations. It is evident, for instance, that under the same influence of international capital, the logistics sector is often more significantly affected than the production sector proper; within production, industry is more readily transformed than agriculture; and within agriculture, the impact on markets and finance is greater than on land tenure and use patterns.

If the comprehensive research method fails to identify and focus on these critical differential points, then the invoked "whole" global economy, the "whole" Chinese economy, and the "whole" of their interaction risk becoming empty abstractions, devoid of explanatory power.

3.2.3 Progressive Research Method

The progressive research method is indeed indispensable for applying the aforementioned sciences to the study of the Chinese economy. It may appear that critical economics, alongside the study of economic history and the history of the Chinese economy, naturally lends itself to this progressive approach. However, two pivotal points require further elaboration.

First, rigorous research on the modern Chinese economy must systematically account for traditional feudal economic factors. It is therefore understandable when some critics question the relevance of such historical inquiry or conflate it purely with economic history. While the feudal economies of Europe have been extensively studied, yielding universally accepted conclusions, the role of China's traditional feudal factors is far from being a settled matter. If these factors were merely peripheral in the modern Chinese economy, perhaps a superficial understanding would suffice. Yet, the reality is that the traditional economy not only remains profoundly significant but also lacks a scholarly consensus on its defining historical characteristics. For a China in transition, the debate on the nature of its society is intrinsically linked to, and a prerequisite for, the debate on its social history.

Similarly, in a world undergoing transformation, this underscores why general economics must be integrated with the study of economic history to be truly effective.

Second, while scientific inquiry strives for simplicity in its objects of study, the Chinese economy presents a case of exceptional complexity. This simplicity is typically found in societies with a uniform socioeconomic base and consistent relations of production. In a mature capitalist society, for instance, where feudal remnants have been largely eradicated and socialist elements are not yet emergent, the economic phenomena, however developed, are fundamentally homogeneous under the capitalist framework. In stark contrast, a transitional society like China's, while perhaps less developed in scale, exhibits a far more intricate tapestry. Its economic fabric is woven with diverse factors from various historical stages, particularly feudalism, which coexist, resist, and adapt in relation to capitalist elements.

The dynamics of such a society must be deciphered precisely through these interactions of constraint and adaptation. Consequently, understanding the peculiarities of the feudal system is not merely a preliminary step but an essential component of the research object itself.

The central aim is to identify the rules and tendencies governing an economy where a strong feudal composition obstructs capitalist development, and where new and old forces struggle amidst growth and decline. Since the Opium War, China's path to economic modernization has been fraught with twists and setbacks. Despite this, a clear historical trend that outlines its current panorama and future direction remains elusive.

To ground these abstract arguments in a concrete example, one might consider the conspicuous expansion of commercial capital during the Anti-Japanese War. This expansion seemed to defy societal censure and restrictions, even transforming associated activities in production, banking, and relief into commercial ventures. The nationwide clamor to suppress commerce ultimately proved powerless. A primary reason for this failure was the tendency to analyze commerce in isolation, detached from its social foundations and historical traditions.

Scholars often overlooked that even before the war, a comprador-oriented commercial system was already hindering modernization and industrialization. Its corrosive influence on various sectors was essentially an expansion of its traditional operational logic.

Therefore, analyzing commercial phenomena in isolation leads to limited understanding. A more effective approach involves first comprehending the unique commercial forms under China's feudal system, then examining their evolution after adopting comprador characteristics.

To thoroughly understand the nature of Chinese commercial capital, it is essential to compare it with capitalist commerce, consider its relationship with the broader social economy, and contextualize it within its historical traditions.

These three research approaches are most powerful when combined, especially in studying the Chinese economy as a whole.

Issues discussed in this section

1. Why do people propose to discuss the nature of Chinese society?
2. What is the essential difference between the research at the first stage and that at the second stage? What are the relationships between the opposing opinions at the previous stage and those at the following stage?
3. Why does the debate on the nature of Chinese society lead to that on the nature of Chinese social history?
4. Why is there difficulty in establishing the Broad-sense Economics?
5. In the developmental history of human society, there is a basic rule that more advanced productivity will correspondingly reduce or weaken the natural particularities among nations and societies. What can we apply this rule to interpret?
6. How does the research on Chinese economic principles and laws benefit the study of Economic History or General Economics?
7. As current proposals for industrial construction seem to mirror those put forward by Li Hongzhang and Zhang Zhidong, etc., how can people avoid repeating their mistakes?
8. Is it feasible to study the Chinese economy according to the principles and methods of the Popular Economics?
9. What are the differences between the several research methods proposed in this part and general research methods?

Part II
Chinese Commodities and Its Forms of Value

Abstract This chapter focuses on the chaotic and backward state of China's monetary system. Its core feature was the co-existence of multiple monetary standards (silver taels, silver dollars, copper coins) alongside countless local and private coinages and paper notes, lacking a unified, stable, state-backed modern currency system. This disorder stemmed from general economic backwardness and political fragmentation. Silver, as the primary standard, was highly vulnerable to fluctuations in the world market price, denying China a stable domestic price mechanism. The currency's dysfunctional nature—its unreliable unit of account, constrained medium of exchange, hampered means of payment, and preference for metallic hoarding—severely hindered commercial development, capital calculation and accumulation, and the establishment of credit systems. This archaic monetary form was both a symptom of underdevelopment and a primary cause hindering the evolution of capitalist production relations.

Chapter 4
Forms of Chinese Commodities

4.1 Commodities as an Economic Form of History

It is evident that commodities have served as a fundamental economic form throughout history. A commodity emerges as the outcome of product development, and when one examines the entire process through which a product—no matter how simple—is developed, or its hidden nature as revealed in basic commodity exchange, it becomes clear that commodities depend on specific social relations for their existence. Not only do commodities reflect concrete social relations, but they also offer a means to measure a society's productivity through the very manner of their formation.

A commodity evolves through several stages, from its initial emergence in simple exchange to its most advanced forms. At each stage of economic development, a commodity possesses distinct qualities and embodies different social relations of production.

Within the same society, commodities from different historical stages of economic development can coexist. If a society distinctly differs from others in its historical stage, or has largely completed a specific phase of development, the dominant modes of production in that society can be identified with little controversy. For example, since Britain is a capitalist society, there is no need to preliminarily study the forms of goods or commodities produced within it to determine its dominant economic character.

By contrast, during the sixteenth and seventeenth centuries, when Britain was transitioning from feudalism to capitalism, the forms of commodity production were far more complex. The coexistence of diverse commodity types made it difficult to distinguish which played the overriding role—that is, which form was dominant.

China has found itself in a similar situation for many years. The debate regarding the nature of Chinese society has not yet been fully resolved. Consequently, among the various commodity forms present today, deciding which type of commodity—or which commodities produced under specific conditions—should be taken as representative of Chinese society remains unsettled. Perhaps the ongoing debate stems

Y. Wang, *The Basic Theory of Chinese Economy*,
https://doi.org/10.1007/978-981-95-6330-2_4

from the fact that the issue of fundamental and decisive commodity forms has been mentioned only by a few scholars and has not been thoroughly discussed, even when considered.

4.2 Commodity Specimen to Identify Chinese Society

A product in society is seldom intended solely for the producer's own consumption; rather, it is generally produced with the aim of being sold to others. This sale serves a dual purpose: first, to acquire other goods the producer requires, and second, to realize a monetary value exceeding the cost of production. In any case, products enter circulation, and while their physical attributes may remain unchanged, their social properties are transformed. The product becomes a commodity—a transition akin to the passage from girlhood to womanhood upon marriage.

When a product is turned into a commodity, it assumes an opposed social character. In a natural economy or one with minimal division of labor, producers manufacture items predominantly for their own use. As products increasingly become commodities, society correspondingly sheds its natural economic traits. This is a prolonged process. Even in a highly developed capitalist society, remnants of the natural economy may persist. In vast rural regions of a country like China, particularly in remote and underdeveloped areas, natural economy elements may still play a significant quantitative role, despite the lack of precise statistics to determine the exact proportions of natural versus commodity economy.

Clearly, even if accurate data were available showing that only a small fraction of products in Chinese society have been commodified, with the rest retaining a natural economy character, it would be incorrect to conclude that China remains a natural economy society. The issue is not solely quantitative but qualitative—it hinges on which form plays the dominant role in society as a whole.

In fact, the question regarding the economic nature of contemporary Chinese society is no longer whether the commodity component surpasses the natural economy component. Rather, it is whether the dominant commodity itself takes the form of pre-capitalist small-scale commodity production or capitalist commodity production.

Commodities entering circulation carry varied social characteristics, derived from the different aims and conditions of their production and exchange. If the majority of products are exchanged solely to obtain other goods for the producer's use—a practice known as selling in order to buy—this mode applies to independent producers who work with their own tools and labor. The commodity production of these producers, such as artisans or small peasants, is constrained by their relations of production, simple tools, unsystematic methods, and low productivity, limiting it to a narrow scope and small scale. Accordingly, this is termed "simple" or "small-scale commodity production." As it historically preceded capitalist society, it is also called pre-capitalist commodity production.

In contrast, capitalist commodity production, though rooted in small-scale production, exhibits markedly different traits. A key defining condition is that all inputs—including means of production and labor power—are purchased as commodities, and all outputs are sold as commodities. The underlying logic is buying in order to sell. This form of production applies where direct producers, separated from the means of production, are employed by the owners of those means, who also control the products.

Despite major differences, both small-scale and capitalist commodity production share a basic similarity: their existence presupposes private ownership of the means of production. The owner of the means of production is also the owner of the products. It is this shared feature that leads some to conflate the two, mistaking small-scale commodity production for capitalist commodity production—especially in a transitional society where both forms coexist, at times within the same industry or even enterprise. When this misunderstanding is applied to the nature of Chinese society, it inevitably gives rise to unnecessary controversies.

Evidently, small-scale commodity production is a multifaceted phenomenon. In terms of its private ownership form, it may appear as an incipient stage of capitalism. Yet, viewed through its production method—based on the producer's own tools and labor—it can be seen as anti-capitalist. If small-scale production is regarded as capitalist, then the capitalist sector in the modern Chinese economy might be considered significant. However, from the latter perspective, small-scale production remains intertwined with local self-sufficiency and feudal remnants. Moreover, the absence of historical prerequisites for capitalism hinders its potential to develop into a capitalist sector. Despite cyclical destruction and regeneration, small-scale commodity production cannot, in theory, spontaneously lead to capitalist economic sectors.

What follows is a concrete analysis of the characteristics of Chinese commodities before further explanations are offered.

4.3 Classifications of Chinese Commodities

The most common products circulating as commodities in our markets today are, without a doubt, industrial and agricultural goods. Following these are more specialized commodities, such as land and labour power. In this discussion, I will focus on the first two categories as they are classified within China's commodity economy, though we will touch upon the latter two for the sake of a more complete picture. This specific focus is also why, in this study, Chinese commodities and their values are often examined as distinct entities.

Now, from a social perspective, land and labour power as commodities are intrinsically linked to basic industrial and agricultural products. Put simply, active trading of land often stimulates the commodification of labour, and vice versa. Similarly, a vibrant trade in labour can help clarify the commodity nature of industrial and agricultural outputs. However, this relationship depends heavily on the specific conditions under which land and labour are traded, and the social relations that allow labour power itself to become a commodity.

When these specific social conditions are absent, the commercialization of land or labour may not lead to a capitalist character for industrial and agricultural products—a reality clearly evidenced by the specific nature of the Chinese economy.

Let me first address industrial products.

Generally, capitalist production methods tend to appear first in industry before spreading to agriculture. China's industrial output comes mainly from four sources: independent handicrafts, household industry, manufacturing industry, and factory-based industry (we'll set aside their intricate relationships for now). For the moment, I won't delve into the incomplete or mixed capitalist nature of large-scale factory products—what we might call their "quality." Instead, let's proceed by assuming they are standard capitalist commodities and focus our examination on their "quantity".

It is well-known that the most developed sector in modern Chinese industry is textiles. Take 1927, for instance, when handicraft products accounted for about 65% to 75% of the national consumption of cotton fabrics.

While some of these handicrafts originated from rural household industries or urban artisan workshops, a significant portion located near large cities had begun to change their traditional forms. Some had even become integrated into factory production or supply chains, having "already become part of factories, manufacturing plants, or the external production segments of warehouses".

If we consider the influence of merchant capital, which reorganised many household industries for manufacturing, the products of this manufacturing sector actually constitute a major part of our total industrial output. Items like straw hats, fans, embroidery, textiles, pottery, and toys were often produced by household industries under the direction of merchant capital.

Given the overwhelming importance of this manufacturing industry, we can only truly understand the nature of industrial products by first understanding the nature of this sector. In terms of scale, it represents an expansion of handicraft production. However, because it still largely relies on outdated methods to extract surplus labour from direct producers, its character is transitional, positioned between small-scale commodity production and large-scale industry.

This form, while long-present in China, has developed significantly in modern times, especially in recent decades.

Why such huge development? The reasons are rooted in China's economic backwardness and dependency.

For example, this manufacturing industry requires little capital and simple tools, making it suitable for conditions where capital accumulation is insufficient. Furthermore, the surplus labour created by the influx of foreign goods was perfectly absorbed by this labour-intensive sector. Secondly, its centralized nature made it easier for comprador capital to control raw materials and product collection compared to scattered handicrafts. Thirdly, in a context of incomplete economic sovereignty and constant foreign market pressure, this industry, with its low fixed capital, could adapt more readily, leading to cycles of disintegration and revival.

For these reasons, some scholars even see it as the industrial form best suited to colonial conditions.

Products from this system have a dual character. They are capitalist in the sense of concentrating capital and workers, yet they retain strong pre-capitalist traits due to the persistence of old production methods. Therefore, a substantial portion of China's general industrial products remains rooted in the pre-capitalist sectors of small-scale commodity production.

Secondly, let's deal with agricultural products.

In the modern Chinese economy, agriculture has maintained a dominant position over industry. When discussing the nature of agricultural products, a quantitative view is insufficient. However, compared to industrial products, agricultural commercialization can more easily take on a capitalist appearance. Estimates suggest that less than half of the average Chinese peasant's output was for self-consumption, with the rest being sold.

In some areas, especially near cities, peasants both bought and sold food grains. The reasons for this went beyond simple exchange, often stemming from acute pressures like usury and taxes, which forced poor peasants to sell grain immediately after harvest only to repurchase it later under unfavourable terms.

One might argue this level of commodification isn't widespread, as most peasants would avoid such disadvantageous practices. However, another factor deepened this process: agricultural specialization driven by the expansion of commercial capital. In branches producing raw materials for export, many peasants grew crops useless to themselves, selling all output and buying all necessities. Yet, even this high degree of commercialization does not necessarily signify capitalist production.

A seemingly stronger argument is that wage labour exists in agriculture, indicating capitalist relations. If the presence of wage labour defines capitalist production, then its existence in rural China would signify a capitalist sector. However, this reasoning is flawed. The nature of production is determined not only by who labours but also by the conditions and tools of production. Outdated labour conditions and traditional tools often underpin pre-capitalist methods.

While limited use of new machinery in some regions indicated emerging capitalist relations, these were often overshadowed by pre-capitalist patterns. Therefore, it is difficult to classify most agricultural products as fully capitalist.

Finally, we turn to the two special commodities: labour power and land.

For labour power to be traded as a commodity, the labourer must be free to sell it. This means they must own their labour power and be liberated from feudal bonds tied to the land.

Historically, the commodification of land generally preceded that of labour. In China, land trade has a long history, with evidence of transactions even under strict systems like the Equal-Field System across various dynasties.

However, relatively free trade of land did not automatically create a free labour market. Traditional industrial forms, such as itinerant artisans ("away work") in China, did not generate a class of wage labourers in the capitalist sense. Peasants separated from the land typically became tenants, not free workers.

After the Opium War, the decline of feudal restrictions, the impact of foreign goods and ideas, and the creation of new markets finally allowed labour power to become a true commodity. Consequently, wage labour became visible in both industry and agriculture.

The commodification of industrial and agricultural products, land, and labour power confirms the existence of a commodity economy in China. However, this does not automatically equate to capitalist commodity production. The capitalist nature of a commodity is determined not by its frequency of exchange but by the conditions under which it is produced.

Capitalist commodities are those produced under capitalist relations, where the owners of the means of production and the direct producers who use them belong to different classes.

Therefore, to truly understand the value of Chinese commodities, we must investigate these underlying production conditions.

Chapter 5
Forms of Chinese Commodity Value

5.1 Commodity, Value, and The Law of Value

As we have discussed earlier, commodities are in essence a historical economic form. It is only at a specific stage of historical development that products become transformed into commodities. When this transformation occurs, the labor expended in their production begins to manifest itself as the value of those products.

The intrinsic and inseparable relationship between commodities and value has always persisted. The simple form of value for a commodity is simultaneously the simple commodity form of a labor product. The development of the commodity form progresses in tandem with the development of the value form.

Since modern capitalist commodity production represents the highest stage of commodity form development, the law of value accordingly embodies the highest development of value within capitalist society. This implies that the law of value is unique to a specific stage of social development—namely, the stage of commodity production.

Whether the products of a society can be transformed into capitalist commodities depends on whether their production and exchange adhere to the law of value. The characteristics of this law can be illustrated through three key features of commodity production.

First, as noted before, what is produced must be sold as commodities and as value, and what is used in production must be bought as commodities and as value. The ultimate purpose of buying is selling.

Second, the value obtained from selling the product must be greater than the value spent on its production—at least in the subjective intention of the seller. This difference in value, known as profit or surplus value, is appropriated by the owner of the means of production.

Third, the commodities used in production—such as tools, objects of labor, and especially labor power, which is the source of surplus value—must be purchased according to the law of value as manifested through competition. Similarly, the

Y. Wang, *The Basic Theory of Chinese Economy*,
https://doi.org/10.1007/978-981-95-6330-2_5

products produced, whether industrial or agricultural, must be sold according to that same law of value, also under the influence of competition.

5.2 Incomplete Forms of Chinese Commodity Production under the Law of Value

Commodity production means capitalist production when it is considered as the representation of the form of a society. The so-called Chinese commodity production refers to the production of commodities with the appearance of capitalism, in addition to the production of small commodities which are sold for buying. Whether this kind of commodity production is pure, complete, and adequate for the conditions of capitalism depends on how it adopts the law of value, or to be exact, on the extent to which it reflects the aforementioned law of value. Now, we can examine the nature of Chinese commodity production from the following three aspects: (1) how the value of Chinese commodities is multiplied; (2) how this multiplied value is realized; and (3) how the realized multiplied value is distributed. The following sections will explore these points in detail.

5.2.1 The Multiplication Process of Chinese Commodity Value

The essential elements of commodity production include tools of labor, objects of labor, and labor power. The monetary expenditure on the first two is referred to as constant capital, or capital that does not increase its original value. In contrast, the expenditure on labor power is referred to as variable capital, or capital that can potentially increase its original value. The capitalist nature of commodity production hinges on the surplus value generated by wage laborers in the production process. In other words, the conditions of wage labor largely determine the entire process of surplus value creation.

Even in regions where modern large-scale industries are concentrated, China has yet to develop a market that allows or demands free competition of labor. Even in the most modern, large-scale industrial factories, some outdated labor systems are still in use: for instance, the sweatshop system where workers take home piecework, the contract labor system where foremen recruit workers for production, the apprenticeship system where rural migrants who flee to cities and temporarily cannot find work are taken in and trained, with their wages being fully or partially claimed by their benefactor for a certain period, and the bonded labor system where unemployed men and women from rural areas are hired at extremely low wages and forced into lifelong servitude. These practices collectively paint a picture of non-modern forms of wage labor. Moreover, in reality, especially in large industries run by foreigners, economic exploitation, coercion, and extortion are pervasive. The comprehensive labor form of manufacturing industry discussed hereinbefore is almost dominated by such backward relationships as relatives, trade associations, apprentices, and sidelines, so it is much tougher to find open markets for labor to participate in free competition. Moreover, there are no more than four million industrial laborers under such backward wage labor conditions. Although the handicraft industry hires many more wage laborers, its modern employment conditions are also inadequate accordingly.[1]

For these reasons, agriculture might be viewed as another study subject. According to the estimate, the maximum number of about 30 million wage laborers are employed in agriculture. The working conditions they rely on surely lag far behind those of industry. Various labor forms are present in miscellaneous ways, including the servant, relative, seasonal, tenant who take up voluntary work, and even exchange work (exchanging manual power, animal power, or tools, etc., with their labor). By summarizing these forms, two features can be generalized. One is that the wage labor of all agricultural laborers largely relies on the land itself rather than on agricultural capital or the capital invested in the land except for rare occasions. The situation is the same for tenant farmers, as well as for laborers employed by rich peasants, and even by semi-self-cultivating farmers and tenant farmers. Rich peasants and self-cultivating farmers use their own land as a tool to exploit hired laborers, while tenant farmers use the land they rent to achieve the same exploitation. Furthermore, agricultural laborers are not hired because of agricultural progress or the adoption of new farming tools and techniques. Instead, they are hired due to the stagnation in agriculture. The less agriculture advances and the fewer improvements are made in tools or the application of scientific methods, the more laborers are needed.

In brief, in Chinese industry and agriculture, wage labor is still shackled by traditional feudal practices and fails to present its modern nature in the free competition of the open labor market. Although its modern nature exists more or less on some occasions, modern wage labor relationships may remain elusive in some ways given that no intrinsic changes have happened to the general environment and the conditions for developed industries are not ready.

However, the lack of modernization in the conditions of wage labor, or the uncertainty in the pricing relationship of labor, does not hinder the formation of surplus value. On the contrary, this may even be a favorable condition for generating a greater amount of surplus value or excess profit. Employers, by exploiting the uncertainty in the labor pricing relationship, arbitrarily lower wages below the necessary wage limit. Whereas, the increased surplus value produced by driving wages below the necessary wage limit, except in a few cases and in industries managed by foreign entities, is rarely realized as excess profit. This requires further explanation.

[1] Further analysis will be presented in the discussion on Chinese wage form.

5.2.2 The Process of Realizing the Multiplied Value of Chinese Commodities

The multiplied value of commodities during the production process can only be effectuated when the commodity is put into circulation or exchange process. As exchange mode has always been corresponding to production mode, there must be some obstacles in the Chinese commodity market for surplus value to be realized in accordance with the activity procedure of the modern market.

In the exchange process, two general forms of economic activity dominate: commodity circulation and monetary circulation. The agents of commodity circulation are commodity traders, namely merchants, while those of monetary circulation are money dealers or financiers. In pre-modern societies, the distinction between these two roles was not clearly defined. With the development of modern division of labor, financiers have gradually separated from merchants to take on their specialized roles. In a society governed by capitalist production methods, merchants typically act on behalf of producers or industrial capitalists, handling the tasks of circulation. In terms of the social division of labor, merchants are independent from industrial capitalists. However, the activities of their capital, or commercial capital, are still subject to the influence of industrial capital. In this relationship, commercial capital is considered subordinate to industrial capital. Industrial capital must maintain a dominant position over commercial capital to prevent it from disrupting production, ensuring that modern capitalist production relations can be established.

The facts tell us that within the exchange process of Chinese society, there are two subordinate relationships at play.

Foreign firms → Comprador commerce → Native commercial capital → Production enterprises.

Foreign banks → Modern banking → Moneylending → Usury business.

As for the two series, the interdependently subordinate relationships between the individual units, as well as the interrelationships between the two series, people with common sense in China must have a good understanding. Except for certain big new enterprises in some areas, all other industrial or even agricultural products are put on the market more or less in unregulated ways, and it seems that most products from the manufacturing industry feature reserved production. In most cases, entrepreneurs consent to transfer their products to businessmen in accordance with predetermined conditions and obtain from businessmen raw materials and capital used to renew laboring tools and purchase labor force. Agricultural products, particularly those from specialized agricultural sectors, are mostly dealt with by means of usury in such ways as advance sale and advance purchase before they ripe. Moreover, there are, of course, some products that are not handled through the aforementioned methods. However, because most products come from small-scale operations, combined with the transportation difficulties for agricultural products and the interference of irregular taxes, these products must be sold at nearby periodic markets that remain in a primitive state. It is very clear that such primitive markets are unfavorable to producers but advantageous to buyers and hoarders in general.

As for the obstructive effects caused by various outdated privileges in the circulation sphere, and the obstacles arising from the reliance on privileges in the circulation of commodities and money, there are countless examples. The practice of merchants and moneylenders driving down prices during the harvest or completion period of raw products and semi-finished goods, only to raise them afterward, is so commonplace that it has come to be seen as normal and acceptable.

Additionally, in foreign trade relations, the industrial hardships caused by incomplete tariff rights, industrial rights, and transportation rights are also clearly reflected in the exchange process.

Numerous examples could be cited, but here we can only mention this in principle and summarize the general characteristics of Chinese commodity circulation in the following three points:

First, commerce turns products into commodities, rather than commodity movement giving rise to commerce. In other words, the comprador-driven commerce, which extensively sources local materials and manages global production, plays a crucial role in the distribution of goods. It forcibly disintegrates traditional agrarian-industrial economic structures, driving the division and specialization of agriculture and industry. As a result, the advancement of industrial division of labor and exchange relations appears to be carried out under the directives of commercial capital (both international and domestic). This phenomenon not only demonstrates that production cannot subsume circulation as one of its own components, but rather suggests that circulation dominates production, limiting it to the extent necessary for exercising control.

Second, the entire process of commodity circulation is governed by unequal exchange relationships. These unequal exchanges can be summarized from both domestic and international perspectives. In terms of international unequal exchange relationships, it is evident that labor products in a less developed country embody a greater amount of labor, and thus hold a higher exchange value, compared to equivalent labor products from more advanced nations. However, due to the constraints imposed by various unequal treaties, the outcome is that we expend more labor or greater value for the foreign products we consume. Both our external purchases and sales are subject to the limitations set by these treaties. Although it may appear that transactions occur in a freely competitive market, in reality, they are conducted under unequal exchange terms dictated by those unequal treaties. As for the domestic market, the unequal exchange between industrial and agricultural products is equally evident. In many modern countries, the organic composition of capital in agriculture is generally lower than in industry, allowing industrial goods to often be exchanged for a greater amount of labor or higher value in agricultural products. However, the situation in China is otherwise. Under the pressure of imported goods, China's industrial sector is in great need of significantly lowering the prices of raw materials, which constitute the most important component of industrial products, as a means of compensation. In a context where both industry and agriculture are subject to commercial control, industry—which has closer ties to commerce—finds it easier to sacrifice agriculture in various ways, even if we disregard the relatively more favorable social conditions it enjoys compared to agriculture.

Third, the realization of excess surplus value occurs not under the law of value but under contrary conditions. It is not driven by free competition based on production prices but rather by deceitful practices such as buying cheap and selling dear. The process is fundamentally characterized by unreasonable and illegal coercion, and, more essentially, by the persistence of feudal labor practices.

5.2.3 Segmentation Process of Surplus Value of Chinese Commodities

In capitalist commodity production, the prices of means of production and labor are generally well-defined. At least, the purchase of these commodities and the sale of their products are influenced by competition in the open market, which allows for the estimation of commodity costs and average profit margins. However, in China, the production and exchange methods are complicated by outdated practices, privileged interests, and semi-colonial interference, making it difficult to determine production prices. As a result, the surplus value of products exhibits significant variability and unpredictability.

What's more, the surplus value of the commodities under commodity production must be realized through an exchange process, and the recipients of surplus value can only confirm their share after this process is complete. In contrast, in China, the surplus value of commodities can not only vary arbitrarily in amount, but also be subject to arbitrary fluctuations in its appropriation or division. This can occur not only during the exchange process but also during the production process.

In a situation where commercial capital (both international and domestic) serves as the central nexus between producers or between producers and consumers, the generation and realization of commodity surplus value do not allow industrial capital or producer capital to play a leading role. Consequently, if industrial capital does yield profits (in reality, many production enterprises generate no profit, and the remuneration obtained in the name of profit is essentially a result of the transformation of wages), these profits are instead residual from commercial capital. Commercial profits are not derived from industrial profits; rather, industrial profits are derived from commercial profits. This mode of surplus value distribution is already quite backward and specific, but when examining the agricultural sector, even more outdated practices become apparent.

In capitalist agricultural production, because agricultural capital has a lower organic composition compared to industrial capital, it generally yields surplus profits above the average profit. However, as previously analyzed, in China, land in rural areas is in an absolutely superior position relative to capital. The profitability of agricultural operations does not depend on the capital conditions but rather on labor conditions, particularly on the conditions under which land is acquired. Rent remains largely in the form of surplus value, and profits are merely a meager fraction extracted from rent. Alternatively, profits are simply a rebranding of the portion of wages extracted from extremely low wages paid to hired laborers.

As the investment in industry, especially in the manufacturing industry, or in agricultural production, is hard to be reliably paid off, social fund is less likely to be drawn in production undertakings, but more likely in non-production businesses, instead. This explains why commercial usury is highly active, and why land becomes the subject of expanded commercial activities. The difficulty in raising funds for production leaves agricultural and industrial businesses no way but to suffer the exploitation of commercial usury and expensive land rent, which provides the prerequisites for further exploitation of them. Herein, it is easy to perceive how the surplus value created during the commodity production is segmented, and why it is segmented in the exchange and even the production processes.

Finally, it must be noted that all forms of extraneous economic exploitation, whether arising from unequal treaties in external relations or from various feudal or irrational regulations in internal relations, directly or indirectly participate in the division of surplus value.

As a matter of fact, the aforesaid various factors involved in the division of surplus value not only partition the multiplied value of commodities but tend to encroach on the original prepaid capital value. Notably, what deserves investigation herein is not so much about how commodity value (prepaid value and multiplied value) is divided, as about how the multiplied value is partitioned and who is the beneficiary.

5.3 General Characteristics of the Value of Chinese Commodities

From the above, we can discern general characteristics of commodities and their value in Chinese society.

Production organizations, especially those focused on use-value, have largely disintegrated and are transforming. However, a significant portion of products, especially primary agricultural products, are still produced mainly as use-value for the producers' own consumption, not for exchange value. We need not compare the proportions quantitatively, but we can assert that the portion produced for exchange value has steadily increased, even without an absolute quantitative advantage. In other respects, the commodity economy component is dominant. International capital has integrated China into global commodity and monetary relations, forcing producers to consider exchange value.

The shift from production for use-value to exchange-value was primarily driven by commercial capital (international, comprador, indigenous) and merchants. Consequently, in domestic and international markets, it is not producers but merchants who compare costs and market prices. Thus, commodity value is determined less by labor expended and more by the whims of merchants, making valuation unpredictable for producers. This is exacerbated by socio-political factors hindering circulation.

Commerce operates on the principle of "buying cheap and selling dear"—a philosophy of deceit. When circulation is restrained by industry, this principle is limited; otherwise, notions of equivalence and the law of value are absent. The only value concept is that bought and sold commodities embody social labor.

Many modern countries experienced a phase where commercial capital dominated. Initially, goods were considered valuable only when bought and sold. But as they broke free from old production relations and industrial capital became dominant, commodity value relations became less unpredictable, and the laws of value movement clearer under competition.

However, due to socio-political reasons, China's modernization has failed to let industrial capital rise above commercial capital. Consequently, commodity production and movement have never been fully governed by the law of value.

Moreover, value forms resulting from industrial underdevelopment inevitably express a larger quantity of labor in a smaller quantity of the same commodity, reflecting greater exchange value in lesser use value. Surplus labor caused by underdevelopment hinders machinery adoption, leading to goods that waste more labor and contain more value.

In capitalist societies, the profit motive drives adoption of new machinery and technology. In China, the same motive takes a different path. Faced with difficulties acquiring capital and machinery, producers prefer exploiting readily available living labor rather than adopting machines. Thus, while elsewhere machines replace labor, in China, labor replaces machines. This lowers productivity, forcing workers to spend more time reproducing their subsistence, leaving less time for producing surplus value. Maintaining the same surplus value requires harsher exploitation or wages below the value of labor power, sustaining a difficult existence.

In summary, the relation between commodities and value is a social relation. Each social formation has corresponding forms of commodity and value. Since China's commodity circulation cannot overcome obstacles from feudal traditions and international capital domination, its value relations manifest ambiguously and incompletely in exchange.

Most Chinese commodities are not initially produced as such for realizing exchange value by producers. They are largely transformed into commodities by a commercial sector subordinated to international capital and its connected usury industry, which drive products originally produced for use-value into the market. These products enter the market not because producers seek average profit, but because merchants (compradors, usurers, officials) exploit disadvantaged artisans, farmers, and manufacturers to extract exorbitant profits.

Thus, while China's commodity value relations have changed during modernization, they remain rooted in pre-capitalist small-scale production. Circulation under this system is not governed by the normal law of value. Production is not initiated by industrial capitalists, so surplus value cannot transform into a unified profit form. Commercial profit and interest are not distributed from overall industrial profits.

Even where labor and capital have diverged in larger enterprises, wages insufficient for minimum living standards do not necessarily ensure reasonable profits for employers. Wages and basic earnings are eroded by commercial capital, usury capital, and other forces of primitive accumulation that control production.

Furthermore, under the influence of international capital, economic interactions typical of a colonial relationship result in commercial, usury, and landed interests being converted—directly or indirectly—into the special interests of foreign capital through unequal trade, foreign debt, and other mechanisms. Thus, the ultimate expropriators of China's surplus value are international capitalists. Domestic commercial actors merely take residual surplus value according to their service to international capital.

Therefore, the analysis of China's commodity value relations is key to understanding other forms within its broader economy—money, capital, wages, and profits.

Issues discussed in this part

1. Why is commodity an economic form of a history? How is commodity formed and how will it perish?
2. Why are the fundamental changes in social production conditions and distribution relationships necessary when the exchange mode is transformed from selling for buying to buying for selling?
3. Why is a society less capitalist where the manufacturing industry dominates the big industry? Please discuss it with the nature of the manufacturing industry in Chinese society.
4. Why does the commercialization of land come before that of labor? Why does the free trade of land in Chinese society fail to bring about the truly free trade of labor force?
5. Why is the general law of commodity value not at play in the multiplication process of Chinese commodity value and the realization process of the multiplied value?
6. How should unequal exchange be understood?
7. What's the essential difference between commerce that forces products to become commodities and the one that is formed by commodity movement?
8. Who gains the surplus products or surplus value produced in Chinese society?

Part III
Forms of Chinese Currency

Abstract This chapter analyzes the unique positions and interrelations of various capital forms within Chinese society. Unlike capitalist societies where industrial capital dominates, in China, merchant capital and usurer's capital—two "pre-capitalist" forms—long held sway. Merchant capital operated independently of production, exploiting small producers through unequal exchange. Its profits were not a share of industrial surplus value but were often extracted directly from the producers themselves, sometimes eroding the potential base for industrial profit. Usurer's capital was deeply intertwined with landownership and commerce, maintaining exorbitant interest rates. Chinese industrial capital, by contrast, was inherently weak, suffered from inadequate accumulation and low technical composition, and was often subordinate to or dependent on commercial and lending capital, struggling to achieve independent development. This capital structure directed surplus value accumulation towards circulation and usury rather than productive reinvestment.

Chapter 6
Basics of Currency

In order to conduct a scientific analysis of China's monetary forms, it is first necessary to clarify the scientific theoretical basis of currencies from a historical perspective. This is because the Chinese monetary forms under investigation here are primarily confined to the period after the Opium War and before the Chinese People's War of Resistance against Japanese Aggression. Although, for the sake of clarity and necessity, it may be inevitable to touch upon periods outside of this time frame, especially towards the end of this text, where I intend to address some of the current issues surrounding the monetary system.

Nearly a century has passed from the Opium War to the Chinese People's War of Resistance against Japanese Aggression. During this period, the form of Chinese currency has undergone significant changes. If one attempts to discuss it from a fixed perspective, it is impossible to grasp the full dynamics of its evolution. Furthermore, judging the currency form of this period solely based on common sense and empirical facts would not allow one to fully grasp its distinctions from both traditional and modern forms of currency. Therefore, to comprehend Chinese currency, it is essential to understand its historical development and transformation trends; without such knowledge, any discussion would be incomplete.

Only from a developmental perspective can we study the facts of development.

Currency has passed through three distinct stages of development. The currency originated from commodities, and its various functions emerged gradually over time, with each function changing in nature as society evolves. Let us now follow this sequence and elaborate on these three stages one by one.

Y. Wang, *The Basic Theory of Chinese Economy*,
https://doi.org/10.1007/978-981-95-6330-2_6

6.1 Historic Development of the Relationship Between Currency and Commodity

Commodities originate from products of labor. A product becomes a commodity when it is produced not for the producer's own consumption but for consumption by others, a process that requires specific social relations and conditions. The emergence of currency is a consequence of the transformation of products into commodities, and it in turn acts as a catalyst that further promotes the transformation of products into commodities.

Currency itself is not merely a product of labor; it undergoes a transformation, first from a product into a commodity, and then from a commodity into currency. Within the limits of the production that needs currency as its medium to become a commodity, the time when the production becomes a commodity is the time when the commodity becomes currency.

Nevertheless, under all circumstances, all products can become commodities, while under no circumstances can any commodity be turned into currency.

In the course of the development of socioeconomic history, it is true that some commodities, such as cereals, livestock, fur, cowries, dried mullets, were coincidentally used as social exchange equivalents within a limited scope and functioned as currency. However, the properties were subsequently dismissed for irresistible reasons along the socioeconomic development and gave way to currency to monopolize the position as universal equivalent. The reason why the currency achieved the dominant position is that the currency, or the precious metal, as people generally perceive, possesses such special functions for exchange medium as durability, ease of melting, and relative scarcity, easy melting, and difficult availability, which enable it to hold significant value in small quantities. These special functions manifested themselves in accordance with objective requirements or were generally discovered in the development process of exchange.

Once currency, among various products and commodities, secured its position as the universal equivalent due to the aforementioned special characteristics, its nature as an ordinary commodity became concealed, while its function as currency was further developed. The more it acts as currency, the less it is viewed as a commodity. Currency and commodities are thus related in an opposing manner. Perhaps for this reason, many people, including some economists, view currency as having no fundamental connection to commodities, believing that currency can exist independently of its tangible commodity basis, merely as a conceptual entity. This belief forms the foundation of the so-called "state theory of money". Paper money further reinforces this theory.

In fact, even after precious metals became recognized as the universal equivalent in the form of currency, appearing to shed their original properties and standing in opposition to other commodities, their ability to serve as universal equivalents arises precisely because they were originally commodities themselves. Precious metals inherently possess intrinsic value and embody the labor of a particular society. Paper money, on the other hand, emerged at a certain stage in the development of a commodity economy as a representative of metallic currency. It functions as a symbol of precious metals, and its relationship to commodity value can be considered indirect; the value of commodities is represented conceptually by quantities of gold or silver, which are in turn symbolically represented by paper money. However, this topic will be discussed further later. For now, it is important to understand that currency maintains a close relationship with commodities. As commodity relations evolve, currency evolves to the same extent. From another perspective, the history of commodity development is also the history of currency development.

6.2 Evolutionary Process of Currency Functions

The development of commodity relations has undoubtedly been facilitated by currency, yet the various functions of currency, when viewed as such, have clearly emerged gradually over the course of commodity development. For instance, today when we speak of currency, we refer to its five key functions that constitute its conceptual framework: the function as a measure of value (along with its associated function as a standard of price), a medium of circulation, a means of hoarding, a means of payment, and finally, the function as world currency. These functions did not all emerge simultaneously with the advent of currency; rather, they gradually developed in response to objective economic demands.

When different commodities are compared and their labor values are mutually reflected, currency serves as the intermediary and universal equivalent, which indicates that currency must first possess the function of the unit of account. However, when it acts as the unit of account, it transforms the values of various commodities into prices, expressed as imagined quantities of gold or silver. For example, one might say that an item is worth a certain number of pounds, while other items are worth respective amounts. But what does this number of pounds represent in terms of actual gold or silver? How many ounces or taels does it contain? At this point, currency must also fulfill the function of price standards, where specific quantities of gold or silver are used to measure or determine other quantities. For instance, China used to take 7 qian and 2 fen (1 qian equals to 3.78 g or so and 1 fen weighs approximately 378 mg) as a unit to measure a silver coin. While the unit of account and price standards are clearly distinct functions, they are closely related and can easily be confused.

When currency functions as both the unit of account and price standard, it inevitably also takes on the role of the medium of circulation. This is because, when a specific quantity of gold or silver serves as the equivalent in the exchange of commodities, those commodities must be transferred from one owner to another through the medium of currency. In this process, currency acts as the means of purchase or circulation. This function naturally arises from the previous function and serves to complete it.

When currency is considered as a means of purchase, it can be used to obtain any other commodities and even any desirable things in addition to commodities. It seems that a special trait is added to it so that it invites the desire of protection and preservation, which is the storage function of currency.

Although the function of currency as a means of payment does not necessarily result from its function as a means of hoarding, the role of the following function is closely related to that of the previous. In the circulation community, as selling and buying tend to come apart, which means that the commodity put to market fails to find a buyer, or the buyer may not pay in full. To accelerate commodity circulation, the function of currency as a means of payment is discovered. Commodities can be transferred in advance with their price paid in installments, or they can be paid once a certain sum has accumulated. As commodity production reaches a certain level of development and scope, this function extends beyond the realm of commodity circulation to broader areas such as contracts, rent, wages, and taxes.

The various functions of currency described above are primarily manifested within the domestic circulation sphere. Once currency crosses national borders, it sheds its local characteristics such as price standards, coinage, and a symbol of value, reverting to its original form as bars or ingots of precious metals. In this context, the physical essence of gold and silver stands in opposition to their processed form as coinage. The latter serves as a means of circulation and payment within a particular country, while the former becomes the universal means of circulation and payment on a global scale, as well as the absolute embodiment of wealth. This function of world currency has existed throughout all eras where economic exchange occurred among nations, though its full development is evidently a modern phenomenon.

6.3 Different Currency Functions in Different Societies

The evolution sequence of the currency functions has been fore-illustrated, and what should be paid attention to herein are the functions of currency with varying natures in the same name in different societies. As currency, like what has been discussed above, is a manifestation of a kind of social relation. The currency in different societies is not represented in its minting, design, the amount of gold or silver, or its weight, the amount of gold or silver, or its weight. The cast coinages of many countries in the past might be more delicate or exquisite than those in modern times. However, there is no essential disparity in these aspects. More correctly, the real difference of currency in different societies lies in the functions with different natures. This is to say, the function of circulation medium or hoarding means is of different natures in various historical eras.

As is known to all, currency functions that presuppose commodity circulation, commodities and their exchange modes are confined to the production situation at that time. Different production status and relations of production in different societies can only demand or allow the currency functions adapting to them, which leads to different forms of currency.

Only once this key point is established can we begin to examine the forms of Chinese currency.

Chapter 7
Special Features of the Chinese Currency

Before exploring the functions of Chinese currency, it is reasonable to briefly describe and interpret the common phenomena of Chinese currency, or the different characteristics of Chinese currency forms in comparison to those of other countries and historical periods.

7.1 Backwardness Reflected in the Silver Standard System

Before the currency reform of 1935, China had always followed the silver standard. Even after this reform, although China formally adopted an exchange control system or a quasi-gold standard for international purposes, domestically, the silver dollar continued to serve as the general unit of account and price unit for circulation and payment. The adoption of the silver standard inherently reflected not only the backwardness of the currency system itself but also the underdevelopment of the commodity economy that relied on it. This backwardness cannot be understood solely by examining the form of Chinese currency in isolation; rather, it must be analyzed in the broader context of the historical evolution of monetary systems in other countries worldwide.

Before the 1850s, almost all countries around the world adopted the silver standard system. However, since then and the end of the nineteenth century, various countries shifted to the gold standard system for the following reasons.

First, given the surge in the output of silver, its value became extremely volatile, leading to the reduction in its function as a unit of account accordingly.

Second, the increase in gold mining made it adequate to settle the debts in international trade. This seems to contradict the first reason. Will the rise of the output of gold lead to the same result just as that of silver has negated its qualification as standard currency? One explanation is that the relatively small amount of gold

Y. Wang, *The Basic Theory of Chinese Economy*,
https://doi.org/10.1007/978-981-95-6330-2_7

will not cause supply to exceed demand when gold is used as standard currency. Furthermore, the most important reason lies as follows.

Third, the greater value of gold makes it more adaptable to the increasing scale of commodity circulation, and can largely reduce the storage and transportation charges returned from settlement.[1]

For these reasons, countries in succession gave up the silver standard system at the request of their developed domestic economy and foreign economic exchanges. The sequence goes as follows:

Britain—late eighteenth century
America—1873
Germany—not sure
Romania—1890
Austro-Hungarian Empire—1892
Bulgaria—1893
Russia—1897
Japan—1898

Although the Latin Monetary Union, organized by France, Italy, Switzerland, and Belgium, put into place the bimetallic standard system, it ended up with failure. In World War I, various countries successively dropped the gold standard system, but once the war ended, they resumed the system (For example, Britain and America adopted the gold bullion standard system, Austria, Hungary, Italy, and the Czech carried out the gold standard system, and Germany, Sweden, Belgium, and Chile implemented the gold exchange system). In 1927, even India began to adopt the gold bullion standard system, and in 1930, only three countries retained the silver standard system, namely Mexico, Spain, and China.

The general trend of the reform of the currency standard system in these countries shows that their departure from the silver standard system was closely related to the development of their commodity economy. The gold standard system was first adopted by major capitalist countries, among which Britain took the lead. As Russia and Japan developed relatively slowly, they were later comers to adopt the system. China is still carrying out the silver standard system, which demonstrates that the Chinese commodity and currency economy is still very underdeveloped.

[1] "The increase in the total value of commodity in circulation will inform nations that settlement with silver is more convenient than copper-based settlement yet less convenient than that with gold. The more prosperous a nation is, the more likely it is to take metal with smaller value as fractional cast coinage and that with higher value as currency" (scc page 191 in *A Contribution to the Critique of Political Economy* translated by Guo Moruo).

7.2 Discrepancies and Uncertainties of the Monetary System

The persistence of the backward silver standard system inherently entailed a disorderly variety of currencies, as well as discrepancies and uncertainties in currency units. Economically backward nations were often left reliant on the silver standard. Yet, these same economies were compelled to participate in the international commodity economy, a necessity which inevitably created conflicts with emerging economic relations and consequently prevented the establishment of a systematic silver standard system. This confusion and contradiction manifested itself in several key aspects.

(1) The Opposition Between Modern and Feudal Currency. This opposition was most clearly observed in the concurrent use of silver dollars and silver taels (a unit roughly equivalent to 37.5 g). Up until 1931, when the tael was officially abolished in favor of the silver dollar, the silver tael remained widely used as a unit of account within feudal financial systems, for tax purposes, and in large traditional transactions.

As exchange relations advanced, the inconvenience of using taels gradually led to growing reliance on banknotes denominated in silver dollars, which were issued by modern banks. However, the silver dollar system itself was complicated by the circulation of various foreign coins of differing purities, such as the Mexican Eagle dollar prevalent in coastal areas, which differed in quality from the larger domestic silver dollars.

Furthermore, the subsidiary currency system based on copper coins was highly fragmented, with nearly every region possessing its own distinct types. These coins were widely accepted because they suited the low purchasing power of the urban and especially the rural working class. Conversely, local feudal powers were particularly keen to mint these easily produced coins, exploiting them as highly profitable instruments.

(2) The Opposition Between Government-Issued and Private Currencies. The tension between state and private currency issuance represents a fundamental dynamic in monetary history. Theoretically, modern paper money should be issued based on substantial reserves of precious metal, emerging as a convenient medium of exchange when a commodity economy reaches a certain stage of development.

However, in a country like China, where a robust credit system was historically underdeveloped, paper money with a purely nominal value existed for a remarkably long time. This allowed the state to engage in profligate expenditure, as the cost of producing such currency was almost negligible, a scenario reminiscent of Mandeville's assumptions about fiat money.

We can see that the use of paper money in China began early. Its implementation, however, was not primarily motivated by the need to facilitate commerce, but stemmed from the power of monarchs or emperors to issue currency arbitrarily. When the central authority exercised this power, it set a precedent eagerly followed by officials, provincial governors, and local aristocrats, who similarly abused the privilege of currency issuance.

This legacy of decentralized and often irresponsible monetary creation persisted into modern times. Leading up to the mid-twentieth century, the country lacked a complete and unified national right to coin currency or issue bonds coherently. The financial landscape was fragmented, with provincial and municipal governments employing various instruments like treasure bonds or guanpiao (official notes). Before a significant move towards currency unification around 1924, large new banks could issue banknotes, and even private businesses and small shops in towns and villages could issue notes with little restriction, illustrating the chaotic coexistence of public and private monetary claims.

(3) The Opposition Between Domestic and Foreign Currency. According to basic economic principles, even metallic currency loses its specific national value outside its country of origin, functioning only as bullion. Yet, in China, foreign currencies—both coins and paper—circulated widely and effectively. For instance, the Mexican Dollar had long been in circulation alongside other foreign silver coins used as standard currency.

Moreover, foreign paper money was often more trusted and preferred by the public than notes from even relatively reputable Chinese banks. In provinces bordering imperialist nations, such as Manchuria, Shandong, and Fujian concerning Japanese currency, or Guangdong and Guangxi regarding Hong Kong and British currency, foreign banknotes were considered more credible than their Chinese counterparts. These foreign currencies were not only circulated within China but were also hoarded by Chinese citizens as representations of absolute wealth.

7.3 The Number and Types of Currencies and Their Development

As is described hereinbefore, there are many varieties of currencies in China. However, the wide varieties do not mean a large volume of circulating currencies, but instead, the total volume will not increase because of the restriction and counteraction among these various kinds of currencies. Besides, as each currency has its local, feudal, and even imperialist background, its circulation scope has to be restricted by the background. Therefore, in China, a country with vast territory, the notes issued by foreign banks reached 560 million yuan until late 1932, while the amount issued by major Chinese new banks only stood at about 583 million yuan until 1934, together with the number issued by provincial and city banks that amounted to 100 million to 150 million yuan. The total value of private notes, mainly copper coin notes, issued by private businesses and small shops was at best tens of millions of yuan. It is true that a large amount of silver and copper coins were circulating in addition to the 1 billion or so paper money, but in the situation where inferior money drove out superior or hard currency in disorder was inevitably scattered among the public and collected in bank inventory, the total value of the silver and copper coins in circulation seemed not to be substantial.

Setting aside the limits imposed by the development of the actual commodity economy and its demands on currency, the existence of various types of currency inevitably restricts the issuance of any single type. Conversely, the reduction in the number of currency types appears to allow for an expansion in the issuance of the remaining currency types. Over the past decade or two, China's monetary system has gradually moved towards simplification. During World War I, China's national economy experienced significant growth, and, in response to this development, modern financial practices began to dominate. These new financial institutions not only gained an advantage over the feudal local currencies but also began to push back against the use of imperialist currencies. For instance, in Shanghai, which was the center of national financial activity, the circulation of foreign banknotes at the end of the Qing dynasty amounted to over one billion yuan. By 1934, this figure had dropped to just 30 million yuan. Furthermore, in the early years of the Republic of China, 70% of the paper currency in circulation in Shanghai was foreign-issued. However, by 1934, Chinese banknotes accounted for 99% of the total circulation of 3.23 billion yuan, while foreign banknotes represented only 1%. This shift can be attributed to several factors.

First, during World War I, China's banking sector, which had long been dependent on foreign influence, began to shift as the national economy showed signs of growth. This change was further driven by the post-war movement to reclaim national sovereignty, which surged in momentum. As a result, financial professionals and entrepreneurs alike came to realize that without gaining independence and autonomy, they would remain under foreign control. This growing awareness had a profound impact on the development and expansion of the domestic banking industry.

Second, many foreign banks went bankrupt amid the World War I, so the wealthy who had adored foreigners started to question the credibility of the foreign banks or their paper money.

Third, as domestic banks grew firm, they were more credible. What's more, the failure of old-fashioned money shops in the competition with a concentrated financial industry which boasted new technology as well as deep pockets could beef up the morale of the Chinese banking industry against its foreign rivals.

Fourth, on the other hand, around 1930, in the aftermath of World War I and during the period when imperialist powers were once again suffering from the global economic depression, they realized the necessity of stabilizing the Chinese currency to maintain control over the Chinese market and ensure a steady outlet for their goods. They recognized that the chaotic and diverse state of Chinese currency, which was hindering commodity circulation, had to be reformed and simplified. The success of the "abolishing the tael and adopting the yuan" initiative and the establishment of a new monetary system can be largely, if not entirely, explained by these imperialist motivations.

Chapter 8
The Functions of Chinese Currency

As stated above, the differences between monetary forms lie not in their outward patterns but in the functions they perform. Therefore, it is necessary to explore the nature of Chinese currency in light of the foregoing representations. It is better to analyze the functions of the Chinese currency to find out how its nature differs from that in capitalist countries, or to identify whether they can perform the functions required of capitalist money.

8.1 The Function of Chinese Currency as a Unit of Account and the Standard of Price

In a commodity-producing society, fluctuations in production prices are considered the only reliable gauge for producers to determine what and how much is needed by society, or what is no longer in demand. For this gauge to be effective, currency—acting as both a unit of account and price standard—must itself possess a stable and universally accepted standard that facilitates transactions and payments across society. However, the aforementioned characteristics of the Chinese monetary system have clearly struggled, or even failed, to fully realize this crucial function.

China's currency system has long been diverse, with various types of currency each possessing its own inconsistent and non-uniform price standards. This lack of uniformity and stability in currency creates significant challenges for producers when calculating production costs. Navigating the highly complex and fragmented monetary landscape of larger markets makes it exceedingly difficult for them to gauge the limits of demand. Moreover, those who control local or specialized monetary authorities can, and often do, manipulate the currency's price standards to serve their own interests, frequently changing its value. In some cases, they even deliberately or systematically devalue their currency to the point where it becomes virtually worthless.

Y. Wang, *The Basic Theory of Chinese Economy*,
https://doi.org/10.1007/978-981-95-6330-2_8

It is true that the silver dollar and silver tael as Chinese standard currency functioned as the unit of account or price standards in large markets, in wider markets and larger transactions. However, the past five decades have seen the extremely volatile price of silver in the world, and China, as a major user rather than a producer of silver, has been constantly exposed to these fluctuations all the time. Although the price fluctuation of silver has little impact on a certain amount of silver serving as price standards, or in other words, it only affects the accomplishment of the unit of account, it is already known that, as fractional currency is used equally as the standard currency in rural retailing markets, the fluctuation of silver price will lead to the price parity of copper coin to silver coin, or foreign price (the market price of purchasing copper coins with silver coins). As a result, it has difficulty effectively performing the functions of a price standard and a unit of account.

Moreover, fluctuations in the global price of silver are not solely driven by the supply and demand dynamics of silver mining but are also intricately intertwined with the monetary conflicts between imperialist nations. When considering this reality, along with the various monetary policies these powers imposed on China—ranging from partial manipulation to full-scale control—it becomes evident that even after adopting an exchange rate management system, China's lack of economic independence prevented it from stabilizing its currency. As a result, both its domestic and international monetary values remained volatile, making it difficult to achieve the consistency and stability required for a unified and reliable unit of account.

However, while the value-measuring and price-standard functions of China's currency, as previously mentioned, are inadequate in meeting the demands of a capitalist commodity economy, they are, on the other hand, well-suited to the needs of a backward economy of small-scale commodity production and an externally dependent economy. The very lack of consistency in the unit of account and price standards provides an effective tool for various privileged groups to exercise economic and non-economic forms of exploitation.

8.2 Chinese Currency Functions as a Medium of Circulation

"The currency necessary to drive a nation's commerce has a certain limit and proportion." "Any amount exceeding or falling short of this will impede commerce and hinder circulation." From this observation, a principle is established: the quantity of circulating currency is determined by the ratio of the total price of the commodity in circulation to the velocity of the currency of the same denomination. However, the application of this rule assumes that the currency used as a means of circulation can effectively perform its role as a unit of account and price standard. If not, this rule needs to be adjusted in practice. In other words, the function of currency as a means of circulation will inevitably be affected by incomplete conditions for its function as a unit of account and price standard. More fundamentally, the function will be made very special because of the incomplete forms of the commodity production.

As China's economy increasingly integrates into the global commodity economy, even though it largely remains in the stage of simple commodity economy, all elements beyond self-sufficiency require currency for circulation. The function of the Chinese currency as a means of circulation naturally emerges from these circulation relationships.

There is no doubt that the sectors of the Chinese commodity economy are increasingly growing stronger, and the currency volume needed for the circulation is accordingly increasing. However, as is indicated previously, up around 1932, the total currency volume in Chinese circulation was no more than 2 billion. It might be astonishing that the small volume of currency (compared to the issued volume of any modern country) could support the commodity circulation of the huge Chinese market, but people will take it for granted when considering that the Chinese natural economy still takes up of the economy.

It is known that one major reason for the development of the commodity economy lies in the advancement of currency. However, the aforesaid representations and forms of Chinese currency, like the discrepancy and uncertainty of the currency system, and the like, blocked the currency-based commodity and the commercialization of currency in many respects. As a consequence, the products that could have been included into and need to join in the circulation process, and the currency that could have been practically adopted in circulation, found them nowhere because of the incomplete conditions of the currency itself. This led to financial depletion in rural areas and the distorted trades like the exchange modes of advance purchase and advance sale. Take the loan mode of barter as an example. It, on the one hand, suffered from inadequate currency supply, and on the other hand, it excluded currency, and in large part reduced the currency value for changing hands. Consequently, the very currency that could have facilitated the commodification of products and accelerated their circulation instead reversed many of the commoditized components into natural economic components.

Surely, the advancement of the currency system is just one factor in promoting circulation relations. To make this factor positively effective, a unified regime is required to provide relevant prerequisites and supplementary conditions for the corresponding infrastructure of security, transportation, weights and measures, and the establishment of a domestic free market. Although the conditions have made progress prior to the Chinese People's War of Resistance against Japanese Aggression (1937), there is still a long way to go before meeting the requirements of the capitalist mode of production and circulation of commodities. Therefore, the currency that needs the prerequisite or auxiliary conditions of the achievement of these aspects for its circulation can only play its role of a means of circulation within the limits set by the progress achieved in these areas. In other words, when Chinese currency is at play as a means of circulation, it has to be restricted by the development of the forms of Chinese commodity production and circulation.

8.3 Chinese Currency Functions as a Storage Medium

Since currency began to play its part of circulation medium, the storage function has come after it. This function is compatible with its functions of circulation medium and even unit of account.

In the infant stage of commodity circulation, only the surplus beyond use value was translated into currency. When currency or gold or silver has become the representation of a rich society, the seller of the surplus is actually the hoarder of currency, which is the simplest form of currency storage. Over time, as commodity circulation got promoted and the currency as universal equivalent exerted great influence on society, the desire to hoard currency was accordingly on the rise. Therefore, the former ideas that there was no difference between value and value form and that the increase of gold and silver storage meant more value have given way to the urge of investing currency to get more currency in return through circulation. Subsequently, it was assumed that the only way to get more currency in the circulation process was to make more products in the production process. At this stage, the original function of currency storage was concealed by the growing investment, and the cunning and hideous desire for currency storage was made invisible by the considerable investment in "social services". As a result, the currency storage at this stage was possibly the amount for a certain production scale and the needed payment within a certain period of time. The first stage featured the function of the currency storage in pre-capitalist society, the second stage was represented by the function of early modern times, and the third stage involved the storage function after the early modern period.

Once we clearly distinguish between these different forms of currency storage, we can proceed to examine the storage function exhibited by Chinese currency.

Viewed in its function as a means of storage, Chinese currency gives a very unclear idea of what it is. In the first place, in the backward places where the traditional subsistence method of production is still dominant, the fixed and limited desires of the general public lead them to engage in the simple storage of currency (silver dollar, silver ingot, or copper coins) obtained from the surplus of value in use. This tendency, which was reinforced by the proliferation of all kinds of paper money without credit, led the people to value coins relatively highly. Thus the habit of cellar storage has been preserved until recently.

In areas with developed circulation or where bank notes have recently been popular, the practice of storing coins in cellars has died down. Average citizens have come to realize that it is wiser to use currency flexibly so as to make more money than to stick to preserving currency. However, the best way for the flexible use of currency is to turn it into production capital, and changing it into commercial capital is the second best choice. If the first choice is deemed to be complicated and may not be profitable in accordance with experiences, and meanwhile the latter is not suitable for personal interest and social status, the old-fashioned money shops and new banks can provide assistance for flexible use of money by providing higher interest rates. Consequently, money shops and banks, especially the banks in the recent decade or so, have become the major pool of currency storage for urban residents. This largely explains why the banking industry has developed at a fast pace nowadays.

The especially wealthy also use money shops as their storage place on certain occasions, whether the money they store is from land rent, taxation, or any other accumulation methods. Although the storage is performing the function of generating interests, its final purpose is to accumulate a larger amount of money so that they can meet the deposit threshold of foreign banks (for example, there was a time when the Hankou branch of HSBC set 100 thousand yuan as the minimum standard). Most strangely, the savings in foreign banks sometimes see no interest at all and instead require premiums. On this occasion, currency not only represents the simplest storage function but abnormally reflects the anti-storage function. This is to say, the storage in this form aims not to accumulate more currency to add to its total value, but to preserve its total value even at the expense of part of its value (factually, the savings of many warlords and politicians in foreign banks are always confiscated with excuses). Related to this kind of storage is the large amount of foreign money hoarded by national people in the safes of foreign banks, which obviously requires premiums.

Moreover, another method to store currency, also regarded as a variation of the simplest one, is to make use of various gold and silver ornaments to preserve the purity of currency. The manner of storage method is prevalent in all backward nations. It is even sometimes used to counter the measures of state-owned gold and silver currency system. After the new currency system took into place in 1935, this storage method has always been witnessed in China.

It is natural that when a commodity currency economy develops to a certain stage and commerce and industry, particularly commerce, are fairly well-founded, there is at least a part of currency stored to reach the amount required by a certain business scale. However, even if the significance of the fact is underscored, it can only by and large justify that the storage function of Chinese currency remains at the aforesaid first two stages, and that of the third stage is merely in the bud.

8.4 Chinese Currency Functions as Means of Payment

The role that currency plays as a means of payment did not start in modern times. It was not until modern times that this function began to flourish.

In ancient times and the medieval period, the payment function of currency was mainly represented in lending relationships. Although the relationship arose from commodity circulation relationships or trade relationships in some cases, the commodity economy at that time was not mature enough to make currency extend its payment function, or in other words, the opportunities and conditions for the development of the function were not enabled in the circulation field itself. Therefore, the payment function of currency from ancient times to the medieval period could get across from the fiercest struggle between creditors and debtors. In early modern times, as commercial activities got promoted and all the conditions (such as public security, transportation, and currency itself) favorable to commerce were increasingly improved, the function of currency as a payment means shifted its focus from the lending relationship to the circulation relationship. In modern society, where commodity production has developed, everything that is produced or used in production has to be sold and bought. The buying of one side means the selling of the other. If problems occur in selling, the same also goes for buying. As general products vary in production time, the season that production depends on, and the distance from the sales market, they need to be purchased before sales and paid after purchase. In this way, the payment function of currency grows stronger with the development of commodity production and circulation. In return, the commodity production assisted by this function can make for the application of currency to the wage labor relationship and rent-tax relationship beyond the circulation field. As a result, the barter and compulsory labor, land rent paid with surplus labor, and so on, can be paid with currency.

The function of currency as a means of payment in China has been hindered primarily by the inherent uncertainty of the currency itself. The lack of precision in the currency's role as the unit of account and price standard already poses inconvenience when it functions as a medium of exchange or means of purchase. When it comes to serving as a means of payment, the difficulties are even greater. For instance, if a product is sold for a price of 100 yuan, and three months later, at the time of payment, the price of silver drops, the seller is naturally expected to bear the loss in proportion to the decline. However, if the amount of silver contained in each yuan, or its purity, is also reduced, the loss becomes even more substantial. From this perspective alone, it would be more advantageous for the seller to receive compensation in goods rather than in currency after a period of deferred payment. If we take into account that the price of silver has been steadily declining over the past several decades, and that currency manipulators have consistently benefited from reducing the silver or copper amount in standard or fractional currencies, the likelihood that credit sellers would reject currency as a means of payment increases significantly.

However, the development of currency relationships goes hand in hand with that of the entire commodity production. In the early stage of commodity production, merchant capital, or the financial capital of comprador commerce in China, had a dominant say. Merchants, in the interest of monopoly, combined usury business with commerce in the circulation process, reversing the relationship between buying and selling that instead acted as the relationship between creditors and debtors. The payment function currency performed herein is not being paid after but before the commodity transfer. By doing so, buyers are no longer debtors but instead creditors. Under this circumstance where production is subject to the restriction, or where merchants control producers by means of advance order or advance sale, etc., the payment function that is hard to be performed in the circulation field is inevitably restricted in the forms of wage, land rent, and even the debit-credit form of standard currency.

It is well known that the payment function of currency performed in wage is sure to grow stronger with the development of the relationship of wage labor, and the development of wage labor is obviously related to how commodity production is developed. Distinctly, Chinese commodity production is obstructed and remains backward. Despite the inherent difficulty in extending wage labor in quantity, its nature is very likely to be very abnormal. Various modes of wage payment, including barter, payment with labor, exchange of labor with animal power, and advance payment on credit, all impede the payment function of currency in wage, not to mention the household and subordinate payment modes.

The same situation also occurs with land rent. In a country like China where the tenant system prevails, if the land rent is paid with currency, the application of payment function will surely be extended. However, this is unlikely, as land rent can be developed into currency-based rent only on the basis of production, or more strictly, on the basis of capitalist production. However, the capitalist production in China, in industry and particularly in agriculture, is still extremely infant.

Definitely, the submission of taxation has long been paid in the form of currency, which serves as another way for the application of currency payment. Indeed, the collection of tax (regular and even extra) may be a powerful driver of the formation of the Chinese commodity economy because original products have to be put into circulation. In this regard, heavier taxation may promote the growth of the commodity economy. However, on the other hand, the destruction of production imposed by taxation or other similar non-economic exploitation methods will definitely confine the Chinese economy and the payment function of Chinese currency severely.

8.5 Chinese Currency Functions Viewed as a World Currency

China has been utilizing silver. The silver dollar as the standard currency (once silver tael) will lose its function as price standards once it goes to foreign countries. It is dispensable in the world commodity market to measure how much pure silver is contained in one dollar. It stands opposite to any commodities in the world with its original form of bar of bullion and internal value, which is like an overcoat or certain pounds of iron are worth how many ounces of silver. In foreign economic exchanges in reality, one should exchange pound or mark with silver dollars before he or she buys a British overcoat or German iron through the foreign exchange market. In this case, the price of silver against pound or mark is measured by comparing how much silver is contained in a silver dollar and how much gold is in a pound or mark, or in other words, the price is decided by the proportion of relative value between silver and gold. It can be interpreted that the silver dollar herein is viewed as the unit of account in foreign places, while its counterparts, pound or mark, also function as the unit of account to the outside world when they are used to exchange silver dollars.

There is nothing different between Chinese and foreign currency, but their similarity only lies in what has been aforesaid.

Before the year of 1933 when America began to drive up the price of silver, the ratio between silver and gold had been falling in the past decades or so. The fall of silver price meant the decreased foreign purchasing power of China, which could to some extent hinder import and promote export. Therefore, domestic production could be enhanced to some degree. However, as a matter of fact, the import surplus in Chinese foreign trade never shrank but instead kept increasing. At the same time, the industry never changed for the better. Since the elevated price plotted by America in 1933, the purchasing power of silver using countries became higher. Those Chinese people that were optimistic about the change believed that machines could therefore be bought at a lower price, and less silver could be utilized to repay foreign indemnities, debts, and the import surplus value, which was to greatly contribute to the economic rejuvenation of China.

In fact, for the industrial development of a country, the volatility of foreign currency value is only one of the promoting factors. What's more, whether the volatility is helpful to the economic prosperity of a country depends on whether it is voluntary or forced. If currency can be utilized as a weapon to fight against foreign countries and the ownership of currency right is under control, the rise and fall of its foreign value are both favorable. Otherwise, the rise and fall both pose threats when the volatility is passive and at the mercy of others.

In modern international economic struggles, tariff right is the first weapon, and monetary right is the second. When tariff right is not secured, the use of monetary right becomes significantly restricted. Moreover, due to the inherent flaws in China's monetary system, particularly the country's economic dependence on foreign powers, its currency not only fails to act as an offensive tool but is also insufficient for defense. In fact, it is often turned against the nation, exploited by foreign powers as a means to undermine China's economy.

In a developed economy with established international credit, a nation's currency serves not as a means of purchase but rather as a means of payment, primarily to settle trade imbalances. In contrast, China's international payments, in addition to its persistent trade deficits, are more significantly directed toward political indemnities and debt repayments. The financial burden imposed by foreign entities' profits and services in China weighs heavily on these payments. Although Chinese nationals have large deposits in foreign banks, which may appear capable of offsetting external debts, as mentioned earlier, these funds are not utilized for long- or short-term foreign lending. Instead, they are reserved for indemnities, insurance premiums, extravagant consumption, and to provide foreign entities with capital for increased speculation and exploitation in China's commodity and exchange markets.

Normally, for a country with frequent import surplus, heavy debt, and the demand for paying tribute to other countries, each year should see a great outflow of silver to close the gap, but since 1918, there has always been an import surplus of silver in China, the import volume saw a consecutive reduction since 1928, and the import surplus reached about tens of millions of dollars in 1932. In light of the aforesaid various foreign payments, this may seem weird. The fact is that China is involved in frequent lending and repaying of money and boasts a large amount of remittance from overseas Chinese, and foreigners invest all their gains from the exploitation economically and non-economically in China to make the best of the money. Under the circumstance where foreign countries manipulate Chinese finance and Chinese foreign exchange market, the application of Chinese currency both domestically and internationally is distorted and hampered. In regard to foreign relationships, China has to adopt some monetary policies that are detrimental to its economy rather than those helpful to its economic development.

Chapter 9
Currency Reform and Special Tendencies of Currency Movement

The aforesaid functions of the Chinese currency obviously take place through Chinese social relationships, and under the production and exchange conditions of Chinese society. There are commodity movement and currency movement in the overall operations of the commodity economy. The performance and representation of currency functions cannot be attributed to foreign exchange or foreign commodity production; it arises within the domestic activities of the commodity economy. As a result, although the flaw of currency itself is to some degree an impediment to the development of the commodity economy, it shouldn't go so far as to remark that the underdeveloped relationships of the commodity economy are mainly because currency fails to perform modern functions to advance commodity circulation as well as the smooth flow of capital. This misleading thought may lead to the illusion that the reform of currency itself could fundamentally change all of its original functions and that the entire commodity economy could therefore develop. This illusion has been dominated discussing in Chinese economic circles, and even now, people attribute, whether intentionally or not, the reform of the social economy to the efforts of "currency reform". In fact, the realistic experiences in the past ten years have long dispelled the misunderstanding. Based on the currency movement over the past decade, it is time to explore what special tendencies have been found after the currency reform.

The new currency system established in 1935 opened a new chapter in the history of Chinese currency. The greatest feature of the new currency system is undoubtedly that silver is collected by the government in a state-owned manner, and the government stocks the silver in preparation for issuing notes for circulation, a measure that has in part rectified many flaws of the original silver standard. The currency of various varieties in the past stood in the way of circulation and issuing, while the current one is unified and has extended its scope of circulation. All feudal, local, and even personal cast coins and paper money have gradually given way to bank notes and fractional currency in some backward areas, not to mention the national metropolis and the areas with convenient transportation. Given that the rights of issuing paper

Y. Wang, *The Basic Theory of Chinese Economy*,
https://doi.org/10.1007/978-981-95-6330-2_9

money and casting coins have largely been unified by the central government, Chinese currency has at least acquired a modern look.

Although it is unnecessary to elaborate on the domestic and international reasons why the currency reform turned out successful, it is necessary to point out, to carry on the statements above, that against the backdrop of the extreme panic about the economy and desolate commerce and industry, the currency reform is not so much adaptive to the requirements of developing the exchange relationships of commodity production as a means to improve the fiscal finance and even commerce at home and abroad. Just by recalling the large outflow of silver, gradual increase in unfavorable balance of trade, and long-term economic panics, the idealistic plan that aimed to increase the inflow of foreign capital in China by stabilizing the Chinese currency system is really evident.

It is therefore erroneous to conclude that the prolonged Chinese People's War of Resistance against Japanese Aggression and the overall chaos that followed the end of the war diminished the role of the new currency system in promoting production development. It has been established that the currency, which was designed with a modern appearance, was in fact used in a way that was incongruous with its outward form during wartime for over a decade.

Its first nature is shown in the fiscal characteristics of traditional politics throughout Chinese dynasties. Currency, due to its easier issuing than other methods to extort taxes, serves as a remedy for fiscal difficulties, and fiscal expenditures can be expanded at random. In this way, the fiscal characteristics become increasingly evident. Amid the long-term chaos caused by war, there are good reasons to be grateful to the currency reform whose result is said to have helped navigate through fiscal predicaments. However, it seems that the very reason why people are now deeply troubled by inflation again is that the currency reform made it more possible to issue currency randomly, so that the current economic crisis has become so overwhelmingly serious and devastating. The consequence carries on.

Its second nature is represented with the commercial characters in relation to the features of the modern Chinese economy. As is mentioned before, currency circulation and commodity circulation reinforce each other, so the interdependency between currency and commerce is clear-cut. However, the final task of modern currency entrusted by commodity and commercial flow is to speed up capital flow and fulfill the function of production. Currency capital should be turned into production capital, then into commodity capital, and finally into larger currency capital. In this flow process, currency serves as a link to induce and expand production, yet it in essence seems to just serve commerce in the case where other social prerequisites for production fall short. The currency which is issued in large amounts for fiscal requirements and whose value is reduced while the issuing proportion is on the rise has always been taken captive in the circulation field, strengthening the activities of commercial capital. Consequently, the trend is reinforced.

Strictly speaking, the above-mentioned characteristics of the currency in its services to fiscal finance and commerce are the inevitable results of an underdeveloped system of modern commodity production, where only the form of currency has changed superficially. However, the unified issue of currency and the promotion of the circulation of currency make people more aware of its special tendency to move as follows.

First, the more the issue of currency is fiscally driven, the more commercial the trend of its internal development is. The fact that the fiscal expenditures of a country are mainly made up for through issuing currency has, on the one hand, revealed that the country is underdeveloped in national economy and production and absent in tax resources, and on the other hand, manifested that its expense is not invested in production, but is outrageously random and wasteful, and encouraged by the convenience of issuing currency. When consumption is expanded on the basis of underdeveloped production, the input of arms and luxury goods will surely be increased and subsequently compensated by various primitive means that will inevitably be adopted to extort raw materials and semi-finished products, whether the consumption is invested in military force or in large-scale construction to pursue extravagance and hedonism. Thus, the crazily expanded issue of currency just seemingly serves to distribute foreign products and purchase original products in various manners. In other words, it merely functions as circulation to serve commerce alone.

Second, the more currency becomes congested in circulation, in accordance with the aforementioned principles, the more its inherent backward functions are exposed. This intensifies the contradictions between its superficial unity and modernization, revealing sharp disparities.

In accordance with the general law of currency movement, the currency or legal tender required by the non-circulation field would flow non-stop in the circulation. The legal tender in constant devaluation is less likely to be stored, and currency will be gradually excluded in payment. What if land rent, or those whose elements are currency-oriented, is paid with concrete objects? Besides, such things as wage, debt or salary have to some extent been the case in many areas. In urban areas, the foreign currency with gold standard acts as the duties of legal tender obviously or obscurely, and in the rural areas adjacent to towns, it is nearly regarded as a routine to view the old silver dollar as the unit of account and price standard for economic exchanges. If the situation carries on, the simple function of legal tender to serve commercial service is hard to proceed.

Third, the more currency drives up the abnormal activities of commercial capital in its flow process, the less likely the circulation and trade of general social commodities (foreign or local) is based on the measurement of value and price by producers according to cost, and the more likely this price is to go up and down at the mercy of the ability and greed of merchants to hoard for speculation. Consequently, producers are increasingly likely to be captured by merchants and usurers. If producers are to save themselves, the only way left is to turn themselves into merchants, wholly or partially. By doing so, the tendency of movement of social capital is subject to this kind of currency movement, which is to be illustrated in the next part.

Issues discussed in this part

(1) Try to respectively describe the relationships between commodity and currency in their historical development.

(2) How should one distinguish the unit of account from price standards? What role do the currency functions of payment means and storage means play in capitalist commodity production?
(3) Why was the silver standard system adopted in China before the currency reform?
(4) Is it the underdeveloped currency relationships that restrict commodity production, or the underdeveloped commodity production relationships that limit the backward functions of currency?
(5) Is Chinese currency reform more conducive to industry or to commerce?
(6) Money is more financial in nature, so why is it correspondingly more commercial?

Part IV
Forms of Chinese Capital

Abstract This chapter reveals the exceptionally high rates and stark diversity of interest practices in China. Three vastly different interest spheres existed: the low rates of foreign bank capital (~4-8%), the higher rates of modern Chinese banks (~9-20%), and the astronomical rates of widespread traditional usury (24%to 300%or more). This disparity reflected extreme economic imbalance and a fractured financial landscape. Usury thrived on the widespread desperation of impoverished small producers seeking funds primarily for consumption, not productive investment. Consequently, its rates were unconstrained by any average rate of profit and were profoundly destructive. Even new-style bank capital often exhibited usurious characteristics. Prohibitively high interest rates drastically increased the cost of industrial capital, devouring its potential profits and acting as a powerful brake on industrial development.

Chapter 10
The General Concepts of Capital and its Occurrence and Development

When it comes to Chinese capital, the general concepts of capital, capital itself and its occurrence and development should be first clarified in the way other Chinese economic forms have been expounded. Although the focus is on the distinctiveness of Chinese capital and what features it possesses compared to the capital forms of general advanced countries, precisely for this reason, seeking differences from common ground is a must and isolated observation method should be avoided. This is because the term "capital" has been defined by almost every economist. The definitions from authoritative economists are as follows.

Adam Smith——Capital refers to the part of property used to make profits.

Roebertus——"Capital (raw materials and tools) means the products used in reproduction".

Böhm-Bawerk——"Capital is a property that aims to generate profits".

These definitions may appear to vary considerably, but they share a common flaw: an inadequate and ambiguous understanding of capital.

It is widely acknowledged that capital can occur in the form of currency, of production and consumption means, and of finished commodities. However, none of these forms can become capital in isolation and can be the polar opposite to capital. As a result, a better perception of capital should be "not an object but interpersonal relationships with objects as media." Such a description may be too abstract for non-economists. But in fact, currency becomes capital only when it forms relationships between the lenders and borrowers, granting the lender the right to demand information from the borrowers. Or in other words, it is production means that helps to forge employer-employee relationships between capitalists and laborers in which employers are entitled to claim profits from employees, thus capital comes into shape. Therefore, the definition might as well go like this: "Capital represents the material means by which its value is multiplied under certain social relationships."

Although capital, as is mentioned hereinbefore, can occur not only in the form of currency but in other material forms seen as commodities and production means. Its concrete representation, or the multiplication of its value, has always centered

Y. Wang, *The Basic Theory of Chinese Economy*,
https://doi.org/10.1007/978-981-95-6330-2_10

on currency in its entire movement process when currency is viewed as universal equivalent. Capital is inseparable from currency, so currency doesn't occur in any society out of a sudden. Given that capital has to play its role by means of currency, people might as well track its origin through monetary relations. Economic historians have informed us that currency could exist prior to the occurrence of capital, bank, and wage labor, and that it is historically true. This is because currency is the inevitable result of the circulation of simple commodities, and it remains the same instead of the form of capital long after its occurrence. If currency is to be developed into capital, the currency itself must have possessed certain conditions, been separated from general commodity, and functioned as universal equivalent. This is to say, commodity circulation and then commodity production must have reached a considerably high level.

The difference between currency itself and currency as capital lies in the form of commodity circulation.

Selling for purchase means that producers sell the products of their own to buy those they need with the currency gained from selling. In this case, currency is utilized as "pure currency" and only plays the role of medium. Opposite to this circulation form of selling for purchase is buying for selling, which refers to the fact that the currency owner makes use of his currency to purchase some kind of commodities with the aim of reselling them to others rather than for his own use. On this occasion, its currency is not used as "pure currency" but serves as a means to multiply value. Or in other words, it is used as capital.

As the social economy develops, commodity circulation converts from "selling for purchase" to "buying for selling". During this process, correspondingly, currency is more likely to be utilized not as "pure currency" but capital, and to become more capitalized.

However, the so-called capital has three main forms, including interest-bearing capital, commercial capital, and industrial capital. The first two capital forms are the so-called ones "pre-capitalist", which only require commodity circulation, so the usury industry and commerce existed in historical times when there was simple commodity circulation. They can act beyond the production to put pressure on or drive production externally. However, the so-called basic form of capital (industrial capital) is different from them in that each of its links has to do with production. The formation and development of production factors lays the foundation for its establishment and imposes restrictions on its development.

Naturally, the entire movement process of industrial capital, just like that of commercial capital or usury capital, begins with currency, but the currency owners want to use their currency as industrial capital instead of commercial or usury capital. They have to find out free workers who sell their only commodity—labor force, in the market, except the simple or even relatively developed circulation relationships of general commodities. Therefore, the emergence of free workers may be the foremost prerequisite for currency to divert from commercial and interest-bearing functions to industrial function. This is to say, even if a person boasts "currency, living materials, tools and machines, but lacks workers, he will not turn into a capitalist". During the early period of the modern industrial revolution, especially in the colonies beginning to undergo capitalist transformation, such as America and Australia, such practice was ubiquitous. Moreover, from a specific perspective in reality, one with currency, production means and living materials, fails to become a capitalist because laborers are not available. But from the general public's term, the failure of finding laborers implies the social production means and living materials are still in the hands of general laborers and have not been turned into capital. The production means and living materials are not capitalized yet when possessed by direct producers. Only when they serve to exploit laborers, they become capital. The fact that laborers are separated from the means and living materials of their own and turn to rely on those of others is neither out of their own will nor others' arbitrary coercion, but concerns a matter of the change in social relationships, from feudalistic to capitalist social relationships.

In a society where this social change has been accomplished, the two pre-flood capital forms, namely pre-capitalist capital forms, will have their nature changed. The commercial capital will no longer act independent of the production field and become a vital factor or link facilitating the circulation of industrial capital in the entire production process. The circulation driven by the activities of industrial capital will be taken into the general production process and subject to the scale and movement law of industrial capital. As commercial capital finishes the transformation, interest-bearing capital will sublate its usury form and change into the form of bank capital, which makes it no longer a persecutor but a booster of production. With regard to the relationships of industrial capital, if the former, or commercial capital, is thought to undertake the business of commodity circulation for industry, it is fair to say the latter, or interest-bearing capital, operates the business of currency circulation for industry, which is what is achieved under the transformation of the two forms.

This historical transformation cannot be accomplished at one stroke in any society, but it varies in requirement of time and particularly adoption of methods given the different natural and historical conditions of each society. In this regard, although extensive discussion is not possible in this book, the pre-capitalist form of capital of some countries can adequately represent the entire picture of the socioeconomic organizations, or in other words, the representation presents a panorama of the social economy of the country. Meanwhile, if the pre-capitalist form of capital of a country has an adequate impact on the development towards capitalism and confines its transformation, there are good reasons to believe that if a society fails to accomplish the historical transformation smoothly, its pre-capitalist form of capital, or the nature of its usury and independent commercial capital, has in fact played a decisive role. What's more, if industrial capital cannot gain the dominant position in a society, its backward capital forms will remain overriding. If industrial capital cannot revolutionize interest-bearing and commercial capital, interest-bearing capital is still with the nature of usury, and commercial capital is still independent. These two capitals will kill industrial capital, instead.

This is what the history of world capital reveals to people.

Chapter 11
An Examination of the Quality and Quantity of Various Forms of Capital in China

11.1 Coexisting Forms of Capital

Various forms of capital, both modern and non-modern, coexist in Chinese society.

It is typical for highly developed capitalist countries to experience imbalanced economic development, as certain backward sectors or fields are inevitably left behind, where pre-modern forms of capital may still thrive. However, the scope of these activities continually shrinks as capitalist production methods advance. These forms have not only lost their decisive role but have also been transformed.

Nevertheless, this is not the case in China. Although modern industrial capital and bank capital have emerged, pre-capitalist forms of capital not only retain decisive influence but also hinder industrial capital and distort bank capital. This is unsurprising, as capital relies on the growth of a monetary economy. However, Chinese commodity production remains largely at the stage of small-scale production, and the currency system is not only diverse but also functionally backward, contributing to the diversity of capital forms.

Before analyzing the characteristics of Chinese capital, two points must be clarified. First, Chinese capital in general includes foreign capital, but for the sake of clarity, it is set aside in the following discussion. Second, the capital forms discussed here refer to those existing prior to the War of Resistance against Japanese Aggression; contemporary capital will be addressed later in this book.

We now investigate the characteristics of existing capital forms.

First, we analyze the most prominent form: commercial capital. There is no denying that Chinese commercial capital has acquired new characteristics during modernization, but its original traits must be understood first. Traditional Chinese commercial capital differed from that of Western Europe in its socioeconomic foundations. The latter relied mainly on a seignorial economy, where land was not freely tradable, and merchants stood in opposition to landowners. In contrast, under China's landlord economy, land could be freely transferred, allowing wealthy merchants to become landowners and vice versa. This close relationship between merchants and

Y. Wang, *The Basic Theory of Chinese Economy*,
https://doi.org/10.1007/978-981-95-6330-2_11

landowners mitigated the fundamental opposition between commercial capital and land ownership, though it did not eliminate it entirely.

For instance, usury capital was often used to acquire land. Originally, foreign trade fell within the scope of commerce, but as merchants gained land rights, their interest in foreign trade diminished. Furthermore, autocratic regimes based on the landlord economy imposed strict controls on foreign trade. Since merchants were unlikely to engage in foreign activities, industry had little direct connection with them. Government-controlled manufacturing and rural handicrafts, integrated with agriculture for self-sufficiency, fundamentally impeded commercial expansion.

It might seem that merchants should have focused on improving land and agriculture, but since land was easy to purchase and served as a symbol of social status, they preferred acquiring more land rather than investing in its improvement. However, modernization has altered the relationships between commercial capital and other aspects of society. Land products are no longer the sole focus of commerce, and land ownership no longer guarantees social status or political power. In recent decades, the trend of land concentration has weakened, as wealthy merchants have shown declining interest in land rights.

This shift has also changed the relationship between commercial capital and foreign trade. Consumer commerce, for example, has fostered closer ties with production enterprises and, through foreign trade, began to disentangle the traditional integration of agriculture and industry. This has created opportunities for merchants to act as intermediaries. Similarly, the relationship between commercial capital and usury capital has transformed. Previously, the commercial capital relied on usury to consolidate land holdings; now, it uses usury to control production enterprises.

However, the comprador commerce that emerged from China's modernization remains limited in how much it can change. Externally, it serves as a submissive link to foreign industrial capital; internally, it fails to dominate domestic production. While the commercial capital has expanded into rural areas, leading to increased agricultural commercialization and the disintegration of the natural economy, its service to foreign capital hinders the growth of Chinese industry. Thus, although it has shed some traditional characteristics, it retains its original nature and may revert to relying on land rights if foreign support wanes.

We now turn to interest-bearing capital, which includes both non-modern usury capital and modern bank capital. In a transitional society where the industrial revolution has not fully taken hold, these two forms coexist and interact. Usury capital seeks modernization to adapt to the new environment, while bank capital is forced to perform functions contrary to its nature in the old environment. Chinese interest-bearing capital exemplifies this duality.

To understand its characteristics, we must first distinguish between the functions and foundations of usury capital and bank capital. Generally, usury capital targets small producers, such as farmers and artisans, while bank capital serves large producers or industrialists. Usury capital relies on personal accumulation and thrives in backward societies with high interest rates, whereas bank capital draws on social accumulation and operates in prosperous economies with lower rates. Usury capital is closely linked to commerce, while bank capital is tied to industrial capital. In essence, the two are opposed, rooted in different social economies—feudal and capitalist.

In China, however, their opposition is not clear-cut but intense and overlapping. Due to underdeveloped industry, bank capital often targets the same small producers as usury capital, leading to competition and interaction rather than mutual exclusion. This ambiguity is compounded by the influence of international capital, which initially leverages traditional usury networks but later excludes them when they prove inadequate. As a result, the old and new financial sectors sometimes coordinate to resist external pressure.

Moreover, the opposition is partial rather than comprehensive. While usury capital remains dominant in vast rural and backward urban areas, bank capital has taken precedence in regions with developed commodity and currency economies. The decline of usury capital in these areas is not due to its incompatibility with industrial development but because of its unsystematic and localized nature, which makes it unsuitable for serving international capital or meeting the demands of national fiscal finance.

For example, traditional finance profited from currency fluctuations and the exchange between silver dollars and taels, but currency reforms aimed at stabilizing the national fiscal system undermined its viability. Additionally, its decline reflects an inability to adapt to new technological, organizational, and capital requirements.

The above suggests that the waning of usury capital's traditional advantage appears to deviate from the typical evolution of interest-bearing capital. Meanwhile, bank capital, now dominant in developed areas, exhibits several distinct characteristics. First, it struggles to shed its usurious nature. Without a solid foundation in heavy industry, Chinese bank capital often operates like usury capital, charging high-interest rates and targeting small-scale producers and consumers.

Second, Chinese bank capital is heavily fiscal in nature. The growth of Chinese banks, particularly after World War I, was closely tied to government debt rather than industrial expansion. Between 1925 and the outbreak of the War of Resistance, while Chinese industry declined, the banking sector expanded in number and scale, fueled by large issuances of government bonds. This fiscal characteristic represents a critical phase in the development of bank capital, though its duration varies across countries.

Third, Chinese bank capital is highly commercial in nature. While banking is inherently a form of commerce, its commercial feature here refers to its close ties to trade, particularly foreign trade, rather than industry. In 1934, for instance, bank investments were directed largely toward commerce (29%) and public organizations, including government debt (41%), with only 13% going to industry. This commercial focus aligns bank capital more with currency and commodity circulation than with production.

Given the characteristics of commercial and interest-bearing capital, we can infer the nature of Chinese industrial capital. Each capital form reflects the general traits of capital, and organic relationships exist among them.

First, the source of industrial capital is inherently deficient. Accumulation typically begins with commercial capital, but in China, the ties between commercial capital and land rights hindered this process. Moreover, the recurring destruction of commercial capital during periods of political upheaval—such as the Taiping Rebellion—further obstructed the formation of industrial capital.

Although the commodification of agricultural products after the opening of treaty ports provided some accumulation, this capital rarely transformed into industrial capital due to unfavorable conditions, including lack of tariff autonomy, transportation rights, and a functional industrial securities market. The characteristics of Chinese bank capital further constrained industrial expansion by limiting investment channels.

In addition to scarce accumulation, the organization of capital was backward. Few enterprises adopted the joint-stock model; most were sole proprietorships or partnerships among relatives. Official or government-supervised businesses also played a significant role, particularly in sectors like transportation and mining. While resembling modern capitalist enterprises in form, they were fundamentally different, arising from an inability to concentrate capital and develop advanced technology rather than from organic growth.

These traits led to a third characteristic: low organic composition of capital. Industrial capital required mechanization and fixed capital, but the small scale of most enterprises—75% had capital under 200,000 yuan—made this impossible. Light industries, which dominated, relied on imported machinery and faced monopolistic pressures from imperialist policies. The absence of external or internal security further encouraged a "guerrilla" style of production, adaptable but technologically stagnant.

Agriculture faced similar challenges. Traditional land ownership relations drained capital away from productive investment, with fixed capital accounting for only 2%–4% of total agricultural expenses. This reflected the same difficulty in achieving higher organic composition.

11.2 Investigation from Quality to Quantity

The characteristics of the forms of Chinese capital that have been previously clarified, with their respective characteristics, not only exhibit a mutual and organic coordination but can also be perceived as the divisions of the distinctive total capital. An analysis of social sciences indicates the existence of certain intimate functional relationships between the quality and quantity of any social matters and phenomena. Indeed, the respective characteristics of Chinese commercial capital, interest-bearing capital, and industrial capital can be seen to allude to their proportions to the total capital.

It is challenging to ascertain with precision the extent to which social wealth can be transformed into capital and the proportions that should be employed to divide it into respective capitals, given that these figures depend on a multitude of social conditions that are ever-changing at any moment. Nevertheless, if people are to ascertain the proportions that indicate the general trend of evolution rather than the fixed figures in a static economic situation, the aforementioned hardship may be significantly alleviated. Social sciences demonstrate that the proportions of capitals vary distinctly between developed and underdeveloped social industries. In an undeveloped society, capital is accumulated from commerce and even from the usury industry. As social credit and transportation that are compatible with the social form are underdeveloped, the turnover of merchants' capital is slow, resulting in a significant proportion of merchant capital in total currency capital. The less developed the production is, the larger the total amount of merchant capital will be in comparison to the total amount of commodity in circulation. It was thus observed by an economist that when production remains underdeveloped, the majority of the real currency capital in a society must be in the hands of merchants. Indeed, whether a society adopts a commercial form or a usurious form in close relationship with commerce, monetary capital is in large part referred to as general capital, given that the small-scale commodity production on which their social foundation is based is not undertaken in the capital form in terms of production cost. In contrast, in a society with developed industry, general capital is accumulated industrially, as well as social credit and new means of transportation that adapt to industrial development. This reduces the amount of currency capital used in business operations. Consequently, the proportion of commercial capital in total social capital is correspondingly lowered, and the amount of commercial capital represented by currency lags behind industrial capital in an inversely proportional manner as industry evolves.

This is the fundamental understanding that enables the accurate interpretation of the proportion of the quantity of the aforementioned Chinese capitals. Furthermore, their actual proportions reinforce the confidence of this understanding.

The previous analysis of the characteristics of various kinds of capital commenced with commercial capital, while the investigation into the quantity of capital herein will commence with industrial capital. In 1924, when Chinese industrial development began to decline from its prosperity period, the total capital of 565 registered factories across China amounted to 224.14 million yuan, among which the investment in transportation and mining industries and foreign industrial investment were not listed. In 1930, the total investment in railways, the most important transportation sector in China, was approximately 520 million yuan. Concurrently, the industrial capital in the national capital before the War of Resistance against Japanese Aggression approached one billion yuan, with the investment in coal mining, metal mining, and shipping collectively amounting to approximately 500 million yuan. This figure is comparable to the statistics presented by Gu Chunfan, who estimated that the capital of the new industries before the war was approximately 3.80781 billion yuan, of which the foreign investment accounted for 2.8 billion yuan, or 74%, while only 987 million yuan was from national capital.

The quantity of interest-bearing capital is incompatible with the industrial capital. In 1925, the total capital of 141 Chinese banks amounted to 158,160,471 yuan, and by 1932, the total capital of the 150 banks had risen to 266,700,000 yuan. In 1935, there were 1347 old-fashioned private banks in China whose total capital amounted to a mere 50 million yuan. The two sections added up to approximately 300 million yuan. However, in terms of the real income, the total amount of paid-in capital of banks, provident funds, savings, and issued notes reached 2.6 billion yuan in 1931. This figure was exceeded by that of foreign banks with a paid-in capital of 516 million yuan, which reached 8.4 billion yuan.

Although it is not straightforward to estimate the commercial capital that was the most convertible and kept converting, the following two facts can be used to provide a rough calculation. Firstly, Chinese commerce after the opening of five treaty ports was of greater magnitude externally than it was internally. It can be reasonably argued that the development of domestic commerce or the commercialized and commodity-oriented agricultural and industrial products was driven by the requirements of foreign trade. In 1864, the input and output of Chinese foreign trade was less than 100 million taels, and by 1914 this figure had reached 920 million taels, with a further increase to 1.8 billion taels by 1924. From the fact that more than one billion foreign trade transactions occur annually, it can be inferred that the commercial capital employed in its circulation must have been considerable. If one considers the underdeveloped social credit and transportation systems, it can be surmised that the amount held by merchants among the total currency capital would be considerable. In 1931, C. F. Remer estimated that foreign investment in China was 3,242,500 thousand U.S. dollars, of which 2,531,900 thousand U.S. dollars was commercial investment and 710,000 thousand U.S. dollars was government loans. Providing the exchange rate of U.S. dollar against Chinese currency was 4 to 1, near 10 billion yuan was invested in commerce among the total foreign investment of 13 billion yuan, apart from the government loans of 3.2 billion yuan. In particular, the so-called commercial investment herein refers to any kinds of capital used to make profits in the form of enterprises, including the aforesaid bank capital and industrial capital. If the two varieties of capital, including bank capital of 1.6 billion yuan (total amount of the items of pay-in capital, provident fund, and issued notes, the balance between the total amount of 8.4 billion yuan and deposits of 6.8 billion yuan) and industrial capital of 2.8 billion yuan, were deducted from the 10-billion commercial investment, the resulting figure would be 5.6 billion yuan. The remaining 5.6 billion yuan would be the commercial capital owned by such trading places of 8000 foreign firms of different sizes as stores, hotels, and even entertainment venues. (Refer to the translation of C. F. Remer's Foreign Investments in China, translated by Jiang Xuekai.)

The aforementioned figures demonstrate that, among the various types of Chinese capitals (with or without foreign investment), industrial capital constituted a relatively minor proportion. Meanwhile, if bank capital that is related to commerce and is actually engaged in business operations is included in the calculation of commercial capital, the overwhelming advantage of commercial capital in quantity would help to identify the relative backwardness of Chinese industrial capital.

11.3 Re-investigation from Quantity to Quality

The analysis presented here indicates that the distribution of various types of Chinese capital was ultimately contingent upon their respective quality regulations. The backward industrial form, which was characterised by limited new operations and in which pre-capitalist small-scale commodity production held a dominant position, had to make way for the independent activities of commercial capital. This law, which has been revealed by the development history of global capital, states that the independent development of commercial capital was in reverse proportion to that of capitalist production.

Not only does the law demonstrate the varying relationships from quality to quantity between commercial capital and industrial capital, but shows the variation from quantity to quality.

Commerce that developed independently was not subject to regulation by industry, and thus was bound to regulate and nurture itself at the cost of the latter. The increase in the quantity of Chinese commercial capital has consistently been based on its exploitation of industries, both new and old. The unfavorable situation for industrial development would not only hinder the transfer of capital to industry, but would also alter the utilization of the capital that has been invested in industry. The smaller the quantity of industry, the more helpless it would be to reverse the adverse prospect, and the more powerful its original characteristics would be.

Certainly, merely theoretical talk does not suffice, and facts should be more powerful, which are presented as follows.

Chapter 12
Accumulation, Centralization and Decentralization of Chinese Capital

Previous chapters examined the forms of Chinese capital and their qualitative features. This chapter extends the analysis by bringing foreign and international capital into the picture and tracing how it entered domestic circuits and influenced the overall movement of Chinese capital.

However, the aforementioned Chinese capital has set aside foreign or international capital in China. In addition to a few necessary exceptions, foreign investment and its role in Chinese capital flows have been largely overlooked and viewed as an external pressure or obstruction, all of which are for the illustrative purposes. The present research on the entire movement of Chinese capital cannot ignore the role of foreign investment, as otherwise it would prove that foreign investment played a decisive role in the entire movement process of Chinese capital.

Therefore, the reasons why foreign investment had such a dominant say have to be elaborated on before one discusses the accumulation, centralization and decentralization of Chinese capital.

12.1 The Role of International Capital in Chinese Capital Movement

One could argue that distinguishing purely between "international" and "local" capital in China is notoriously difficult, a point many researchers of Chinese economics have emphasized.

The two were often intimately intertwined, creating a cycle where extraction was problematic. For instance, Chinese comprador merchants accumulated significant wealth facilitated by foreign capital, which was then often deposited as savings in foreign banks. These savings, in turn, could be deployed by those same banks to fund their business operations within China. Profits generated from these ventures

Y. Wang, *The Basic Theory of Chinese Economy*,
https://doi.org/10.1007/978-981-95-6330-2_12

could subsequently be channeled into sectors like mining, which, while potentially operated by Chinese national capital, completed a deeply integrated cycle.

However, studying this phenomenon requires moving past isolated examples. We need to abstract a general understanding of their respective roles from these intricate, specific contexts. Without this, we cannot clearly differentiate Chinese capital from foreign investment, nor can we distinguish industrial capital from the other capital forms it interacts with in circulation. Therefore, we cannot discuss the entire capital movement in overly broad terms. A productive discussion must be predicated on first understanding the specific functional scopes and limits of each capital type within the overall movement.

To understand foreign capital's role in China's capital movement, we must first address two prerequisite questions. The first is whether the will of foreign capital's operators was unified—in other words, did they play a consistent role? The second is whether foreign capital owners could unify their intentions regarding capital development in China and consistently implement them in practice.

The first issue concerns the economic demands and prospects that imperialist countries imposed on backward nations. These specific demands varied significantly due to the unique natural conditions and historical relationships between the imperialist and underprivileged countries. Given the disparate interests of different imperialist powers, it was challenging for them to implement a uniform imperialist policy; sometimes, their approaches were even diametrically opposed. However, as imperialist states, they all shared certain fundamental requirements for a backward economy like China's. This makes it possible to identify their common policies, which often transcend their temporary, partial conflicts. Furthermore, while the conflicts arising from differing demands tend to draw focus, the common ground or balance of interests reflected within these conflicts is often overlooked. The history of foreign capital investment in China over the past century provides ample evidence of this phenomenon.

The second point has been debated frequently. The most convincing view is that while capitalist countries might adopt different policies at different stages—sometimes even appearing to facilitate the growth of Chinese capitalism—their ultimate goal was not necessarily China's successful independent development. For example, before the imperialist stage, feudal production methods were prevalent in backward areas. However, during the imperialist stage, there was a clear aspiration to maintain or co-opt feudal relations in underdeveloped areas to suit their own economic needs. This theory is sound but often misses a key point: when imperialists implement policies, they must do so based on objective conditions on the ground. Our following study will proceed from this crucial aspect.

Regarding our analytical procedure, we must shift our focus from the imperialist attitude towards Chinese economic development to the actual growth trajectory of Chinese industrial capital. The outcomes of Chinese industrial capital development over the past century were largely shaped by external factors, though these factors inevitably worked through China's existing socioeconomic structures. The obstructions and setbacks encountered by Chinese industrial capital can thus be interpreted through this lens.

Firstly, it is evident that imperialist countries did not permit or genuinely expect a backward nation like China to develop robust independent industries. They feared this would negatively impact their own markets for manufactured goods, their supply of raw materials, and the outlets for their surplus capital. While the first two reasons are straightforward, the last requires elaboration. Successful industrial development in a country leads to expanded reproduction and the accumulation of large amounts of domestic capital. This, in turn, can create a barrier to the inflow of surplus capital from other countries, a point we will elaborate on later.

Secondly, one might ask: even with the aforementioned obstruction, wouldn't it have been in their interest to allow some controlled industrial development in China to secure a more favorable position in the market, utilize cheap labor and raw materials, and address their own problem of surplus capital? While they may have entertained this idea, putting it into practice consistently proved unfeasible. Establishing an industrial unit in China often risked sidelining the same industry in their home country. Thus, competition from their own domestic industries was the first obstacle to the random expansion of industry in China. Furthermore, the intense rivalry between imperialist countries meant that any industry one country developed in China would face competition not just from Chinese capital but from the interests of other imperialist powers. For instance, if Japan transferred its textile industry to China, it would face competition not only from British-owned mills in China but also from Lancashire imports. China itself could neither fully defend its own industry nor offer protection to any particular foreign industry. This inter-imperialist rivalry was the second difficulty. Moreover, while each imperialist power had its own sphere of influence in China, the convenience this offered was countered by the difficulties of controlling labor, sourcing raw materials, and managing sales markets across a vast and politically complex country. Recently, these spheres of influence grew increasingly unstable due to fierce struggles among the powers, revealing the third difficulty. Finally, the backward production relationships and the resultant challenges in security, transportation, currency stability, and purchasing power that hindered Chinese national industry also posed significant challenges for imperialist industries operating in China. This constituted the fourth major difficulty.

Faced with the objective reality that they could neither successfully drive China's full industrial development nor simply replace it, imperialist powers naturally sought to exploit any and all privileges available to guide the movement of the Chinese economy and Chinese capital in a direction that suited their own interests.

A country's financial system exerts a pivotal influence on the overall movement of its capital. Through their control over indemnities, foreign loans, the gold standard, public debt, and the foreign exchange market, imperialist powers held Chinese finance largely at their mercy. This control systematically impeded the diversion of domestic funds towards industrial development.

They would only invest in Chinese industry out of necessity or when significant profitability was assured, often using their control over financial and securities markets to prepare for mergers and acquisitions or to lure Chinese capital into sectors only to absorb it later. Moreover, they actively strengthened the role of Chinese commercial capital, often at the expense of industrial capital. A "harmonious" division of labor emerged: the export trade in raw materials, initially dominated by Chinese merchants, saw increased foreign involvement after the treaty ports opened, while the import trade in manufactured goods, initially managed by foreign entities, saw growing Chinese participation. This comprador commerce flourished precisely because Chinese finance was under foreign control. The social conditions fostering this type of commercial capital forced other sectors to adapt. When an overwhelming external force dominates the economy, the development path of indigenous capital is inevitably constrained or distorted. Understanding this dynamic is the pivotal issue we must address before we can truly investigate the movement of Chinese capital.

12.2 The Accumulation Process of Chinese Capital

In the entire movement of capital, the process of accumulation—both historical and contemporary—must be clarified from the outset. Capital accumulation constitutes the fundamental dimension of capital movement and serves as a key to deciphering the nature of Chinese capital.

To facilitate an understanding of the various forms of capital accumulation in China, it is useful to briefly introduce the two most frequently confused types. Capitalist accumulation and pre-capitalist (or primitive) accumulation are polar opposites in nature. The former is based on the surplus value created by industrial laborers, which is transformed into capital. When reinvested in the reproduction process alongside the original capital, it enables expanded reproduction. Under conditions of free competition, each industrial capitalist is driven to adopt new and cost-heavy machinery to gain a competitive edge, reduce production costs, and convert as much surplus value as possible into capital. Consequently, the pursuit of industrial expansion becomes a form of forced accumulation.

However, accumulation did not always take this form. To grasp the origins of industrial capital, we must turn to the other method—commonly referred to as primitive accumulation. In contrast to the capitalist mode, this method relies primarily on the surplus product or surplus value generated by small independent producers. On this foundation, the activities of commercial capital and usury capital emerge and intensify. As these activities deepen and extend, it becomes increasingly difficult to convert the surplus product into capital; in fact, the original capital—or more precisely, the original factors of production—may even be eroded. While reproduction on this basis may sometimes expand or remain unchanged in scale, the accumulation achieved does not stem from internal expansion of industrial demand or from economic coercion alone. Instead, it depends heavily on extra-economic forces such as public debt, taxation, commercial policy, and modern banking policy operating outside the industrial process.

This basic framework of accumulation allows us to examine the nature and principal forms of capital accumulation in China.

Chinese industrial capital gained some momentum in certain light industries during the last imperialist war, when external pressure eased slightly. However, once the war ended, pressure resurged, and sectors with weak industrial foundations were easily absorbed by foreign-invested industry. It is true that some sectors enjoyed abnormal prosperity even as Chinese national industry declined or was taken over. Yet, as the above analysis suggests, such prosperity was generally short-lived. Moreover, the limited capital accumulation that did occur still relied on non-economic privileges and was aided by primitive methods. Not only foreign capital, but even part of the accumulation within national industry depended on such primitive assistance. When capitalist relations of production have not yet become dominant in a society, or remain subordinate to traditional modes from an overall perspective, capitalist accumulation tends to lean on primitive methods. In fact, in the early development of capitalist countries, nearly all gains from industrial operation were made possible indirectly through government protectionist policies or funds raised by primitive means by the state.

Up to the present, China remains at a similar stage. The principal mode of capital accumulation is still primitive, based on the surplus labor of small independent producers. This implies that accumulation in a capitalist form may have been sustained under the shelter of primitive accumulation—even if not directly due to official protectionist policies, then because of the privileges imperialism enjoyed within the feudal setting.

It is precisely because of the primitive character of capital accumulation in China that its level and scale cannot be simply or directly read from the scale of production. Instead, accumulation is indirectly reflected in the scale of comprador commercial capital, modern usury capital, and the abnormal fiscal capital intertwined with it.

Although statistical data on the various forms of Chinese capital may give a general picture of the scale of accumulation, several issues require further analysis.

First, we should not focus solely on the accumulation of capital in its various forms. As the evidence shows, while the scale of production—the real basis of accumulation—may have expanded for a very small number of small producers, many struggled to maintain simple reproduction, and the majority saw their scale reduced or were forced to shut down entirely. Sectors where production was cut back or ceased clearly yielded no accumulation; indeed, they consumed accumulation previously achieved. Much of what appears in the statistics of Chinese capital is not the result of new accumulation, but rather the outcome of original capital being swallowed up and redistributed through exploitation. The widespread bankruptcies in both rural and urban areas reveal the core of the problem. Unfortunately, whereas in capitalist accumulation the expansion or contraction of the overall production scale largely reflects whether accumulation has occurred, in China's primitive accumulation the picture is obscured by the involvement of other capital forms that claim to represent accumulation. This is a key reason why the prevalent phenomenon of bankruptcy has failed to attract sufficient attention from the public and even from some economists.

Second, it is evident that capital forms other than industrial capital—such as commercial capital, agricultural land capital, and old and new financial capital—lacked stability and could shift rapidly from one form to another. Land rent, for instance, constitutes a basic form of rural capital accumulation. In its unmodernized form in China, it absorbed not only potential profit and wages, but even income from rural sidelines and the necessary living expenses of peasants. Given the interrelation between landlord extravagance and the growing concentration of land ownership, land rent served as the operational basis for commercial capital and usury capital (or capital of a usurious nature). Though commerce and usury employed distinct accumulation methods, land rent played a pivotal role in enabling their accumulation. Such circulation or collaboration was a natural outcome of the socioeconomic conditions that had developed in Chinese society. Furthermore, these capital forms could be artificially inflated through credit, making their statistical figures an unreliable gauge of the real accumulation of social wealth. Nevertheless, many Chinese economists have been all too ready to take the growth of bank capital as a sign of economic prosperity, as if social capital could spring directly from bank vaults and account books, without the need for industrial expansion.

Third, if the essence of capital accumulation remains obscured in the spheres of commerce, agriculture, and finance, it becomes completely confused when expressed through public debt, taxation, and currency systems dominated by fiscal policy. In a country like China, which lacked a modern industrial base, earnings and accumulation in private commerce and finance were inevitably tied to government fiscal policy, and especially to the commercial and financial framework imposed by imperialist powers in China. In the case of Chinese commerce and finance, accumulation was highly dependent on non-economic forces emanating from abroad. The more that commerce, usury, and banking benefited from fiscal channels such as taxation and public debt, the more these tools were used as instruments for double exploitation or outright expropriation of small producers. For example, the notable expansion of bank capital over the past three decades relied heavily on special government favors. When the government borrowed from banks through public debt, there was a large gap between the par value of bonds and the actual amount received by the treasury. Beyond the gain from this difference, banks earned high interest on the debt, and could use government bonds as note-issuing reserves. From the lending relationship alone, banks could reap quadruple profits—this is how much of bank capital was accumulated. To secure creditors' rights in public finance, the state had to resort to taxation, since borrowing new debts to repay old ones could not continue indefinitely. As a result, extra-economic coercion became the lever of accumulation. Although the accumulation of Chinese commercial capital did not rely as visibly on coercive means as bank capital, it was no accident either—especially when we consider its reliance on multiple forms of unequal exchange, its ties to officialdom, and the forced transactions that prevailed in remote and backward areas, regardless of cost or market conditions.

Clearly, many would rather justify this mode of accumulation in China than be disillusioned by it, seeing it as the same path taken by all early capitalist countries—where primitive accumulation paved the way for modern accumulation. Yet what is regrettable is the time lost in this process. The internal linkages between the accumulation of Chinese commercial and financial capital and imperialist commerce and finance in China will be explored in the following discussion.

12.3 Centralization Process of Chinese Capital

The accumulation form of capital is subject to the regulation of certain socioeconomic conditions, as is the centralization form of capital. It can be fairly asserted that the centralization of capital is determined by the accumulation of capital.

It is evident that capitalist capital accumulation develops through the self-inflicted mandate in the internal organization of the capitalist economy. In order to sustain and outperform its competitive counterparts, a business organization or production unit must seek to improve technology and replenish equipment, or in other words, to seek the expansion of the reproduction scale. As expansion becomes a vital prerequisite for survival, the centralization of capital emerges as the fundamental principle underlying capitalist commodity production. This law plays a role in the operation of capitalism, and capitalist commerce and finance are no exception. Regardless of the specific form of centralization adopted by an enterprise, the centralization of industry or production business must serve as its foundation. Although extensive exchange processes related to the activities of commercial capital are included in such monopoly organizations as Trust and Cartel, industry remains the core activity, with commerce playing a subservient role. Even for the considerable financial capital of the modern era, it will become nothing but a superficial existence when centralized industry is detached.

In return, the centralization in the form of primitive accumulation extends beyond the domain of industry or production to that of exchange, in particular. It is already recognized that although only independent small production scale exists in a society with backward industry, the expansion of its commercial capital is not therefore impeded. Economic scientists indicate that independent commercial capital may develop in inverse proportion to industry. This implies that the decentralization of industrial capital may, in certain instances, give rise to the centralization of commercial capital.

This reveals the truth concerning the centralization form of Chinese capital.

The Chinese commercial capital developed to an extent that was not compatible with the industry before the commencement of its modernization. Among the factors why capital was easily centralized in commerce, the superior economic status of merchants in a backward society rose to prominence. They exploited the ignorance and disunity of independent producers to become decision makers on the price of simple commodities. The philosophy of buying cheap and selling dear works all the way through commerce. In many cases, their speculative activities persisted. Furthermore, they were assisted by the necessary social associations, the development of the usury industry and even the financial industry at its early stage. To further develop the argument, it is necessary to consider the collaborative relationship between Chinese land capital and commercial capital, as well as the fact that merchants traditionally intended to approach officialdom and become officials almost effortlessly. It is therefore not difficult to comprehend the fact that social capital was quickly centralized by merchants with no obstacles.

The argument that a certain quantity of centralized commercial capital should undergo a qualitative change must be described from two aspects. One of these is the issue of capital decentralization, which will be discussed in the next section. The other is that the centralization of modern Chinese commercial capital includes its relationships with imperialist commerce and finance. The contact method of Chinese domestic and foreign trade, as previously discussed, indicates that foreign trade in China was manipulated by foreigners, while domestic trade afflicted with foreign trade turned out to serve foreigners. Normally, foreign trade is not inherently different from domestic trade, as in both cases, the commodity of one party is transferred to the other, resulting in a shift in currency. Here, industrial goods are neither superior nor inferior to agricultural goods. However, a society that mainly exports industrial commodities and one that focuses on the export of agricultural commodities are on the whole in unequal statuses, so their commodities are therefore placed differently, and agricultural commodities (or semi-manufactured products) with larger value are forced to trade with industrial commodities (and even some agricultural commodities) with smaller value. This unequal exchange will be bound to induce the Chinese economy to be international-oriented and enhance the subordinate relationships between the Chinese commodity and currency economy and international commodity finance. In the end, an abnormal movement of capital centralization is formed in the recurrent Chinese foreign commodity and currency movements. In the seven decades from 1864 to 1934, only a few years saw export surplus with the rest witnessing import surplus whose amount reached 53.9 million taels from 1871 to 1928. The currency value needed for the huge amount of import surplus is reflected by the centralization process in which Chinese social capital flowed from rural areas to cities, national financial organizations, and foreign banks from which part of the capital also went abroad. Certainly, the capital accumulated at any of the stages did not flow along with nothing left and see no return back. In fact, this largely shows how the total investment volume (1934), 3,242 million U.S. dollars accumulated by imperialists, was centralized. The centralization form of modern Chinese commercial finance capital took shape with the shelter of the large movement of centralization, and in return it laid the foundation for the latter.

Nevertheless, there is no doubt about the fact that the bankruptcy and decline of commercial finance was not eased up but instead more aggravated because of the centralization movement. The bankruptcy and decline of commercial finance provided the basis for proportional or fractional centralization and expansion. This illustrates the crux that not all commercial finance, both old and new, experienced periods of prosperity, while both old and new Chinese industries went bankrupt. The reason why some could grow stronger and others went downhill in commercial finance would rather be attributed to the qualification and capital available to employ privilege relationships than to the obtainment of imperialist or feudalistic privilege relationships. The greater the influence or larger the investment of the imperialist powers in China, the greater the scale of or more centralized capital that would be demanded from Chinese commerce and finance in return for their services.

12.4 Decentralization Process of Chinese Capital

Superficially, decentralization appears to be the opposite of centralization. However, the decentralized form of capital is constrained and regulated by its centralized form. With regard to the centralization of capital in industry, it is important to note that this extends beyond the industry itself to encompass the activities of commercial finance, which are designed to meet the requirements of industry. Conversely, when capital is mainly centralized in commerce, it can be decentralized into industry only on very special occasions in accordance with the commercial principle of independent activity. Otherwise, it will certainly expand its activities, the activities similar to or intimate with themselves, in other words, it will expand financial activities to maximize their interests.

Consequently, despite the considerable capital centralized in Chinese and foreign commerce and financial sectors, a relatively small proportion was allocated to rural areas, where raw materials and semi-manufactured products were sold. The circulation of capital was time-consuming, and trade was inevitably influenced by security and transportation. Even if various privileges could be exploited to enhance the profit margin of unequal exchange, this would only become apparent to Chinese and foreign commerce and finance when raw materials or semi-manufactured products were required in order to gain greater interests. What concerned them most was the trade objects that could lead to greater profits just by changing hands, so the formal business. Consequently, the formal business sector, which encompassed currency and commodity movements, sought to disassociate itself from capital centralized in commercial finance. It attempted to make ends meet by turning to the standard gold market, foreign exchange market, public debt market, and various marketplaces that were farther from the production process. Furthermore, real estate operations represented another speculative target of profit seekers.

The decentralization form of Chinese capital nearly reached its climax in the years before the outbreak of the War of Resistance against Japanese Aggression when economic crisis and even political crisis posed threats both domestically and internationally. Any normal trade relationships were inclined to fall into pieces, which further reinforced the aforesaid speculative activities. However, the capital that was quickly decentralized by means of speculation was soon centralized in the same way, which made the pool where gold flowed more likely to experience a spillover effect. Therefore, the so-called overwhelming surplus of fluid capital which raised a tremendous stink then was displayed in a seriously abnormal way in the difficult decentralization process.

It is true that there was also a traditional decentralization method for the capital to be centralized in Chinese commerce. The money earned by Chinese merchants was partly used to purchase land in addition to the investment in commercial expansion, and they were allowed to trade land freely in the special feudal economic relationships of China, as has been repeatedly expounded hereinbefore. This method of decentralizing capital to land could be perceived as viewing land as a special objective of commercial activity and including the income from land in one of the special methods of commercial accumulation. Further analysis will be illustrated later on. It is sufficient to demonstrate that, after the opening of the five treaty ports, the decentralization method was gradually neglected by general business operators in areas of relatively developed commerce, and they regarded land outside urban and suburban areas as a burden due to the greater scope for operations and variety of objectives available in commerce. Normally, situations differ in underdeveloped areas. However, as the modern economy of commodity currency becomes increasingly influential and more extensive, there are good reasons to suggest that the method of capital decentralization has become less important compared to the situation before the war.

If purchasing land with the capital accumulated in commerce became an outdated way of investment before the war, traditional usury activities related to it also saw a reduction in their absorption of capital. There is no doubt that the vast bankrupt rural areas serve as an arena for usury activities, but when capital finds a more favorable way out, it will not be obsessed with the ever-changing territory mired in chaos. This is a powerful explanation for the shift of capital from rural to urban areas.

Naturally, all these evolutions developed in a gradual and imbalanced manner. Prior to the comprehensive reform of the Chinese social economy, capital accumulation and centralization in commerce were inevitable, and accordingly, commercial capital was decentralized to land investment and usury activities. Nevertheless, the accumulation and centralization of commercial capital is more about the unequal interests of imperialist powers in China than about feudalistic privileges, while its capital decentralization has to force original land investment to become urban property investment, and traditional usury activities to be those of bank capital, with the old typical path blocked out. Furthermore, as was the case with the association between land investment and usury in the past, the speculation in property was also related to the activities of the capital of new banks that were of usury nature. The description of capital decentralization led to a return to the very starting point. The aforementioned phenomenon of surplus fluid capital remains prominent in the movement of capital decentralization.

Until the years prior to the outbreak of the War of Resistance against Japanese Aggression, the fluid capital that went rampant in urban areas and banks started to force the so-called national capitalists to shift their focus to rural areas, and since then agricultural loans emerged as a new program in the movement of capital decentralization. Nevertheless, the transfer of capital to rural areas was designed to facilitate further accumulation and centralization. The production undertakings in rural areas could have been profitable, but its nature and quantity were restricted by agricultural loans before other social conditions favorable to agricultural production ended up somewhere. According to the normal procedures in modern times, agricultural loan develops from being long term to short term. In a society that has recently embarked on the journey of modernization, land represents a significant proportion of the expenses incurred in agricultural production. Consequently, it is necessary to adopt long-term loans in order to relieve farmers of the burden of land ownership, thereby enabling them to utilize middle-term and short-term loans to enhance land quality and adjust their yearly prepaid capital. However, the agricultural loan in China commenced with a short-term loan, which was not applied to production but rather served as a land surtax. There are many theories concerning this, among which the most well-grounded one seems to be that the social production relationships in rural areas were not mature enough to create the social conditions for long-term loans, but the more important is that the surplus capital in urban areas was neither adequate nor qualified or effective to be decentralized to vast rural areas in terms of quantity and quality. This will be discussed in more detail subsequently.

12.5 General Tendency Displayed in the Entire Process of Capital Movement

From the investigation above, the accumulation, centralization, and decentralization in the entire movement process of Chinese capital are all imprinted with a commercial mark rather than an industrial one. The commercial activities that accumulate and centralize are mostly currency property, which has been previously elaborated. The centralization movement in which capital flows from rural to urban areas, Chinese and foreign banks, and foreign countries, also belongs to the movement of currency property. Now, readers may question whether, given that commercial activities include currency movement and commodity movement, the aforementioned process of centralization of currency viewed as capital must be accompanied by the reverse movement of commodity viewed as capital. Furthermore, it could be argued that a large amount of material inflow must accompany the capital flowing outwards in regard to foreign trade relationships. With unequal exchange put aside, the quality of imported materials alone can be the answer. The import of materials in China was not intended to meet the needs of industrial expansion, but to meet the need of enlarged commerce. In other words, the importation of materials was not for the purpose of production, but rather for consumption-- the hedonic consumption having nothing to do with production. The consumption in major Chinese cities was mainly supplied by foreign countries. Consequently, even if unequal exchange relationships didn't exist, the considerable capital paid for import surplus resulted in unnecessary domestic waste that was not beneficial to actual capital. Therefore, despite the increase in imports and import surplus year on year, and the expansion of the commercial scale, the increase in quantity failed to lead to that in quality, due to the rising waste.

However, there is something more severe. To compensate for the capital outflow resulting from a considerable import surplus, three ways are available: (1) yearly remittance from overseas Chinese, (2) foreign investment in China (political investment or foreign debt), and (3) export of gold and silver bullion. It may appear odd that despite the prevalence of natural disasters, civil wars, and bankruptcies in China, major cities witnessed a surge in extravagance and enjoyment, as if the resources expended could be replenished from a seemingly inexhaustible source. Even the most optimistic assumption, namely that the general production in Chinese society, especially in rural areas, could on average maintain the basic reproduction scale, would fail to explain the increasing nationwide extravagance by various means. It is true that many Chinese people experienced a poorer life. However, the material factors that were introduced as a result of the "bitterness" could be employed to address the increased material factors caused by more waste. Even for foreign trade, the materials obtained from the poorer people were employed as a means of exchanging those materials for waste. The point was to offset the import surplus, or the import that could not be balanced by improved export in various ways. As the value of the import surplus might be alleviated or reduced beforehand by the poorer life of Chinese people, which was helpless to remedy the import surplus value that had already been established in some cases. In addition to the remittance of overseas Chinese and foreign investments, the import surplus already formed had to be balanced by the shipment of gold and silver bullion to foreign countries. Despite the lack of precise data regarding the volume of gold and silver bullion shipments, it is evident that these volumes were substantial in the years around the war. In recent years, gold and silver, which were previously regarded as social assets and national treasures, representing absolute wealth in society, have been centralized by foreign countries through the banking system at home and abroad in the aforesaid movement process of capital centralization.

Although gold and silver and even the social materials in China were constantly abstracted and absorbed by foreign countries, Chinese commercial and financial capital measured by currency kept expanding and especially pervading. which can be easily inferred. In the aforementioned decentralization of Chinese capital, it has been posited that as Chinese commerce and financial business matured, they were more likely to target public debt, land property, standard gold, and foreign exchange, etc., as the primary objects of their activities. Actually, the increased value of the capital on these occasions only meant the amplification of value marker. Take public debt as an example. The major capitalists and bankers in China held a considerable amount of credit currency that could be transformed into national bonds. When they acquired interests in the given period, the property was no longer consumed as capital and had long vanished, or it just occurred as conceptually virtual capital, even if it was viewed as capital or, more accurately, interest-bearing capital, which was because it was regarded as capital for lenders in regard to the generation of interest. Consequently, the expansion of such creditor rights is not so much about tangible capital, but rather about virtual capital.

As for the investment in real estate, the fluctuation in the currency price of the real estate, for example, the price of land in Shanghai surging from 1 to 5 billion yuan which later dived to 2.5 billion, was hard to indicate the expansion or contraction of capital, if the real investment in real estate was not at play and the change in the marker of value was speculatively manipulated. Although the assets of the real estate owners increased in line with the surge in land prices in Shanghai from 1 billion to 5 billion yuan, they ultimately received only the nominal increase registered in their account books. Other prices rose accordingly, more metal currency would be needed to buy clothes, tools, and carriages, as Hume in Britain ever put.

However, when large amounts of Chinese metal currency flowed to foreign countries, neither the increase in commercial assets value nor that in financial one was symbolic of and could symbolize greater amounts of metal currency. It might in large part aim to adapt to the abnormal circumstances, or to address the contradiction that asset value rose while metal currency kept flowing to foreign countries (the two of which are actually not contradictory), which made people realize it was pressing and essential to unify the issue of currency. Therefore, currency reform became an inevitable result of Chinese capital movement in the critical period before the war.

After the implementation of the currency reform, the representative assets of Chinese commercial finance capital were more likely to expand, but it simply occurred on the eve of the outbreak of the war. In this sense, the result of the expanded assets did not begin to manifest itself until during the war.

Chapter 13
Capital Movement Laws in and after the War

The movement of capital is regulated by its nature. During the ten more years from the outbreak of the war, there were no obvious reasons to state that the nature of Chinese capital was fundamentally changed amidst the turbulence of the war. The representation of the Chinese economy underwent significant changes during wartime and in the post-war period, resulting in the emergence of distinctive characteristics within Chinese capital activities. However, just as all changes are centered around the fundamental nature, although a number of unprecedented new factors, such as wartime economy, state-operated enterprises, materials from enemy and puppet regimes, foreign loans and large-scale relief goods, etc., were added to the capital movement in the past ten-odd years, they in fact confusingly complicated the original capital movement to some extent and in some cases. When observing internally, it is not hard to identify that they in essence continued and reinforced the existing capital movement. This will be illustrated in the following notable aspects in brief.

13.1 Conversion from Industrial Capital to Commercial Capital

About the investigation in this regard, a prerequisite perception should be made clear that there must be Industrial Capital before Industrial Capital can convert into commercial capital. Only when Industrial Capital keeps increasing or expanding, can it keep turning into commercial capital. Otherwise, how can the conversion become a frequent movement tendency?

The answer to the question is that China has always been developing its industry in various ways along with modernization, attempted to build some industries in support of the war, and taken over a number of factories from the enemy and puppet regime in the post-war period, but the achievements have so far collapsed or are breaking

Y. Wang, *The Basic Theory of Chinese Economy*,
https://doi.org/10.1007/978-981-95-6330-2_13

down presently. Although more endeavors can be made to enhance industry, they will be doomed as long as general social production relationships remain unchanged. That's because this may be more likely to be attributed to the destruction of the civil and foreign war, but more importantly, it has something to do with the tendency of Industrial Capital converted into commercial capital, which is an objective condition bringing irresistible pressure.

The characteristics of the various kinds of Chinese capitals have been analyzed before. In Chinese commerce that is closely connected with international capital, Chinese merchants, enjoying superior status in the social economy, manipulated and exploited producers as outsiders using backward and traditional methods, which foreshadowed the future of industry. From the beginning of the war till now, the increasingly serious inflation has made the industry that has already been inferior more disadvantageous, and superior commerce (comprador and bureaucratic commerce) more advantageous. Under the influence of hyperinflation, the industry that was lacking motility to adapt to the market and required longer circulation time has already been in deep water, regardless of the original superior position of commerce. To make matters worse, the foreign trade policy that took advantage of foreign materials and cheap goods in recent years to lower domestic prices has fueled the urgency for large and small industries. Consequently, the strategy of "cultivating industry with commerce" or "converting industry into commerce" has emerged as a valid approach for general industrialists to escape their seemingly inevitable fate.

13.2 Conversion from National Capital to Bureaucrat Capital

In the civil and foreign wars, small and large industries, facing significant challenges, consistently sought governmental assistance and financial support, in addition to employing the aforementioned strategies, to ensure their survival. However, with severe fiscal constraints and a reliance on the printing of notes to maintain spending, how could the government lend a helping hand to them? Obviously, inflation caused by notes from printing presses would make production enterprises suffer more, and more assistance to production enterprises would aggravate inflation, which was like a painful but not pure repetition in which a magic hand would inevitably and frequently appear to change the original relationships of ownership and application. The circulation saw many enterprises controlled, merged and manipulated. In addition, private ownership might also become public in the name of state-owned or state-operated enterprises, or become official with such temptations as preferential subsidies and other special conveniences. Regardless of the method or combination of methods employed, the industries that originally belonged to the national people became partially or wholly official in a direct or indirect manner.

Indeed, when war rendered intervention and unified control necessary in the economy, the aforementioned prosecution and deprivation fell upon industry, as well as profitable commerce. The government was able to impose restrictions on commerce in a number of areas, including transportation, credit, foreign exchange, taxation, and so on. Hoarding for speculation as well as evading tax or customs was a violation of the law. Consequently, if commerce were to engage in business activities in accordance with the stipulations set forth in legislation, it would be no better than industry. It can thus be realized that the special earnings in commerce since the outbreak of the war was due to its specialization, the guarantee for law breaking, and the tacit permission, assistance, and support of the powerful, or in other words, the tendency of "cultivating industry with commerce" or "converting industry into commerce" was bred by the fact of "government assisting commerce" and "converting public enterprises into commercial ones". In this way, the Industrial Capital became bureaucratic, so did the commercial capital.

Until now, general national capital continues to convert into special national capital, or bureaucratic capital. The conversion has become a well-acknowledged tendency, as well as a movement law with irresistible power.

13.3 Conversion from National Capital to International Capital

With the two aforementioned tendencies of capital movement, the third—the conversion of national capital into international capital—inevitably emerged. In fact, this movement has already been strong, and its formation is based on the following facts.

If a country enjoys abnormal prosperity in commerce despite its sluggish production, its commerce must focus on transporting and distributing foreign goods, and currently on American goods. This style of commerce is specialized in serving foreign industry, which clearly reveals its comprador nature. Under the circumstance of "cultivating industry with commerce" or "converting industry into commerce", part of Chinese national capital has been turned into foreign capital operated in the name of Chinese people. It is true that the import of foreign goods might be helpful to national industry, but inflation and other conditions unfavorable to production make imported foreign goods less likely to be constructive production methods and more likely to be destructive consumption materials. Without reference to official figures and types of materials published by the customs, every market will be shockingly flooded with daily accessible products and convenience goods supplied by foreigners, especially Americans, such as cigarettes, alcohol, cosmetics, clocks, watches, fountain pens, and other dispensable goods. The less likely imported goods are to be means of production, the more likely they are to be consumption materials or luxuries. The interaction will lead to a tendency that only comprador capital and other capital forms compatible with comprador commerce exist in Chinese society. Furthermore, the war resulting from the commercial finance of the comprador and the ensuing hyperinflation forced production enterprises that emerged on the industrial basis of the enemy and puppet regime, as well as social assets preserved in various forms, to flee to other countries directly or indirectly, obviously or vaguely. The bureaucracy and the comprador even jointly facilitated this evasion in a reprehensible manner. Consequently, despite the Chinese government's efforts to seek assistance from foreign countries, Chinese domestic property, foreign exchange, gold, and land are consistently transferred to countries perceived as saviors. This ridiculously contradictory phenomenon is unfolding itself in front of people. It is worth noting that the fleeing capital is not forever gone and will return to this pitiful homeland as long as it finds an opportunity to gain higher earnings and more power at home. However, when it comes back, it has not been and will no longer be viewed as national capital to take root in China but as international capital, or something related to real international capital that strives to make its presence in the Chinese economic arena.

From the aforementioned tendencies, it can be comprehended that the movement of Chinese social capitals after the war is, in essence, consistent with that before the war, although a few new factors have been added and it became more complicated and twisty. To see nature profoundly, or find the internal key that capital movement hinged upon, further analysis of the forms of the social profit and interest becomes a necessity.

Issues discussed in this part

1. Why can't general popular concepts of capital be used to elaborate the difference between capitalist society and non-capitalist society?
2. Why is it always hard for China to realize capitalist commodity production even if China has long witnessed the trade of labor force and possessed surplus labor force, which are the basic prerequisite conditions of capitalist production?
3. What are the characteristics of Chinese commercial capital throughout history compared to modern commercial capital and European commercial capital in the past?
4. What are the essential differences between usury capital and bank capital, and those between bank capital and financial capital?
5. Why is the majority of currency capital in the hands of merchants in a society with less developed production?
6. Is it because of merchants or other reasons that the commercial capital in Chinese society refuses to be converted into industrial capital but turns to invade the latter?
7. Why do the foreign-invested industries in China also lack momentum for development as Chinese national Industrial Capital?
8. How can the accumulation process of capital decide the decentralization or transformation process of that?

Part V
Forms of Chinese Interest and Profit

Abstract This chapter explores the pathological relationship between industrial and commercial profit. In a normal capitalist economy, industrial profit regulates commercial profit. In China, the opposite occurred: weak industrial capital allowed merchant capital, leveraging its monopolistic control over markets and channels, to consistently secure super-profits far exceeding any industrial average. These commercial profits were extracted not only from consumers but, more fundamentally, from producers via depressed purchase prices. This excessive commercial profit became the de facto benchmark for all capital returns, making it difficult for industrial profit to reach a level sufficient for accumulation. Furthermore, foreign capital operating in China enjoyed super-profits through privilege, further distorting profit rate formation. This profit structure incentivized capital to flow into commercial speculation rather than industrial production, stifling industrial advancement.

Chapter 14
Interest, Profit and Laws

In the previous part, it is described that interest and profit have restricted the entire movement process of Chinese capital. The two economic categories have not been formally expounded yet, and it is indispensable herein to undertake the discussions in a specialized and systematic manner.

The two economic categories were planned to be discussed respectively, but this style of investigation would leave out many important arguments, making collective discussion a necessary research method, which in fact facilitates better comprehension. In this way, people will be aware that respective and independent forms of interest and profit should be clarified in the entire process of their correlated development. In particular, Chinese general capitalist interest and profit in extremely special forms need to be explained in their process of historical development.

Only by investigating the entire evolution of interest and profit can their forms be revealed and discovered.

When it comes to interest and profit nowadays, it seems that they belong to two completely distinct dimensions. If the development process of perception of economic objects and the development process of economic objects are closely correlated, the evolution of the perception of interest and profit can plainly indicate that, before modern times, their internal relationships were not represented with their respective independent forms as are perceived in the present day.

In the early modern period, interest was still regarded as the general gain or the gain itself, when the term "profit" was not yet widely known. In 1758, Quesnay, a pioneer of physiocracy, published his masterpiece, *Tableau Economique*, which divided capital into two categories: original advance and annual advance. The compensation or remuneration for the former is referred to as interest on fixed capital, rather than profit. The interest he referred to means profit as is termed today, of which he obviously had no clear concept. Stuart gave his book, *An Inquiry into the Principles of Political Economy* published in 1767, a subtitle "Domestic Policies in Free Nations", which especially focuses on population, agriculture, trade, industry, cast coinage, interest, circulation, banking, public debt, and taxation. The special title

Y. Wang, *The Basic Theory of Chinese Economy*,
https://doi.org/10.1007/978-981-95-6330-2_14

encompassed almost all economic contents but profit (despite the ignorance of land rent), because he believed that profit was represented by interest.

Indeed, prior to the quasi-modern writers, even Scholastic scholars were not aware of the distinction between the two. Antoninus proposed that "currency had no interest in itself, and did not produce interest unless it was employed by merchants", and rationalized interest with the possible mutual benefits of borrowers and lenders, which hinted at the reasonable existence of profit. However, it is Turgot, a physiocrat, who then distinguished profit from interest. He held that there were five functions of capital, namely, purchasing land, paying in advance for manufacturing industry, agriculture, and commerce, and the loan with interest, each of which needed to be repaid with benefits, and interest was one of them.

Nevertheless, the awareness of profit independent of interest was still at the infant stage. In contrast, the existence of modern capitalist interest is reflected by the profit of the same nature. The crux was firstly discovered by Joseph Massie in 1750 who stated in *An Essay on the Governing Causes of the Natural Rate of Interest* that people had to pay interest in order to use what they borrowed, and this interest was a part of the profit they could produce. In 1776, Adam Smith elucidated in *The Wealth of Nations* that interest paid with general currency had to be subject to the profit obtained with general currency. Subsequently, Gilbert identified in *The History and Principles of Banking* in 1834 that those who borrowed money to make profits should give part of the profits to their lenders, which was a self-evident, natural, and fair principle.

It is obvious that the evolution of perception of the relationships between interest and profit could not be accounted for with genius and talent but was based on realistic development. In the past, interest was regarded as the gain in general, as well as the capital in general and the capital itself, due to the fact that loaned currency was considered to be capital in general. *Bible* puts blame on interest in particular which covered the proposal of commercial profit, because the commercial operators then were used to sheltering their demand for gains with that of usurers. From then onwards, especially in early modern times, commerce and industry embraced a boom, so that the proportion of functioning capital in society became larger than that of interest-bearing capital. The main targets of activities underpinned by interest-bearing capital were no longer those who borrowed money for subsistence or leisure, but rather those commercial and industrial undertakers. The exploitation of usurers on the latter became less harsh than it used to be on the former, because the undertakers of commerce and industry would not continue to borrow money if they saw no return on their investment or suffered losses. However, there were more fundamental reasons underlying the reduction in interest rates. As commerce and industry developed, the accumulation of social capital would accordingly increase the amount of interest-bearing capital to be issued, so the expected interest of interest-bearing capital would have to be lowered. Given the low interest rate of interest-bearing capital, small amounts of loan or the loan from personal savings could hardly maintain the livelihood of lenders and also failed to keep pace with the increasing scale of production enterprises. Therefore, the usury industry in interest-bearing capital was replaced by the banking that emerged to meet the demand of new production enterprises. At the same time, with the support of the banking industry, The production capital could expand their scale and raise their accumulation, and began to become dominant over commercial capital. The commercial capital profit and even the interest of interest-bearing capital whose source has always been not easily identified started to clearly indicate that they were divided from the profit of Industrial Capital.

From the aforementioned objective evolution, economic science has pinpointed several basic principles concerning interest and profit.

Firstly, in the societies prior to capitalist ones, it was the interest rate that determined the profit rate, while in capitalist societies, it is the profit rate that decides the interest rate. The establishment of this principle not only relies on comprehending some confusing phenomena but requires to be confined to the functioning scope of the principle. Apparently, the interest rate in any society is generally fixed and well known, while profit is difficult to define, and the uncertainty is also true for the average profit in a capitalist society. It is much more likely to impress people that the profit rate is subject to interest rate, but the truth just lies in the opposite. On some occasions and within a certain period, the fixed capitalist interest rate is benchmarked against the previous profit rate of the same place, and the interest rate as benchmark refers to the general but not additional or special one.

Secondly, the interest rate in a country actually represents that of profit rates, in reverse proportion to the development level of the industry. Even in a society with a developed economy, its development is imbalanced, and in some backward areas in rural areas, the interest rate is generally higher than that in urban areas with developed transportation. The interest rate can be employed as a measure of how developed a society is, provided that the underlying principles are applied flexibly.

Thirdly, compared to Industrial Capital, the larger the merchant capital is, the smaller the profit rate of Industrial Capital will be, and vice versa. This principle is applicable to the stages of a society, or to societies with different levels of development.

With the basic principles concluded previously, preparations and basis for further description of Chinese forms of interest and profit have been ready.

Chapter 15
Forms of Chinese Interest

The expositions above have informed that the research has to begin with the forms of interest.

The so-called interest refers to the repayment within a certain period in addition to the principal of the loan and it is universal in any society. However, under the influence of Jesus commandment in old European society, obtaining interest through loan was generally blamed and even banned, and in the areas where the injunction was implemented, the interest tended to be higher in order to make up for the possible loss of lenders which was usually apportioned by and transferred to borrowers in advance. This is to say, the policy of banning and limiting interest never achieved the desired effects. The situation was different in China. Although Chinese dynasties repeatedly suppressed and forbade merchants who "opened stores to sell goods and made profits by special means" (the suppressing and forbidding led to the result similar to that in Europe), the usury industry seemed to rarely come to their notice. Certainly, this was not because of the disdain of those influenced by Confucianism, but for the fact that the majority of the Confucianist scholar-bureaucrats throughout history were both landowners and usurers. They also engaged themselves in commerce, but their status became an obstacle. The involvement in the usury industry could be kept a secret, so that they could maintain nobility in public.

Interest surprisingly seemed to be covered by the fig leaf of feudal rituals and was especially connived at.

Why did suppressed commerce become rampant while the spoiled usury industry never achieved greatness in history? Further comprehension is required.

Although usury capital as a source of interest in China was inextricably tied to land capital and commercial capital, forming a "trinity", the usury industry often served as a means of expanding commerce and centralizing land. As long as the usury industry gained accumulation, it would be spent as commercial capital, especially as land capital. Therefore, amid many social changes throughout history, what came to attention was the scourge brought by commerce and land rights rather than the usury industry, which was in fact the root cause, and was an effective method employed

Y. Wang, *The Basic Theory of Chinese Economy*,
https://doi.org/10.1007/978-981-95-6330-2_15

by merchants to control small independent producers or small landowners, and to make profits and centralize land. In fact, the position of usurers against borrowers was more advantageous compared to that of merchants against goods buyers and sellers, as well as to that of those in need of land against land owners. Land sellers and goods traders could select whom they conducted business with, but borrowers, in particular the poor who tried to maintain their livelihood, were confronted with very limited choices. Hence, willfully high interest rate became an intangible indicator of commercial profit rate and land rent rate, although the latter two might raise the indicator with abnormally high rate under especially favorable circumstances.

When China began to be exposed to modern capitalism, the situation kept changing. It is known that commercial capital has long shaken off its classical form. With the new changes brought about by commercial capital, land rights have also changed or moderated the centralization trend that could have been induced in this respect. However, major changes mainly took place in coastal areas and those with developed transportation, and in rural areas, the simple commodity-currency relationships were expanded, which led to the separation of outdated agriculture and handicraft industry, and changed its form within all-round bankruptcy. With regard to the usury industry, not only did it keep sustaining its traditional relationships with land rights, but it became increasingly rampant when bankruptcies increased and social funds were attracted to urban areas.

Simultaneously, as the aforementioned Industrial Capital could not normally develop in other aspects, Chinese people deemed production undertakings as an arduous journey, and many new parvenus in urban areas were therefore urged to specialize in financial activities. The occurrence of the financial industry was driven more by the need to adapt to the demands of those reliant on interest income than for meeting the requirements of the expansion of new commerce and industry. Regardless of the underlying motivation, those living on interest were no longer the bankrupts in rural areas, but rather those who had benefited from windfalls and sought to spend, as well as industrialists, officials, and those engaged in speculation. Obviously, the interest level of rural usury industry couldn't be applied to these activity objects.

Additionally, the third financial circle has to be mentioned herein, which is set by international financial capital which conducts top financial business and the objects of financial activities are merchants, industrialists and Chinese financiers, which requires another kind of interest benchmark. It will be of greater necessity, provided that the taking of the deposits of Chinese people was the most profitable business for their financial organizations.

In China, there are three interest benchmarks at play.

Firstly, the interest benchmark of foreign banks in China ranges from 4% to 8% according to experience. Within this range, there are several facts about the differential rates to be pointed out. Initially, the interest rate of foreign banks is closely associated with the general interest rate and financial status of the foreign countries, and their capital policies towards China. For instance, compared to Japan, the financial status of Britain is sounder, the interest rate of its domestic banks lower, and its credit for Chinese people more reliable, so the interest rate of Japan-invested banks in China is higher. In terms of taking deposits, Japan has to accordingly raise the interest rate of bank deposit and loan when competing with Britain. However, the general interest rate of British banks is rarely lower than 4%, below which it will be deprived of its function of controlling finance, and that of Japanese banks is rarely higher than 8%, over which the superior position of Japan will be hard to sustain because their rate is too close to that of Chinese banks. In addition, foreign banks differentiated their treatment of Chinese and foreign individuals with regard to loans and savings, particularly during wartime when Chinese depositors gained no interest but had to pay premiums. However, this differential treatment is subject to the capital policies they impose on China. Moreover, the manipulation of banks towards standard gold of the foreign exchange and securities market will incur the changes of interest rates at any time.

Secondly, the interest benchmarks of Chinese banks and money shops range from 9% to 20%, as is indicated by experience. In this respect, some facts about the differential rates should be made clear. Firstly, new banks and the old-fashioned money shops themselves have already implied the differential rates. Although the interest rate of small banks is higher than that of large money shops, it can be perceived that the interest rate of banks is relatively lower after studying their respective financial objects. Money shops often seek financial help from banks, and their main customers are composed of small industrialists and businessmen and normal usurers. Secondly, as the Chinese financial industry is mainly related to commerce, the nature, turnover speed and the risk level of commercial activities influence its profit rate, thus resulting in the change of interest rate to some extent. Finally, when rivaling against foreign counterparts, Chinese banks have to lower their interest rate, and when threatened by traditional money shops, they have to increase the rate. Given the financial business with various competition and restrictions, it is certainly not easy for its interest rate to be fixed on the same benchmark. It is no wonder that although some Chinese banks have taken on a modern look, some of them still retain their strong nature of usury.

Thirdly, the interest benchmark of the traditional Chinese usury industry falls between 24% and 300% based on evidence. One apparent explanation for the differential rates is that, the closer to urban areas, the more likely to follow the prevailing interest rate there. Conversely, in more remote and isolated locations, the rate appears to be largely unregulated. A similar phenomenon may be observed in the context of commerce. As long as peasants have money available, they are likely to consider interest rates in light of the current economic conditions. They have to sell or buy in advance to make a living or sustain their production process, which would be another story. This is more a matter of commerce than of the usury industry. Under extremely favourable circumstances, the usury industry may exploit others to raise its interest rate to 300%, or even extort randomly without consideration of practice. Nevertheless, the interest rate will never be lower than 24% regardless of the circumstances, as the accumulation of usury capital is employed in commerce or land rights. Although commercial profit is somewhat uncertain and it is challenging to forecast future profit rates with current ones, particularly in such a turbulent society, the rate of land rent is fixed. As previously discussed, those engaged in usury activities are primarily individuals who have already accumulated significant wealth through land rent. When the interest rate of usury may be far higher than that of land rent, they are willing to divert capital to the usury industry, but once the earnings from the usury industry fall to the same or similar as the land rent rate, usury capital will flow back to land. The land rent rate herein refers to the ratio of the yearly land rent amount to the land price. In other words, the value of the land rent rate is determined by the multiple of the land price into the yearly land rent. If the latter is determined, the land rent rate will decrease when the land price increases, and vice versa. It is estimated that the land price in China is approximately ten times that of the annual rent, with the land rent rate consequently representing only 10% of the total. Consequently, the interest rate in rural areas has to be lower than 10% before capital can be diverted from usury to land. It should be noted, however, that land rent is the most reliable form of revenue. Even if land rent cannot be collected because of flood or drought, the land price, which represents capital, remains stable. However, in terms of loan, both the interest and the principal may be lost. Therefore, when the interest rate is significantly below the land rent rate, or 10%, capital is allocated to land purchase. This is the primary reason why the threshold interest rate in rural areas is restricted at 24%.

As previously indicated, there are three interest benchmarks coexisting in China. The characteristics of interest rates can be discerned from this fact.

Firstly, from a comprehensive perspective, Chinese interest rates vary from 4% to 300%. The considerable discrepancy and variation within the extensive scope is never seen in any other country. Even in a highly developed capitalist country, the discrepancy in economic development or the relative backwardness of a sector or area cannot be entirely eliminated. The uneven development is one of the reasons why its domestic interest rate of interest-bearing capital is hard to be uniform. However, the difference and change in interest rates rarely exceed the range of 1% to 10%. If the stability of the financial market and the consistency of the interest rate benchmark are a must for the industrial development of a country, it is evident that the forms of Chinese interest impede the growth of the industry.

Secondly, when interest represents its variation and change on an excessively large scope, to make it balanced or normal has been impossible. Furthermore, the respective special ranges and bases of the aforementioned three benchmarks make it even more challenging to attain the aforementioned goal. The capital in a society is continually reallocated from sectors with lower interest rates to those with higher rates. When the interest rate reaches a certain high level and attracts more capital than is sufficient, it will decline, directing capital towards areas where a lower interest rate has caused a capital shortage, which in turn leads to an increased interest rate. This tendency towards equilibrium is a prerequisite for a normal interest rate. It is evident that the conditions for the free flow of capital are absent in China, so a balanced interest rate fails to be formed. Even within the respective financial activity circles formed based on the aforementioned three benchmarks, how normal and balanced the interest rate is varies a lot. In general, the interest rate of foreign banks is more likely to be normal despite the obstacles to capital circulation set by other countries. By contrast, the interest rate in the Chinese financial sector leaves some leeway for being balanced within its functioning areas, particularly in urban areas where currency-commodity relationships are relatively well-developed. However, the social relationships in these areas are significantly different, making it challenging to establish normal point-to-point connections between urban financial sectors. As for the interest rate of usury in rural areas, it is even hard to balance.

Furthermore, although it is challenging to achieve a balanced and normal interest rate in China, the interactive regulation on the interest rate of different benchmarks cannot be denied. It can be seen that the interest rates of foreign banks, the Chinese money industry, and usury in rural areas range from 4% to 8%, 9% to 20%, and 24% to 300%, respectively. This implies that the lowest interest rate of the Chinese money industry connects with the highest rate of foreign banks, and that the highest rate connects with the lowest rate of usury, which suggests the possible interaction among them. In fact, this may be the reason why the capital policy imposed by imperialist powers has become a dominant force in Chinese society, forming a chain that cannot be ignored. However, it is strange that the interest rate gradually declines from rural areas to urban areas and foreign banks, yet Chinese social capital is not concentrated in areas with high interest rates, but rather in the opposite direction. This abnormal phenomenon demonstrates that capital requiring not only a high interest rate but also stability is not guaranteed when amassed by Chinese individuals in rural and urban areas. Consequently, the financial shortfalls in rural areas easily lead to a high interest rate. From this perspective, it is not because high interest rates drive capital away; rather, it is the result of capital being attracted and concentrated under the imperialist capital policy that rural finance is depleted and the interest rate is elevated.

In addition, it has to be pointed out that only three benchmarks of Chinese interest rate are put forward, but the lending modes are various. When the interest rate is lower, the lending procedure is simpler, more modern and currency-based, while in the rural areas with the highest interest rate, many primitive credit modes prevail. The lending and repaying forms are various, including repaying with objects for borrowed money, repaying with money for borrowed objects, repaying principal with objects and interest with money, repaying principal with money and interest with objects, and even repaying both principal and interest with physical objects. The varieties are brought about by the following two aspects. On the one hand, capital falls short in rural areas and currency relationships have never been established. On the other hand, usurers tend to adopt various lending and repaying forms in order to extort more. The high interest rate in rural areas is in large part underpinned by the complicated means of lending and repaying.

Chapter 16
Regulating Effects of the Chinese Interest Forms on Profit

How will the aforementioned forms of interest influence profit?

For the present discussion, "profit" refers primarily to industrial profit, and the relation between interest and profit must be reconsidered. It is clear that profit in China has not liberated itself from the forms of interest.

In current society, the relationships between production capital interest and industrial profit should be comprehended from the relationships between production capital and Industrial Capital. In addition to the substantial capital required for initial startup costs, modern industry necessitates a significant financial investment for ongoing operations. Moreover, the currency generated from the production of commodities or value in exchange is more than the earnings derived from small independent production in the past. Therefore, if an industrial capitalist desires to facilitate the turnover of his Industrial Capital as quickly as possible, he will not only rely on businessmen to operate commodities, but will also require financiers to manage currency for him. Ultimately, he has to allocate profits to the businessmen and interest to the financiers in accordance with the convention, in his final outcome of his production. If he chooses to conduct trade and finance on his own, the final gains accrue to him directly, all of the final gains will be his income irrespective of any influence. Nevertheless, in contemporary society where labor division is common, the net income of the industrial capitalist has to be divided into industrial profit, commercial profit and the interest of interest-bearing capital, even if he can continue his operations through the aforementioned means. The relationship between industrial profit and interest of interest-bearing capital is evident, irrespective of commercial profit. Whether the industrial capitalist operates an individual industry or concurrently engages in the finance needed for his business, he will use his business to seek the normal or average profit of the capital he has invested. In addition, he also demands the interest available. Otherwise, the interest demanded by the capital he has borrowed or diverted will be deducted from his normal profit or average profit. And this is the crux of the matter. If the interest of the capital to be borrowed or diverted hinders the normal or

Y. Wang, *The Basic Theory of Chinese Economy*,
https://doi.org/10.1007/978-981-95-6330-2_16

average profit in his business, he will put an end to the industrial operation. In this case, profit is freed from interest.

Nevertheless, the growth of Chinese industrial profit has historically been constrained by the influence of interest. The relationship between interest and profit in the modern era cannot be fostered at random due to the restriction of many social conditions. In vast Chinese rural areas, the interest benchmark ranges from 24% to 300% (Wargnier of Germany analyzed the usury burden of the peasants in Shandong Province and noted that they had to pay as high as 200% and even 300% interest to survive, and the benchmark was also agreed by Magyar). The appallingly high interest rate doesn't make sense just because of capital shortage in rural areas. The fundamental lies in that borrowers aim to cover their basic living expenses, rather than engage in production and business operations. Part of the expenditure of independent producers in rural areas is undoubtedly regarded as the spending on production and at least for covering the life expenses during the production process, but idle wanderers in rural areas are not qualified to borrow money. If the producers who are burden-free in life borrow money purely to maintain production spending, update agricultural tools, purchase fertilizers, and employ laborers and animals, they will undoubtedly consider whether the increased income from production can be in surplus after the interest on borrowed capital is repaid. In the absence of a general profit rate, producers may be temporarily satisfied with surplus benefits. However, when there is no such pitiful benefit, they will make production as simple as possible and be unwilling to borrow money. In such circumstances, they still have the option of selecting the interest rate. To put it another way, if the owner of interest-bearing capital wishes to retain their capital, they will have to consider the benefits of borrowers. Regardless of land rent and industrial profit, interest cannot encroach on all industrial earnings.

If the aforementioned producer can manage to be self-dependent on the aforementioned production factors, such as agricultural tools, animals, seeds and fertilizers, yet encounter difficulties in covering basic living expenses prior to the harvest, there remains the possibility of resisting really high interest rates by pawning these items, such as animal power, seeds and even agricultural tools and halting the employment of laborers, for life expenses, when it is necessary, in order to cover living costs. If the borrower has the ability to resist, he may expect lenders to lower the interest rate, and when the rate is reduced, he can thus gain enough living expenses. If he fortunately generates surplus in addition to the production cost and interest of the borrowed funds. In this case, when the interest rate is a little bit lower, part of the surplus value may be termed as profit.

If this peasant producer sells most of their simple production means because of suffering abnormal natural disasters, diseases, or other man-caused calamities, leaving no means of support and having little qualification to borrow money, they have no choice but to perish immediately or the high interest rate will threaten their survival later on. There is no profit at play at all herein. Namely, the reason why profit is absent in this case is not so much about high interest rate as about the absence of capital that profit is built on. If poor peasants are left to rely on their labor force and nature alone to maintain production, high interest will not be the reason for profit, and is the most profound reason in fact with which the prerequisite conditions for profit to exist cannot be induced.

While there are miscellaneous factors influencing the establishment of loans in rural areas, in addition to those already discussed, to understand why interest rates in rural areas are high and different, and how they hinder the achievement of profit, cannot be gained by considering these factors as the basic picture of peasants' loans. Certainly, it is true that modern forms of profit derived from the interest paid for the capital employed to engage labor are absent in rural areas. As previously stated, the interest paid by peasants who borrow money to enrich their production means may have the rate minimized by lenders, so that surplus viewed as profit is allowed to exist hereby. However, this is partial. It is imperative to consider the labor conditions of peasants and land rent when establishing modern profit.

Perhaps, the establishment of modern capitalist social relationships spread gradually from urban to rural areas. The interest benchmark in urban areas ranges from 9% to 20%, far lower than that in rural areas. If the lowest interest rate in rural areas may allow for the emergence of profit, and the urban loan whose lowest interest rate is lower than the highest one in rural areas, it will definitely not restrict the occurrence of profit. The facts speak for us.

First of all, it has to be clarified that the nature and lifestyles of urban residents are different from those of peasants in terms of borrowing conditions. Especially in emerging urban areas, residents come from everywhere, and most of them are not relatives nor socially connected and have no residence, especially without fixed land to confine and restrict them, whether the land is self-owned or rented. People like them can be categorized into two parts generally, proletarian laborers who are finding jobs or have been already at work, and businessmen and industrialists who own certain assets of various forms. With regard to loan, the former is in general not qualified, or at least not the major objects of urban loan, while the latter, businessmen should be temporarily excluded. Those who engage in industrial undertakings include independent handicraftsmen, manufacturers, modern industrialists, etc., and urban independent handicraftsmen and a small number of wage laborers may be the foundation for rural usury industries in urban areas. The majority of the remaining manufacturers and industrialists operate businesses to make profits rather than make a living. When the business is profitable, or when their production and operation can provide them with satisfactory earnings or profits, they will take delight in doing it. However, should profit become uncertain, and should high interest rates cause this uncertainty, they will cease borrowing and halt their business activities. Instead, they will invest their property as a borrowing basis into the principal in the financial industry, where it will cost less effort to reap fruits.

Secondly, the capital accumulated through land rent, usury, or other primitive methods in rural areas is expected to accumulate more in some way, but the worrying turmoil there leads it to be concentrated in urban areas. Nevertheless, the capital amassed and centralized in urban areas by this means has, in essence, constrained the intention of its owners for the application of it. Land rent and interest are both the income that comes from the toil of others. Consequently, it will be challenging for those who are accustomed to a life of leisure to adapt to an unfamiliar city and engage in an unfamiliar production process. The lifestyle most suitable for them is certainly the one living on interest.

The wealthy are reluctant to undertake production and operation and would like to engage themselves in the financial industry, and those qualified to borrow money are willing to be involved in the financial industry if the interest rate is too high to gain profit. Eventually, the supply of finance exceeds demand, and the interest rate should be reduced. In fact, the interest rate in the urban financial industry is much lower compared to that in rural areas. However, this reduced interest benchmark does not help a lot for the formation of Chinese industrial profit.

The interest rate, which ranges from 9% to 20%, is indeed lower than that in rural areas. However, it remains significantly higher than the rates in foreign countries and even those of foreign banks in China. There are several issues to be figured out herein. Firstly, why the interest rate in Chinese finance sectors is unable to be reduced to a level that is in closer alignment with the interest benchmark of foreign banks in China. It is necessary to take the aforementioned comprador commerce and the high commercial profit to be described hereinafter into consideration. The capital concentrated in urban financial sectors can only be invested in industry, in addition to being used in interest-generating activities, and its industrial profit has to be taken into account for the sake of interest. If commerce is available for the deployment of capital, in addition to finance and industry, the capital will, in essence, favour commercial activities based on the aforementioned capital source and its concentration process. The preferred commerce will rely on the profit gained in various special conditions to seek interest with commercial profit instead of industrial profit as the standard. Therefore, the interest of Chinese interest-bearing capital cannot be further lowered.

Subsequently, even if an emerging industry in a country causes no external destruction, it initially enjoys numerous advantages over traditional industries. This is because its social advantages have not taken shape and the required social conditions, such as technology, capital, and market, are not ready. Consequently, during the early modern period, the industries of countries could make profit by overcoming the obstruction of backward relationships was mostly assisted and promoted by the states. Among the protective methods, three are related to interest: the circulation capital with low interest, grant capital that does not require interest or principal repayments, and the orderly diversion of capital to industry aided by the central bank to control the interest rate market and unify financial procedures. Measures to award industry were implemented in the past, but neither commonly nor realistically, and the industry most worthy of rewards fail to benefit. The method of low-interest circulation capital commenced approximately in the past decade or so amid the implementation of industrial loan. Furthermore, China lacks effective conditions to unify the financial market, which is to be investigated subsequently.

Accordingly, even if a new industry in China is confronted with no external obstacles, it will not obtain reasonable profit with its interest benchmark unless under extremely favorable circumstances like World War II.

In the process where high interest rate restricts "reasonable profit", and low interest rate plays a negative role, foreign banks in China provide allocated funds to their invested industries in China at the interest rate of 4% to 8%, while to the same

Chinese industry over 10% interest rate. With other circumstances being the same, the unequal interest rate alone will make Chinese people suffer losses in industrial profit. However, foreign industries enjoy various privileges in China, while domestic industries are bothered and confined by unfavourable conditions. Technology, capital and operation expertise are all different between the two, and the unfavorable result and losses resulting from the unequal interest rates will be far more serious.

Furthermore, for social and political factors, foreign banks do rely on low interest rate instead of high interest rate to take large number of deposits. By taking advantage of various privileges, they manage to create an abnormal social psychology in the Chinese wealthy class who are convinced that a high interest rate reflects less reliability and that a low rate, even zero rate, and sometimes required premiums mean better reliability. As a consequence, most social capital of Chinese people is turned into the illusory Arabic numbers in the books of foreign banks. If the abundance of capital is effective in lowering interest rates, foreign people will depend on such capital policies to constantly draw capital accumulated by China through primitive methods under any favorable circumstances, which will make the interest rate of Chinese banks remain high all the time. This may lead to the question: Can Chinese banks use low interest policy to outplay their foreign counterparts? The answer is "No" absolutely. Interest cannot explain the abnormal phenomenon that a large number of deposits are taken with low interest rate, because a series of special privileges also play their part herein. Chinese banks can always hold on to an adequate number of deposits because of their high interest rate. Especially for those who are very wealthy and sensitive to the financial market, high interest rates still serve as an effective way to take deposits. However, higher savings interest will surely lead to elevated loan interest. It is obvious that the raised interest rate aims to counter the pressure of low interest rate imposed by foreign banks.

Most significantly, the financial policy that facilitated the flow of social capital to industry at a low interest rate, cannot be smoothly implemented because of the unique interest benchmark adopted by foreign banks in China. In the past, the interest benchmark of usury existed in vast rural areas, but the experiences concerning the centralization and decentralization of social capital in the past two decades have demonstrated that scattered and unsystematic usury, and even the money shops that represent modernized and centralized usury, cannot play a decisive role in social capital turnover. Instead, they can be at the mercy of the new financial industry. In other words, the reason why China is unable to implement a low-interest policy that would be beneficial to industry is that, financially, foreign banks have another low-interest benchmark to manipulate the entire financial activities of China. As for China-based foreign industries sheltered by the low interest rate and other privileges, they achieve not only profit but excess profit, and that kind of industrial profit is the very crux that Chinese normal industrial profit cannot be formed.

Similarly, Chinese industrial profit is hit and destroyed by the high interest rate of usury that represents extremely backward relationships as well as the low interest rate of the capital of foreign banks that reflects highly developed social relationships.

Chapter 17
Regulating Effects of the Forms of Chinese Commercial Profit on Industrial Profit

In broad terms, if industrial profit cannot regulate interest and is instead constrained by it, industry also fails to regulate commerce and becomes subordinated to commercial profit.

A lot has been expounded about the forms of Chinese commercial capital. These forms themselves have shaped the relationship between commercial capital and Industrial capital, and thus the relationship between the profit of commercial and Industrial Capital is also determined. These relationships are abnormal in modern society but normal in the past. The high interest rate that is led by commercial profit of high rate to exert influence on industrial profit can be perceived as a means for commercial profit to suppress industrial profit directly or through interest. It is necessary to illustrate the entire process of how it impedes and holds back industrial profit, as a mere partial explanation is inadequate.

The production of independent producers engaged in industrial activities in rural areas is obviously small-scale and scattered, and may not be self-sufficient. It is therefore necessary for them to take advantage of the surplus products in order to exchange those that they require and which cannot be fully consumed by others. In other words, they are compelled to rely on the market to a certain extent, yet it is challenging for them to gain access to the market and ascertain reliable quotations. Therefore, merchants emerge as the intermediaries responsible for facilitating the exchange of goods and services, as well as for comparing prices. Consequently, the process, which is more or less based on value or production price, or the process of equalization of profit, is typically only reflected in commerce within the field of circulation. Whether an industry is profitable or not and how much profit it achieves become little known and insignificant. Furthermore, the fact that commercial profit is based on the surplus labor of independent producers is glossed over, because they do not produce for profit essentially. In the meantime, business operators simply exchange the commodities for which they are reluctant to be at risk to shoulder the burden in some cases unless profit drives them. As a result, even if industrial

Y. Wang, *The Basic Theory of Chinese Economy*,
https://doi.org/10.1007/978-981-95-6330-2_17

operations gradually change their forms to reveal the budding desire for profit, thus the profit only derives from commercial profit.

This is the universal rule prevailing in any society in the past.

If Chinese commercial capital exhibits distinctive characteristics compared to its foreign counterparts, its profit, subject to this rule, can be regarded as a variant or reinforcement of the practice.

The relationship between Chinese commerce and land rights has been investigated previously. If land rights are presumed to be the foundation of feudal political power, Chinese business operators will be more susceptible to exploitation and plunder compared to European businessmen who are in opposition to feudal authority. In the context of European capitalism, Chinese commerce begins to disassociate itself from its traditional relationships with land rights, during which it lands new patrons, and is supported by international capital or imperialism. It is deprived of traditional privileges and compelled to seek new ones. It seems that it can continue to demand benefits at random to expand its earnings as it used to, but some preconditions of restrictions on the earnings are created in the progress of the change.

Firstly, at the time when commerce and land rights were inextricably linked, the main objective of commerce was to transform the surplus products of independent producers into commodities. Consequently, the most vulnerable groups affected were peasants and handicraftsmen, who were susceptible to exploitation due to their lack of awareness and potential for arbitrary deprivation. At the stage when commerce was attached to the nature of the comprador, a considerable number of products in urban areas were produced as commodities. Even in rural areas, different sectors of agriculture have become specialized and commodity-driven in order to adapt to the requirements of the international market. In other words, the objects with which merchants conduct business are no longer at their mercy. As a result, it becomes simpler for them to gain access to the market, and they become increasingly aware of the significance and value of industrial profit as a result of the gradual transformation in production methods. The process of profit equalization has at least spanned from commerce to emerging industries and manufacturing industry. People have at least realized that industrial profit is as significant as commercial profit, but it is still hard for ordinary people to notice the different roles of the two, which may be because it's not allowed to reverse their social relationships in reality. China still stays at this stage currently.

The occurrence of modern industry in China is obviously a precondition for the existence of industrial profit. Nevertheless, its existence and actualization are two distinct concepts. The former pertains to the nature of industry. Any industry operated in the methods of modern production seeks profits, but how it can achieve its demand of profit may be possibly a matter of the quantities of industries. There is no doubt that new industrial operation has been witnessed in China, but the issue of quantity is likely to arise as China has been used to replacing the observation of quantity with that of quality.

The change of production methods, from the production forms centered on independent handicraftsmen and smallholder peasants to large-scale production, didn't come easily, and took place slowly from sector to sector and area to area. Therefore, the prerequisites of industrial profit were created slowly, but the corresponding equalization of profit were not necessarily or couldn't be consequently adopted. In an isolated emerging industry based on outdated production methods and even in a new industry with an isolated department from other traditional departments, the application of the average industrial profit was not feasible. It is only when the quantity of new industries has overtaken that of backward and traditional industries in all respects that the law of average industrial profit can be applied. Obviously, Chinese industries still have a long way to go to reach the stage. It is therefore reasonable to conclude that the law of average profit cannot be applied to Chinese industrial profit.

However, there is a seemingly self-contradictory proposition herein. New industries need to obtain overwhelming social advantages before they can enjoy reasonable average profit. Many conditions that constitute reasonable profit, or favorable conditions of new industries compared to traditional ones, cannot be formed under the control of old production methods. However, in order to enlarge their social advantages, new industries must achieve a reasonable profit in order to facilitate further reproduction. In the modern era, nations have resolved this contradiction by leveraging national political power to increasingly destroy old relationships and protect new relationships. In the description of interest forms, the methods of capital turnover with low interest rate and grants are proposed, and it is time to review the protective methods for commerce herein. If the infant industry of many modern countries has earned a profit higher than expected, it cannot be asserted that this is simply due to the greater advantage of new industries over traditional industries. Rather, the major reason for this should be attributed to the support provided beyond the economic sphere. This support is represented by new features in taxation, in addition to the various privileges of interest and commercial policies. The most important of these is the contribution made to the exploitation of the labor force, in explicit or implicit ways.

This is how new industries in modern times are "born". After the initial stage, they gradually attain advantages over commerce in terms of gains and surpass traditional industries in social status. During this process, numerous conditions pertaining to industrial development have changed, and then the equalization of profit shifts from commerce to industry. Commerce has been at play as an industrial organization, and its profit is defined by how it "serves" industry. Consequently, the social situation and the various social relationships undergo a significant reversal.

The aforementioned description seems excursive, but it shows the opposite side of the relationships between Chinese industrial and commercial profit. Modern industries indeed existed in China and developed under favorable circumstances. However, as Chinese industries embarked on the journey of modernization, they did not receive any support from but were blocked by the non-economic force in profit instead. The comprador nature of Chinese modern commerce is in essence exclusive of industry. Under the influence of international capital, Chinese commerce performs the task of serving foreign industries, so it does not have to or cannot serve Chinese ones, which fundamentally prevents commerce from serving Chinese industry. Furthermore, the profit aided by foreign privileges serves to exacerbate the foolish arrogance of comprador commerce towards national industry. Under this circumstance, it is doubted whether the "warm" assistance granted by various countries to their industry in modern times in finance, commerce, taxation, can elevate industrial profit to the level of commercial profit, or even surpass it. A thorough resolution is needed herein to cast commercial capital away from general social foundation, and to further eliminate the basis on which imperialist policies are built. If the aforementioned basis remains in effect, it will impede the cultivation of industrial profit through finance, taxation, and other aspects. In the majority of cases, it is likely to transform the cultivated "benefits" into a pressure and burden of industry. This is no longer theoretical but factual.

If it is a principle that the formation of the social advantage of industry over commerce relies on political power to influence their profits, countries like China, coerced by foreign power, must flexibly apply the principle to making the social transformation come true instead of adopting the same methods and steps as modern European countries that only need to break down their domestic traditional social relationships.

However, in general, it seems that China observed the principle too rigidly or failed to accurately understand the principle, so it partly followed the example of advanced countries. As a result, the industries that were established through various opportunities failed or went bankrupt due to the absence of sufficient profit. Furthermore, many prospective industries ceased or languished during their transition to manufacture for the same reason. The industries struggled but failed to expand and reproduce based on their original accumulation, which made it impossible for them to gain an advantage in quantity and become superior in quality. This resulted in a cul-de-sac.

Furthermore, new industries could not gain momentum for development, backward industries were on the verge of complete breakdown under the influence of emerging industries at home and abroad. Meanwhile, traditional agricultural and industrial communities that were disintegrated, and independent production organizations, such as people and objects, lost functions opened up more profound and extensive ways for the activities of commercial capital, although they could not be included in new industries. In this way, not only was commercial capital not helpful to the growth of new industries but destroyed old ones. When the independent development of the capital was attached to the nature of comprador, it became rampant with redoubled strength. Although its high profit rate was still based on shattered industries, old and new, it could still gain high profit with the assistance of foreign privileges, which were like its cultivation of the fruits of commerce on the ruins of industry. Eventually, the commercial scale expanded through the accumulation of high profit rate, especially through the role international capital played, brought about the social advantages it boasted to arbitrarily order about industries. Although industry was more valued and industrial profit was viewed by some people as more important than commercial profit, when it turned to serve commerce, the profit for its "service" would have to divide from the total earnings of its "master".

This was the situation prior to the outbreak of the War of Resistance against Japanese Aggression. Clearly, exceptions did occur within this general context. For instance, some industries managed to overcome difficulties and even demonstrated a tendency toward growth in certain cases, while other businesses failed early on or went bankrupt. Neither scenario was exceptional.

We will investigate the former case—those industries that showed growth—further in the subsequent chapter. For the sake of a clearer illustration, that discussion will be developed together with an analysis of wages and land rent.

The bankruptcy of commercial ventures, even those with high profit rates, can be explained by the characteristics of Chinese profit structures. The overall advantage of commerce over industry did not guarantee the prosperity of every commercial activity. Within the commercial sphere itself, the accumulation and centralisation of capital often occurred at the expense of weaker counterparts. It was common for large-scale commerce to absorb smaller businesses, especially in an environment where commerce operated independently, without the regulating influence of a strong industrial sector.

Furthermore, if commercial profit was tied to imperialist privileges, its sustainability depended on the existence and intimacy of that very relationship. Needless to say, changes in the commercial policies of imperialist powers had a significant impact on the earnings of those who relied on them.

Additionally, many comprador-style commercial businesses were closely linked to national industries. This was especially true for industries established during the advantageous period of World War I. These commercial entities were often the first to suffer panic and losses when foreign trade declined. It is estimated that the shutdown of numerous shops in major cities prior to the War of Resistance was largely attributable to prevailing industrial crises.

The foregoing analysis suggests that it was impossible for Chinese commerce to develop in complete isolation from industry. Ultimately, as commercial profit derives from the industrial products created by surplus labour or surplus value, the erosion of both traditional and modern industries would inevitably deplete the very source of that profit.

Chapter 18
Comprehensive Investigation into Chinese Interest and Profit and their New Current Forms

The aforementioned description has presented the forms of Chinese interest and profit, which are the indispensable products created in the movement of commodities, currency and capital, although they play the role of regulation or adjustment in the process in the meantime.

Interest and profit could have been interpreted as the conditioning factors related to capital circulation, which are both the cause and result of capital circulation. No matter where capital comes from and how it is used in society, being Industrial Capital, interest-bearing capital, or commercial capital, it always views profit rate (industrial and commercial) or interest rate as the indicator of circulation. Once the application of capital has been determined in accordance with the standard of profit or interest rate, the remuneration received will be commensurate with the indicator of circulation, whether that be profit or interest. The remuneration may be higher or lower than the circulation indicator. Nevertheless, the circulation of capital can only be made to function effectively within a society where the relationships between commodities and currencies that are characteristic of capitalism have been established. To put it another way, the process can be made to function when a society has identified the assistance of interest-bearing capital and commercial capital, which conduct currency operations and commodity operations respectively for Industrial Capital throughout the entire production process.

In a society such as China, where commodities are still confined to the form of simple commodities, even if some products are unavoidably involved in the process of circulation, the objective is evidently not profit. It can be seen, therefore, that the value of the production means and labor force produced is not yet deemed to be capital. Furthermore, currency retains its form as a means of simple commodity circulation. Its application is not intended to remunerate the value of production means and labor, nor to realize the surplus value of commodities. These forms of commodity and currency have inherently constrained the nature of capital circulation that could be transformed into.

Y. Wang, *The Basic Theory of Chinese Economy*,
https://doi.org/10.1007/978-981-95-6330-2_18

Should Chinese commodity and currency assume the aforementioned form, the circulation of capital within society will be confined to that between usury capital and commercial capital. In this process, usury interest and commercial profits (land rent is temporarily put aside) serve an uncertain regulatory function.

Nevertheless, the relationship between commodity currencies has historically facilitated the social existence of industrial capital. Yet, the very factors regulating capital circulation—namely, usury interest and commercial capital profit—have come to assume a role of great significance, often standing in for industrial profit.

Research indicates a recurring pattern: industrial capital tends to develop in a form antithetical to usury and commercial capital, yet remains constrained by them. This is particularly evident when industrial capital fails to gain control over these forms, allowing them to continue acting in concert to resist being subordinated to industrial logic.

For instance, when interest rates experience significant fluctuations and establish multiple benchmarks, the equalization of a general profit rate for industrial capital becomes impossible. In such conditions, it becomes easier for commercial capital profits to encroach upon industrial earnings through various means, exploiting the absence of a uniform profit rate.

Moreover, when commerce leverages external forces—such as imperialist privileges—to constrain industries in multiple ways, the latter face further pressures. Lacking sufficient accumulation for expanded reproduction, industries find themselves restricted by the multiple, differential interest rates of usury capital, new-style bank capital, and even foreign bank capital.

At its core, commercial capital and usury capital share a common demand for collective operation against new industrial capital. This demand manifests in many ways, but the decisive factor is that commercial capital's application is most easily altered—more so than industrial capital. The same holds true for usury capital and even bank capital.

Therefore, when industries embark on a bumpy path and profit becomes uncertain, the association between interest-bearing capital and commercial capital grows more intimate. Commercial profit and the interest rate of interest-bearing capital together hold the key to the circulation of social capital, with the interest rate often serving as the norm for commercial profit.

It is no coincidence, then, that amid a sluggish industrial and securities market, the financial market, public debt, and the real estate market experienced an unexpected boom. This phenomenon informs us, in both true and misleading ways, about the distorted dynamics of capital in this context.

Given the large fluctuations and gaps in interest rates—which obstruct industrial capital—do they also hinder the formation of a general profit rate for commercial capital? This is easy to answer. When commercial capital takes independent form rather than becomes an auxiliary part of Industrial Capital, although the task of comparing market price and production price should be performed by commerce in some cases, merchants themselves still hope to conceal the underlying truth. Their philosophy is to deceive others in the absence of legislation and regulations (although it especially needs them when the other conditions for its transformation into modern commerce are well ready). Therefore, the large distinction in interest rate can be made use of as an advantageous condition. Consequently, the large distinction in interest rate can be made use of as an advantageous condition. Even if it is ultimately unsuccessful, the flexibility and adaptability of commercial capital will enable it to effectively adapt to different interest benchmarks. For the same reason, common commerce is still at ease although new industries and even manufacturing industry and independent handicrafts industry find it difficult to deal with the changing interests across the nation.

After the outbreak of the War of Resistance against Japanese Aggression, the general picture of the Chinese national economy has varied, along with the changes in interest and profit and in the relationships between the two. However, no matter where the changes have taken place, the aforesaid principles remain unchanged and even get reinforced.

During the early period of the war, social capital required high earnings and rushed more swiftly along the past centralization route to Shanghai and Hong Kong where foreign forces were. Because of the currency reform and unified issuance, physical gold and silver were shipped to foreign countries through the maintenance of foreign exchange and the escape of capital in various ways, while the virtual capital represented in bills and bonds was especially pervasive. Ever since the order on the restriction of withdrawing deposits was issued, Chinese banks and money shops were the last place to go for those living on interest, and commercial speculative activities became overwhelmingly violent. Commerce gained hundreds of times of interest by employing the advantages amid the wartime, and the interest of interest-bearing capital turned out to be overshadowed.

Following the successive occupation of Shanghai and Hong Kong, and the subsequent cessation of foreign trade, the comprador nature of commerce was temporarily halted. However, this suspension did not result from industrial development. Meanwhile, the feeble foundation of industries broke down with the loss of comprador nature, which made commerce randomly utilize existing modern commodity-currency development as well as any backward relationships retained and strengthened due to underdeveloped industries to give full play to its functions of speculation and manipulation. The excessive profit or high profit rate in commerce minimized Industrial Capital profit and even the interest of interest-bearing capital owing to inflation and surging prices. It seemed that social capital only saw the special commercial profit in some sectors or some areas as the norm of its centralization. Not only did the financial measures adopted by the government, such as elevating interest rates and rewarding saving, exert little effect, but the industrial profit that received assistance and support in various ways became conspicuous, as if the interest of interest-bearing capital and Industrial Capital were deprived of their regulating effects on capital circulation.

Anyway, interest-bearing capital and commercial capital resemble twins in their operation. If the high profit rate of commerce primarily benefits merchants at the expense of other social classes, the resulting poverty and financial inadequacy will inevitably create opportunities for the expansion of interest-bearing capital.

Meanwhile, when social capital becomes concentrated in commerce, it leads to a paradoxical situation. On one hand, there appears to be a surplus of fluid capital; on the other hand, this does not mean that merchants or prospective business operators have adequate capital at their disposal.

As commerce becomes more centralized and operates on a larger scale, it tends to leverage backward social relationships to hoard goods for speculation. In such conditions, merchants want to retain large amounts of money for purchases, even as they struggle to maintain the value of their capital amid currency devaluation. This means that every social class—including the merchant class itself—faces a constant need for money.

Does this then present a sound opportunity for interest-bearing capital? Historically, banks failed to absorb deposits effectively because of the significant gap between the interest rates they could offer and the prevailing rate of commercial profit. The industrial sector, meanwhile, could only provide minimal interest, making the turnover of industrial capital problematic.

Money was simply better deployed as commercial capital than as interest-bearing capital, since it followed the speculative trend and faced fewer obstacles. If money was to be lent, lenders naturally demanded interest rates closer to the level of commercial profit.

This high interest rate was often ensured through physical forms of repayment. The practice of repaying loans in kind—such as returning physical goods for borrowed goods or money—was once limited to backward areas but has now become widespread, spreading from rural to urban areas like an "infectious disease."

For example, a loan of one dàn of grain (about 50 kg) or its cash equivalent might require repayment of two dàn within a year—a nominal interest rate of 100%. But when grain prices rise, the real rate escalates dramatically: if the price doubles, the real interest rate reaches 400%; if it quadruples, the rate hits 800%.

Under such conditions, the returns to interest-bearing capital can rival the high profits of commercial capital. When the commercial capital itself engages in transactions in kind, merchants hope for continuously rising prices. Similarly, when interest-bearing capital is lent in physical form, both lenders and borrowers become speculators on price inflation.

In this mode, interest-bearing capital effectively functions as a subspecies of commercial capital. Lending becomes a form of hoarding—but with a crucial difference: whereas ordinary hoarding profits only from price increases, this method multiplies the hoarded value through the leverage of debt and compounding real repayment obligations.

Nevertheless, no matter how interest-bearing capital tried to adapt to the governance of commercial capital, many changes have taken place in its realistic activities. The interest rate of interest-bearing capital has no longer been a norm of commercial profit but the other way around, implicitly or explicitly. Amid the changes in reality, the three interest benchmarks in the past have long surpassed the original boundary. The occupation of Shanghai and Hong Kong during wartime resulted in the loss of territories for foreign financial activities, and the subsequent termination of unequal treaties following the war had a significant impact on these activities. Not only was the wide gap of interest rate between the Chinese urban financial industry and rural usury industry made light of by the abnormally high commercial profit, but even the renewed interest rate of usury demanded by the new banking industry could be forgiven out of sympathy by ordinary people. The changes have made it not applicable to gauge the current interest with the evaluation in the past. However, no matter how they have changed in form, how commercial capital regulated the interest of interest-bearing capital during the wartime, and how the current horribly-high interest rate of interest-bearing capital is influencing the profit of commercial capital, the huge profit in any aspect, or the excess earnings gained through interactive competition, will in the end sacrifice the production enterprises of various sizes in China.

Issues Discussed in this Part

1. Why did the occurrence and discovery of profit forms normally come after interest forms?
2. What are the respective influences of interest rate deciding profit rate and profit rate deciding interest rate in the development of the social economy?
3. How did the past different interest benchmarks prevailing in Chinese society interact with each other? What were the consequences?
4. Why could Chinese industrial profit not get rid of the shackles of interest? How is it related to the segmentation of surplus value?
5. Try to explain the encroachment and control of commercial capital over industrial capital from the perspective of commercial profit depriving of industrial (capital) profit. Why did Chinese bank capital assist commercial capital other than industrial capital?
6. Have the original tendencies changed or been reinforced at present?

Part VI
Forms of Wages in China

Abstract This chapter details the pre-capitalist characteristics of wage labor in China. Despite a large pool of hired labor, its nature differed fundamentally from modern free wage labor. Pervasive systems like apprenticeship, labor contracting, and indentured servitude created various forms of personal and economic dependency on employers; labor power was not fully commodified. Wage levels were extremely low, often barely sufficient for the individual worker's subsistence, let alone supporting a family, thus preventing workers from becoming significant consumers and expanding the domestic market. The widespread use of women and child labor to further depress costs was common. These depressed wages and poor conditions were both a result of weak industrial capital and meager profits, and a cause of constrained market demand, trapping industrial production in a vicious cycle.

Chapter 19
Forms of Labor and Wage

Wage is the reward paid to workers for their labor over a certain period—in other words, the monetary form of the price of labour-power. From this simple definition, we can see that: (a) Wages are based on the existence of laborers who have achieved formal independence and are thus free to sell their labor as a commodity; (b) The fact that wage-earners are willing to sell their labor, and employers are willing to buy it, shows that the means of production with which labor operates have already been separated from the workers and transferred to the employers; (c) Paying the price of labor in money over a period of time presupposes the development of commodity-money relations—otherwise, payment would take other forms.

These three conditions are interrelated, and together they form the basis of what we call the modern wage system. The difference between this modern wage and earlier forms of labor compensation lies not so much in the content or amount of payment, but in the conditions under which laborers work and are paid. Thus, it is the form of labor that ultimately determines the form of wages.

In a society based on private ownership, the form of labor has evolved through several stages—from slave labor, to corvée labor, and finally to wage labor.

Under slave labor conditions, the slave is regarded as a living tool, belonging to the owner just like physical tools. What the slave receives for subsistence can hardly be called "payment"—it is no different from fertilizer for the land or feed for livestock.

Under corvée labor, the situation is markedly different. Here, the serf's labor is divided into two parts: labor for themselves and labor for the landowner. The serf works for the landowner in order to gain the right to work for their own subsistence. If the part of labor spent on self-sustenance is enough to maintain the serf and their family, then the labor performed for the landowner constitutes surplus labor. In economic terms, the former is called necessary labor, the latter surplus labor.

Surplus labor is undoubtedly the source of the landowner's income, while necessary labor sustains the serf. Yet, in those times, the product of necessary labor was by no means considered a "payment" given by the owner to the laborer. Instead, the product of surplus labor took the form of tribute paid by the laborer to the owner.

Y. Wang, *The Basic Theory of Chinese Economy*,
https://doi.org/10.1007/978-981-95-6330-2_19

Whether one gives or receives, the object and the real basis are clear—even though the owner could arbitrarily increase or decrease the share of necessary labor and surplus labor.

For the product of the laborer's necessary labor to take the form of a wage, labor conditions must undergo a fundamental shift—from corvée labor to wage labor. Under wage labor, the social situation changes entirely.

Previously, power and wealth were bound to the land, and landowners had every incentive to keep serfs tied to the estate to secure a continuous supply of tribute. But capitalists, as the new masters of society, needed to liberate the serfs. Only with free laborers could the expansion of capital proceed. Thus, the slogans of freedom and equality were raised against feudal privilege, and relations of commodity production were established.

Laborers no longer offered surplus labor as tribute in a relation of subordination. Instead, they began to sell their labor as a commodity on the basis of formal equality. This is how the modern wage system came into being.

That said, I will not delve here into the question of whether this formal and superficial equality is preferable to real subordination, or whether the control exercised by capital is more convenient than the constraints of the land.

In the evolution of labor forms, wage labor is, after all, a progressive stage. Yet the emergence of this form—that is, the establishment of capitalist wage relations—is far more intricate, convoluted, and twisted than what a few abstract principles might suggest.

Whether in industry or agriculture, the historical transition from corvée labor to wage labor has been, for the laborers, a history of hardship. Their work under the old system was a kind of suffering; their struggle to adapt to the new system often brought another kind of pain. And if they were caught in between—stuck in a transitional stage—they might not only miss the dubious benefits of "fake equality but real subordination," but also experience a double dose of suffering. Their labor takes on the appearance of a commodity, yet remains tribute in essence.

The wage forms we see in China today offer a telling illustration of this reality.

Chapter 20
Traditional Chinese Wage-Labor Relationships

If people comprehend the formation of modern wage as the most basic part of the overall capitalist production relationships, and this painful transitional stage is what the laborers of all modern countries must have experienced. The duration and the painful extent of this transitional stage can vary from country to country as the natural and historical conditions of these countries are greatly diverse.

Today, when discussing Chinese current wage forms and its formation process, people should at least briefly describe the traditional relationships of wage labor which exert great influence on that presently. If the traditional relationships are rather special and largely remain in all kinds of current labor forms, then it is more necessary to undertake the description.

One issue requires particular attention, namely the wage labor relationship as the basis of production. As has been noted previously, this represents the final form of the evolution of social labor within a context of private property. In other words, this phenomenon should not have manifested prior to the advent of modern society. The aforementioned general principles of labor evolution would be undermined if such labor relationships existed in previous societies. Indeed, this issue has been previously addressed. L. Delevski asserted that slavery, serfdom, and free labor existed concurrently, and at times, it was challenging to discern which was the predominant form. He asserted that during the peak of slavery in ancient Rome and Greece, there were also significant numbers of free laborers. Furthermore, as Edonard Meyer has asserted, the existence of free labor has a history as long as that of slave labor. In other words, the history of slaves in medieval times was as long as that of serfs and free laborers in urban areas. In America, slaves and free laborers worked shoulder by shoulder. Delevski thus drew the conclusion based on these facts that "history did not give rise to rules". (Refer to p9–10, *Outline of Socioeconomic History of China* compiled by Wang Yucun).

It seems a sound theory with "full evidence", but it fails to distinguish the following two arguments clearly. Firstly, the division of the history of social labor is based on the main mode of production of each society as well as the basic production relationships

Y. Wang, *The Basic Theory of Chinese Economy*,
https://doi.org/10.1007/978-981-95-6330-2_20

stipulated in that mode of production. For instance, people have to realize, in ancient societies, whether the luxurious and extravagant life of the ruling class and free citizens was supported by a small number of free laborers who were occasionally and reluctantly engaged in production, or the filthy and exhausted laborers of the vast slave groups. Secondly, the essential difference between the so-called free labor existing in ancient societies and medieval times, and the free labor or wage labor of modern times, is what people have to clarify. The former is a matter of quantity, while the latter quality. By raising these two issues, people can not only refute the fallacies concerning the development history of social labor, but also clarify whether there could arise the relationships of wage labor in the past societies.

Around 180 years ago, renowned Adam Smith raised the issue of the wage of Chinese workers in his great book *The Wealth of Nations*. He stated that in the travel notes of many travelers who traveled to China before and after the time of Marco Polo, it was generally recognized that Chinese labor wages were low and laborers could barely support their families. Farm laborers could be satisfied with earning a little money for food with their hard work. The situation of craftsmen was the worst. He added that unlike European craftsmen who could be seated comfortably in their shops and wait for customers to come, craftsmen in China often carried their tools and peddled door to door just like beggars. Furthermore, he summarized that the lower class in China was even poorer than the beggars in Europe. Why? Herein, he pointed out a fact that Chinese were used to witnessing but sounded a little shameful. He stated that at the ports of Guangzhou, the Chinese people were scrambling for the unclean food abandoned by European merchant ships. Even if the bodies of dead dogs and cats were somewhat smelly, the Chinese people pursued them as much as the people of other countries pursued the most hygienic food. He remarked that although the lower class of China were so poor, China once became one of the richest and most prosperous countries in the world a long time ago. His description of a rich country with an extremely poor lower class went that although China had big fortune, it had stopped growing for long, so the labor wages were not supposed to be very high, or be raised.

Smith employed Chinese wage level to demonstrate his theory of wage dispersion. He held that the wealth level of a country did not necessarily mean its high wages or wage increases. Only the countries that ceaselessly increased their wealth could see continuous wage growth, and only the countries that ceaselessly had their wealth reduced would see continuous reduction. He cited the developing situation in America as an evidence of wage raise, and the backwardness of East India and other British colonies as an evidence of wage cut. China, on the other hand, was regarded as staying in a static state of neither going forward nor going backward, and the wages would make the ordinary laborers fail to sustain their lives. His opinion can be concluded with his words that "the generous reward of labor is the natural symbol of the increase of national wealth, the meager means of living of poor laborers is the natural symbol of overall stagnation, while their hunger is the natural symbol of ultimate decline".

The theory of wage dispersion proposed by Smith is not to be discussed herein. As for all his descriptions of Chinese wages, it is true that the wages were too low for the laborers to support their life. Nevertheless, this explanation is too broad and insufficient to account for the emergence of low wages in China without considering the broader context of societal stagnation.

First of all, it must be pointed out that the relationships of wage labor in China have been present for a long time. However, the social conditions for its presence are quite different from those of Western European countries which also have existed over the centuries. Therefore, its form and nature are quite distinct.

In an agricultural society, industry is generally attached to agriculture and thus proves to be subordinate to agriculture. The industries located in rural areas are mostly in the form of handicraft industry. This handicraft industry is operated in three ways. Firstly, it is as a sideline, or for the operators' own consumption, or for sale; secondly, it is as their main business and also as agricultural activities; thirdly, it is as a profession and becomes an absolute handicraft operation. This absolute handicraft industry can be divided into independent handicraft industry and "wage operation" which is not independent enough, based on whether it has tools and raw materials or not.

What is to be done herein is to disclose the handicraft form of "wage operation" and its characteristics in China. Originally, wage operation was in two ways. Firstly, the operator provided equipment for operation, and allowed the customer to bring raw materials to its own workplace for production. The compensation for the cost of the equipment was required upon the completion of the production, but the point was to demand a wage from the customer. Therefore, this operation was named "home wage operation". The mills or flour mills in which customers took wheat to grind, the dyeing houses in which customers took clothes to dye, the grain mills in which customers took rice to grind and oil mills in which customers took rapeseed or cottonseeds to extract oil were in similar forms. On the contrary, some craftsmen did not own equipment. They could only carry their simple tools they needed to find customers door to door, such as blacksmith, coppersmith, tinsmith, bowl mender, cooper, carpenter, mason, plasterer and seamstress, or wait for employment at home, such as craftsmen, dressmaker, mason and plasterer, and the like. They usually worked at the customer's home and got paid from their customers. Therefore, this form of operation was also known as "away wage operation". Of course, this "away wage operation" today is mixed with something "modern", but in comparison, Chinese society has always regarded this operation form as the primitive form of wage labor. (See *Outline of Socioeconomic History of China* compiled by Wang Yucun).

These two labor forms seem simple, while their formation process has exerted a great impact on the subsequent development of labor forms.

Generally, "home wage operation" has advantages over "away wage operation" in terms of remuneration. If craftsmen wait for customers to come to them, they may miss job opportunities. Besides, some customers will not go to craftsmen's until they have no way out. If they go to visit customers, their chances of getting hired can be increased. Some customers may probably hire them even not out of necessary demands. But in terms of remuneration, the former is less constrained by daily wage needs, whereas the latter depends on wages for subsistence., while the latter must obtain adequate prices. Moreover, in the case of home operation, not only the operation procedures and time can be effectively adjusted and arranged by the operators, so that when there are no customers in the short run, the regular operation may well not be suspended. In addition, they can make better use of raw materials. However, those away wage laborers are not free. No matter he waits or seeks to be hired, operation time, scope and procedures are all controlled by others. One day without work probably means one day without food. Taking these situations into consideration, the remuneration for away wage operation is doomed to be much lower.

Furthermore, "home wage operation" was not voluntarily adopted by handicraftsmen at that time; rather, it resulted from prohibition. The Craft Guilds of the Middle Ages in Europe exercised considerable authority within their respective industries. In order to eliminate internal competition, the scope of their activities was limited in various ways. An important item stipulated in Guild regulations was that no one in the same trade was allowed to operate freely and they should work within a certain scope. Under such restrictions, the number of home wage operators would not exceed the needs of the public, and their wages could be raised accordingly. However, in Chinese society, the Craft Guild was not organized rigorously enough. It can even be stated that the Craft Guild like the European type was never established at all in China. All the regulations similar to Guild put emphasis on sacrifice, contact, mutual aid and special local relations. Therefore, away wage laborers could move freely without any restrictions, and their number could not be limited within the range of need. As a result, their remuneration had to be lowered accordingly.

Herein, the origin of this kind of laborers may be helpful to point out what a disadvantageous position those away wage laborers were in. The Chinese rural economy has been more volatile than that of Europe, which is a significant factor contributing to the underdevelopment of hereditary occupations in China. The Chinese form of landlord economy that has been mentioned from time to time on other occasions, that is, the fairly free relationship in the transfer and sale of land, could easily facilitate land concentration in the hands of a few people, and Chinese special commercial capital has further contributed to this trend. Consequently, when a peasant who had previously lived on land, whether as an owner or tenant, was forced to leave their former land and unable to secure land under more unfavourable conditions, there were only two potential avenues for them to pursue. Firstly, they could regard their handicraft work, which had previously been a secondary occupation, as their primary business and profession, thereby becoming an independent handicraft laborer. But what kind of independent craftsman could he become? In the past, ordinary people took land particularly important. With land, he would be a peasant rather than a craftsman. Meanwhile, when he was forced to leave the land due to poverty or debt, he was naturally unable to provide any kind of industrial equipment for operation, and had to choose a job that required less skills and simpler production tools. This is the form of away wage operation, and this path is obviously the most difficult. In addition to the above-mentioned reasons for wage cut, here it is necessary to indicate a key point. That is, if their work was limited to simple and easy operations, they would find not only unrestricted competition within the trade, but that all scheming peasants competed with him. The peasants in the past featured that they adapted their production to their own consumption, they fed on the food they grew, drank the wine they made, wore the clothes they sewed, and even repaired their doors and windows, walls, drawers and cages all by themselves. Especially when ordinary peasants were in extreme poverty, they would not call for workers as long as they could make do with whatever was available and did it by themselves. Therefore, among away wage laborers, the situation for those who waited to be hired was better than those who peddled their craftsmanship. After all, they chose this kind of work because they lost or did not get land at all. As for those apprentices who had years of training, they made such a bad decision because they expected no land for farming or they were not suitable for the occupation.

Furthermore, there was a way out for those who lost land in rural areas. That was to exchange food with their labor with the landowners and even land users (i.e., serfs). They were the lower class, wandering men or food-seeking vagrants who were known for their labor, diligence and thrift among the villages. They were loaned with seeds and residence and became servant peasants similar to slaves before they were reduced to private belongings of their masters. They were less than semi-free and their status was even lower than those day laborers who had simple operation tools. Therefore, their earnings with their labor were even less "modern" than that of away wage laborers.

In addition to the aforementioned industrial and agricultural labor wage relationships, it may also be necessary to describe the labor form of official industry throughout Chinese dynasties. There were two types of official businesses, one is the business that needs higher technology and large-scale equipment, such as salt making, mining, porcelain burning and paper-making, etc., which was mostly run or supervised by the government. Its main purpose was not so much to assist production as to increase fiscal revenue, so it represented the nature of monopoly. This kind of enterprise form quite resembles the modern manufacturing industry. Although, by nature, the laborers working in this cooperative mode still relied on manual labor rather than machines, they were more likely to benefit from division of labor and cooperation and enhanced their labor force compared with the independent craftsmen who needed to complete all operations as each of them was only responsible for only one aspect of all operations. Only in this sense, the laborers who engaged themselves in such operations were likely to receive more remuneration. Whether they were hired, forced or they volunteered, they did not have to provide simple production tools for themselves like independent handicraftsmen, which indicates that they were more similar to modern wage laborers.

The other one was related to the consumption of feudal monarchs, nobles, bureaucrats and even some special monks and Taoists. Long ago, the Chinese government began to name the handicraft industries producing these kinds of goods as "Baigong (all craftsmanship)". Among all, there were 7 branches of wood-related craftsmanship, Yu (舆), Lun (轮), Gong (弓), Lu (庐), Jiang (匠), Che (车), Zi (梓); 6 branches of metal-related craftsmanship, Zhu (筑), Ye (冶), Fu (凫), Zhuo (桌), Duan (段), Tao (桃); 5 branches of fur-related craftsmanship, Han (函), Bao (鲍), Hui (辉), Wei (韦), Qiu (裘); 5 branches of color-related craftsmanship, Hua (画), Hui (缋),

Zhong (钟), Kuang (筐), Huang (慌); 5 branches of polish-related craftsmanship, Yu (玉), Ye (椰), Diao (雕), Shi (矢), Qin (磬), and 2 branches of ceramic-related craftsmanship, Tao (陶) and Yi (旊). Officials were designated to take charge of every category of craftsmanship (the systems can be referred to in *Rites of Zhou: Record of Craftsmanship*). It is believed that the labor division and organizational system seemed impossible to be so complete at that time. However, as the special needs of the upper class or officials of all dynasties were not easy to be met by non-governmental institutions, they must be planned and arranged by the government as a whole. The categories and objects of the production varied from time to time. For instance, after Buddhism was introduced to China, people's needs for such articles as bronze bells, Buddha statues and perfumes began to emerge. Moreover, when the needs of a small number of upper classes gradually became the general needs of society, the goods previously made for the officials were expected to be produced by the folk. However, no matter how it evolved, every dynasty had its own official industry regarding the production for its special needs. Although the handicraft laborers working in these kinds of official industries were "official slaves", their remuneration was generally better because their craftsmanship was prominent. Obviously, They created use value instead of exchange value and only served royals and nobles. They might as well be named "noble laborers", but their number was limited. And they were not classified by Adam Smith as Chinese poor wage laborers.

Chapter 21
Evolution from Traditional to Modern Wage-Labor

The previous brief discussion on wage labor in China serves mainly to understand what role this form of labor has played—and will play—in the transition to modern wage relations: whether promotive or obstructive.

First, this section examines the widespread "away-work" system. It can be seen as both a result and a cause of the weakness of craft guilds.. The fact that artisans were scattered across the countryside does not deny that workshops once existed in cities, but rather shows how workshop-based craftsmen could be reduced in number and dispersed geographically. To adapt to modern labor conditions, these artisans first had to negate their own status: a small minority would become bosses or capitalists, while the rest turned into wage laborers with no means of production left to rely on except those of the few capitalists. Clearly, many social factors facilitated this modernization of labor relations, among which pre-existing wage relationships were one of the most powerful.

If independent artisans had been firmly organized within guilds, they could have restrained internal competition and strengthened their collective bargaining power, thereby accelerating the growth of their interests. In Europe, guild cities once served as strongholds against feudal aristocratic power. There, at least before early modern times when commercial capital began to dominate, craft guilds held a dominant posi tion (modern merchant guilds often evolved from craft guilds or alliances of them). Through such organizations, artisans were concentrated in certain towns. Although journeymen and apprentices within the guilds may have had limited freedom, their development as a social group was largely protected—something that can be observed from several angles.

Let's first consider their internal relations.

Independent artisans, though confined to certain towns or markets, usually operated under a "home wage" system, often with their own tools. They lived relatively stable lives and could focus their efforts. Any profits they made could be used to expand their operations—forming a prototype of manufacture. Free from scattered

Y. Wang, *The Basic Theory of Chinese Economy*,
https://doi.org/10.1007/978-981-95-6330-2_21

pressures and with greater concentration of mind, they could more easily improve production techniques and business methods, even without guild supervision.

Now, as for their external relations:

When organized, guild artisans could agree on the type, quality, cost, and price of products. Custom-ordered production and open-market supply could be planned and coordinated. This greatly restricted the ability of merchants—engaged in transporting and selling goods inside and outside the cities—to manipulate the market. Thus, the influence of merchants in most European guild cities remained limited. Except in a few major trading centers like Venice, Hanseatic cities, or certain English towns, the craft guilds' social power was hard to ignore. Guilds could make collective demands to feudal lords and sometimes even successfully confront merchant capital, creating favorable conditions for industrial and labor development.

Thanks to these supportive internal and external social conditions, the transition to new wage-labor relations in Europe was considerably shortened.

What about China's situation?

The scattering of independent Chinese artisans across the countryside weakened their collective industrial strength. The quasi-guild organizations I mentioned earlier served mainly ritual, mutual aid, and social purposes, with little active effort to expand members' economic interests. Meanwhile, merchants in the same cities took advantage of the artisans' lack of organization, while also leveraging their own ties to officials and landlords, to dominate urban economic life. Industry gradually became subservient to commerce. The less protection urban artisans enjoyed, the less incentive they had to gather in cities—leading to further rural dispersal. Cities thus became consumption centers dominated by merchants and officials, laying a historical foundation for commercial supremacy over industry.

Moreover, those "away wage" workers scattered in the countryside, even if they earned enough beyond subsistence to save, rarely invested in equipment or industrial expansion. Instead, savings went into moneylending or land purchase. Hence, industry was hindered not only by commerce but also by the pull of agriculture and land rights. This explains both the low earnings of independent artisans and the difficulty of forming modern wage-labor relations in China.

China did witness relatively advanced cooperative industries or "quasi-manufacture" at times. But as the analysis above suggests, their evolution differed from Europe's. Normally, industry evolves from household craft to independent handicraft, then to manufacture, and finally to factory industry. In China, however, cooperative or manufacturing enterprises often did not grow out of independent handicrafts; in fact, they sometimes hindered the latter's development. Most successful larger-scale workshops or manufactures were officially supervised or directly run by the court to meet government consumption or fiscal needs. The political weakness of Chinese craft guilds historically prevented artisans from articulating demands for protection or autonomy. Thus, ordinary laborers in state-supervised industries remained politically and economically muted.

Furthermore, monopoly rights were common in official industries. Prominent sectors like salt, silk, and porcelain were dominated by official operations, leaving little room for private growth. Luxury goods for the elite also fell under government purview, limiting profitable markets for private artisans. This further obstructed the transition from independent handicraft to manufacture. In addition, profits from state-supervised industries were usually treated as fiscal revenue or used for luxury spending, rarely reinvested to improve production or expand operation. That explains the repeated failure of official monopolies throughout Chinese history.

Finally, a special form of agricultural labor—where landowners or even tenant farmers provided land, tools, seed, and huts to landless laborers to farm under supervision, or where the poor worked in exchange for minimal subsistence—also hindered modern wage-labor relations in several ways. First, it encouraged land concentration but also land fragmentation, preventing the scale of operation needed for modern wage systems. Second, those who lost land became dependent laborers or semi-serfs rather than independent artisans or beggars. This type of employment was not exactly slavery—employers didn't own the workers but still controlled them through subsistence guarantees. Nor was it serfdom, which involved clearer mutual obligations. In China, the relationship remained ambiguous, allowing landowners to use threats of withdrawing tools or food to extract maximum surplus while providing minimal subsistence. Landlords and even rich tenants took advantage of these "food-seeking vagrants," reducing them to a subordinate status. Establishing formal wage-labor relations in agriculture was thus historically difficult—for many reasons, but this semi-feudal form played a key obstructive role.

If we are concerned not only with what these labor forms were, but what they ought to become, we may note that of all the traditional forms, the last one—the dependent agricultural laborer—has proven especially resistant to change. Taken together, these forms created major obstacles to the emergence of modern wage relations in China.

Since the arrival of modern capitalism, Chinese society has undergone certain transformations. But when we analyze these changes in light of earlier production relations, it becomes clear that pre-existing social and historical conditions heavily constrained subsequent development.

First, merchants and their organizations—traditionally accustomed to subordinating independent producers—were given new life as compradors. While their targets of domination shifted (as rural cottage and handicraft industries accelerated their decline), and while some official enterprises converted to private operation under comprador conditions, these new industries remained concentrated in a few large cities. Together with newly built Chinese and foreign factories, they altered the consumer-city character of old urban centers. Traditional merchant guilds also transformed, yet merchant dominance over workers—and even industrialists—largely continued. Chambers of commerce acted as intermediaries with foreign powers. Most urban and rural production units operated under commercial capital; many urban factories were run directly by merchants or indirectly through raw material control. In the countryside, handicrafts tied to foreign and domestic trade fell under merchant and usury capital. Laborers in these systems became, in effect, "merchants' slaves." Even urban workers paid by factory bosses were often indirectly controlled by merchant capital behind the scenes. Compared to industrial capitalists, merchant exploitation tended to be cruder and less restrained. The "commercial" character of urban wage labor was often masked by a modern exterior—a point we'll return to later. In short, comprador-era merchant domination over industry exploited the older social foundation of merchant guilds dominating craft guilds, only in a more dependent and unfavorable form.

Second, it is widely recognized that modern manufacture in China did not evolve gradually from independent handicrafts, nor did it grow out of older official or cooperative industry. Instead, it seemed to leap over historical stages, being implanted from outside the normal industrial progression—whether by accident or special demand. This origin made it inherently vulnerable in technology, capital, organization, and experience, restricting the sound development of wage-labor forms. Moreover, unlike bosses who rose from artisans to capitalists, the new merchant or bureaucrat-industrialists lacked understanding of or sympathy for labor management. Not coming from production themselves, they often left foremen to freely bully workers. But that's only one side. Even worse, although old official enterprises could not evolve into modern large-scale industry, many early official-run modern factories (e.g., arsenals or military-supply plants) inherited the operating methods of traditional government manufacture. As economists note, any state-run industry not based on a developed private industrial foundation easily becomes a "gravy train," and its workers could be treated as "government slaves"—a phenomenon seen not only in China but also in countries like Japan, where feudal residues were strong.

Finally, we should examine the role of the traditional "colonus"-type labor in rural wage-relation modernization. It's well known that rural China was backward, but not unchanged. As foreign trade penetrated the countryside, the small peasant economy combining farming and handicraft was gradually dissolved by commodity-money relations. Traditionally, land concentration rates were often offset by urban capital concentration. Landlords grew attracted to urban life. Urban lifestyles spread to the country—including, relevant here, the practice of controlling means of production and hiring laborers for money wages. This seemed beneficial to landowners (landlords or owner-peasants) and even tenants, since in turbulent times it was safer than entrusting land to "vagrants" who might farm carelessly. Gathering workers under supervision also allowed some division of labor. But there was another side: the decline of rural sidelines and urban handicrafts left landless peasants with little choice but to seek urban employment. Many did find work as servants, coolies, or factory workers—sometimes together with their wives and children. This made them less willing to accept semi-serf dependence in the village. Even those staying in the countryside might prefer to work for landowners or tenants on a short-term, monetized basis. Pushed by monetary relations, rural labor forms began to change. Yet, in the relation between landholders and agricultural workers, the change often worked against the latter. When urban industry stagnated and workers returned to the village, they fell back into the "vagrant" pool. Despite monetary relations, their status remained inferior to the traditional colonus; they received minimal necessary product, now in money form, while providing maximum surplus—this was the essence of the "change."

Thus, we can see how traditional labor forms in China distorted and hindered the modernization of wage relations. This is only one part of the picture, but it helps explain why, under capitalist influence, Chinese wage labor developed in such a deformed manner. Had it not been for the historical legacy of "merchants' slaves," "official slaves," and semi-serfs, modern wage relations in China would not have taken the abnormal form we see today—or at least, they would look different.

Chapter 22
Quality and Quantity of Chinese Wage-Labor

It is necessary to provide the statistics of Chinese wage laborers for better description herein.

Statistical evidence indicates that over 50 million people in China derive their livelihoods exclusively from manual labor. It is assumed that the national population is 400 million, which would mean that wage laborers in China account for 1/8 or 12.5% of the total population. In comparison to countries such as Britain and the United States, where the proportion of industrial workers is 78% in Britain and 74% in the United States, the ratio in China is remarkably low. It would be misleading to subdivide the category of laborers without clarifying their underlying relations. It's estimated that (see Xu Shenzhi's *Research in Industrial Labor in China*, Issue 2, Volume 2, *Culture Magazine*), among the 50 million people who solely live on manual labor, more than 30 million are wage laborers in agriculture (this is close to the figure in Wang Yichang's *Capitalist Land Rent of China*, Issue 9, Volume III, *China's Economy*, which quotes the number of wage laborers in China in the first issue of the *Quarterly of Zhongshan Culture and Education Center*. In other words, it can be estimated that between 6% and 20% of the total rural population in China is engaged in wage labor, representing more than 10% of the total agricultural population on average. If the population of the whole country is 400 million, and according to estimates, Chinese peasants account for 80% of all, then the number of agricultural wage laborers should be about 32 million). Additionally, there are over 1.5 million urban dock workers, railway carriers, street sweepers, rickshaw pullers, sedan chair bearers, boatmen, and so forth (based on experience, the actual number of such workers may be considerably higher); about eight million are family industrialists and independent handicraftsmen, and 6 to eight million are workers in various traditional handicraft workshops and traditional pit workers, particularly in the salt, tobacco, oil pressing, porcelain burning, and traditional textile factories industries. In addition, 3 to 3.5 million are new-style industrial workers. Except for the last kind, which still has incomplete statistical basis, the number of most of these workers is calculated or estimated. On the whole, it could be comprehended that,

Y. Wang, *The Basic Theory of Chinese Economy*,
https://doi.org/10.1007/978-981-95-6330-2_22

among the Chinese population of about 400 million, there are about several tens of millions of wage laborers, and among whom, there are less than 1/10 of industrial workers.

That is the ratio of the industrial workers to the national population.

If the number of modern industrial workers can be regarded as an indicator of the degree of social development and a test of the progress of capitalist production methods in conquering backward production methods, people might as well investigate the possible characteristics of the tens of millions of wage laborers except industrial workers, and the possible characteristics of those industrial workers themselves, based on this rough ratio.

The adoption of capitalist production methods cannot simply be achieved by copying other countries mechanically. Every new mode of production must develop out of the social conditions inherited from the old society.

Take the United Kingdom, for example—a country with a long history of capitalist development. When the British attempted to introduce capitalist practices into Australia, they found that the necessary preconditions were absent: the local peasant-proprietors lacked the means of production, the technical foundations, and above all, the willingness to become a wage-earning labor force.

Similarly, when Britain tried to implant capitalism in the United States, even though the settlers brought machinery and technical know-how, many of them showed little interest in working for capitalists. Instead, they found it easier to acquire wealth by reclaiming wasteland and hiring laborers themselves.

This illustrates a crucial point: for capitalist production to take root, there must first exist a broad class of people deprived of their means of subsistence—a proletariat, in other words. Without this essential condition, all other factors that might otherwise support capitalist development remain non-capitalist in nature.

In China, by contrast, such a condition was indeed met. On the one hand, traditional processes of land concentration continuously stripped peasants of their means of production. On the other, the massive influx of foreign goods dismantled the traditional union of agriculture and handicraft industry in the countryside. Together, these forces created a vast number of impoverished laborers—the indispensable precondition for capitalist production.

Yet, in practice, China still lacked other internal and external conditions required for modern industrial or commodity production to flourish. While a large proletarian class is essential to capitalism, it cannot alone give rise to capitalist relations if other social and institutional foundations are missing.

Thus, among China's approximately 50 million wage laborers at the time, only a small fraction—about one-twentieth—were true industrial workers. The rest survived mainly by manual labor, but under conditions that fell far short of capitalist norms. Lacking the social structure of free and equal exchange, these laborers could not truly sell their labor as a commodity. Though their work took on the superficial form of a "commodity," it still carried the essence of "tribute."

In older and newer forms of manufacture, in distorted cottage industries, and even in what remained of independent handicrafts, the labor force often took on the character of "merchants' slaves" or "debt slaves." In agriculture, it manifested as a type of "special serf" or colonus—bound, dependent, and far from free.

In fact, it is true that the laborers in the aforementioned backward industrial sectors cannot work in modern conditions of wage labor. Even those lucky enough to be admitted to new industrial sectors cannot work and have not worked in sufficient modern conditions of wage labor either. One of the most fundamental reasons is that industrial modernization is based on the all-round reform of a society as the premise. For an entrepreneur undertaking any new industrial operation, no matter how complete his equipment is, how regular their operation mode is, if his factory is set up in an environment where no social reform has been achieved, he is bound to lower the purchasing cost of labor force as much as possible for his self-interest. This is what every capitalist country experienced in the early modern period.

Secondly, if the wage labor conditions of Chinese industrial workers, no matter how non-modernized, are generally better than those of handicraftsmen, coolies and even colonus-type dependent laborers, indicate that for these three million or more industrial workers, there were nearly 20 or more times the number of industrial reserve forces or alternates who were eager to replace them and ready for capitalists. Under the increasingly serious situation of rural bankruptcy, it was very obvious how this increasing pressure would have an adverse impact on the employment conditions of industrial workers.

In addition, it should take into consideration foreign-owned enterprises in Chinese new industries and even the sectors operated in the name of foreigners. The businesses operated by foreigners in China put the factor of extremely low Chinese labor prices in the first place at the very beginning. Moreover, as for the exploitation of labor force, foreign industrial operators are even more immoral and unethical compared to their Chinese counterparts. That is to say, they are more merciless. In addition, imperialists began to treat colonial people, especially the toiling masses, as dirt a long time ago, and various forms of privileges of those foreign capitalists gave rise to the fact that they treated Chinese wage laborers inhumanly without scruple.

When people investigate the whole picture, they may perceive that even those specified industrial workers in the Chinese broad wage labor group are not employed completely in modern conditions of wage labor.

Certainly, these are merely theoretical explanations. Facts are to be given for substantiation.

Chapter 23
Forms of Wages: A Realistic Basis for Exploitation

In China, industries operated by foreigners were able to generate excess profits. Interest-bearing capital and commercial capital could yield considerable interest and profit rates, while the rate of land rent was exceedingly high. Such facts, of course, need to be described from many aspects, and the most basic and essential must be perceived Chinese forms of labor and wage.

To begin, we will examine the comparatively new industries.

One early rationale for the adoption of machinery under capitalism was its compatibility with the employment of women and children. In other words, capitalism exploited the low remuneration rate of women's and children's labor, while simultaneously using this to reduce the wages of adult workers. Many of the achievements of modern capitalism have been made possible by the exploitation of women and child labor. The majority of criticisms levied against capitalism, along with the formulation of factory laws and regulations designed to restrict the proliferation of capital, have focused on the labor of women and children from the outset. This may serve as a suitable point at which to commence an investigation into the wage-labor conditions of Chinese industrial workers.

Those who can be regarded as the workers in Chinese new industries can be classified into three categories: railway workers and seafarers, miners, and factory workers, especially textile workers. Among them, the workers of the third category account for an absolute majority. The research as follows mainly focuses on this category.

According to *China Labor Yearbook* published in 1933, among the 2,000,256 wage laborers in 23 provinces and cities across the country, more than a quarter of them were women and children. Take Shanghai as an example. If the non-factory workers and family operators were included, there were 550,000 women and children among the 600,000 workers in the satin industry alone. According to the report of Shanghai, there were 168,885 child laborers under the age of 14 in the city. The most direct indication of such a large proportion of women and child laborers is that even if they shoulder the same workload as adult male workers, their remuneration is far

Y. Wang, *The Basic Theory of Chinese Economy*,
https://doi.org/10.1007/978-981-95-6330-2_23

lower. For instance, in Shanghai in 1930, according to the survey of the Ministry of Industry and Commerce, the average monthly wage of all industries was 15.28 yuan for male workers, 12.50 yuan for women, and 8.70 yuan for child workers. Such a great wage gap between men, women and children may be because, on some occasions, the workload of men is heavier than that of women and children or the work of women and children could be simpler. However, despite how complex or simple the work was, an adult male worker must be paid by the wage standard of adult male. So, replacing men with women or children could undoubtedly save the expense of wages.

But the advantages of employing women and children go beyond that. When women and children do the same jobs as adult male workers, adult male workers immediately feel the competition and exclusion from their wives and children, which serves as an excellent disguised way to lower the wages of adult male workers, and in turn, those of women and child workers.

Furthermore, women and children are easier to control than adult male workers. It can be inferred that the labor control and supervision methods adopted in emerging industries in metropolises like Shanghai, such as the foreman system, contract system, grade system, shift system, exploitation system and clear punishment system, are closely related to the large employment of women and children. Stress always stretches towards the less resistant respects. For instance, in 1923, the Municipal Council organized an investigation committee to investigate the status of young laborers in Shanghai. The results of the investigation were presented to the General Bureau of the council the following year, which indicated that in the 274 factories in the industrial area of the city, there were 22,000 children under the age of 12 who worked from 6 a.m. to 6 p.m., or from 6 p.m. to 6 a.m. It was common for them to work for twelve hours a day. The committee also reported that many child workers were just six years old or younger, and some of them were even employed under the age of five. Sometimes they even worked day and night.

The report undoubtedly informs of misery. However, if people disclose the whole living conditions of those children in terms of food, housing and clothing, and all kinds of inhumanity, insult and damage suffered by the workers in the accommodation area near the factory, the picture would be even more shocking. Given the long working time of the children, it's not hard to imagine the working conditions of their parents, elder brothers and sisters.

Certainly, China has never enacted legislation pertaining to labor. In the 12th year of the Republic of China (1924), the Ministry of Agriculture and Industry of the Beijing Municipal Government announced the provisional general rules for factories, and the rules for the treatment of miners in the same year. In the subsequent year, Dr. Sun Yat-sen announced the Regulations on Trade Union as Grand Marshal in Guangdong. In the 18th year of the Republic of China (1930), the Nanjing Municipal Government promulgated the factory law. These decrees have many similarities with the early labor laws of modern capitalist countries. If the regulations and decrees had been strictly observed, it might not have been difficult to compulsorily modernize Chinese employment labor conditions. However, this was impossible. For instance, for the children who could not go to work because of failing to reach a specified age, the labor remuneration of their parents must be capable of maintaining a minimum standard of living for the family. Otherwise, the employment of child labor would not be a sin, but a "favor" and a "grace" worthy of being obtained through bribery. Factually, many were employed through bribery. The report of the British imperial consulate also openly affirmed that it was safer to keep children with their parents in factories than to let them wander on the streets. Of course, they had a "glorious" history of buying a large number of children from poverty relief homes and orphanages to raise their capital value. They showed no pity for the children and women in the colonies. Therefore, in June 1933, although China proposed in the 17th International Labor Conference that factories set up by foreigners in China should be subject to the labor laws and regulations stipulated by the Chinese government, the conference rejected the proposal. This indicates that the laborers in the foreign factories in China never enjoyed modern wage labor working conditions. The International Labor Conference, which aimed to protect the interests of capitalist powers, would certainly not rashly block the source of excess profits of their industries in China at the request of the Chinese government.

It is true that Chinese employers were more constrained by some habits, public opinions and morality than foreigners in the illegal exploitation of the labor force. However, as their business was not for charitable purposes, and at the same time, their industrial profits were subject to astounding high loan interest rates, commercial profits of high rates and various other non-economic extortion, it is more necessary for them to bargain in terms of wage labor conditions than foreign employers. Therefore, all effective exploitation methods adopted by foreigners in their factories immediately "infected" Chinese factories. For protecting national industries, it was not easy for the government to inspect and ban the factories in the foreign concessions, especially foreign manual factories. As for Chinese factories, the government could only "let everything take its course", encouraging workers to develop national industries.

However, the way of employing women and children labor in large quantities to exploit and raise surplus value was not entirely copied from foreigners. Let alone the fact that "actual gains make people wise", employers in China would not forget the various methods of enslaving production workers adopted by the traditional autocratic regime. Many foreign "China Hand" scholars, such as Wittfogel, considered that Chinese industrial workers suffered far more miserably than those in any country in the early modern era. Only people who were used to the humiliation under the traditional autocratic authority could be "submitted" to the abuse and all kinds of humiliation they received in their work and life. In China, the reason why foreigners did not hesitate to adopt all exploitation methods of extreme insult and oppression was only because they were used to the scenes where the Chinese upper class arbitrarily trampled on their compatriots, which is somewhat undeniable.

If machinery represents the most apparent distinction between the new industrial and the original forms, various cooperation industries that utilize primitive handicraft tools, such as salt, porcelain, sugar, tobacco and tea industries. Additionally, there are numerous workshops, including oil mills, dyeing facilities, wood and leather workshops, and, most notably, all kinds of traditional textile workshops, such as silk, linen, cotton and textile workshops. It is crucial to acknowledge that these operations often exploit women and children, a phenomenon that intensifies under the influence of capitalist production methods. In their various industrial operation modes, generally, the following wage labor systems are applied, although they vary from one to another due to the variant natures of their operations.

The first one is the common apprenticeship system. All these production sites (even some modern factories) have young workers. Some of these young workers are apprentices, and some even work in the name of apprentice. Although they work daily from five a.m. to eleven p.m., that is, 18 hours a day, they can only get a little rough food and are not paid.

The second kind of labor system is the patriarchal system closely related to the former system. Under this system, a number of apprentices assemble for a boss and a number of employees as the teachers of these apprentices, all of whom act in accordance with the will of the boss. The length of work hours and the amount of work remuneration are almost not clearly defined. Whether the work goes well, whether the boss is diligent in business, and whether the boss likes or dislikes them are the most reliable criteria for whether they can get paid with some money in addition to food.

The third kind of labor system is the sweating system, the most exploitative piece-rate form of labor in the form of taking work home. In traditional industries such as firecracker production, porcelain manufacture, and various textile industries, especially in the match and cigarette industries, a large number of handicraftsmen gather in each production unit. Due to their different regions and the nature of their industry, some of them live exclusively on such labor remuneration, while others operate them as sidelines. However, their wages are unbelievably low. If they rely on this kind of labor to make a living, they have to work day and night. It is also very natural for them to encourage all their families to produce.

The fourth kind of labor system is the contract system associated with the previous one. Of course, this system is very classical, but is also somewhat modern. It is a by-product of the piece-rate system. The work is contracted by the contractor from the manufacturer, and then allocated to ordinary laborers through some subcontractors. The old and new construction industries, including some mines, salt farms and even textile factories all adopt this system. This kind of labor system not only breaks the time limit like the sweating system, but also maximizes the exploitation of workers.

It is not difficult for people to understand that all industries with such labor systems might have other more barbaric forms of exploitation, but what it needs to explain herein is their common internal relationships. With the competition between and oppression of the operation of foreign and new factories, as has been described on other occasions, manufacturing industries which are easy to centralize and decentralize, and even various forms of workshops, are more likely to exist than independent handicrafts. Their possibility of existence is mainly limited by two facts. Firstly, the scale of the manufacturing industry and various forms of workshops are just ideal for comprador capital. Large-scale new industries are not willing to be controlled by it, and the excessively decentralized independent handicraft industry is very difficult to control, either. Only medium-sized manufacturing industries and workshops are easy to be effectively controlled and manipulated in operation, raw material allocation and product concentration. Commercial capitalists can successfully turn the bosses of the industries into their own agents. Therefore, in the industrial field, Chinese comprador business almost mainly adopt this form of industry as a hotbed for capital proliferation. However, why can this kind of industry support commercial capital (and the high interest rate of usury capital) is another point that needs to be explained herein. In manufacturing plants and various workshops, although the workers still mainly work manually, they are anyway gathered in one operation unit. Time is saved through the division of labor and practical results are obtained through cooperation. Compared with independent craftsmen, they have higher labor productivity and produce more products of surplus labor. However, although the products of surplus labor are increased, the necessary labor production as their remuneration is forced to be relatively reduced under the aforementioned working conditions. Their non-human life reflects their nature of "businessmen's slave" and even "debt slave".

Finally, it needs to give a brief introduction to the characteristics of the approximately 15 million aforementioned employed farmers.

A small part of individual laborers are characterized by being separated from traditional means of production, land, and subordinated to a new means of production, capital or machinery. In this transformation, direct agricultural workers no longer have relations of production with land owners, but with the owners of other means of production, especially the owners of machines or agricultural capitalists. To put this another way, after this transformation, the tool employed to exploit them is no longer land, but capital.

In Chinese rural areas, whether the agricultural operators are landlords, rich peasants, small and middle peasants and even tenant peasants, they typically engage in small-scale agricultural practices. Their main or most important means of production is naturally land. More and larger land means more powerful tools for exploitation. Rich peasants, landlords and middle and small peasants, are of course the polar opposite of direct producers as land owners. As for tenant farmers who rent other people's land, when they hire laborers temporarily or on a long term, they are also polar opposites as land lessees and land users from those direct producers who cannot own or keep land and have no choice but to be employed.

If this fact is evident and undeniable, then the 15 million wage laborers in Chinese rural areas are not employed because they have been deprived of land and have no means of production other than land. They are employed because their land has been deprived of and they are incapable of using it. Therefore, although the identities of the three pillars that constitute the lowest stratum of Chinese rural society, namely, small peasants, tenant peasants and employed peasants, are overlapped and interactive on many occasions, as three categories respectively, on the one hand, small peasants have no alternative but to give up their small patches of land only under extreme circumstances, and this is the case with tenant peasants. On the other hand, it is extremely difficult for tenant peasants to obtain a small amount of land, and it may be even more difficult for employed peasants to rent a small amount of land. Consequently, employed peasants find themselves at the lowest rung of the social ladder in rural areas.

Generally speaking, the ultimate purpose of Chinese agricultural operators undertaking land management is to obtain more land. Once their wish is fulfilled, they are unwilling to continue to take on this troublesome work and become rent collectors who are only interested in consumption. That is to say, except for a very small number of rich peasants, those who employ laborers are almost all small and middle peasants and tenant peasants who do not even have the necessary simple farm tools and live in great difficulties all the time. They do not hire laborers because they have better farm tools and livestock. On the contrary, they often use labor force to reinforce and replace these working conditions which they cannot afford. This shows that on average, the price of labor force should be lower than that of animal power and the cost of agricultural tools, so that it is possible for them to be employed. If not so, unlike the price of livestock and farm tools, which needs to be paid at one time, the price of labor can be paid in parts or at the end of a certain employment period.

All kinds of backward and bizarre wage labor relationships therefore emerge. Readers can find out what wage labor conditions are in effect in the Chinese countryside on their own.

Many people draw a conclusion of labor commercialization from the phenomenon of the widespread existence of wage labor in rural China. In fact, the form of monetary payment and the fact that general rural laborers lodge at the employer's home rather than their own are not powerful explanations of whether the labor force is truly commercialized. The key is whether the laborer is subject to land or capital for their work. However, as has been analyzed previously, they are not employed for the lack of capital, but rather for that of land. Therefore, all the people with land, the owner or the lessee, may use the land to exploit others. In this way, small peasants and tenant peasants in Chinese rural areas can exploit others, which accounts for the widespread existence of wage labor.

Obviously, Chinese tenant peasants are generally not like modern land lessees. They relate themselves to landlords with labor instead of capital. Therefore, with their dependence on land to some degree, they inevitably become subordinate or serfs to landlords accordingly. This is one of the basic reasons for the emergence of corvee. However, although the general tenant peasants are still serfdom to some extent, this does not prevent them from exploiting those who fail to rent land. On the contrary, he may have to rely on the labor of others to offset the heavy burden of the high rate of land rent for renting and keeping land. Herein, after all, the existence basis of Chinese extremely heavy land rent has been found out.

Issues Discussed in this Part

1. Why is the division of necessary labor and surplus labor not recognized by ordinary people and economists after the adoption of wage?
2. Is Adam Smith's understanding of Chinese wage correct?
3. What are the advantages and disadvantages of "away wage operation" and "home wage operation" for the future industrial development?
4. Why can't the wage labor condition in Chinese new industries become modernized?

5. The various extortion relationships in Chinese society generally view various wage labor conditions as the basis of their reality. How to explain this?
6. There is an essential difference between the small tenant peasants in rural China and the land renting agriculturalists in a capital society. Why are they qualified to exploit farm laborers?

Part VII
Forms of Chinese Land Rent

Abstract This chapter argues for the central role and backward nature of land rent in China's economy. Feudalistic rent in kind prevailed, characterized by extremely high rates often claiming 50% or more of the harvest. This extracted not only the peasant's entire surplus product but frequently encroached on necessary product required for their subsistence. The development of money rent was constrained underdeveloped commodity-money relations. This high rent, based on landlordism and small-scale tenant farming, was the primary form of wealth accumulation for the landlord class. It drained the agricultural surplus, preventing capital accumulation and technical improvement within agriculture itself. Furthermore, landownership was intrinsic linked with merchant and usurer capital, forming a "trinity" of exploitation that collectively suppressed agricultural production and peasant livelihoods, locking the rural economy into a state of simple reproduction and long-term stagnation.

Chapter 24
The Evolution Process from Feudalistic to Capitalistic Land Rent

The concept of land rent is more challenging to grasp within the field of economics. Firstly, for the convenience of description or analysis, the field of economics tends to focus on commodity production within the industrial sector. This is due to not only the gradual expansion of modern capitalist production methods from the industrial to the agricultural field, but that the development of the capitalist economic form in the industrial field is generally more mature and purer than that in the agricultural field. Land rent is generally an economic category of agriculture. Therefore, it is more likely to retain some backward factors, which causes the hardship in analysis. Secondly, in the research procedure of economics, the finding of commodity analysis in the industrial field is applied to that in the agricultural field. The key difference between agricultural commodities and industrial ones is that in the value of the former, there includes one excess profit which can be realized and converted into land rent (industrial field also includes the category of land rent, but the importance of land rent is extremely reduced with the centralized development of industry). If the theory of commodity value is the key to economics, people must firmly grasp the key to the understanding of land rent. In this sense, all economic theories can help the comprehension of land rent.

However, although the difficulty in perceiving land rent once dazzled many excellent economists, such as Adam Smith and Ricardo, in the 17th and 18th centuries when capitalism began to emerge, some first-class scholars like Petty took this issue extremely easily. This is because they lived in a period that was almost feudal, and thus did not intuitively regard land rent as the general form of surplus value. Furthermore, capital land rent was not yet an established form that could perplex their analysis. a century later, the category of land rent as the research object of Adam Smith became so complicated as a transition between the old and new forms. Half a century later, in the research object of Ricardo, the category of land rent, the new form achieved a dominant position while the old was still somewhat in effect. Therefore, although Adam Smith established many economic laws with his profound genius, he was particularly vague about the concept of land rent. He was not born in the right

Y. Wang, *The Basic Theory of Chinese Economy*,
https://doi.org/10.1007/978-981-95-6330-2_24

time. Neither was Ricardo, although it was he who eventually established the basic law on the theory of land rent.

Generally speaking, there are three forms of land rent, namely, labor rent, in-kind rent and money rent. The former two are feudalistic, while the third capitalistic. Although in the pre-capitalist society, in-kind rent was often converted and collected into money to a certain extent, capital land rent was often converted and collected into materials to some extent, the general capital land rent must be money rent.

Labor rent is the most primitive form of land rent. In order to utilize the land of another party, the direct producer allocates a portion of his time each week to work for the landlord on the land in question, under the supervision of the latter, without receiving any remuneration. The situation differs somewhat with regard to in-kind rent. In order to utilize the land of another party, the direct producer is required to provide the landowner with a specified quantity of land products at the end of the annual harvesting period. In this sense, the landowner can no longer obtain the surplus labor of the direct producer, but can only do so through the land products. Therefore, direct producers are not required to engage in labor or deal with their products of surplus labor under the supervision of the landlord. This transformation of land rent has not given rise to the change of the nature of that it is the only form of surplus value or surplus labor.

However, everything would change provided in-kind rent is transformed into money rent. The direct producer does not provide the landowner with his products but the price of the products. It seems simple but at least the following social preconditions need to be achieved.

Firstly, for the price of labor products to be regarded as land rent, it is essential that all or part of the direct producer's output be transformed into commodities and subsequently into money. The commercialization of agricultural products thus presupposes considerable development in commerce, urban industry, general commodity production, and monetary circulation. Moreover, these products must be sold at market prices closely corresponding to their intrinsic value.

Secondly, with the legalization and monetization of the relationship between landowners and tenants, a fundamental shift must occur in rural social production relations. On one hand, the direct producer must be freed from traditional feudal obligations to the landowner, emerging as an independent and free agent. On the other hand, the non-land working conditions he has traditionally used—such as tools, seeds, and livestock—must become fully his own property. Only under these conditions can a tenancy relation based on contractual agreement be formed.

Within this new framework, some better-off direct producers become fully independent owner-peasants, as they possess the means to acquire land ownership along with other necessary instruments of production. Those less fortunate, lacking both land-purchasing power and non-land productive assets, are reduced to proletarians or agricultural wage laborers.

What distinguishes this new arrangement from the old is that in the past, dependency stemmed from lack of land; now, it arises from the lack of means of production apart from land. Once rural social relations take this form, the significance of land—once the paramount condition of production—gradually diminishes, giving way to capital. The tenant, now owner of agricultural capital, appears in the role of a capitalist. With the emergence of the capitalist tenant-farmer mediating between the landowner and the actual tiller of the soil, all relations rooted in the earlier mode of rural production begin to dissolve.

Finally, a further crucial precondition for the full transition from rent in kind to money rent is that the monetary relationship should not arise arbitrarily or sporadically, but be grounded in objective social conditions. The division of the surplus value generated in agriculture between the tenant-farmer and the landowner must be determined not by extra-economic coercion, but with reference to the average rate of profit formed in non-agricultural spheres—serving as the benchmark for capital allocation.

With this average profit as a reference, the tenant-farmer can determine the return expected from investing capital in agriculture, and thus ascertain what portion of the agricultural surplus value should be paid to the landowner as rent. Likewise, the landowner can estimate what portion of the surplus should be left to the tenant to maintain agricultural investment, and how much he himself may claim. If the landowner demands too much, the tenant may shift capital to non-agricultural sectors. If the tenant retains too high a share, the landowner may sell the land and invest elsewhere.

Thus, the average profit rate outside agriculture serves as an objective basis for negotiation in lease agreements.

The particularity of agricultural production lies in its lower organic composition of capital compared to industry, enabling it to yield more surplus value—specifically, an excess profit above the average social profit. This excess, attributable to the monopoly of land as a natural factor, is transformed into land rent. What was once conceived simply as a form of surplus value now appears under capitalist conditions as a portion of the total surplus value, subordinate to the prevailing average rate of profit.

The aforementioned is the whole process of the transformation from feudal land rent into capital land rent. Although this transformation is reflected in the change from provision in kind to that of money, the essential reform underlying this phenomenon can be summarized as follows. (a) At least a large part of agricultural products are produced as exchange value instead of use value; (b) the most important agricultural working conditions are the means of production other than land instead of land; (c) the persons agricultural laborers directly rely on or have a relationship with are no longer the owners of land but those of other means of production other than land; (d) the remuneration of agricultural operators is not restricted by land rent conversely, the remuneration of land owners is limited by average profit and transformed from excess profit; (e) the surplus value of agricultural labor takes profit instead of land rent as its general form.

However, all these changes are based on the completion of capitalist land rent and its transformation. At the start of or during the process of the transformation, either aspect of the aforesaid changes would inevitably take on extremely complex unfinished forms. In accordance with the previous research on the various aspects of Chinese commodity-currency capital, it may be especially indispensable to point out those unfinished forms, but in order to avoid repetition in narration, herein it only points out the different characteristics and transformation process of feudalistic land rent and capitalist land rent, which can also serve as grounds of arguments hereinafter.

Chapter 25
General Phenomena Forms and Characteristics of Land Rent in China

Land rent is also an ancient economic form in China. The evolution of land rent is, of course, closely related to other long-standing economic forms. Throughout Chinese economic history, land has long been treated as the most fundamental issue; therefore, analyzing land rent as the core of the land question is crucial for understanding many economic phenomena in Chinese history. On other occasions, I have discussed more than once the relationship between Chinese land ownership and commercial capital and usury capital, or the relationship between land rent and commercial capital profit and interest-bearing capital interest. However, the characteristics of Chinese land ownership or its more realistic manifestation—land rent—can only be manifested herein.

Among China's major economic phenomena, land rent has perhaps remained the most traditionalTo put it another way, the rights of the landlord to the tenant as well as the obligations of the tenant to the landlord. It seems that it is not only due to that economic reform in rural areas, which generally lags behind the urban areas, but also to the trend of Chinese industrial development in urban areas, which generally has the effect of inhibiting the fundamental changes in rural land relations. Nevertheless, Chinese patterns of land rent have not been consistent. In recent decades, Chinese and foreign scholars have made a lot of contributions to the current investigation and theoretical study regarding Chinese land rent. Here, I only need to cite the most general phenomena and forms for the discussion in this part.

Firstly, land rent is one of the most widespread economic phenomena in contemporary China. Although the situations vary across the country, that is, in some provinces or regions, the rented farmland is more common than the self-cultivated land, while others exhibit the opposite pattern. On the whole, however, rented farmland accounts for roughly sixty percent of all cultivated land in China (This assessment is based on the estimates of foreign scholars with different views. According to Mazar, landlords in southwestern provinces own sixty to seventy percent of the cultivated land; fifty to sixty percent in the Yangtze River basin; fifty percent in Henan and Shaanxi; thirty to forty percent in Shandong; ten to thirty percent in Hubei; fifty to seventy

Y. Wang, *The Basic Theory of Chinese Economy*,
https://doi.org/10.1007/978-981-95-6330-2_25

percent in the northeastern provinces. According to Rahiman, the owner-peasants in the twelve provinces in southern China account for only twenty-three percent, while the semi-owner peasants for twenty-five percent and the tenant peasants for forty-three percent). Of this vast area of rented farmland, only a very small amount belongs to public land such as official estates, school fields, clan properties, and temples and the disintegration is accelerating, while the rest is owned by private landlords. This indicates that the form of pure feudal land ownership can no longer be maintained, while the landlord economy, with its capitalist appearance, is developing.

Secondly, in line with the aforementioned development of the landlord economy, all these leases are generally formalized through contracts, that is, the lessee has a contractual relationship with the landlord, although in relatively backward areas, there are still oral contracts, on very small-scale and fragmented lease occasions. Certainly, let alone the oral contracts, the contractual terms themselves vary depending on the location, time, and individuals involved. While there is one common feature herein, that is, the rights and obligations stipulated in these contracts are generally one-sided. To put it another way, the rights of the landlord to the tenant as well as the obligations of the tenant to the landlord. It is true that there are so-called perpetual rent, fixed-term rent, and non-fixed-term rent in the provisions of years, and so-called charter, sublet, and sublease in terms of the form of tenancy. It seems that the landlords are also bound by the restrictions of these tenancy conditions themselves, but a closer analysis reveals that these contents are all for the benefit of the landlords, or at the very least, they leave room for landlords to "act conveniently."

Thirdly, the land rent paid by the lessee or tenant peasants to the landlord is still generally in rem or in kind. Undoubtedly, money rent has arisen in certain special regions, such as the newly developed northeast, or in specialized cultivation areas, such as those for cotton, tobacco, bamboo, wood, and horticulture, as well as areas in the vicinity of urban areas. However, money rent takes a small part in all, just as labor rent. Naturally, we do not deny that the trend of the monetization of land rent is progressively advancing. However, at the same time, we must admit that such progress is very sluggish, and, in essence, it serves as a deformation of land rent in kind rather than its transformed form, which we will describe below.

Finally, we need to discuss the rent rate of in-kind rent. The rate of land rent is the ratio of the total land price to its annual rent. However, there is another common calculation, which is to divide the total land price by its annual rent amount of land, to obtain the "purchase year," which indicates how many years of annual rent are required to recover the purchase price of the land. The fewer the purchase years, the higher the rent rate. The general rent rate in China differs based on the abundance of land, the economic status of both parties of tenancy, and other various factors. However, it always accounts for more than fifty percent of the land produce, with some cases reaching as high as seventy to eighty percent. Converted into the number of purchase years, the maximum is sixteen years, the second is twelve years, and the minimum is five years (see *Introduction to Chinese Rural Economy* by Mazyar). So, the average purchase year is about eleven years, that is, the land rent rate is generally more than ten percent (Wagner, a German, analyzed the current economic situation of the peasants in Shandong and found that their rent amounted to eighteen percent of the total land price, noting that this was not the highest rate in China, while the rent paid by Prussian farmers to the state was only three point five percent). The purchase year in Britain during the Industrial Revolution was twenty to twenty-five and was reduced to twenty-seven to thirty after World War I. In Germany, it was twenty-eight to thirty-two in the Bismarck era, and was raised to about twenty after World War II. By comparison, the land rent rate in China today is significantly higher than that in any country in the modern world.

We may as well employ the aforesaid four points to briefly summarize the general phenomena of the land rent in China. Land rent is mainly collected by private landlords. The tenancy procedures have generally taken the form of contracts. The in-kind rent has become dominant, and the rate of land rent is incomparably high in China. Superficially, it seems that the first two might give us the impression of being "modernized," while the latter two might give us the impression of being far from enough modernized. Factually, the issue should be investigated from a holistic perspective. Instead of conducting piecemeal investigation into the various phenomena and forms of Chinese land rent to assess the extent of its modernization or capitalist development, we would rather focus on whether the general social conditions required for capitalist land rent can be located in Chinese society from a broader perspective. Therefore, the research on Chinese land rent is not about investigating what characteristics its various phenomenon and forms can imply, but about what characteristics its various social conditions surrounding it can permit.

Chapter 26
The Shadow of Absolute and Differential Land Rent as Expressed in the Limits of Development of Commodity-Monetary Relations

In economics, capitalist or capital land rent is classified into two categories: absolute or general land rent, and differential land rent. The former generally occurs on all leased land (in fact, it also happens on the peasant's own land, but the recipients of the special land rent are the peasants themselves instead of others). The reason is that the capital composition in agriculture is generally lower than that in industry, and the surplus value of commodity production in agriculture is generally greater than that of industrial products. Just as the surplus value in industry has to provide industrial capitalists with average profits, the greater surplus value in agriculture can provide agricultural capitalists with excess profits. Under the conditions of equal competition among capitals, the earnings of agricultural capitalists above their average profit will inevitably be converted into land rent because, in such cases, the land ownership has justification to regard this excess profit as the fruit of utilizing the land. In short, general land rent arises from the competition between Industrial Capital and agricultural capital. As for the occurrence of differential land rent, it arises as a result of the competition among various capitals in the same agricultural sector. When the same amount of capital is invested in the same area of land, the reward will vary depending on the quality, location and other conditions of the land. Landowners of superior land or more advantageous locations naturally demand higher land rent. According to this explanation, we know that the occurrence of both absolute and relative capitalist land rent is only possible when the law of average profit is in effect. The land rent converted from the excess profit above the average profit is the essential difference between capitalist land rent and pre-capitalist land rent. Given that the role of the law of average profit assumes the development of the commodity-currency economy as a prerequisite, We should examine and determine whether the land rent in Chinese society has a capitalist nature by investigating the following aspects respectively:

1. Whether the majority of agricultural products in China are produced as commodities.

Y. Wang, *The Basic Theory of Chinese Economy*,
https://doi.org/10.1007/978-981-95-6330-2_26

2. Whether our currency, as a means of commodity circulation, has largely fulfilled its function as a unified and dominant standard currency within the country.
3. Whether the land that is bought and sold in our society can be freely transferred as a commodity, unconstrained by traditional hereditary relationships.

Obviously, if agricultural products in a society are primarily produced as use value rather than exchange value, then it will be baseless to pay land rent in terms of price and currency, and the differential value between agricultural products and industrial products—where the former can provide more surplus value to the latter, thereby generating excess profit above the average profit that can be converted into land rent—cannot be realized. Namely, absolute land rent cannot be achieved. Certainly, if agricultural products need to have a market price and are sold at a market price close to their value, then a unified form of currency is required to assume the mission. Certainly, it alone is not adequate. As agricultural products are produced from land, the natural conditions (in terms of soil fertility), social conditions (in terms of investment in the ground), and even the combined natural and social conditions (in terms of proximity to usable rivers or the markets for sale) are the basis for the difference in purchase and sale price of land, the basis for the rate of land rent (the total land price divided by its annual rent) and the basis for the occurrence of the so-called differential land rent. However, the reliability of this basis depends on whether the conditions above can function as the standard of the market price in land transactions without being affected by non-economic factors.

Of the forms of Chinese commodity and currency economy, I have provided an analysis in the second and third parts of this book. Under the conditions of increased foreign economic dependence and the growing demand for money across rural society, not only have such originally specialized agricultural products as cotton, tobacco, tea, soybeans, and tung oil become further commercialized, but even the most self-sufficient products like rice and wheat are being sold on the market in increasing quantities and proportions. Many take this as strong evidence of the development of commodity production in China. I have previously mentioned the ratio of commercialized to non-commercialized land products in China; in truth, however, this ratio is of little material significance.

Strictly speaking, whether something constitutes commodity production does not depend solely on whether the product is made for one's own use or for others, nor merely on whether it serves as a use-value or an exchange-value. What matters are the conditions under which the product is supplied to the market and produced for others as an exchange-value. If exchange relations are generally governed by production relations, then the conditions under which production takes place are the most decisive indicator of whether land products have truly broken away from simple commodity production. The actual conditions and general state of production in our rural areas will be examined in detail in later chapters of this part. What I wish to emphasize here is the sequence in which commodity production develops in a society.

Generally, commodity production first emerges and grows in urban industry. Then, through inherent connections between urban industry and agriculture, it gradually induces agriculture to adopt capitalist methods of production. Thus, from the lagging and fragmented state of urban industry in China, we can already infer certain characteristics of rural production.

However, to maintain a clear line of argument, let us set aside that relationship for the moment and first examine the conditions under which products from our rural areas enter the market as commodities. Factors such as transport, weights and measures, the tax system, and even the peasants' knowledge of the market—all these undoubtedly affect the realization of the value of agricultural products. But the most crucial factor, in my view, is currency.

Even before the outbreak of the War of Resistance against Japan, the most basic functions of currency—as a measure of value and a standard of price—were already so unstable and irregular that ordinary products, especially land products, could hardly obtain market prices reflecting their actual value in the process of circulation. Here, we need not explore whether backward monetary forms stem from traditional social relations of production that hinder the development of modern monetary relations. Instead, we may examine how these traditional relations take advantage of monetary weakness to obstruct the full commodification of land products.

We observe that Chinese comprador-merchant capital has long been active in the manufacturing and specialized agricultural sectors. In collusion with usury capital, it has manipulated and controlled the rural economy, particularly in specialized agricultural production. A large portion of the ordinary peasant's output is disposed of in advance through hoarding or forward purchasing even before it is produced. The remainder is sold piecemeal in local primitive markets. In other words, whether the peasant sells in bulk or retail, he rarely has access to a stable or average market price for reference. In any given locality, the commercial manipulator becomes the de facto price-setter.

The aforementioned objective factors—poor transport, complex taxes, and inconsistent weights and measures—furnish the conditions for this price-setting power. What is more, the variety of currencies in circulation and the instability of their values work particularly to the advantage of these manipulators, serving as the most effective means of confining agricultural product prices within a favorable range.

Thus, in such a context, modern monetary relations have not been established. The transformation of agricultural products into money, or of money into agricultural products as means of purchase or payment, is inevitably interrupted or fragmented by coercive factors external to the circulation process. What emerges are disconnected, irregular, and artificially determined market prices.

To be sure, in daily life we may observe something like a prevailing price level in trading activities centered around large cities—a phenomenon that may seem puzzling at first. Yet closer analysis reveals that the formation of that price level conforms to the pattern described above: in a backward society, it is determined by merchants who compare production costs and market prices. It results from a rough equalization of profit in the process of circulation, premised on the direct producers' lack of market knowledge, isolation from the market, or inability to engage with the market directly. This kind of price formation differs almost entirely in category and nature from the market prices of agricultural products and the average profit of agricultural operators required by capitalist ground-rent.

In short, due to the underdevelopment of China's commodity-money relations, agricultural products cannot be normally commercialized and monetized. As a result, land rent cannot be smoothly converted into a monetary form and remains stubbornly tied to payment in kind.

That said, as noted earlier, the form of land rent in China has indeed been monetized in certain specific regions and for certain commercial crops. Moreover, could the occasional use of rent conversion methods nationwide be seen as a gradual trend toward monetization? My answer is yes, but we must be clear about the nature of this monetization.

Commodity-money relations in China are undoubtedly expanding. The demand for money—that is, the commercialization of agricultural products—does make rent in kind an inconvenient form for both tenants and landlords. But this alone cannot fundamentally transform the nature of rent. Furthermore, rent in kind and money rent are not always purely what they appear to be. What is collected in kind may in essence be a form of money rent. In the United States and other regions, rent is sometimes still paid in kind due to special circumstances, but it is converted into a monetary value. In ninety-nine out of a hundred cases in China, the so-called rent conversion system serves as a means for the landlord to extract additional earnings or to secure a self-determined income. Since the value of money fluctuates, and since landlords generally have better market knowledge, they can choose to receive rent in kind when prices are favorable and insist on conversion to money when that is more advantageous. They always control the timing and terms to their benefit. Therefore, this kind of monetization can never truly change the nature of land rent.

As for monetized rent in the Northeast and some other special regions, even where the degree and method differ, the logic of "conversion" still applies. For example, in bamboo-producing areas, there is no market price reflecting the actual value of bamboo. Instead, its price is generally set by reference to the grain rent commonly used in adjacent areas.

From this, it is not difficult to see how the modernization of Chinese land rent is constrained by backward commodity-money relations. If we further consider land itself as a special commodity, the characteristics of our land rent can be even more clearly revealed.

We have repeatedly emphasized that a major feature of the Chinese feudal system is the landlord economy, and thus the "free trade" in land. For land to be freely traded, natural differences in land quality must be reflected in land price, and thus in the rent rate—that is, the ratio between the total price of land and its annual rent. It should be acknowledged that this represents a progressive aspect of the Chinese feudal economy.

However, the "freedom" implied in our free land trade differs considerably from that required by capitalist ground-rent. Under a manorial economy, land is granted through enfeeffment rather than bought and sold. Generally, only those with special status—nobles, monastics, vassals, knights—could obtain land, and those who obtained land were assigned a corresponding status. This is a fundamental distinction between the manorial economy and the landlord economy.

By contrast, the "freedom" of land trade under the landlord economy is only relative: it means that individuals without special status can obtain, hold, and even sell land. That is the limit of such freedom. As for free trade in the modern sense—the conditions under which land is obtained and transacted, and whether buyers and sellers bargain on a truly equal footing—it must be said that this has not yet been achieved in China.

In our society, various types of public land—such as state lands, school lands, and clan properties—have always been beyond the scope of arbitrary disposal by individuals. Even with privately owned land, the consent of family and relatives was traditionally required before a sale. Only if they were not interested in buying could the land be sold to outsiders. Moreover, a restriction was often attached: when the land was resold, the original seller retained a right of redemption. Under the system of permanent tenancy, although the landlord could transfer land ownership, he could not freely sell the right of use. Conversely, the tenant could transfer his right of use but could not involve land ownership.

Admittedly, such customary restrictions have been gradually relaxing in recent times, especially near large cities. Yet the lack of freedom in China's land trade stems more from broader social obstacles encountered during transfer. In comparison, the above points seem secondary. For instance, if the seller or buyer was a dominant figure within the family or locality, these restrictions did not really apply. Conversely, if the party lacked power or status, he often had to pay "tribute" to local magnates. Worse still, when transactions occur between parties of vastly unequal status and power, non-economic coercive factors—stemming from social status rather than the land's natural or economic attributes—inevitably become embedded in the transaction price.

In fact, the land price paid by most direct producers who lose their land is often forced upon them in advance through debt repayment or rent arrears. Buyers frequently use loans or leases as a way to acquire land eventually. Consider: are the buyers in our rural areas not mainly landlords, usurers, merchants, and officials (with a small number of hardworking peasants)? Are the sellers not mostly small peasants oppressed by debt, taxes, and rent (along with a few bankrupt well-off families)? In such transactions, it is difficult for the land price to reflect the real fertility or location of the land. Likewise, the rate of rent may not truly indicate land quality.

According to this analysis, what is "free" in our traditional land trade not only falls far short of the freedom required by capitalist ground-rent, but also hinders its realization in the following two ways: on the one hand, it has sharply reduced and dispersed popular resistance to feudalism; on the other, it has strengthened the ties between backward capital (like merchant-usurer capital) and landownership, thereby increasing the resilience and flexibility of the feudal system.

In short, to the extent that capitalist ground-rent must take the form of money rent, the development of China's commodity-money relations remains insufficient to establish either absolute or differential rent. In particular, the law of average profit has never functioned between industrial and agricultural capital, let alone among various agricultural sectors. While surface obstacles appear to lie in underdeveloped commodity-money relations, the root constraints lie in the production relations of industry and agriculture themselves.

Chapter 27
The Development of Modern Land Rent Regulated by Forms of Land Ownership and Land Operation

Due to the traditional "freedom" of our land trade, coupled with the promotion of modern currency-capital relationships, modern private land ownership, at least superficially, seems to have been established. However, as we have analyzed hereinbefore, the process of land trade has not eliminated the traditional Chinese method of annexation, but has pursued the scope of activities of acquisition and plundering to those in Europe and the United States in the early modern period (which was particularly prevalent in the newly developed wasteland turning into cultivated land, silted lake field area, and various types of public land areas). Then, the land ownership formed in the process of this style of acquiring land inevitably abnormally represents the characteristics of the transition stage. The predominant form of land ownership is large-scale land ownership. However, it has not been accompanied by large-scale farming operations. Consequently, alongside large-scale land ownership, there exists a form of small-scale land ownership that, rather than corresponding to it, is complementary to it.

We shall now examine the two forms of ownership within the limits of relating to the development of land rent. For the sake of convenience, we will start with the so-called small-scale land ownership.

It has been demonstrated previously that rented farmland accounts for approximately sixty percent of all cultivated land in China. In other words, the proportion of self-cultivated land is approximately forty percent. In the case of self-cultivated land, those belonging to small-scale land ownership must account for a considerable proportion, given that in the past, most of the middle and rich peasants would appear as landlords. Superficially, it seems that this form of land ownership appears to be unrelated to the issue under discussion herein, as owner-peasants are also the free owners of land under all styles of this land ownership. For an owner-peasant, land is his primary means of production and the indispensable site for utilizing his labor and capital. Not only does he not pay land rent, but the surplus value he generates from his production does also not appear as rent. However, if this form of small-scale land ownership is to function as a social system, it will inevitably exert an impact on the

Y. Wang, *The Basic Theory of Chinese Economy*,
https://doi.org/10.1007/978-981-95-6330-2_27

general land rent in various aspects. This is particularly evident when we analyze the various conditions of this form of ownership in China.

The first characteristic of small-scale land ownership in China is that the majority of the land is inferior in quality, which is generally observed consistently both nationwide and in various individual regions of the country. In a relative sense, the land in the Yellow River Basin of China is generally not as fertile for intensive cultivation as that in the Yangtze River Basin and Pearl River Basin. Therefore, the proportion of small-scale land ownership in the former region is also higher than that in the latter two regions. It is especially the case across the country. Fragmented mountainous areas, gravelly lands, low-lying lands, barren lands, and all regions vulnerable to water and drought damage are typically less attractive to land grabbers. However, once such barren lands are converted into cultivated land, fragmented plots are consolidated into whole plots, or low-lying areas become fertile through silt deposition, a small-scale landowner will immediately become aware that these improvements could lead to his misfortune. Consequently, a small-scale landowner will be more attached to his land when he acquires more fertile land and his production and situation improve. In practice, it is not unlikely that a small peasant could advance to a medium or even rich peasant. However, its limitations would not likely to significantly affect the general concept that small-scale landowners mostly own less productive land.

The location of land of the small peasants is quite disadvantageous. Additionally, as for the amount of land they hold, the area of paddy fields cultivated by each household, excluding the animal husbandry areas, is only five to ten mu in the southern rice paddy areas, while it is no more than ten to fifteen mu in the northern loess areas.

Since the land therein is insufficient, sporadic, and infertile, low profitability is to be expected. Moreover, as they are free owners, all the burdens, such as multifarious and exorbitant donations, taxes, levies, labor obligations, and various onerous burdens, which should otherwise be apportioned and transferred, fall heavily on their shoulders. Even in the absence of natural and man-made disasters, their meager incomes are not enough to cover the costs of marriage, funerals, sicknesses, etc. They are generally bound to become debt slaves to usurers. In this case, their production becomes impossible even if they rely solely on human labor and natural resources. In a word, they are engaged in production under extremely unfavorable conditions. Nevertheless, through donations, levies, taxes, usury, and the most irregular and expensive retail trade, they make substantial contributions to society. They provide a great many surplus labor products beyond their essential means of subsistence. This, however, does not result from increased production, but rather from their greater poverty and a standard of living that is markedly below ordinary people.

At this point, we have oulined the adverse impacts of small-scale land ownership on new forms of land rent. Firstly, the commonest viewpoint, of course, is that small-scale land ownership exists within a certain social scale, and within the limits of its existence is to fundamentally prevent the emergence of land rent. Secondly, small-scale land ownership generally represents the most self-sufficient system. The products that make up the majority of the consumption of small peasants are produced by themselves. They are compelled to engage in all possible handicraft sidelines in order to make up their constant shortfalls in expenditures. Herein, the commodity-money relationships, which is a prerequisite for the emergence of modern land rent, has been correspondingly hindered. Thirdly, the scattered existence of small-scale land ownership will inevitably exclude the social form of labor and the social accumulation of capital... All these are precisely the basic prerequisites directly required by capital land rent.

However, there are several key points we should pay special attention to here.

Firstly, the widespread existence of small-scale land ownership consistently serves as a "reserve" for land annexers and a source of primitive accumulation for land rent—which is often not reinvested in agricultural improvement, but used to acquire yet more land. In the process of land concentration, the most attractive targets are not the plots of poor small peasants, but rather the lands of middle peasants and small landlords. That said, small peasants ultimately have the weakest capacity to resist. As middle peasants and small landlords are squeezed out and their lands—often of relatively better quality—are transferred, small-scale ownership easily becomes an appendage to large-scale landholding.

Secondly, the prevalence of small-scale land ownership poses a serious threat to the tenant class. Small landowners are generally eager to acquire more land; in reality, many are liable to become tenant peasants at any time, and a considerable number already work part-time as tenants. As discussed earlier, they are able to provide a significant amount of surplus labor product to society even under highly unfavorable conditions. This makes them more likely to offer an even greater surplus to landlords in exchange for access to better-quality land. In effect, their widespread presence, and the land system that supports it, pushes the rent rate to a level where it absorbs nearly all operating profit—since small-scale ownership and operation are not profit-driven, and often leave little room for profit generation.

Thirdly, while some small landowners may have the chance to rent additional land and work part-time as tenants, such opportunities are scarce. Landowners typically assess the operational capacity or capital of potential tenants, which puts small landowners at a significant disadvantage compared with full-time farm laborers. If they do engage in part-time tenancy, their willingness to accept high rents diminishes profit margins for other operators. If, instead, they work as agricultural laborers, their pre-existing subsistence basis allows them to accept far worse conditions than ordinary peasants, thereby driving down agricultural wages to extremely low levels. In other words, if they take the former path, agricultural profits become hard to achieve; if they take the latter, reasonable wages for laborers become unsustainable. Under such conditions, land rent ends up absorbing not only all potential profit but also a large portion of wages.

Fourthly, this mode of small-scale land operation provides an ideal "model" for large landowners who practice decentralized small-scale leasing. Fragmented small plots run by subsistence-oriented households can yield substantial surplus product and sustain high rent rates. From the landowner's perspective, this eliminates the need to shift toward large-scale operation; indeed, it often makes small-scale leasing appear more profitable. And reality, as it unfolds, seems to confirm their expectations.

In China, landlords—making up only about 4% of the rural population—own approximately 68% of cultivated land. Rich peasants, who account for another 6%, own about 18%. This means 10% of the rural population holds 86% of the land. On the other hand, small and middle peasants, who constitute 90% of the rural population, possess only 32% of cultivated land (these figures, compiled by Tao Zhifu in his article "Land Issues at the Present Stage of China," synthesize data from multiple sources; while not perfectly precise, they reflect the general picture). From these numbers, we can glimpse the degree of land concentration in China.

As noted earlier, this level of concentration emerged in a context where comprador commerce, following contact with capitalism, drew social funds into cities, somewhat alleviating further concentration in the countryside. While large-scale land ownership is normally a key precondition for capitalist farming—with large-scale production being its first slogan—under a system of private ownership, this requires not only large ownership but also contiguous plots suitable for unified management. In China, however, a notable feature is that land concentration has mainly meant concentrated ownership, not consolidated operational units.

Several factors explain this. The prevalence of small-scale ownership naturally obstructs the formation of contiguous tracts. Especially in southern paddy-field regions, where tenancy is most common, terraced and uneven terrain adds natural obstacles. That said, such barriers could be overcome if more fundamental social prerequisites were in place. The real issue is that Chinese landlords have typically acquired land not for the purpose of large-scale capitalist farming, but based on their experience of the profitability of small-scale leasing. From the outset, they assume decentralized tenancy rather than unified management.

Although some might prefer contiguous estates to facilitate control and display authority, the capital required to purchase large integrated properties is substantial, and resale is cumbersome. More importantly, the profits from estate management often fail to justify the transaction costs. Tenants on larger estates also tend to have more stable livelihoods and stronger bargaining power, making them less compliant with landlord demands. Barring exceptional wealth or specific operational needs, most landlords prefer holding numerous small and medium plots over a few large estates.

This preference is reinforced by China's traditional system of equal inheritance among sons. While equal inheritance among landowners has contributed to the fragmentation of ownership, its effect among land users (tenants and owner-cultivators) has had an even stronger impact on operational fragmentation. When a landowner dies, his heirs may continue collecting rent collectively and maintain the existing tenancy arrangement. But when a tenant dies or his household divides, the operational unit is typically subdivided. In this sense, it is not so much concentrated ownership as fragmented operation that has hindered the emergence of large-scale farming. Overly subdivided management does not fundamentally prevent land concentration, but it does obstruct the transition to capitalist agricultural production.

Traditionally, large-scale land ownership of the wealthy with extensive fields connected by roads has been a common form in China. In modern times, it has undergone deformation to some extent and seems not to have been acquired by means of a special status but, at most, by taking advantage of some political and economic privileges. However, by nature, it is still regarded as the primary means of capital accumulation, rather than as a secondary means of promoting other labor conditions beyond land. Centralization of land ownership and decentralization of operation, or large-scale land ownership and small-scale operation, is seen as a characteristic phenomenon. Consequently, in the absence of pressure from large-scale operations, the feasibility of adopting the form of small-scale operation under small-scale land ownership is achieved. In turn, it serves as a powerful incentive for large-scale land ownership to adopt small-scale operation. In this context, the large-scale land ownership and small-scale land ownership, which are clearly mutually exclusive, coexist in parallel as two intrinsically interconnected forms within the current overall land ownership system. In accordance with the trend of Chinese land rent discussed in Chap. VII, if the large-scale land ownership of the capitalist system, designed to facilitate large-scale operation, fails to decisively replace the current form of the large-scale land ownership of small-scale operation in China, then the continuation of small-scale land ownership remains a viable possibility.

In economic science, this form of small-scale land ownership was originally considered a transitional form. As capitalist agriculture progresses, the advantages of large-scale operation become increasingly apparent, leading to the gradual obsolescence of small-scale land ownership due to its inherent disadvantage that excludes the social development of capitalist labor. Naturally, agriculture, being inherently conservative, has undergone very slow reforms in every aspect. Even today, although small-scale land ownership is declining day by day, it still stubbornly persists in the interstices of capitalist production in advanced countries. The situation of small-scale land ownership in advanced countries is quite the opposite of that in China. Our small-scale land ownership survives under conditions of underdeveloped capitalistic operations. In contrast, in advanced countries, small-scale land ownership is simultaneously subjected to the pressures of the operation of the capitalist system and benefits from the general development of capitalist production relations. As capitalist production relations advance, all backward privileges that harm the interests of small peasants will gradually disappear. There are market prices for agricultural products, the interest rate benchmark prevailing in rural areas has also been relatively lowered, which relatively mitigates the incidental exploitation imposed on them by commercial and usury capitals. At the same time, the tax system, which is most criticized by small peasants, has also been unified under the capitalist order. This is originally required by large capital, but it dialectically benefits the survival of small peasants. It is evident that, setting aside the advantages and disadvantages, in a society where large-scale production is overwhelmingly dominant, small-scale land ownership is nothing more than the product of a transitional society. It persists as merely a relic of backwardness in advanced countries. Whereas, small-scale land ownership in China, which was neither protected by the capitalist order nor subjected to large-scale operation oppressions, still has its "merits".

Here, we should not ignore the existence of the class of the middle peasants and small and middle landlords between the large-scale and small-scale land ownership. The middle peasants are owner-peasants who own significant amounts of land, many of whom are also landlords, small and middle landlords, many of whom are also part-time land operators. Their "characters" are to be analyzed hereinafter. Regardless of the various ways in which they retain land, they fail to create an intermediate form of land ownership. In a transitional society, which is characterized by turbulence, has lost its equilibrium, the tendency toward polarization is typically more pronounced.

We cannot detect signs of capitalist land rent in China by examining the various conditions constituting the land ownership system; therefore, we must shift our focus to another perspective.

Chapter 28
The Peculiarities of Land Rent Expressed by the Composition of Agricultural Capital and Agricultural Wage Labor

The capital composition and wage labor of agriculture were originally closely linked to agricultural operation. Even under large-scale landownership, agricultural operation is generally decentralized and small-scale; this provides a preliminary explanation for the issues discussed here. However, Chinese landowners or landlords have traditionally maintained a traditional pastoral style, which means that they may well retain part of their land for direct cultivation. In recent times, the growing prosperity of the urban areas and the increasing unrest in rural regions will undoubtedly seriously reduce their interest in it. Whereas, until today, it seems that many landlords, regardless of the amount of land they own, still lease out only a portion of it and retain the remainder for their own operation. However, this practice is generally limited to small and middle landlords, while large landlords increasingly have less time to engage in such activities.

The proportion of land retained by a landowner to the land he leases out determines his status in the rural areas. If he leases out only a small portion of his land, he is a landlord and agricultural operator. If he retains all of his land for his own operation, he is a pure rich peasant, and he is a pure middle peasant if he has less land. It is now clear that that in rural areas, in addition to tenant peasants and small peasants, those engaged in agricultural operations are middle peasants, rich peasants and some landlords. These are the groups most likely to adopt the capitalist operation.

We understand that the benefits of large-scale or capitalist operations can only be manifested when all the required social conditions are largely in place. These social conditions are embodied in the transformation where such social production relations have achieved a dominant position. Regardless of the industrial development in urban areas, both large-scale and small-scale land ownership in Chinese rural areas is practicing the form of small-scale operation. At least, the objective conditions necessary for demonstrating their advantages or superiority of large-scale or capitalist operations have not been created. This fact largely indicates the mode of operation that rich and middle peasants, as well as some landlords who concurrently engage in agriculture in rural China, are likely to adopt and are required to adopt.

Y. Wang, *The Basic Theory of Chinese Economy*,
https://doi.org/10.1007/978-981-95-6330-2_28

It is true that rich peasants, the landlords who have retained sufficient land for their own operation, and even a small number of tenant peasants who have leased sufficient land, will naturally avoid subdividing their operations since they possess adequate land for large-scale operation. But here, we must comprehend that the large-scale operation in the modern context is not solely defined by the size of the land of an operation unit. If a certain area of land is an indispensable prerequisite for large-scale operation, the amount of capital invested in a certain area of land is the most reliable indicator of whether the land is effectively utilized for large-scale operation.

Now it is time to discuss the agricultural capital in China.

In the field of economic science, land is not typically regarded as a capital factor. Consequently, the organic composition of agricultural capital refers to the ratio of constant capital, which encompasses machinery, farming tools, agricultural construction, seeds, fertilizers, and other items, to variable capital, which is utilized for wage payments. The organic composition of agricultural capital, defined as the ratio of constant capital to variable capital, serves as an indicator of the extent to which capitalist operations in agriculture have been realized.

In China, machinery is so scarce that it can almost be considered a negligible factor in the concept of agricultural capital. In addition to machinery, other working conditions that should be included in production costs, such as farm tools, animal power, seeds, fertilizers, irrigation ditches, etc., can also be referred to as capital, specifically as constant capital. It is quite a challenge to maintain these conditions and to ensure their constant replenishment and renewal after consumption and degradation. Perhaps only the landlords who are also engaged in agriculture, only rich peasants, some better-off middle peasants and a very small number of tenant peasants are able to maintain such operating conditions. For the inferior peasants, it would be a considerable achievement if they could secure seeds for cultivation, hire animal power from others, retain a few rudimentary and worn-out farm implements, and obtain grain rations to feed their families at exorbitant interest rates during periods of temporary scarcity.

Why, then, do rich peasants, landlords who also farm, and a very small number of better-off tenant farmers not seek to improve their means of production? Some may challenge this assertion, citing customs data on agricultural machinery imports and cases of machinery-based production in certain regions of Jiangsu Province. However, if we consider general production in China's rural areas as the object of research, rather than a few demonstration farms or agricultural experimental institutes, our analysis of this issue should emphasise the following facts. Firstly, the implementation of new-style agricultural operations, or the application of machine production in agriculture, is not easy to achieve in isolation from the general state of social development. For instance, the requirement for peace in the production process free from any political and social disturbance, the guarantee of the market for selling products, and so on, which is not too extensive a problem, In terms of technical conditions, the coordination of various aspects is required. It is challenging to cultivate technical operation directors, and it is similarly difficult to encourage operators to cultivate the entrepreneurial spirit without the prospect of significant benefits.

Secondly, with regard to land, the technical integration of individual parcels of land within reasonable limits is achieved in many countries through the enactment of legislation known as the Act of Land Splice and Exchange. However, we always place technical issues in a secondary position. The application of the new style of land operation requires that the price of land itself be relatively low. The tendency of high land prices in China is caused by the continuous investment of funds originally accumulated in society in land purchase. As a result, operators spend so much on land that only a relatively small proportion of their total operating costs is left for use as regular capital. Of course, for the rich peasants and landlords who own land, the cost of land may appear to be practically nil, but if they are not naive, they will make a calculation of the proportion of the land price in their total operating expenses according to the "year of purchase" or the general rate of land rent. Undoubtedly, tenants who rent land for farming and who have accumulated considerable assets in their hands are more likely to feel the squeeze of land costs on both constant and variable capital when they buy new land in the hope of engaging in agricultural activity.

Thirdly, the pressure of high land costs on agricultural capital is reflected in the low organic composition of agricultural capital, i.e. the degree of labor intensity on the land. The less machinery is used to work the land, the greater the reliance on labor. Therefore, the operating expenses invested in rural land in China can also be called capital, and this type of capital is mainly composed of variable capital invested in labor. Under the above restrictions, and under the conditions of surplus labor and low labor wages caused by high land prices, these agricultural operators are not willing to increase the composition of constant capital to replace the variable composition of capital. Instead, they prefer to use manual labor rather than machines. In this context, labor is not displaced by machinery, but it displaces and oppresses the machinery.

In some cases, especially in areas near the major cities, where labor is so expensive that it is not worthwhile to hire more labor, there are other options. A landlord who also farms can become a pure landlord. A rich farmer can become a land tenant. Nevertheless, there are always people who have hope for the land. If they believe that the direct employment of labor is beneficial, they will engage in farming. If they think that the indirect use of labor is more beneficial, they turn to land tenancy. Sometimes, if they think that stopping the land operation in part may result in wasting some agricultural tools or difficulties in disposing of animal power, they will choose the subleasing method of leasing agricultural tools and animal power at the same time. In this respect alone, they are free to choose.

In fact, such evolutionary changes have been ongoing in our rural areas. One phenomenon that is more or less obvious here is that the more land a landowner owns, the more likely he is to withdraw from farming and become a land renter. The less land he owns, the more likely and necessary it is for him to become a land operator. This is because in the former case one can completely withdraw from the production process, since one neither has to work personally nor supervise the workers, while in the latter case one not only has to supervise the workers, but sometimes has to participate in the work personally.

However, both the land-operator and the land-tenant have one thing in common: their profits and their appropriation of the surplus products of the land are not based on the labor conditions other than the land, but on the land as the main means, or they are not primarily based on the capital used on the land, but on the land itself.

From the previous conclusion, not only can we see the backwardness of Chinese land rent from the composition of agricultural capital, but also the labor conditions associated with this capital composition expose the backwardness of our land rent in terms of agricultural labor relations.

The modern worker is characterised by his detachment from the old means of production, the land, and his attachment to, and turning to, a new means of production, the machine. This phenomenon is evident in both the industrial and agricultural sectors. In this transformation, land, which had traditionally been the primary means of production, gradually became secondary. In this same transformation, the direct producers no longer entered into a productive relationship with the owners of the land, but with other means of production, especially with the owners of the machines or the agrarian capitalists. In other words, it was no longer the land that exploited the workers, but other means of production.

From the investigation into the composition of our agricultural capital, we comprehend that in Chinese rural areas, regardless of the agricultural operators, landlords, rich peasants, middle and small peasants, or tenant peasants, they all adopt small-scale operation or small-scale operation on a slightly larger scale. Their primary or important means of production remains land. Owning more land means possessing more powerful tools for labor exploitation. It is evident that rich peasants and landlords who also engage in land operations, and even small and middle peasants, are positioned in opposition to direct laborers as landowners. Even tenant peasants who rent land from others, whether on temporary or longer-term wage labor occasions, as land retainers and users, are also opposed to those direct laborers who can neither own nor retain land and are compelled to be employed by the former.

If this is an evident and undeniable fact, the 15 million wage laborers who are generally counted in Chinese rural areas are employed not because the land is deprived of and they have not obtained means of production other than land. Rather, they are employed because the land is deprived of and there is no opportunity to use it. Therefore, although the three pillars that constitute the lowest stratum of Chinese rural society, namely, small peasants, tenant peasants and hired peasants, are interchangeable and overlapping on many occasions, each of them should be regarded as a distinct category or aspect, respectively. On the one hand, small peasants are compelled to give up their small plots of land only as a last resort. This phenomenon also occurs among tenant peasants. On the other hand, while it is extremely difficult for tenant peasants to acquire even a small amount of land, and it may be even more challenging for hired peasants to rent a small plot of land. Consequently, hired peasants have become the most disadvantaged group within the lowest stratum of society in rural areas.

According to the previous analysis, the ultimate purpose of our agricultural operators in operating land is to acquire more land. Once this aspiration is achieved, they are unlikely to continue engaging in this burdensome work and instead become those who live on land rent and focus solely on consumption. Namely, with the exception of a small number of rich peasants, those who are wage laborers are almost small and middle peasants and tenant peasants who often lack even the necessary basic agricultural tools and have consistently lived in difficult conditions. They do not hire laborers because they have better agricultural tools and capable draft animals. On the contrary, they cannot afford these working conditions, so they hire laborers for the supplement. This indicates that, on average, for a laborer to be hired, his price of labor should be lower than that of animal power and also less than the cost of agricultural tools. Furthermore, the price of labor, unlike the price of animal power and agricultural tools, which require one-time payment, can be paid multiple times, or may not be paid until the end of a specified employment period.

Various kinds of backward and bizarre wage labor relations have thus emerged. We can leave it to the readers to independently testify what kind of wage labor conditions there are in Chinese rural areas. To enumerate the most basic forms of wage labor relations, it is advisable to first begin with the paternalistic mode of wage labor. In this mode, employers can make arbitrary decisions regarding both work and its intensity, and they even have certain rights over the personal dignity of the employees. Generally, the employers of small-scale farms are more able to restrain their employees than the owners of various production factories. Setting aside all other aspects, the strong traditional feudal relationships in agriculture grant employers greater parental-like authority. When an employee has worked for a long time, especially if there is a clan relationship with the employer, or if the employee belongs to a younger generation, he will not simply view the employer as his master, but also as his guardian. Secondly, there is the mode of helping servants. In this mode, the employee has not established the aforementioned wage labor relations with the employer and may help the employer as a relative. He may, out of desperation and without options, work for the employer as a helper temporarily. Additionally, he may offer assistance in exchange for animal power or to repay accumulated debts. All these occasions are limited to temporary and short-term employment. In addition, there is a mode of attending servitude. In this mode, the tenant peasants are obligated to provide labor for the landlords in accordance with the rent rules or customary practices as required. Their labor is not only limited to production, especially when the landlords do not concurrently engage in agricultural operations. It should be noted that this labor is not necessarily unpaid. When all factors are comprehensively taken into account, including the payment period (mostly settled at the end of the year or before the Spring Festival), The payment procedure, the work intensity and the labor occasion (which often requires temporarily putting aside their urgent work), then the remuneration is significantly lower than that of ordinary agricultural laborers.

A considerable number of individuals take pleasure in the widespread prevalence of wage labor in rural China, and assume that the Chinese rural economy has undergone modernization and improvement. In particular, the observation that the wages in many areas are mostly paid in the form of currency reinforces their view that this is a sign of the commercialization of labor. In fact, whether labor is truly commercialized cannot be solely determined by payment in currency on the one hand, or the fact that ordinary rural laborers basically eat and reside in their employers' homes rather than their own. The key distinction lies in whether those laborers rely on land or capital. As we have analyzed previously, they are not employed due to a lack of capital, but rather because of a lack of land. Therefore, all those who possess land, whether as tenants or owners, may exploit others through land. In this way, small and middle peasants and tenant peasants in Chinese rural areas acquire the capacity to exploit others, which serves as the foundation for the widespread existence of wage labor.

It is clear that our tenant peasant generally is not a modern land-renting agriculturist. He engages with the landlord with labor instead of capital. Consequently, he inevitably forms a corresponding subordinate or serfdom relationship with the landlord due to his dependence on land. This is one of the basic reasons for the formation of the aforementioned mode of wage labor. However, although the general tenant peasant still possesses characteristics of a serf, it does not prevent him from exploiting those who fail to rent land. Conversely, he may have to rely more on the labor of others to alleviate the excessive burden he is obliged to bear for renting land.

Land remains the hub for all social production relations in rural areas. It is not used to leverage labor instead of capital. Land continues to be the primary means of capital accumulation in agriculture. All these facts illustrate that our land rent is still in line with the assertion put forth by William Petty, an early economist who had not yet witnessed the modern forms of land rent, "Land is the Father and active principle of Wealth, (the product of surplus labor represented by land rent), as Labor is the Mother." Capital merely plays a supporting role in extremely limited circumstances.

Chapter 29
Accumulation and Transformation of Land Rent

In a backward society with underdeveloped industry, land rent is the most basic form of accumulation, or serves as the basis for all other forms of accumulation.

In such a society, the most productive industry is agriculture, not industry. Both industry and agriculture rely on simple tools for labor. However, agriculture makes more efficient use of natural resources. Consequently, the same amount of labor can produce significantly more surplus products in agriculture than in industry. Moreover, agricultural products are the most basic products that everyone needs to consume. People in industry and other occupations benefit from the high productivity of agriculture. It allows them to obtain their basic needs without spending excessive amounts of labor time. They are therefore able to produce some products of surplus labor while still meeting their basic needs. This principle remains valid even in a society in which the tools of labor have become highly advanced, i.e. a society in which machines are used for production. However, it presupposes that the agricultural use of natural resources for production continues to significantly reduce the necessary labor time or increase the surplus labor time of industrial workers. Nevertheless, it cannot be concluded that agriculture is inherently more productive. The full and unrestricted use of social labor productivity reduces the relative importance of natural labor productivity.

In short, the agricultural products of surplus labor are the foundation of wealth in a backward society. When the land (the natural resource utilized in agriculture) is owned and monopolized by private ownership, such surplus products will inevitably be provided to landowners by means of land rent. Therefore, the accumulation of wealth in such a society can be said to be equivalent to that of land rent.

As has been aforementioned, our rural society generally relies on land to facilitate the natural productivity of labor. The advantages in both quality and quantity of leased cultivated land over self-cultivated land have made it clear that the products of surplus labor in our society have been largely absorbed into the hands of landlords under the guise of land rent. If we further investigate the high rate of land rent, which even absorbs part or most of the profits and wages, we comprehend that

Y. Wang, *The Basic Theory of Chinese Economy*,
https://doi.org/10.1007/978-981-95-6330-2_29

land rent is not only the general and routine form of the surplus value of surplus products, but also encompasses the part of the necessary labor products required for the minimum standard of living of the direct producers. This concerns the leased cultivated land. It is not necessary for rich peasants to acquire the products of surplus labor on their land through land rent. However, as previously mentioned, both rich peasants and landlords absorb or exploit the labor of others by means of land. In this context, although their income is not labeled as land rent, it clearly has the nature of it. Essentially, he evaluates his income from land operation against the prevailing high land rent rate. In the event that his income is less than that of land rent, or even not significantly greater than the potential land rent, he will promptly lease the land to others. Moreover, most of the small peasants and even some middle peasants in Chinese rural areas need to rent a small amount of land to supplement their insufficient cultivated land. Compared to the poor peasants who have nothing, they are more likely to rent land. In the event that they are unable to do so, they need to be employed to produce products of surplus labor and contribute to land rent directly or indirectly. Therefore, the accumulation of land rent is typically that in Chinese rural areas.

However, throughout the history of the Chinese economy, especially the accumulation of land rent in modern times, it did not occur in isolation. Commercial capital and usury capital have consistently acted as its two guardians, and supporting and propelling its advancement.

Originally, in a progressive society, land rent may gradually increase due to population growth and the rising demand for land products as raw materials and food. The power of land ownership may also be enhanced by the development of the conditions that enable agricultural products to transform into commodities and value, as well as that realization of value. Therefore, a larger portion of the continually increasing value may be converted into land rent without incurring any costs.

However, there may be signs of increasing accumulation of land rent in certain specific regions of our society, reflecting the expansion of the market for land products and the gradual development of the conditions that enable land products to be transformed into commodities or value. Nonetheless, even in such cases, it is evident that the increase of accumulation will not completely eliminate the influence of the activities of usury commercial and other forms of rents and taxes. In certain instances, these activities may inevitably conflict with the interests of individual landlords, but when viewed as a social-scale activity, they will directly or indirectly contribute to an increase in the rate of land rent. The relationship between the high rate of land rent and that of interest in rural areas, as well as that between usury interest and commercial profits, has been discussed previously. An increase in the profit rate in one aspect will immediately attract or affect the other aspect. Naturally, there is a limit to the increase in their mutual attraction and affect. This will be discussed in the next part. Herein, we will briefly discuss how our accumulated land rent was disposed of.

As previously mentioned, after engaging with modern capitalism, Chinese rural society has increasingly demonstrated a keen interest in the urban areas. The prosperity and relative stability of urban areas would obviously drive the transfer of the wealth accumulated in rural areas, or its general manifestation—land rent, to urban areas. This kind of transfer may take the form of currency or physical objects, but when the rural areas are viewed opposite to the urban areas, both forms can be regarded as the escape of rural capital. Once this capital had escaped, it rarely flew back. The escape in the currency form may promote the monetization of in-kind land rent, allowing land to be sold to tenant peasants in the form of rent conversion, which was more profitable than selling in the market, where costs for storage and transportation were incurred. As for the capital flowing into the urban areas, in addition to indiscriminate consumption, it could be most appropriately and conveniently outlets in the land market, financial market, and bond market. Once a capital takes this path, it increasingly distances itself from its origin. As for the escape portion that was in the form of physical objects, it may initially be accumulated through hoarding, allowing land rent to be directly converted into commercial capital, which was then ultimately transferred to the urban areas.

On the other hand, we should also consider that the lifestyle of those who live on land rent has likely determined their use of wealth accumulation through land rent. They will not engage in the business operations that they are unfamiliar with or unaccustomed to, especially in industrial operations. The same lifestyle also constrains them, making them reluctant to transfer their savings to urban areas from which they feel deeply alienated, or even disapprove of and fear. They remain attached to the real estate, wealth and honor they have acquired in the rural areas, as well as the bond of feudal kinships, unless there are significant fortunes, opportunities, or necessities. Of course, the savings remaining in the rural areas continue to be used in the traditional way: either for purchasing land or for lending. (In fact, the capital invested in land is already interest-bearing capital. As land price is capitalized, the land rent obtained at that price each year is interest-bearing. Therefore, when land rent is fixed, the price of land is adjusted by the interest rate). However, in recent times, some landlords with an entrepreneurial spirit have also engaged in rural manufacturing industries directly related to raw agricultural products, such as rice milling, sugar making, wine making, oil extraction, and weaving. Of course, more landlords also preferred to operate the stores at rural markets. Nevertheless, the accumulation through land rent used in these industries will soon flow back to land in much larger amounts. We can even say that the owners of these rural enterprises are more likely to return to being landlords as a consequence of their accumulation of wealth in their enterprises.

In conclusion, our land rent is largely accumulated through traditional means and is also largely used in traditional ways. The manner of capital dispersion is determined by the way it is concentrated and accumulated. Without fundamental changes in the process of accumulation and concentration of land rent, there cannot be significant alterations in its dispersion or transformation. We have found another principle regarding land rent that, in certain circumstances, such as when wars happen in the rural areas, it is very difficult to avoid the additional burden like conscription and levies in kind when one owns land. In such situations, land may be a target easily to be neglected. According to experience and statistics, during the prolonged period of inflation from wartime to post-war, the rate of increase in the prices of physical items being bought and sold was relatively low for land. However, this can only indicate that the original transformation tendency of the basic accumulation of our society, land rent, may be temporarily hindered, that is, its dispersion path may be temporarily changed. However, before the fundamental reform occurs in our social general mode of production or accumulation, this aforementioned alternation would amount to little more than a significant increase in the proportion of land rent allocated to pure consumption, along with a prolonged duration during which that land rent remains in the form of usury capital or merchant capital.

Issues discussed in this part

1. The study of land has often posed significant challenges for even the best asset economists. However, in the early modern period, many considered this study as relatively straightforward. Why is that?
2. What is the alteration of the nature of land rent when it transitions from physical object form to currency form?
3. Why are capitalistic absolute and differential land rents unable to manifest within commodity-money relationships in China?
4. How can we explain the coexistence of large-scale and small-scale land ownership? Why does small-scale land ownership hinder the emergence of modern land rent?
5. Rich peasants in Chinese society face significant challenges in becoming agricultural capitalists. What are the fundamental reasons for this?
6. The motto "Land is the Father and active principle of Wealth, as Labor is the Mother" can still be used to explain the formation of the land rent in Chinese society. What accounts for this?
7. Why is it that the wealth accumulated through land rent in Chinese society is particularly difficult to convert into Industrial Capital but more easily converts into commercial capital, usury capital, or land capital?

Part VIII
Forms of Chinese Economic Crises

Abstract This chapter concludes that China's economic crises were uniquely rooted in its backward mode of production. Unlike capitalist crises of overproduction, China's were essentially crises of "underproduction." Intense feudal exploitation (high rent, taxes, usury) rendered the small peasant economy incredibly fragile, unable to withstand natural disasters or social upheaval. typical manifestations included declining agricultural productivity, widespread peasant bankruptcy and displacement, the collapse of handicrafts, and the major socio-political convulsions these triggered. In the modern era, this traditional crisis pattern intertwined with influences from the world capitalist economy: fluctuations in international agricultural prices, dumping of foreign manufactured goods, and volatility in silver exchange rates exacerbated internal weaknesses, creating crises of greater complexity and depth. These cyclical crises catastrophically damaged the productive forces, fundamentally impeding a transition to a modern economic structure.

Chapter 30
Differences Between Two Typical Forms of Economic Crises

From a historical and socioeconomic perspective, whether feudal or capitalist economies inevitably experience crises or panics in the whole process or as an inevitable result of the movement. If these crises or panics can be overcome, this social form will continue or expand, otherwise, it will be historically replaced or terminated.

The feudal economy is overthrown by its insurmountable internal crises. Although those forms of crises vary across countries with different natural and historical conditions, and do not display the same content or process of subverting the economic system, they share common characteristics as a category. A similar phenomenon can be observed in the context of the capitalist economy as well.

Capitalist society has accumulated great wealth. Although the accumulation of this great wealth is full of elements of primitive accumulation, over time, capital increasingly becomes the primary means of accumulation rather than land. With regard to the capital, there is an extensive expansion of the constant capital, which is composed of machinery and equipment as the core. This expansion, driven by an increase in labor productivity, results in a relatively reduction of variable capital required for purchasing labor. Eventually, although laborers, as a social class, produce more commodities and surplus value for capitalists as producers due to the increasing amount of constant capital. However, due to the relative reduction of the proportion of variable capital to constant capital, they are unable to purchase the commodities provided by capitalists to the market as consumers. Consequently, it is not feasible for them to assist capitalists to realize their surplus value. On the side of laborers, this manifests as overpopulation relative to industry, unemployment, poverty, and hunger, while on the side of capitalists, it appears as the danger of overproduction of their products, closure of factories, credit bankruptcy, and financial stagnation. In a capitalist society, the disconnection in this regard is latent even in the most prosperous period, serving as a condition for both prosperity and rapid concentration of capital. However, once this state of crises shifts from a singular and local instance to a general and notable phenomenon, the entire social order will descend into chaos, leading to

Y. Wang, *The Basic Theory of Chinese Economy*,
https://doi.org/10.1007/978-981-95-6330-2_30

political and social crises. Whether this kind of political and social crisis can lead to overthrowing the capitalist system primarily depends on the capitalist production relations of each society and the possibility and flexibility for further development of its labor productivity. When there is still this possibility or flexibility, production stagnation, credit bankruptcy, unemployment, and hunger of laborers are considered as the preparations for the economic recovery and renewed prosperity. Therefore, the capitalistic economic crises generally have the following characteristics.

Firstly, it is primarily rooted in the socioeconomic system itself rather than in natural or political relationships. Although occasional natural disasters or unpleasant political disturbances may sometimes induce or contribute to such crises, the capitalist economy itself is more independent of natural factors. The politics of capitalist society has long been regarded as an integral component of capitalist production relations, and its stability or chaos is merely a political manifestation of the economic state.

Secondly, it is generally manifested through the market by an excess of supply over effective demand as well as an excess of production over effective consumption. Capitalist commodity production, driven by the pursuit of profits or greater profits, does anticipate a certain level of consumption. However, as the projected target buyers of a certain commodity producer often overlap with other commodity producers, they have a clear strategy for reducing costs, lowering prices, and attracting buyers. However, they fail to account for the broader implications of their actions. As they reduce costs and expand production, resulting in an increase in constant capital and a relative decrease in variable capital, and thus social purchasing power is reduced. Therefore, the further the capitalist system develops, the more this overproduction will become an inevitable phenomenon beyond their will.

Thirdly, it is generally regularly manifested as periodic morbidity. As economic crises are regarded as an inevitable tendency of the interplay among the laws of the capitalist economy, the more mature the capitalist economy becomes, the fewer occasional and non-economic disturbances arise from the interactions, and the regularity of its underlying maladies becomes increasingly apparent.

Whereas, the economic crises under the feudal system take on a different form.

The typical feudal economy is originally represented in the form of natural self-sufficiency, with underdeveloped transportation, as well as monetary and credit relationships. Agricultural production is nearly the most general form of production in this society. Therefore, "live at the mercy of the elements" has become the best known proverb of life among them. Natural conditions always play a decisive role in production, and the low social productivity is so incapable of controlling natural disasters such as floods and droughts. Therefore, social economic crises of this type not only show greater naturalness but greater fortuity compared to capitalist economic crises. This so-called fortuity lies not only in the incapability of controlling nature, but in the political powers in this kind of society having a major impact on the economy. For instance, the wanton waste of warlike feudal lords and the wars they wage, which result in hundreds of thousands of deaths both in rural areas and the cities, for land and their honor, will immediately lead to economic crises akin to natural disasters due to the lack of labor. The crux of the crisis is largely reflected in the fact that production is insufficient and many people are unable to secure adequate food and clothing.

Originally, both the feudal economic crises and the capitalist economic crises shared a common feature: direct producers experience starvation. Feudal lords had "fat meat in the kitchen" and "fat horses in the stables" in ancient China, and similarly, capitalists have large quantities of products that cannot be sold and rot in their warehouses. But generally, the feudal economic crises are ultimately due to the insufficient food production of ordinary serfs. Normally, they are self-sufficient. In times of chaos and turmoil, they have no means to sustain themselves. Moreover, the goods they produce are not typically for exchange, or at least the majority is not for exchange. Therefore, crises of this type are not represented in the market. Moreover, under the natural and self-sufficient economic conditions, general economic sectors are not closely and organically connected with each other. Therefore, the natural and man-made disasters in a certain place do not necessarily have a severe impact on the overall economy. And widespread major crises generally do not occur. This is one of the reasons why many feudal societies experience crises from time to time yet are able to endure for a considerable duration. In addition, it should be noted that although the crises in feudal society erupt occasionally, the periodic regularity of their occurrence cannot be definitely ascertained from the interval between periods of their occurrence due to the significant influence of external sporadic factors during the formation of the crises.

The aforementioned are the viewpoints concerning the typical feudal crises and capitalistic crises, respectively, but what we should focus on herein is the form and characteristics of crisis under the economic situations during the transition from feudalism to capitalism. The discussion of these two forms of typical crises is precisely a preparation to describe the third type of crisis conveniently.

It is evident that the crises of a transitional society undoubtedly embody the dual characteristics of feudalism and capitalism. However, the underlying and fundamental explanation of this duality is not mechanical. It is insufficient to merely point out the feudalistic crisis factors on the one hand and the capitalist crisis factors on the other.

If we analyze the economic crises in modern China as a specimen of this form of crisis, the explanation of all the economic forms previously discussed, along with their historical origins, will serve as the basis for the argument presented here. This approach allows the Chinese economic crises we discussed to be presented as the general trend of the general economic movements, and our theory of crisis can be viewed as the conclusion of a general theory of the Chinese economy.

Chapter 31
Characteristics of Economic Crises in Traditional China

If we treat economic crises in traditional China as crises within a feudal system, certain distinctive features emerge, some unusual characteristics are bound to emerge. The reasons for this should be explained in terms of the inherent characteristics of Chinese feudalism itself.

Firstly, on the basis of landlord economy, China established a centralized feudal system ever since the Qin and Han Dynasties. The fundamental fact of this feudal system is that the local leaders of the entire country below the supreme sovereignty, whether they are feudal lords with manorial estates or provincial officials, are deprived of the right of "awarding feudal lords and land." The land within their jurisdiction does not generate direct rents and taxes for them, which are instead contributed to the supreme sovereignty, and then allocated to them in the name of salary by the supreme sovereignty. The local economic independence has been restricted, making it difficult to establish the form of a decentralized and centrifugal feudal system. However, what we are focusing on here is the agricultural products, as typical products of labor in a backward society, must have a portion contributed to the central authority. Even if this contribution is in the form of physical objects or is often converted locally into salaries and allowances, the portion that leaves the hand of direct producers and is not directly used to support the local feudal lords and officials, namely the portion that forms the basis of central fiscal expenditures, inevitably needs to be converted into currency through the market. In previous dynasties, various measures, such as equal distribution and market exchange, were taken to deal with this tribute of agricultural products. However, over time, as the tribute of peasants was gradually monetized, the majority of the gains in the form of in kind were largely reliant on the market. The extensive market of agricultural products within the unified market was one of the fundamental reasons for the prosperity of commerce in China.

Secondly, through centralized feudal politics, not only did the vast areas with accessible transportation in ancient China become the scope of commercial activities, but also the various national or comprehensive facilities directly or indirectly related

Y. Wang, *The Basic Theory of Chinese Economy*,
https://doi.org/10.1007/978-981-95-6330-2_31

to the economy under the unified political power were able to adopt more uniform standards in terms of currency weights and measures and tax system, which indeed provided a framework for supporting and connecting for the backward economy.

Furthermore, one of the characteristics of the landlord economy in China is that the ownership of land is not inherently tied to a specific social identity. Regardless of background or status, as long as he possesses the currency to acquire land, then he is able to be the owner of land. Although, during extremely brief periods in several dynasties, merchants were prohibited from acquiring land, under the so-called Equal-Field System, there was still a considerable duration in which land transactions were only permitted within a very narrow range. Moreover, even in legally sanctioned cases of free land transactions, traditional customs imposed restrictions, not to mention the coercive effect of feudal privileges. Nevertheless, in general, the transfer of land in China is relatively free. The most fixed and ubiquitous land can be freely used as the object of transactions among individuals across all social strata, which has not only loosened the class rigidity and solidity of this feudal society, but also endowed the general economic system with greater organic vitality. The free movement of labor accompanied by the free transfer of land further highlights the vastness, mobility and organic nature of our feudal economy.

Perhaps it is precisely for this reason that the historical rhythm of rises and falls in Chinese feudal societies appears both regular and rhythmic and is repeatedly performed through the alternating relationships of rise and fall between the dynasties throughout history. In this context, the circularity of the economy is still regarded as the realistic basis of the rise and fall of the dynasties in politics. All dynasties were overthrown as a result of irreparable economic crises.

After the establishment of each new dynasty following a period of great turmoil, the founding emperor—eager to consolidate the economic foundation of the realm—typically pursued policies of fiscal restraint and actively promoted agricultural development. Key measures included improving water conservancy, advancing farming techniques, reducing penalties and taxes, and striving to ensure that every peasant had land to cultivate. These were regarded as essential tasks for any promising ruler of a new regime.

As a result of these efforts, agricultural output increased, which in turn boosted state revenues from taxes and rents, while also expanding the volume of goods available for commerce. With rising consumption, the scope of taxation widened, and the imperial court gradually shifted "from frugality to extravagance." Large-scale construction projects, military displays, and campaigns to subdue noncompliant regions—all reflected a growing inclination toward ostentatious consumption.

The greater the court's pursuit of consumption, the less attention it paid to production. Historically, it was precisely this overemphasis on consumption that gradually drew resources and focus away from productive activity. Consequently, earlier policies of light taxation and thrift unintentionally gave way to oppressive tax regimes.

During this transformation, the merchant class seized various opportunities. They profited from the court's expanding demand for daily necessities, entertainment, and luxury goods. They also took advantage of heavy taxation by trading the agricultural products peasants surrendered as rent or tax. Beyond economic gains, merchants established close ties with the court and officialdom, gaining political influence and privileges. Monopolies once controlled by the state gradually passed into private commercial hands.

In the cities, merchant guilds increasingly overshadowed craft guilds, turning urban centers into hubs of consumption for officials and businessmen. The absence of a clear boundary between commerce and officialdom—coupled with the fact that many officials came from merchant backgrounds—contributed to administrative decline. Agriculture was neglected, taxes were levied arbitrarily, and the peasantry grew increasingly impoverished, creating ideal conditions for usury. Whether the moneylenders were merchants, officials, or scholars, the outcome remained the same: accelerated land annexation.

Once the decline began, imperial decrees intended to restrain commerce, promote agriculture, or prevent land consolidation became empty words. As governance deteriorated and water conservancy was ignored, natural disasters struck more frequently and severely. Lacking preparation or effective relief, these calamities sharply accelerated the downward spiral. As the ancient saying goes, "The old and weak died and were left in ditches; the strong fled their homes in all directions." Banditry surged, ambitious warlords seized the moment, and the empire descended into widespread chaos.

Social productivity was severely undermined, court revenues collapsed, currency depreciated sharply, and commercial activity stagnated. The economy became paralyzed and fragmented, approaching a state of near-anarchy. In this context, the dynasty was ultimately overthrown, and the capital accumulated by merchants and usurers was largely wiped out. Before, there had been laborers but no land for them to till; now there was land, but too few people left to work it.

Out of the devastation, land redistribution became the foremost task of the next new dynasty. And it was from this point that economic recovery began anew.

The rise and fall of each dynasty throughout Chinese history is in accordance with this changing relationship of the economic cycle. Herein, we will not explain whether this economic cycle is constant or continuously evolving. We will first examine the characteristics it exhibits.

The first apparent feature is that, compared to the economic crises in any other feudal society, it is more comprehensive. This is undoubtedly closely linked to the fact that the Chinese economy was integrated into a large unit under a centralized feudal system. Nevertheless, further analysis reveals that merely having nominal unity is not sufficient. As we previously mentioned, its internal mobility and organic nature are the more fundamental reasons for the outbreak of more comprehensive crises across a vast area.

The second apparent feature is that, compared to the economic crises in any other feudal society, it exhibits a great degree of sociality. This so-called sociality is contrasted with naturalness. In other words, the formation of crises is not primarily attributable to natural disasters, such as droughts, floods, insect disasters, and epidemic diseases. Rather, it is largely a consequence of man-made disasters. The question thus arises as to whether the society in question is capable of taking the necessary measures in advance and afterwards to prevent and relieve such disasters. Chinese historians often perceive natural disasters as divine punishment of moral failings and poor governance. In fact, natural disasters strike any dynasty indiscriminately, rather than targeting specific regimes. The floods and droughts in the "prosperous period of the Ming Dynasty" were not necessarily less severe than those that took place during the chaotic period. Whereas, the so-called "prosperous period of the Ming Dynasty" placed significant emphasis on various "benevolent policies," including "paying attention to water conservancy," "reducing penalties and tax levies," and "being concerned about the worries of the world before one's own;" and these "benevolent policies" were viewed as "benevolent strategies" for relieving disasters and "heading off a disaster, turning danger into safety." In some instances, the extremely terrible natural disasters in specific regions can be alleviated by the favourable outcomes of agricultural production in other regions. Relocating people to the borders, providing them with food is the traditional approach to disaster relief in China, which is related to the aforementioned vastness of Chinese crises. The mobility and flexibility of the internal economic organization of large feudal countries prevent them from falling into irreparable crises due to misguided political actions. In a vast territory, the impact of natural disasters is necessarily limited by variations in climate, soil, and other natural conditions, making it relatively easy to devise ways to cope with them. Therefore, economic crises in ancient China were relatively less natural, although feudal economic crises were generally characterized by natural elements.

The third apparent feature is that, compared to the economic crises in any other feudal society, it possesses a greater inevitability, followed closely by the aforementioned characteristic of its greater sociality. If natural disasters or sudden wars play a decisive role in an economic crisis, they are mainly accidental and occasional and externally imposed. The natural role in economic crises in ancient China, as previously mentioned, was not particularly severe. Moreover, the dangerous and destructive wars were less a consequence of "prolonged peace and prosperity in the country" and "insufficient military preparedness." Instead, they stemmed from the country's increased wealth and prosperity, which led to expanded consumption, the "neglect of agricultural production," heavy taxation, land concentration, and a significant number of peasants becoming disruptors of social order. However, this kind of war is typically induced when "granaries are full and stables are well-fed," and they may serve as a catalyst for the decline of the feudal economy during prosperous times. But the war at the end of the dynasty was generally manifested as the end of an uncontrollable economic crisis. Wars and natural disasters should be expounded in a social context and included in the process of the inevitable development of the social economy, which is the prerequisite for perceiving the universality of the connotation of Chinese feudal economic organization and its relative lack of certainty.

The typical centralized feudal economy of China serves as the realistic foundation for economic crises in traditional China, which is fundamentally defined by the special form of landlord economy in China.

Chapter 32
Traditional Economic Crises and Economic Modernization

Starting from the landlord economy, the economic changes in Chinese history, despite their greater comprehensiveness, sociality, and inevitability, exhibit a melody or rhythm that cannot be manifested in any other feudal society. The landlord economy is categorized as a feudal economic system and is limited by more comprehensive laws of the feudal economy. When compared to modern economic crises, its features can be readily identified as local, regional, spontaneous, and accidental. The signs of periodic changes associated with the rise and fall of the imperial dynasties appear rather ambiguous and irregular in terms of both duration and the contours of change.

However, what we should particularly pay attention to is not the superficial discrepancies mentioned above, but rather the ultimate and most essential cause of these phenomena, as well as the possible outcomes of their cyclical evolution and transformation. The whole structure of the feudal economy is built upon land, and social production relations are formed on the foundation and key element of land. Whether the land is allowed to realize its natural productivity, or whether the direct producers on the land are allowed to harness their social productivity is a major issue determining the self-sufficiency or prosperity and decline of the feudal society. Therefore, the economic crises in feudal society are consistently manifested in the reality that land products are insufficient for consumption and the direct producers are unable to obtain the most essential means of subsistence. Naturally, individual direct producers or peasants may sometimes be excessively exploited through heavy taxes and rents and usurious commercial practices, resulting in their inability to retain the means of consumption for their minimum standard of subsistence. But on the whole, the core of the crisis is insufficient production for consumption, and the severity of the crisis is almost determined by this factor. In a society with underdeveloped exchange relationships, there were no essential differences evident. If we want to identify the real differences, it can be noted that the crisis under the feudal system in Western Europe was not as large in scale as that in China, nor was its influence as profound and destructive as that in China. The reasons should also be explained by the characteristics of the Chinese feudal system.

Y. Wang, *The Basic Theory of Chinese Economy*,
https://doi.org/10.1007/978-981-95-6330-2_32

As we mentioned above, the industry in Chinese society has been hindered and oppressed in various ways by the autocratic politics based on the landlord economy. Foreign trade, which was closely linked to industry, has always been subject to state control. All cooperative industries or large-scale enterprises related to the handicraft industry were mostly in the form of official commerce. The domination of commercial guilds, based on their various privileges over craft guilds in urban areas, has further severely limited the development of industry and the accumulation of Industrial Capital. On the commercial front, it has undoubtedly demonstrated prosperity and a massive scale of accumulation more than once. However, its development has been constrained not only by the decline of industry and the tendency to convert resources into land, but also intrinsically tied to the rise and fall of the dynasties. In the process of the overthrow of each dynasty, all commercial accumulations are "doomed to the same fate," much like "a louse will die if its host dies." This was quite different from European society, where commerce in European feudal society was generally in opposition to the feudal lords. Although commerce and industry were destroyed by the struggles and wars among the monks and nobles for power and profit, at the same time, they took advantage of their existing accumulation, developed in the process of the collapse of these nobles and lords or on the ruins of their demise. As for commerce and industry itself, commerce in European feudal society generally did not achieve the same social status and privileges as it did in Chinese society. Therefore, aside from a few exceptional cities, such as Venice, which once established a merchant regime, the power of worker guilds in other cities should not be underestimated and some even gained an advantage over merchant guilds. Therefore, those cities are not consumption-oriented or politics-oriented, but rather production-oriented.

These essential differences between commerce and industry in the feudal society of China and those in Europe not only influenced the nature of their respective economic crises, but also had a significant impact on the nurturing and development of new economic forces in the collapse and crisis of the old society, which we must mention here. Therefore, it is not difficult for us to find the most accurate answer as to why European economic modernization and capitalization occurred earlier than that in China.

In the late Han Dynasty, the late Tang Dynasty, the late Song Dynasty, and even the late Ming Dynasty, China suffered widespread and destructive warfare in the extreme economic crisis. The decline of the dynasties was accompanied by that of the merchant class, and the destruction of agriculture also led to the decline of commerce and industry along with its accumulation. This mode of evolution clearly struggled or failed to cultivate new productive forces that could replace the existing production relations during the collapse of old social production relations. In the end, the old productive force had no choice but to allow the old productive relations adapted to it to gradually recover, thereby providing an opportunity for regeneration. The so-called eternally unchanging Chinese society (as emphasized by many famous European scholars, such as Adam Smith and Hegel), or the constant reproduction of Chinese feudal dynasties, was mostly based on the inability of new productive forces to be nurtured and developed amidst the collapse of old production relations.

Nevertheless, one fact should not be ignored herein: regardless of whether the economic crises at the end of the aforementioned dynasties were increasingly severe or whether the resulting wars and destruction were more comprehensive, it must be acknowledged, from the perspective of the longer-term historical evolution process, that the preconditions or potential factors of capitalist production methods were generally in a state of development. This includes the promotion of the domestic market, the increase of commercial organizations and accumulation, the increase of handicraft workshops as the prototype of the manufacturing industry, and the decrease of traditional constraints on land transactions, among others. Such developments could be regarded as changes within the unchanging and development within the stagnation.

We need to grasp the crux of both positive and negative aspects in order to comprehend that our modern economy and its crises did not develop purely on their own, nor were they suddenly imported from abroad. Traditional and specific social causal relations have consistently been at play in this context.

Chapter 33
Expansion of Market Relations and Manifestations of Modern Economic Crises

Since the arrival of modern capitalism, China's traditional economic forms have undergone significant transformation—sometimes rapidly, sometimes gradually. As a result, the content and manifestations of traditional economic crises have also shifted. But if we take a comprehensive look at China's modern economy, we see that the inevitability, regularity, and universality found in capitalist crises have not truly appeared within the internal development of China's own economic organizations. At the same time, what we might call the broader cyclical rhythm—the relatively predictable inevitability that once characterized feudal economic crises in China—has been fragmented, distorted, or thrown into convulsions under the expansion of market relations. This expansion has not enhanced those unique features; on the contrary, it has produced consequences quite contrary to what one might expect—a point we'll come back to later. For now, let me outline the general manifestations of economic crises in modern China.

What we see first is that throughout the entire process of modernization, economic crises—expressed through natural disasters, wars, peasants leaving the land, unemployment, destruction, and famine—have seemed to accompany us constantly. It has become like a chronic, recurring ailment. We've grown so used to it that we no longer see it as a pathological condition, but rather as a kind of inherent weakness or unsoundness.

China may be said to have been "founded on agriculture," but the area of cultivated land—the very basis of that foundation—grew by only one percent over the sixty years from 1873 to 1934, according to statistics published in Shun Paoin 1935 by the Central Agricultural Experiment Institute. What's more, in the latter half of that period—from 1903 to 1934—there was no increase at all. Meanwhile, if we take the amount of cultivated land converted to wasteland in 1914 as a base of 100, it had reached 323 by 1930. The call to "reclaim wasteland while preserving cultivated land" is no longer just a wartime concern.

Y. Wang, *The Basic Theory of Chinese Economy*,
https://doi.org/10.1007/978-981-95-6330-2_33

Now, we can't grasp the true nature of this chronic crisis just from changes in cultivated acreage. As I discussed earlier, the gradual fragmentation of farm operations and the difficulty ordinary peasants faced in renewing even simple tools made the agricultural foundation increasingly vulnerable. In modern times, even as population fell sharply due to disasters and wars, China imported large quantities of rice, wheat, and flour—clear evidence of a steady decline in agricultural productivity. Still, this primitive form of crisis was often overshadowed by other, more visibly "modern" crises that played out explicitly in the market. Some even argued that once this modern crisis was alleviated, the economy would recover. But that, in my view, was clearly an illusion.

A second phenomenon is that as modern times advanced, our economic crisis took on a dual character. On one hand, it seemed mired in its own internal disasters, appearing unrelated to the economic ups and downs of the capitalist world. On the other, it was increasingly regarded as an organic part of international market crises—arising and developing as a component of the capitalist world.

In reality, the prosperity of the capitalist world—the so-called industrial revival—not only failed to help China's economy develop healthily, but was often nourished at China's expense. What's more, economic crises in the capitalist world ended up aggravating China's existing crises in a kind of transferred form.

China originally served as a source of raw materials and a market for commodities and capital. But under the influence of international commerce, certain specialized agricultural products—especially export monocultures like silk, tea, tung oil, soybeans, peanuts, cotton, and tobacco—became increasingly dependent on the international market and the foreign industries that needed them. When those foreign industries slowed, demand for raw materials slumped. A sharp drop in exports of these specialized items triggered widespread unemployment and bankruptcy among the peasants who grew them.

At the same time, we were forced to make sacrifices on multiple fronts amid fierce international conflicts over currency and tariffs. Our potential exports were hindered, while foreign surplus goods—often moldy or damaged—flowed easily into China through unguarded coastal ports. Foreign capital that couldn't find productive use at home seized the chance, shifting from "commodity investment" to "capital investment" to exploit China's cheap labor. They also took advantage of the Chinese government's financial difficulties to depress prices of raw materials and gain commercial and industrial privileges.

So amid profound crises in Chinese cities, you could even spot signs of what looked like abnormal prosperity—which brings me to a third feature.

The last phenomenon I'd note is that, under the interplay of this duality, economic crises in China appeared especially uneven, multifaceted, and ambiguous. Even though China was part of the world market, strong local features remained, and natural factors still mattered.

In particular, the traditional crisis of under production coexisted with the modern crisis of overproduction—often in the very same sectors. For example, before the war, "peasants along the Yangtze were impoverished by falling grain prices. In 1932, rice prices in those provinces dropped 30%—what's often called 'hunger amid abundance.' But in Guangdong, chronic food shortages meant 14.4 million dan of rice were imported each year through Kowloon, Shantou, and other ports. Meanwhile, North China had huge wheat stockpiles—no less than 10 million dan piled along the railways—while Shanghai imported large amounts of foreign wheat every year" (as cited in "China's Rural Crisis and Rural Conditions," Chinese Economy, vol. 3, no. 11).

Similarly, Chinese tea was overproduced as world markets slumped, yet we imported tea from Ceylon, India, and Java. Raw silk output exceeded demand, yet silk fabrics were imported in quantity from Japan and India. Guangdong and Jiangxi had sugar gluts, yet sugar from South Asia and Japan flooded the national market.

These imports should reflect low domestic productivity, yet they caused local overproduction. And if we look at industry, things get even more paradoxical: Chinese factories closed while foreign firms in the same sectors expanded. The crisis was so multifaceted that it became hard to tell what was really happening, either over time or in terms of its expressions.

Now, on the surface, these crisis forms seem fundamentally different from traditional ones. But look closer, and you'll see that the expansion and reorganization of the market offer a compelling explanation for the change. In fact, all the crisis phenomena I've mentioned were tied to market relations.

No wonder many people, focusing on circulation, concluded that China's crises were mainly commercial or technical—tied to the external trappings of capitalism, not its internal laws.

I don't want to dismiss that view entirely. But we should also ask: can it really uncover the root causes of economic crises in China?

Those who analyzed China's crisis mainly from technical and commercial angles placed their emphasis on the circulation process. They argued that the inability to regulate the market uniformly was a key cause, and they pointed to the lack of protective tariffs, poor transport, and non-uniform currency as major triggers.

I don't deny these were direct or indirect factors. But the key question is: what underlying relations determine their scope and limits?

From a circulation perspective, China's market relations do look peculiarly anarchic. The coexistence of gluts in export monocultures and shortages in staple food, for instance, seems especially ironic: surplus in one region couldn't relieve deficits in another, yet large imports arrived from abroad. But look closely, and this situation becomes understandable.

A truly integrated domestic market, in the modern sense, never really existed in China. In fact, some border regions had closer ties with neighboring countries than with inland China or even each other: the Northeast, Shandong, and Fujian were strongly linked with Japan; Outer Mongolia and Xinjiang with Russia; Tibet and Guangdong with Britain; Yunnan and Guangxi with France. Coastal regions also had extensive ties with Southeast Asia, the Dutch East Indies, the American Philippines, Japanese Taiwan, British Hong Kong, and Malaya.

Trade along these external routes was often easier than domestic exchange. Even trade between inland provinces was too weak to form a national market.

Transportation—and, to a lesser extent, currency—was key. Most new transport infrastructure was built with foreign capital and served foreign interests. Nearly every border province had railways linking it to neighboring countries. Inland railways were mostly extensions of foreign lines. Coastal and inland shipping served as feeders.

So as transport developed, China's market relations grew more fragmented, not less. International capital used transport and currency to divide and control the Chinese market. Along foreign-controlled railways, foreign currencies often circulated. Controlling currency and transport let foreign interests regulate trade to suit their needs, not China's.

That's why surplus rice from the Yangtze couldn't prevent imports from Annam, Siam, or Taiwan, and why North China's wheat stockpiles didn't stop flour imports from the United States. Beyond the border regions, foreign capital also manipulated trade, finance, and industry in cities like Shanghai, Guangzhou, Tianjin, and Hankou—using their economic privileges to suit their need for manufactures and raw materials.

The result was that China could neither regulate its own supply and demand nor be uniformly regulated by any single capitalist country. The more fragmented the market relations, the more multifaceted the crises became.

But control over transport, currency, and other economic means could only fully shape commodity flows if paired with influence over tariff policy. China never had full tariff autonomy. Even after very low treaty tariffs were revised, foreign creditors often secured claims against Chinese tariff revenue and transport rights. What's more, tariff revenue was the top source of fiscal spending before the war. These complex financial-capitalist ties gave foreign powers real influence over China's tariff policy.

The result: they fought tariff wars among themselves, dumping their surpluses—even unsold raw materials—into China. Many people say the lack of industrial protection is the clearest cause of China's economic crises. There's some truth in that.

But that still leaves a question: why do economic crises persist in countries with tariff barriers? (In capitalist countries, after all, tariff barriers are seen as both a symptom and an aggravating factor of crises.) So we have to ask: is there a strong link between protective tariffs and fundamentally preventing crises?

There's still quite a bit of wiggle room in answering that. One scientific view is that the Chinese-style crisis is fundamentally different in type and nature from the modern crisis abroad—so the two shouldn't be conflated.

And that is precisely the argument I have tried to clarify here.

Chapter 34
Causes and Consequences of Crises Under the Interplay of General Economic Laws

The duality of contemporary economic crises in China, as I have discussed earlier, presents a complex picture. On one hand, regardless of global economic fluctuations, China has continually struggled with a persistent, recurring economic ailment. On the other hand, precisely because of this chronic weakness, it remains particularly vulnerable to external influences; a downturn in the capitalist market almost immediately worsens our domestic situation. This cannot be explained in any simple or dualistic terms. While the bottlenecks in the circulation process—which we have already examined—do show how China's economic crises are negatively affected by world economic crises, that perspective alone cannot explain their chronic and recurrent nature.

What we truly need is to shift our viewpoint from the circulation process to the production process. Only then can we arrive at a unified understanding of this duality. When exploring the causes of China's economic crisis, the first step should be to ask not so much why it occurs, but what it essentially is. It is through its dual character that the crisis takes on such divergent manifestations: urban traits alongside rural elements, overproduction coexisting with insufficient production, ties to international economic cycles while also displaying continuity and constancy. If we wish to grasp the underlying unity behind these seemingly contradictory phenomena from within China's own economic structure and across the full course of its movement, it is reasonable to conclude that the fundamental crisis can be characterized as rural in nature, rooted in insufficient production, and persistent over time. If that holds, then the opposite set of phenomena—urban, marked by overproduction and cyclical fluctuations—can be seen as developing on the basis of this more fundamental crisis. Clearly, we cannot reverse the logic and claim the latter produces the former.

In earlier chapters, I have analyzed the nature of the Chinese economy by looking closely at the various forms of its economic components. If we regard economic crisis as the inevitable outcome of the movement of the economy as a whole, then we must examine those individual economic forms within a holistic framework.

Y. Wang, *The Basic Theory of Chinese Economy*,
https://doi.org/10.1007/978-981-95-6330-2_34

The value form of commodities constitutes the central axis of the entire economy. I began my analysis from this starting point previously, and I shall do the same now in examining how China's economy functions in its process of reproduction.

As I have noted before, the Chinese economy has largely moved beyond a purely natural economy. Although most products are still made for their use-value rather than exchange-value, the general trend has powerfully pushed toward commercialization. The commercialization of specific products depends on many objective preconditions—markets, currency, and transport, to name the most obvious. In fact, we have already described the obstacles to commercialization in China in these areas. However, whether a product can become a commodity, to what extent, and what kind of commodity it becomes—these questions are not decided only when it enters exchange after being produced. They are shaped by the conditions and mode of production themselves. Most commercialized products in China are made under the conditions of small-scale commodity production. This not only limits the market scope of these products but also defines their inherent attributes and types. Small-scale commodity production is confined essentially to agricultural products and handicrafts.

In a society where small-scale commodity production prevails, the surplus value that forms the foundation for reproduction or the source of social accumulation generally originates from the land. This is because, in such a society, agriculture—being better able to utilize natural forces—is more productive than handicrafts or even manufacturing. Moreover, industry is still largely regarded as subordinate to agriculture. Therefore, the general form of surplus value in agriculture appears not as profit, but as land rent. (Even where land is not leased out, the surplus labor performed on owner-cultivated land can be understood in this light.) Our society treats the accumulation of land rent as the ultimate source of social accumulation, and the potential for reproduction also lies here.

But this is only a general observation. In reality, whether the volume of output from the land increases each year—that is, whether a real surplus exists for accumulation—cannot be judged merely by the amount of agricultural product converted into land rent. We must also consider the living and production conditions of the peasants. Even if land rent remains unchanged or increases, social accumulation may fail to grow or may even shrink if the peasants' conditions worsen. Conversely, even if land rent falls, an improvement in the peasants' livelihood does not necessarily mean a decrease in social accumulation—it may even increase it. In a society where market relations are underdeveloped and agricultural products are not fully commercialized, the surplus from agricultural labor remains uncertain. It is possible for output to increase as the direct producers' living conditions deteriorate, or to decrease as their conditions improve. Regardless, the test of whether social accumulation has genuinely increased, and whether that increase is used to expand agricultural reproduction, can generally be made by looking at the living and production conditions of the direct agricultural producers. For the moment, however, it is not urgent to review the living and production conditions of our peasants. Instead, we should first ask what conditions the general movement of our economy provides for them.

We have stated that the dispersion or application of capital is determined by the manner of its accumulation and concentration. This law also applies to the accumulation and use of land rent. In other words, land rent, as the foundation of accumulation in our society, is typically used or dispersed in the income generated from land and in various primitive accumulation activities connected with acquiring land. Similarly, profit, as the basis of accumulation in capitalist society, is generally used by capitalists to purchase elements of accumulation linked to acquiring capital.

Commerce is one of the most prominent of these primitive accumulation activities. Under generalized commodity production, all elements of production become objects of purchase and sale. The movement of commodities being bought and sold constitutes the substance and manifestation of commerce, which is itself rooted in the production process. In the context of small-scale commodity production, however, commerce operates outside the immediate production process and actively promotes the conversion of products into commodities. This leads to a tendency for commerce to dominate industry, with commercial profit regulating industrial or agricultural profit. As a result, industrial or agricultural profit becomes subordinate to commercial profit. Commerce, in turn, does not dominate interest but is rather regulated by it. In this context, the claims of usurers, and even the fiscal demands of the state, not only align with commerce in dividing the agricultural surplus, but also promote the conversion of products into commodities—whether for tax payments or debt settlements. As foreign trade expands, products become commodities not only for the domestic market but for the international market. Moreover, rising imports—due to increased individual and state consumption—require more exports to balance foreign payments. The unequal exchange that arises from trading agricultural products for industrial products has itself become a major cause of the chronic trade deficit. Consequently, a considerable part of the surplus agricultural product or its value, which should form the basis of social accumulation, is either concentrated abroad through comprador commerce or invested as international capital in commercial enterprises in China's coastal cities.

The urban prosperity that comes with increased imports and the corresponding modernization of the country is based directly or indirectly on various forms of primitive accumulation—commerce, usury, taxation, and even land rent. (In this work, I have not undertaken a direct, detailed analysis of taxation. But in a backward country, taxation, as a factor in primitive accumulation, significantly impacts the entire economy. Its destructive effect on the livelihood and production conditions of the direct producers in China is substantial. One problematic feature is its uncertainty. The direct producers, as the main taxpayers, do not know how much tax will be levied each year, and often neither do the tax collectors themselves. One British author estimated that taxes collected by local officials were more than five times the amount remitted to the central government; another British expert put the figure at three times [see the Chinese translation of Radek's Theoretical Analysis of Chinese History, p. 235]. Combined with other backward means of primitive accumulation—such as high land rent, usury, and merchant capital—the destructive effect is easy to foresee.) This system continuously increases the burden on the countryside—the primary and ultimate source of social accumulation—draining potential wealth from the rural areas to the cities and ultimately into the pool of international capital, thereby linking up with the concentration process mentioned earlier.

Naturally, this concentration of social wealth does not happen "all at once." It is a continuous process. Precisely for this reason, some capital must remain in the countryside to sustain primitive accumulation. In this context, it is local commerce (as opposed to comprador commerce) and usury (as opposed to modern banking) that undertake the most grassroots accumulation activities. And because these activities operate in the most backward rural society—which is also the most easily exploited and where privileges are most easily enforced—the high rates of profit and interest profoundly influence the accumulation and use of land rent drawn directly from the land. In the eyes of the merchant, land is a particularly profitable commodity; in the eyes of the usurer, land rent is disguised high interest. Consequently, the agricultural surplus product or its value that remains in the countryside inevitably circulates and is utilized through these three channels.

Therefore, even though part of the wealth accumulated from the land remains in the countryside and is even used on the land, this accumulation is not employed as capital but for purchasing more land. The more peasants are compelled to pay for land under the pressure of high commercial profit, high interest, and other non-economic coercion, the less they can save from their total income to maintain production conditions or improve their livelihood. The poorer they become, the more they depend on the land, and the more they must pay for it. Peasants with no capital or means to acquire land are forced to work for wages below the minimum subsistence level. This, in turn, leads to a situation where labor displaces machinery. Consequently, labor productivity on the land gradually declines, and the output of agricultural products—especially grain—diminishes.

Thus, our economic crisis—characterized by insufficient production, chronic recurrence, and agrarian features—is formed through the interaction of several laws evident in the economic movements we have described: small-scale commodity production, the transformation of products into commodities by commerce, the domination of industry by commerce, the excess of commercial profit over industrial profit, the regulation of profit by interest, various forms of unequal exchange, the concentration of capital in cities and foreign countries, the interplay of different forms of primitive capital in the countryside facilitating their circulation, and labor displacing machinery and even animal power. Within this crisis, we can certainly recognize traces of classical economic crises. However, we can easily misinterpret the severe economic crises induced in China by world economic crises as the true form of our own crisis. Hence, when the world economy enters a period of recovery or boom, we may get the illusion that our own economy is also reviving. This illusion is reinforced by a superficial observation: the belief that a constant or increasing amount of rent and tax signifies social accumulation, as does a constant or increasing amount of agricultural product representing surplus labor.

In reality, especially in a society like ours, an increase in rent and tax not only can coexist with a decline in social labor productivity, but can even be a direct cause of it. Consider that during prolonged turmoil and destruction in wartime and even after, despite the fact that industry—both old and new, large-scale and small-scale—stood on the brink of collapse and the rural economy was in ruins, the burden on the producers was actually increased through rent, taxes, corvée labor, mercantile operations, usury, and other crude forms of extortion, all exacerbated by hyperinflation. Although people often praise the "diligence" of the Chinese people—for instance, their having to substitute wild herbs, tree bark, and white clay for grain, and human labor for tools and draft animals—the fact is that all forms of rent, tax, commerce, and usury eventually reach their limit of exploitation. Even corvée labor reveals its limits when the "able-bodied men," physically exhausted and debilitated, become incapable of any work. The wars and upheavals that have marked Chinese history are manifestations of the classical crises that have punctuated its development. The current crisis is different in content and essence, and the resulting disorder incorporates new factors. These changes and new factors can be explained by the duality of the crisis and the semi-feudal, semi-colonial character of the economy.

These crises stem from the complex interplay of various relationships within the modern Chinese economy. To some extent, wars can be seen as both direct and indirect consequences of these crises. Regardless of whether wars are fought at home or abroad, and regardless of their outcome, if the basic production relations in Chinese society remain unchanged by the war, and if the social status of the producing masses is not generally raised through a transformation of the mode of production, then the economic principles and laws we have discussed will persist, continuing to entrap China in a chronic and deepening state of crisis.

Issues discussed in this part

(1) What are the different basic characteristics of feudal and capitalist crises?
(2) What are the different characteristics of the form of economic crises in traditional China compared to those under the general feudal system?
(3) How can the duality of economic crises in modern China be explained?
(4) Should Chinese economic crises be seen as the inevitable result of the interaction of the general laws of economic movement? Try to give a comprehensive explanation of the movement rules or tendencies in the aspects of commodity value, currency, capital, profit, interest, wages, and land rent as discussed above.

Part IX
Special Forms of Chinese Capital and Reflection on Economic Theory

Chapter 35
The Historical Evolution and Limits of Chinese Commercial Capital

35.1 Main Focus of the Entire Text

Those who are concerned about the current economic situation in China, regardless of their level of objectivity, will inevitably express discontent and disapproval of the prevalent activities of commercial capital. Indeed, if we examine the root causes of China's current economic challenges solely from the perspective of commercial capital, our analysis may not fully address the most essential and fundamental aspects, but it will undoubtedly encompass the most essential and fundamental issues.

From the perspective of ordinary people, the activities of commercial capital, as a socioeconomic form, may appear abnormal, exceeding the needs of the general society and further becoming antagonistic to the economic series of the whole society; however, commercial capital itself is under the principle of "doing what it is obliged to do" for each of its activities. Its dynamics cannot be dictated by the desires of ordinary people or even by the intentions of its subjects, i.e., the merchants. In some situations, merchants appear to host or dominate the commercial capital they possess, while in other situations, they simply follow the inevitable trend of their capital. This is akin to a horse pulling a carriage: When going uphill, the carriage is undoubtedly being pulled behind the horse, and the horse leads the way. However, once going downhill, the horse does not seem to be pulling the carriage but is instead being pushed forward by it. The reason is that as the capital of each individual merges into the commercial capital of society, the activities of the capital of each merchant cannot determine their respective directions. Instead, they must depend on the overall trend of all commercial capital in accordance with certain socioeconomic laws to guide their directions.

With this kind of understanding, no matter how openly and harshly we condemn commerce and commercial capital, it merely leads to greater mental disturbance for ourselves, doing no harm to the whole commercial capital or its embodiment, the merchants and the merchant class, nor does it contribute to resolving the overall economic problems. Moreover, from the perspective of the evolution of the whole

Y. Wang, *The Basic Theory of Chinese Economy*,
https://doi.org/10.1007/978-981-95-6330-2_35

society, the identity of merchants is not necessarily fixed to being merchants, just as their capital is not necessarily fixed to being commercial capital. If an individual is engaged in commercial activities, he is already considered a merchant. Although the legal and moral concepts may be weakened by a strong desire for profit, we cannot simply view him as a fixed entity defined solely as a merchant. Moreover, especially in the context of contemporary China, a merchant is not merely a merchant. He may operate for his own interests as well as the benefit of others. In the former role, we can accuse him of neglecting social laws and morals, while in the latter role, we cannot deny that he is a supporter of the social laws and morals. Since a merchant can embody both of these two personalities, it is difficult for us to regard him as someone who is indifferent to social laws and morals.

However, I do not make this deduction to exonerate merchants or commercial capital from their responsibility in making a fortune out of national calamities. What I am expressing is that law and morality are both social products that can only function under certain social conditions. In terms of regulating merchants or commercial capital, focusing solely on phenomena, creating severe laws and regulations based on emotions, or applying moral pressure may not yield the desired results.

The activities of commercial capital operate independently of the will of individual merchants and manifest as an irresistible and necessary trend for merchants. In order to curb these trends with morality and law, it is first necessary to recognise the socioeconomic laws of causality that give rise to them. This applies not only to merchants but also to those who might be considered quasi-merchants or even preparatory merchants. In order to gain a comprehensive understanding of the various laws that govern commercial capital, it is essential to engage with the entire field of economics, or even the broader concept of economic theory that differs from the narrower, more modern approach. Commercial capital is an economic form that has existed in all societies since the primitive era. Its entire history reflects the underlying laws that shape its activities.

35.2 Crucial Role of Commercial Capital in the Rise and Fall in the History of Chinese Socioeconomic Development

Indeed, the ascendance and decline of each dynasty in Chinese history has been almost concomitant with the rise and fall of commercial capital. This close connection may lead to the assumption that commercial capital is a prerequisite for the rise and fall of each dynasty. However, the reality is that commercial capital is regenerated by the opportunity presented by the rise of each dynasty. As it expands, it effectively erodes the material foundation of the dynasty through which it was regenerated.

The Chinese commercial capital began to emerge during the Shang and Zhou Dynasties, which are positioned in the early feudal stage in the history of Chinese socioeconomic development. In the subsequent two thousand years, it was largely trapped within a stage of a typical centralized feudal system. The centralized feudal system in China has served as a hotbed of the activities of commercial capital because, in a negative sense, commercial capital needs social backwardness, but if the society is too backward or remains in pre-feudalism, it is impossible for commercial capital to develop. Conversely, in a positive sense, it requires social progress, but if society is too advanced or is moving towards capitalism, it is impossible for commercial capital to achieve a dominant position (In capitalist societies, commerce is generally subordinate to industry, a point that will be elaborated below). However, the feudal system in China has a particularly life-and-death relationship with commercial capital. In the history of Chinese socioeconomy, commercial capital seems to have consistently acted to trap the economy in a feudal state. More than once, it appears willing to perish with the dynasty rather than allow Industrial Capital to assume a dominant social position. This is a major reason why Chinese industry has been underdeveloped and why China has not embarked on the path of capitalism for a long period of time.

Naturally, this explanation is the result of investigating the history of commercial capital in China and assessing its objective performance. However, the activists of the commercial capital throughout the dynasties were not only subjectively unaware of these realities, and their knowledge at that time also did not permit them to recognize them.

At this point, we can further explain the necessary laws underlying the evolution of commercial capital in China.

The ascendance of each dynasty in Chinese history has occurred in the wake of considerable societal upheaval and the subsequent decline in social productivity. This phenomenon can be observed in several prominent dynasties that succeeded the Qin Dynasty, including the Han, Jin, Tang, Song, Yuan, Ming, and Qing Dynasties. If the complete destruction of the social productive forces is the fundamental reason for the downfall of a dynasty, then at the beginning of the formation of a new dynasty, the rulers are inevitably motivated to do everything possible to promote the recovery or regeneration of the social productive forces. In all feudal societies, agricultural production constituted the material foundation. Consequently, the wise monarchs and officials of each dynasty accorded priority to the benefits of peasants and agriculture. This was achieved by paying attention to water conservancy, improving agricultural production techniques, reducing tax levies, appointing officials to promote agriculture and farming, and so forth. These measures were implemented by the founding monarchs and officials of all dynasties.

In the context of feudal nobles, lords, and officials, who were sustained by agricultural surplus products, the emphasis on agricultural production was undoubtedly essential for their survival. In theory, they were supposed to be hostile to commerce, and in practice, they consistently implemented measures to contain commerce because commercial activities had to inevitably share part of agricultural surplus products. The more commercial activities expanded, the more agricultural surplus products had to be shared. Therefore, the general economic policy of feudal societies has always been to stress agriculture and restrain commerce as its backbone.

However, the policy of stressing agriculture and restraining commerce across all dynasties seems to indicate to us a fact from the opposite side, that is, the reason why "agriculture" needs to be particularly "stressed" is that it has previously been neglected, and why "commerce" needs to be particularly "restrained" is that it has been too "indulged." A political commentator in the Han Dynasty once cried out to explain the fact that "the law devalues merchants, yet merchants have already become rich; the law respects peasants, yet peasants have become impoverished." In essence and practice, all feudal dynasties promoted agriculture while simultaneously opening the door to wealth for merchants. That is not due to a lack of foresight, but rather a failure to understand the inevitable logic of facts.

The development of commerce is contingent upon the existence of favourable external conditions, namely public security and transportation. Conversely, the determination of the medium of exchange and the proliferation of objects of exchange serve as the internal conditions that facilitate commerce. The unified situation of each new dynasty and the rest and recuperation that it was bound to achieve under unity, including the "opening up of fields, the rule of the roads," and all the concurrent policies to improve the people's livelihood, although mainly aimed at increasing agricultural surplus products and rehabilitating the peasants, contributed significantly to the prosperity of commerce. Commerce undoubtedly facilitated the circulation of agricultural products under certain conditions and to a certain extent. However, as commerce developed, it transformed its original role of supporting agriculture into one of undermining it. At the very least, its original supportive role was overshadowed by its increasingly destructive effects.

The industrial production in feudal society was merely viewed as a sideline to agriculture. Almost all objects of commercial exchange were limited to agricultural products, primarily those supplied by peasants to feudal lords, nobles, and officials under the guise of land rents and taxes. The more advanced the development of commerce, the greater the influence of the facilitation of circulation across regions, the more objects were consumed. As a result, the consumption desires of the feudal upper class increased, and the peasants were forced to contribute even more of their agricultural surplus products under the guise of land rent and taxes. In other words, the necessary products that allowed peasants to continue to labor and produce will be reduced. Whether the rents and taxes eroded on the living expenses of the peasants or on their production expenses, the scale of reproduction would consequently be restrained or reduced. Once the reproduction could not be maintained, the economic foundation from which the rent tax was derived would inevitably be weakened. In this context, there were only two avenues for the feudal upper class to continue to maintain unproductive and consumptive waste: one was to intensify the exploitation of peasants, thereby further destroying their parasitic economic foundation; the other was to raise funds through various means, such as borrowing, to finance their wasteful consumption. Regardless of which avenue was chosen, the result would be the concentration of land in the hands of merchants and wealthy individuals, with the peasants driven away from the production process.

The movement of commercial capital into and out of land undoubtedly received assistance from the usury capital that it had previously transformed into. However, the transfer of funds from commerce and usury to real estate was not the central focus of the activities of commercial capital; it was a further expansion. This was because the income generated from land and even usury could constantly be reinvested as capital for commercial activities. Some people argued that commercial capital, usury capital, and land capital formed a "trinity," which is quite appropriate. In any backward society, these three types of capital would manifest themselves in various ways as three functions of a whole.

However, why did merchants, land-rent earners, usurers, and rich individuals refuse to invest their funds in agriculture and industry, choosing instead to circle around these aspects? This was not because they possessed the foresight to see that investing funds in production and the development of production and industries was a denial of their existing status and interests. Rather, it was the various traditional laws, regulations, and consciousness of the feudal society that hindered productive activities. Consequently, they weighed the pros and cons and were more easily attracted by the current substantial profits and the potential social status that could be achieved along with the profits.

In fact, the activities of commercial capital extended beyond the socioeconomic field. Its embodiment, or merchants, not only "amass wealth and exploit the poor" and made "feudal lords bow their heads and rely on them for support," "because of their wealth, they interact with nobles and princes," but also leveraged their substantial fortune and experience of practical operation to directly step into roles of financial management in government, taking advantage of the empty treasury of the dynasties. Thus, "the absence of an examination requirement for official appointments, coupled with the fact that a significant proportion of officials were merchants." In such situations, the traditional policy of restraining commerce in feudal society was temporarily set aside, and a compromise measure acceptable to merchants and wealthy individuals was adopted. In fact, within the limits of in-kind rent became the basis of commodity exchange, the recovery and development of social productive forces, inevitably accompanied by the conditions that favor the accumulation of wealth and the prosperity of wealthy merchants. Consequently, the peasants had to be compensated for the loss of the merchants incurred by the policy of restraining commerce. Under various forms of pressure, the peasants had no choice but to contribute their only means of survival, land, to wealthy merchants and landlords under increasingly unfavorable conditions.

If feudalism reached a stage where it had to yield to wealthy merchants and landlords, compromise with commercial capital, and allow these wealthy individuals to participate in the political regime and determine the economic policies, etc., thus entering a stage of self-commercialization, it inevitably set aside all measures that benefited agricultural production, such as water conservancy, improvements of agricultural equipment, etc. Meanwhile, due to the increase of waste and non-production expenditures and the decrease of rents and taxes caused by the mass exodus of peasants from villages as well as tax evasion of wealthy merchants and officials in multiple ways, they had to impose increasingly ruthless exploitation on the remaining peasants struggling to survive in rural areas. At such a stage, natural disasters, floods, and various forms of plague inevitably consistently oppressed the hungry peasants, forcing them into exile everywhere, and they could not help but lose all the constraints imposed on them by the feudal consciousness of living in their proper sphere and to choose the dead end of "going out of their way to take the risk." As a result, wars broke out everywhere, and the social productive forces were fundamentally destroyed. The foundations of in-kind land rent and commodity-money relationships were completely lost. Not only nobles and lords, but also wealthy merchants and officials, were sacrificed to the centralized feudal system of their generation.

The dead end faced by the commercial capital was certainly not expected by the merchant class. However, throughout the process of Chinese socioeconomic development, they had been trapped in this inescapable fate countless times. At the end of the Han, Tang, Song, and Ming dynasties, the merchant class had once flourished and then followed the same path of demise as their predecessors at the end of the previous dynasties. These bloody episodes seemed to offer no valuable lessons to them. This fact cannot be simply explained with the idiom that "merchants are blinded by profits." Even those wise monarchs, scholars, and officials of all dynasties who regarded the interests of merchants as insignificant failed to realize why the feudal regime based on which their dynasties were founded ultimately succumbed to fragmentation and collapse.

If the essence of a society had not changed, all the laws that shaped this society and achieved its historical existence would be enforced with an ironclad consistency, regardless of people's desires. The law of the movement of commercial capital was an important sector of the law of the movement of the feudalistic economy. The key to the rise and fall of the aforementioned commercial capital in the past dynasties can only be explained by the role of the law of the development of the Chinese feudal society, which is also the research finding of the Broad-sense Economics in modern times.

35.3 Commercial Capital After the Opium War

The Opium War is generally recognized as a turning point in the modernization process of Chinese society. After this event, feudal social organizations in traditional China gradually tended to disintegrate, and at the same time, the commercial capital associated with this gradually disintegrating feudal society also relatively expanded its scope of activities and changed its form.

However, the process of disintegration of an old social organization was not complete until the new system, conceived in its womb, emerged from its chrysalis. Until the outbreak of the Anti-Japanese War, the difficult emergence of a modern social system in China resulted in the more or less retention of feudal remnants throughout the country. If the retained elements were necessarily related to the broadest, most conservative, and most foundational aspects of the organization of social production in rural areas, and, consequently, the disintegrating elements were necessarily related to the narrower, more changeable, and more upper-level of the urban economy. Although the form of Chinese society had changed, its essence remained fundamentally unchanged. Consequently, commercial capital, which was dependent on societies such as ours, despite the fact that the scope of its activities had been expanded and its form of activities had been changed; however, by and large, its underlying laws of movement had always functioned.

Naturally, since the gateway of our ancient empire was forcibly opened by the cannons of advanced countries, various forms of manufactured products have been imported to China in various ways. Meanwhile, a wide range of land products in China had been exported to advanced countries. The expansion of foreign trade relations had indeed ushered in a new era for Chinese commercial capital, or, new blood had been injected into the original metabolic cells.

Of course, Chinese foreign trade did not begin at that time. As early as the Western Han Dynasty, we had already engaged in trade exchanges with countries in the west. At that time, we mainly exported raw silk, and "unsophisticated" western scholars (see *The History of China's Social Development* written by Shahanov) even gave us the term "raw silk imperialism." Since then, most of the trade between China and the West, introduced by the Ararabians in northwest China, was emphasized on sea routes. This led to the establishment of many foreign trade ports in southeast China, such as Jiaozhou, Guangzhou, Mingzhou, Yangzhou, etc. The establishment of the "Bureau for Foreign Shipping" and "Fanfang" (a place for foreign merchants to congregate) served as clear evidence of the expansion of foreign trade at that time. Until the founding of the Great Yuan Empire, the land transportation between China and the western regions of Central Asia was once opened up, but after the collapse of the Great Yuan Empire, this route was blocked again. During the Ming Dynasty, due to the rampant activity of Japanese pirates, overseas navigation was prohibited, leading to a complete cessation of overseas trade. However, adventurous navigation flourished in Europe during that time. The Portuguese and Italians successively discovered the east–west shipping routes, and Europeans rushed to Asia. The Portuguese in the 12th year of Ming emperor Wuzong Zhengde (1517 AD) and the Spanish in the 3rd year of Ming emperor Shenzong Wanli (1575AD) had already come to China to exchange trade. Therefore, overseas trade in China, originally obstructed by Japanese pirates, gradually reopened in the late Ming Dynasty and early Qing Dynasty. From the above brief description of China's foreign trade relations, we can comprehend that the activities of Chinese commercial capital in the past were not entirely confined to the domestic market, nor were they exclusively focused on the trade in original products of the land. However, The intermittent foreign trade at that time, in terms of its scope and scale, was insufficient to change or have much impact on the historical orientation or inevitable law of commercial capital movement in China. Furthermore, the nature of the foreign trade was strictly restricted by the state.

In the Tang Dynasty, a tariff of three-tenths of the total price of the imports was levied, while in the Song Dynasty, a tariff of one-tenth to four-tenths of the total amount of imported goods was levied. Additionally, during the Song Dynasty, imported goods were required to be sold firstly to the bureau for foreign shipping and subsequently by the bureau for foreign shipping or by the government to the public. This enabled the government to generate substantial profits from the discrepancy between purchase and sale prices. Therefore, "those who engage in trade with foreigners for the first time are liable to punishment if the transaction volume reaches 100 qian (copper coin) and will be subjected to a more severe penalty if the volume reaches 15 guan (a string of 1,000 coins). In the latter case, they will be tattooed on the face and exiled to islands." Up until the Yuan Dynasty, Kublai Khan unified the regions south of the Yangtze River and stipulated that all coastal prefectures would collect a tariff of one-tenth on goods exchanged with foreign countries and one-fifteenth on raw materials. Subsequently, the government utilized its own ships to transport all goods traded with foreigners, and profits were divided into ten parts; the government took one-tenth of the total profits while traders received three-tenths. To ensure the monopoly of the state on foreign trade profits, even the powerful families were prohibited from using their own money for foreign trade; those who violated this rule would face penalties and have half of their family property confiscated. It can be inferred that foreign trade during the Song and Yuan and other dynasties was largely monopolized by the state, significantly hindering the activities of commercial capital. At that time, the imported goods were primarily luxury goods for nobles, such as perfume, ivory, coral, amber, etc., while the exported products were mainly gold and silver, copper, iron, lead, tin, and silk. Since the objects of trade were limited to these luxury commodities (the outflow of metals, indeed, had disturbed the currency system at that time), even if commercial capital was allowed to operate freely, it seemed that it could not exert a decisive influence on the economic foundation of society.

However, after the establishment of the five-port trading, there were significant changes in foreign trade in China in all of the aforementioned aspects. These changes were not primarily due to our country abandoning our traditional foreign trade attitudes or policies. Instead, they were largely influenced by the fact that the country with which we traded did not allow us to adopt the traditional attitude and policy of foreign trade.

Commodity production is one of the most distinctive characteristics of the modern economy. Every further development of the modern economy has been accompanied by an increase in the degree and scope of the commodification of products. By the middle of the nineteenth century, all the advanced and backward capitalist countries had almost developed their commodity production to such a degree that not only did the goods they produced be put on the market as commodities, but also the goods used for production were purchased from the market as commodities. Consequently, the expansion of the market became a prerequisite for commodity production. The domestic market was bounded, so the expansion or creation of markets had simply become the most basic and important national policy for capitalist countries. Under the guidance of such national policies, their exports to their trading targets, or China, which we are talking about here, were no longer limited to luxury, such as spice, ivory, and amber. Instead, they began exporting a wide range of daily necessities as well as novel and expensive luxury items to China. Through coercion and inducement, they intended to explore a market for all these commodities in every possible corner of China, as if they were serving the Chinese society in the manufacture of commodities and turning into factories for China. And in conjunction with this kind of demand, the two-pronged approach was that because of the commercialization and industrialization of their production, the raw materials that they needed for industrialization were more and more insufficient in their own countries. At the same time, in China, which was in the flood of their commodities, even the old-style handicraft industry tended to decline as manufacturing was replaced by foreign production. Its agricultural products, especially those produced as raw materials, became the best supplement for industrial countries lacking raw materials, almost as if God properly arranged. In terms of the division of labor in the world economy, it seemed that "each does his best" and "each takes what he needs." Therefore, the characteristics of the economy in China can be illustrated by the advertising slogan of a large department store in Shanghai, which is, "wide collection of local products and unified handling of global goods."

However, the formation of these economic features in China was not without barriers from the traditional political and economic conditions and even the general social and national consciousness. To break through these barriers, many battles and a series of unequal treaties were created successively. With these, the characteristics of the Chinese economy were further safeguarded. Undoubtedly, in the process of capitalist production methods shaping the world according to its own model and destroying the old feudal production methods in various ways, China gradually developed a considerable amount of new-style manufacturing and factory industries, though in a contradictory and irreconcilable way. More than half of these modern enterprises were directly operated by advanced capitalist countries with the industrial privileges they obtained in China in order to exploit our raw materials and labor at the lowest cost and with the least effort. The aforementioned economic characteristics of China appeared to be dazzling and ambiguous as a result of their operation.

Here, we have seemingly devoted considerable space to describing the process and characteristics of the formation of the Chinese economy. The description is necessary because the commercial economy, or the form of commercial capital, is a branch of overall economic forms or one of its important sectors in China. Under the economic conditions with the aforementioned characteristics, the activities of Chinese commercial capital have shown a different division from those in the past in the following respects.

Firstly, the objects of commercial activities have increased and extended. A large number of imported industrial products of various styles had been put into circulation, which was very different from the past when agricultural products were the sole object of commercial activities. Moreover, in the past, only the part of agricultural surplus products that were largely contributed to the landowner (whether state, government, or private) as land rent would be put into the market, while the part that was kept by peasants themselves for self-sufficiency had not been or did not need to be converted into commodities. However, at this time, due to the specialization of certain agricultural products, all products, whether surplus or ultimately necessary, would pass through the market and become the objects of commerce. Additionally, all kinds of bills, securities, and foreign exchanges—the most intangible but the largest-scale exchange items in the exchanges—as well as the more tangible real estate were a paradise where the commercial class found its joyful dance in the new era. As for individuals (coolies or prostitutes) being purchased, recruited, or pledged for "import" or "export," it was never a small-scale commercial sector, which "has existed since ancient times," and now it has expanded in scale and changed in form.

Secondly, the scope of commercial activities had been greatly expanded, which was closely related to its objects of activities. The import and export of Chinese agricultural products to and from every capitalistic corner of the world, although in foreign countries, may not necessarily or even not be the result of Chinese commercial capital activities. However, in China, even in the remote and backward areas, the presence of commercial capital had been discerned, both directly and indirectly, through the development of new means of transportation and new financial and exchange organizations. Moreover, even in urban areas, the various exchanges aforementioned have opened numerous new avenues and fields for commercial capital.

Thirdly, the nature of commercial activities has changed significantly. Before the invasion of modern foreign capital into China, Chinese commercial capital operated independently and developed along paths permitted by the socioeconomic realities of Chinese society. However, after that, its activities, willingly or unwillingly, became entangled in the whirlpool of international capital and increasingly became subordinate to it. Regardless of the invasion methods employed by international capital, its activities were primarily focused on promoting manufactured goods and purchasing raw materials, but this task was not directly undertaken by the so-called national commercial capital. In 1930, the total number of foreign firms, both large and small, reached more than 8000, and they acted almost as masters or supervisors, using all the privileges available to promote the activities of the whole circulation sector in China. In fact, the commercial activities carried out by these foreign firms in cooperation with compradors in China had extended beyond the circulation process; that is, they had invaded into the production process. They not only promoted manufactured goods and purchased raw materials, but also seized control of both manufactured goods and raw materials through political and financial means. In large cities and their surrounding areas, the quasi-capitalist family industries, and even the agricultural products produced exclusively for certain purposes, were almost dominated by merchants.

Taking the aforementioned facts into consideration, on the one hand, Chinese commercial capital has not only changed its form and content but also its original nature. However, on the other hand, the change in its nature had not reached a stage where it had been deprived of exercising its dominance over the Industrial Capital. Instead, in some situations, it seemed that commerce was subordinate to industry in some new-style factories and industries in the metropolis, as in advanced countries. Nevertheless, disregarding its essential form, its role as a subordinate was significantly narrower in scope compared to its dominant position in all industries, particularly in vast rural areas.

Furthermore, in recent times, the strategies employed by advanced capitalist countries for economic aggression against China have increasingly precluded the possibility of allowing Chinese commercial capital under their wings to follow the path of active progress, namely, the transformation into industrial capital or the path of affiliation with industrial capital. The preservation and expansion of raw material supply land and commodity promotion areas are the indispensable prerequisites for the establishment and development of comprador commercial capital. Although the requirements of capital export in the imperialist stage, that is, the requirement of engaging in industrial activities in backward regions, had the tendency to weaken the momentum of the activities of comprador commercial capital. Even if part of the export of capital was to utilize the resources and manpower of the backward regions, and thus, to an appropriate extent, part of the raw materials did not require to be exported and part of the manufactured goods did not need to be imported. However, this part of raw materials and products made in China still needed to be distributed by the commercial capital. Moreover, in fact, as the imperialist stage intensified its competition for the commodity market and raw material supply land, a larger proportion of capital export would be allocated to political investment, while a smaller proportion was towards economic development. The impact of commercial capital generated from the former cost of investment through the financial market, government bonds, and securities was significantly greater than that of industrial capital derived from the latter part of investment.

In summary, throughout the extended period between the Opium War and the Anti-Japanese War, Chinese commercial capital, defined by its submissive and dependent nature, expanded and diversified its domestic operations while undergoing a transformation in its traditional form. However, due to its comprador nature and subordination to international capital, it underwent certain changes that did not alter its fundamental essence. These changes occurred within the confines of the "reform" permitted or demanded by international capital or imperialist policies within the broader Chinese economy.

35.4 Commercial Capital After the Outbreak of the Anti-Japanese War

To gain a more fundamental understanding of the aforementioned commercial capital in the process of Chinese modernization, the limit of the transformation of the commercial capital before the Opium War, it is advisable to examine the commercial capital after the war, in what scope and extent, and under what limit of deformation and deterioration, has reverted to the historical form before the Opium War.

As mentioned previously, Chinese commercial capital, as is customary, or more appropriately, in accordance with the historical trajectory of its activities, is closely connected with usury capital and land capital in a "trinity." When merchants earned money, they leveraged usury activities to acquire land on more favorable conditions to acquire land and became landlords. The income of landlords from land, aside from a small portion allocated for personal consumption, was used for purchasing more land, lending at interest, or engaging in commercial activities, or these three activities simultaneously. The question is how the current real profits (or what he subjectively understands to be real profit) are guiding them. He can also become the owner of his self-cultivated farms or workshops.

Since the invasion of foreign capital, Chinese commercial capital initially stubbornly maintained its traditional way of activity, but later on, with the gradual expansion of its scope of activities and the continuous increase of objects of its activities, its attention and interest had been distracted by many temptations. Meanwhile, the international capital had also forced huge pressure on China, compelling or urging Chinese commercial capital to a new world of pleasure, "Epicureanism."

Moreover, the poverty, unrest, and turmoil in the rural areas of China caused by various forms of imperialist aggression were both the result and the cause of the concentration of commerce, usury, and land in the past, but now, the emerging cities of "ten miles of foreign market" are regarded as an ideal paradise for the "trilogy" of refuge, pleasure, and wealth and have absorbed a large amount of commercial capital, which would typically flow into land.

Naturally, in the vast rural areas and even in the market towns far away from the city, there were still many merchants, usurers and local tyrants. Within the limits of the national upper class, the comprador class and foreigners in China, whose consumption was primarily based on the products of surplus labor in rural areas, while wealthy merchants, as the exploiters of the grass-roots laborers, might feel the need to intensify their activities in rural areas. However, because of the foreign merchants, the major landowners, and emerging financiers, a significant portion of potential rural funds has been directly or indirectly siphoned off. The concentration of land in rural areas had not ceased and had even intensified in the vicinity of the cities. However, taking into account the rate and scale of land concentration at the end of the past dynasties and also taking into account the narrow scope of commercial and usurious activities at that time, the trend of land concentration in rural China in the decades before the Anti-Japanese War was to a considerable extent eased by the fact that a large amount of floating capital was concentrated in the large cities. Undoubtedly, the continuous unrest in rural areas has affected the interest of merchants and magnates in land, the kind of property that was particularly important in the past for raising their status so as to get close to officialdom and step on the rank of the officials. In this new era, while land still holds value for those seeking power in rural areas, if he wants to be a celebrity or a dignitary in a big scene, he would certainly feel that land is not a very necessary condition anymore.

According to the aforementioned description, in modern times, the Chinese commercial capital seemed not only to have expanded its objects and scope of activities but also to have changed its methods of accumulation or to have distorted the traditional way of transformation. Therefore, the law of the movement of commercial capital in traditional China had inevitably been modified to a considerable extent in its application. However, at present, the Anti-Japanese War in this great era, at least superficially, had satirically and dramatically reversed the historic course of commercial capital and made it back onto the old path.

The new scene and dynamics of Chinese commerce, resulting from the invasion of international capital, were premised on the correlation and dependence of the overall Chinese economy on international capital; the maintenance of this external correlation or dependence is based on China's access to take advantage of the major coastal ports and the trade, finance, and industry in those ports as the pivotal point of its linkage. In the early stage of the Anti-Japanese War, the ports from the Bohai Sea to the entire South Pacific, that is, the foreign liaison ports from Tianjin to Xiamen, were largely blocked or occupied by the enemy. Meanwhile, Shanghai, because of its special characteristics, managed to maintain intermittent connections with Hong Kong and even directly with the mainland through various roundabout routes. As a result, Chinese commercial capital remained quite active for a period, experiencing unprecedented activity in foreign exchange, standard gold, and import and export trade. However, since December 1941, when Britain and the United States declared war on Japan, the foreign traffic ports from Hong Kong to Yangon were consecutively occupied by the enemy in less than half a year. As a result, almost all export and import trade was severely blocked. Meanwhile, with the occupation of ports such as Shanghai and Hong Kong, the so-called "floating capital" used in foreign exchange, securities, and local products became ineffective. Therefore, the object and scope of commercial capital activities are significantly reduced. With the severance of the foreign correlations, the dependence on and subordination to foreign capital had been accordingly detached in some respects. That is, the commercial capital in China, except for the illegal activities in the enemy-occupied areas, seemed to have acquired an independent or more classical traditional form.

In such a situation, if the industrial construction of China had a foundation, or if the existing industrial foundation of China was sufficient for commercial capital to be placed on it and to be dominated by it, then a large amount of commercial floating capital released directly or indirectly from the circulation due to the severance of foreign correlations and the stagnation of all speculative activities may be able to choose its own favorable way to be diverted to the industrial sector. Unfortunately, over ninety percent of the few existing industries in China, even those operated with foreign capital, were built in the enemy-occupied areas and had been consecutively plundered and destroyed by the enemy. Since the Anti-Japanese War, although the Chinese government had made efforts to rescue or relocate industries to the rear areas in various ways and had encouraged industrial production in various areas in the rear, the achievements were far from being sufficient to offset the significant pressure exerted by commerce on industry. Commercial capital was rampant.

At present, commercial capital is like reversing the wheel of history, retracing its old paths to develop. All the new objects and fields of commercial activities previously brought by international capital have been consecutively lost. Meanwhile, the limited domestic industries have not been able to provide any important avenues of activity for commerce. As a result, commerce has "repeated the same old tunes," taking land and land products as its most probable and profitable object of speculation. This appears to be an inevitable trend and was indeed encouraged and urged by a series of coincidental events.

For instance, firstly, in response to the demands of the government in terms of military service, road administration, and various critical government affairs during wartime, the local administrative organs at all levels were strengthened, and the

Party, government, and military organs were not only increased but also more widely distributed in the interior regions. As a result, the rear areas during the wartime, even in the more remote areas, showed a state of stability that had not been seen for years. Therefore, land in the rear areas appeared particularly stable, making it attractive to floating capital.

① (From the time of expropriation and loan in kind to the present time, when the vast rural areas were embroiled in the turmoil of the civil war, land has once again become a target that cannot attract too much attention. For this, please refer to the last chapter of the part *Forms of Chinese Land Rent*—June 1947 supplementary note.)

Secondly, the soaring prices of commodities increasingly added fuel to the fire to stimulate the barter movement. However, with the increase in wartime demand, the inevitable shortage of goods caused by the severance of external supply and inadequate transportation conditions, and the artificial scarcity caused by the large-scale hoarding and small-scale accumulation behaviors resulting from the barter movement itself, forced the owners of floating capital or special profits to shift their attention to the land, which was available everywhere.

Thirdly, large-scale hoarding and small-scale accumulation of general goods in the market were extremely important to the danger of bombing by enemy planes. Naturally, the materials and population have continuously been dispersed to the villages in the vicinity of the cities in more remote areas. This growing interest of ordinary citizens and officials in rural areas served as a significant incentive for land to become an object of investment, which made the combination of commercial capital and land capital even easier.

Fourthly, usury capital, in terms of its social role, has always served as an intermediary or auxiliary form between commercial capital and land capital. Land and land products, as the objects of commercial activities, are relatively tangible and secure. However, it is not yet easy to establish ownership of the usury, even if it is carried out by means of mortgages. Consequently, the revenue generated from usury is either reinvested in commerce or used to purchase additional land. It would be reasonable to conclude that the significant price fluctuations that occur during wartime present the most unfavourable conditions for lending capital. This is because, for a given amount of currency, the longer it is held, the less its relative value becomes in comparison to its in-kind value. Furthermore, this can impede the circulation of currency. Nevertheless, if the approach is to lend in currency and receive in kind, or to lend and receive in kind within a relatively short period, then these shortcomings can be avoided. Indeed, this is the most common form of lending currently. This form is evidently more conducive to the concentration of commercial floating capital on the land. However, the most important point is as follows.

Fifthly, although land investment is not as rapid or dynamic as commercial activities in terms of turnover, it offers three key advantages that can attract high-interest commercial capital. Firstly, the price of land is increasing at a rapid rate in conjunction with the elevated cost of goods. Secondly, the price of land products is also increasing. Ultimately, the volume of land rent can be augmented for a number of reasons, including an increase in the rental rate itself. This can be achieved by capitalising on the backwardness and irrationality of Chinese tenancy relationships.

The transformation of commercial capital into land is significantly facilitated by the reduction in the size of the commercial activity object and the rapid increase in price. It is evident that in this transformation of commercial capital, the re-emergence of land as a significant form of property, coupled with the prevalence of social and political factors that favour land concentration, should not be overlooked. Land is, by its very nature, a fixed and immobile asset. Consequently, its transfer, absent the influence of non-economic coercion, is a challenging endeavour, particularly when seeking to satisfy the voracious appetites of merchants and tycoons.

Furthermore, it is important to acknowledge that despite the fact that commercial capital primarily focuses on land and land products, it should not be assumed that all commercial capital is ultimately transformed into land capital. The accumulation of land rent does not necessarily cease to be transformed into commercial capital. Indeed, the accumulation of land rent can serve not only to enhance the capital strength of commercial activities but also, indirectly, to increase the concentration of land through the expansion of commerce. However, the core issue is not the extent to which commercial capital will be converted into land capital, leading to the capitalisation and concentration of land. Rather, it is whether commercial capital must be converted into land without any other more favourable method. By grasping this key point, we can better understand the extent of the harm caused by current commercial capital and the limited effectiveness of the current strategies for controlling commercial capital.

35.5 Dangers and Limits of Present Commercial Capital

The current situation is characterised by a multitude of risks and challenges associated with the presence of commercial capital.

However, an analysis of the emotional and rational comments made by ordinary individuals regarding the prevalent behaviours of commercial capital suggests that the penalties imposed upon it are not commensurate with the extent of its actions. The assessed risks and hazards appear to be significantly lower than the actual risks and hazards that it has caused. This implies that if commercial capital is held responsible for the current social and economic challenges, it seems that commentators have yet to identify its actual responsibilities.

At present, the soaring prices of commodities have become an urgent problem for both the whole society and the government's finances. Because of the personal suffering of overcoming this difficult problem, it is naturally easy for the whole country to lament and detest the wealthy merchants and tycoons who manipulate the prices without human or national conscience. No one will come to the defense of the commercial capital when the soaring prices are attributed to its unreasonable and illegal activities. But the most concerning aspect is that if the commercial capital of merchants or quasi-merchants bears too many superficial accusations in this regard, its more essential destructive effects in other aspects are likely to be overlooked. Up until today, although the destructive effects of commercial capital have become very evident from various perspectives, there is no room for suspicion. However, the general public is still reluctant to reveal the truth according to its essence.

"Manipulation" and "hoarding" are the commonest crimes imposed on merchants. A step further of these crimes is merely the blocking of the general process of circulation, withholding goods that could have been quickly supplied to the market, thereby creating a situation of supply shortages that drives prices up. However, if criticism is limited to this extent, we must differentiate between legitimate and illegitimate merchants. An illegitimate merchant can easily find numerous excuses to rationalize and legitimize his behavior. In fact, in the case of the individual merchant, whether he is truly "hoarding" or "manipulating," does not necessarily depend on his ethical conception regarding such behavior but rather depends on the necessary conditions he possesses for such behavior. We can say that, as a merchant, within the limit of being one of all merchants and within the limit of his capital being one of all commercial capital, his personal intentions are essentially those of the capital he uses for commerce, and this individual capital of his is, in turn, influenced by the overall trend of the entire commercial capital. Therefore, while the most blatant illegal acts of a small number of merchants are severely punished, the destructive effects of the whole commercial capital are tolerated. As a result, this is similar to when we once viewed certain ruthless Japanese soldiers as Japanese imperialism to overthrow them, or we regarded some stubborn Northern Warlords as all warlords to overthrow them. Even if those whom they wished to overthrow were to "fall by the hand of the sword" and "fall by the sound of the voice," they could not have any decisive impact on the whole of Japanese imperialism and the warlords. It is the same as some certain specific merchants in relation to the whole commercial capital.

If it is asserted that certain specific merchants engage in illicit activities that impede the flow of goods and raise prices on occasion, and that such activities are not only enabled by the entirety of commercial capital in the process of circulation but also supported by the destructive role of the entirety of commercial capital in the process of production. The criminal activities of commercial capital in the context of circulation are predicated upon the criminal actions it has already perpetrated in the sphere of production. It has been established that Chinese commerce has exerted a dominant and controlling influence over industry, thereby limiting the scope for its own development. From the perspective of general causality, it can be argued that if the industrial sector is underdeveloped, the commercial sector will also be underdeveloped. It can therefore be concluded that the development of industrial capital is a prerequisite for the growth of commercial capital. It is difficult to envisage any objection to the proposition that an increase in the number of products to be produced will inevitably lead to a corresponding increase in commercial opportunities. However, as we recognise that commerce is the master of industry in a pre-capitalist society and the servant of industry in a capitalist society, it becomes evident that, regardless of our subjective views or aspirations for commercial capital, commercial capital itself takes the underdevelopment of industrial capital as a historical prerequisite for its own development. This phenomenon can be observed in any society or country in the world.

Of course, there are more fundamental and extensive reasons for China's industrial backwardness, and the detrimental effects of commercial capital in the role of traditional international capital obviously cannot be overlooked. Whereas, as previously implied, the commercial capital, after the opening of the five-port trading, and the commercial capital before that time, play destructive roles of destruction in the process of production in distinct ways. Namely, the former was subordinate to the international capital, on the one hand, acting as a servant for the international commercial and industrial capital, selling their manufactured goods and sourcing raw materials for them, while on the other hand, it acted as the master of the national industries. The latter adopted a more independent form, more directly and concentratly hijacking and manipulating all domestic industries. There is no essential difference between these two ways of industrial destruction; however, in terms of perception, the former is more perceivable, while the latter seems to be particularly able to obstruct people's perception. Therefore, even someone with a bit of economic common sense can convincingly discuss the disadvantages of commercial capital in the process of circulation, while a scholar who claims to be an economist may struggle to grasp the disadvantages of commercial capital in the process of production. Perhaps for this very reason, the current commercial capital, which has reverted to its traditional form, has been accused of its crimes only in the process of circulation. However, the reasons why these crimes occur in the process of circulation, which should be explored in the process of production, have generally been ignored.

The control of commercial capital over industrial capital or production was originally a characteristic of the classical style. However, in the context of the war, this control function has expanded to an unprecedented extent, capitalising on the favourable circumstances. Its activities in the field of industrial production effectively stifled and undermined the vitality of both new and established forms of industrial production. It can be reasonably deduced that a conventionally operated new-style factory, unless it undergoes a partial and ingenious transformation in its nature, will inevitably lead to its downfall. This is due to the fact that it will be unable to compete with other, more efficient forms of production, such as the purchasing and storage of raw materials, rather than the manufacturing of them. There has been a gradual increase in state-owned and provincial-owned enterprises. In order to assess whether these enterprises are prosperous, it is necessary to analyse the proportion of the commercial sector to the productive sector. In such instances, the paradoxical effect of commercial capital encroaching upon industrial capital manifested as a façade for the rescue of industrial capital. Concurrently, the loans provided by the government to salvage private industries through banking institutions became subservient to commercial capital in a multitude of circuitous manners with regard to the technologies of industrial commercialisation.

In the field of agricultural production, the destructive effects of commercial capital appear to have manifested in a more circuitous manner. The land and its products represent the primary object of commercial activities, which have the potential to disrupt the stagnation observed in rural areas. The frequent transfer of land and the surge in land prices will have a direct or indirect impact on the increase of land rents. In general, the costs incurred by owner-peasants and tenant peasants in maintaining their land holdings have increased, while their expenditures on non-land inputs, including seeds, agricultural tools, fertilisers, animal power, manpower, and even irrigation, have been reduced or, in some cases, eliminated. Consequently, the scale of agricultural reproduction will inevitably diminish alongside the gradual development of commercial capital. The destructive effects of commercial capital are such that even if the government were to offer greater support to owner-peasants and extend loans in rural areas, the reality is that agricultural loans have already been converted into commercial capital, either partially or fully, through a variety of indirect means.

The destructive effects of commercial capital in industrial production have created the premise for the accumulation of capital in two distinct forms: large-scale hoarding and small-scale accumulation. As the scale of social reproduction continues to diminish on an annual basis, the greater the inconsistency in supply and demand, and the more pronounced the commercial hoarding activities will become. It is evident that hoarding has a significant impact on rising prices, which in turn exerts considerable pressure on production. However, it is important to distinguish between cause and effect, and to recognise that while circulation is a potential hazard, the production process itself also presents significant risks. Indeed, it could be argued that production is of greater importance and fundamental to the economy than circulation. If the commercial capital did not impede or inhibit production activities, its activities in the circulation process would be considerably constrained.

It appears that the complex relationship between inflation and other economic factors should be addressed at this juncture. The prevailing view is that the destructive force of commercial capital appears to be driven by an involuntary movement in line with the tide of inflation. Given that inflation causes prices to rise and that rising prices lead to commercial capital becoming active, it can be surmised that the merchant class must have a reason to exploit this phenomenon to condemn inflation while proclaiming their innocence to the world. However, this line of reasoning is likely to prove confusing to the general public, but not sufficiently so to obscure the truth. Let us call upon history to bear witness. The economic disintegration and fragmentation that occurred during the mid-periods of the various Chinese dynasties were not necessarily attributed to the inflation that occurred during those respective periods. Conversely, the proliferation of commercial capital has led to a significant increase in the scope and extent of consumption. Concurrently, the diminution of agricultural surplus products resulting from these activities engenders the disjunction between production and consumption in society and the destruction of production and the foundation of rents and taxes on consumption, thereby precipitating the disarray of the currency system. It is evident that the disarray of the currency system may markedly reinforce the momentum of commercial capital, enabling it to "fish in troubled waters." Nevertheless, we are unable to reverse the causal relationship; commercial capital is originally precipitated by inflation.

It is currently unnecessary to disguise the fact that there has been a notable increase in the rate of inflation in currency. Nevertheless, an examination of the historical development of currency issuance since the Anti-Japanese War reveals that even those who adhere to the theory of phenomenal causality and disregard the underlying issues of production can discern that the destructive impact of commercial capital activities has shaped the evolutionary trajectory. It could be argued that the current Anti-Japanese War is so extensive in its scope and consumption that it is essentially beyond China's existing production scale and conditions. In other words, it is inevitable that difficulties will arise in meeting the demand for production to supply consumption and in generating sufficient government revenue to offset expenditures. It thus appears that the commercial capital should not be held responsible for the increased issuance of currency in this context. This, however, is also an argument that is based on a false premise. In this context, it is essential to differentiate between the consumption patterns of the general population and the consumption directly related to the war effort. This distinction is crucial to understanding the underlying contradictions. A comprehensive and comparative observation of the consumption patterns in the front and rear areas of the war reveals that unreasonable consumption hindered both the achievement of victory and the production of goods and services necessary for the war effort. It is therefore reasonable to conclude that the merchants and the capital they use bear responsibility for the creation and manifestation of all unreasonable consumption.

The destruction of production by the activities of commercial capital has existed since the past. The difference between contemporary commercial activities and those of the past lies not so much in their exploitation of the special circumstances of the wartime conditions—such as the destructive effects of war and the urgent needs for materials and inflation—but rather in their utilization of modern financial organizations of China, along with social status and relations. This situation is further complicated by their ties to foreign economic and political connections. Additionally, they capitalize on the expansion and deepening of currency economic relations in rural areas. From these perspectives, it is evident that the current unprecedented rampancy of commercial capital is not a coincidence. If we allow it to develop smoothly and naturally, its destructive effects are likely to lead to crises similar to those that arose after the mid-period of all Chinese dynasties. However, at this point, we cannot ignore the impact of the government's restraint on commercial capital activities in the circulation process in recent years.

Since the third year of the Anti-Japanese War, the significant pressure exerted by the price problem has compelled the central and local governments to implement a range of general and specific policies and methods aimed at stabilising prices and regulating commercial capital. These include the blocking of the circulation of goods between provinces and counties, the establishment of parity organs at all levels, and the creation of the Central Bureau of Materials. The Economic Committee of the Theater (which was subsequently abolished and its functions assumed by the Economic Operations Department) was responsible for the establishment of institutions for the purchase of materials at all levels by enterprises in various provinces. In addition, it promoted various monopoly undertakings, including the establishment of a new tax system, and implemented strict controls over transportation and finance. The aforementioned policies and methods are largely designed to address the issue of rising prices. When viewed in isolation, their positive impact on the current economic situation is evident. However, while acknowledging their effectiveness, it is crucial to consider the potential limitations of their impact, particularly the possibility of adverse effects during their implementation.

In a previous statement, it was asserted that the individual capital activities of a merchant are subject to the overall dynamics of the entire commercial capital. Piecemeal prevention is an inadequate approach to addressing the issue, as it may inadvertently exacerbate the problematic behaviour of commercial capital by impeding the commercial activities of specific merchants, regions, or sectors. For example, the inter-provincial and inter-county control obstacles may result in some losses and inconveniences for the commerce or merchants directly under their control in the short term. However, this has the effect of increasing the difficulty of circulation and has the same impact as hoarding. Even if the government's intention is to purchase materials with the aim of stabilising prices and eliminating the monopoly of merchants, thereby adjusting the balance between social supply and demand, it is evident that the government lacks both the financial resources and the robust procurement, storage and distribution institutions that would be required to implement such a strategy. Furthermore, given that it is frequently driven by the need for immediate financial resources, it is inevitable that it will result in the promotion of commercial activities. Thus far, the monopoly and the various new tax systems aimed at suppressing merchants have only succeeded in providing merchants with a stronger rationale for raising prices. Furthermore, the financial control that has been gradually strengthened since the fourth year of the Anti-Japanese War has not been as effective as it could have been. In conclusion, the aforementioned policies and methods for controlling commercial capital are, on the one hand, evidently founded upon China's underdeveloped economic foundation. The political units at all levels, the various economic departments, and the various geographical areas are divided into different routes. It is evident that the strict organisation, determination of procedures, and division of powers and responsibilities required for effective control cannot be achieved in China without significant improvements in technology. It is because, even if we were to attempt it, it would be impossible to compel a young person, whose physiological organisation is not yet fully developed, to undertake the responsibilities typically associated with adulthood. The modern controlled economy emerges at a highly organised stage of the development of the modern capitalist economy. There is still scope for improvement in our methods of control, which are currently limited. It is possible to allow for the establishment of that form of inconsistent or uncoordinated control methods.

Furthermore, on the same backward economic basis, commercial capital is not only likely to flourish in the gaps of the aforementioned incomplete and loosely structured controls, but it can also use its multi-controlling function over industry or production to reinforce the restrictions on various production undertakings.

To illustrate, numerous production undertakings that are subject to the policy of nurturing, including the planting of tung trees and tea, the various necessities in the mining industry, and the production of tungsten, antimony, coal, iron, gold, and silver, are all monopolised by commercial capital under the pretext of state control.

These facts collectively indicate the following two points:

First, commercial capital in China is distinct in nature and function from that in advanced capitalist countries. Consequently, the measures for its control cannot be identical. Even if technical conditions warrant attention, a fundamental remedy cannot be achieved by focusing on technology alone. Similarly, while efforts in the process of circulation may be necessary, a fundamental solution cannot be found by focusing exclusively on that process.
Secondly, the efficacy of any control method cannot be determined in isolation; rather, it is contingent upon the fulfilment of the requisite prerequisites for its implementation and the extent to which other concurrently implemented methods can reinforce it. The aforementioned monopoly system, in conjunction with transportation and financial controls, represents a potent instrument for curbing the activities of commercial capital. However, the efficacy of such measures cannot be contingent upon the transient interests of those who exercise control over them.

35.6 Limits of the Activities of Commercial Capital and Possible Means for Its Transformation into Industrial Capital

The activities of Chinese commercial capital are based on the characteristics it has acquired from Chinese society and the special favorable historical conditions it has acquired. Then, for its limits, it is necessary to consider these aspects.

As a matter of fact, in the recent stage, the commercial capital appears to be a spent force. This trend is bound to give us two ambiguous views. First, the control methods have indeed been effective, and if they strengthen and tighten the control accordingly, commercial capital will surely be subdued. Second, it seems that commercial capital is on the decline; even if it is allowed to continue its activities, it will inevitably fulfill the old adage, "To do evil often, one must face the consequences oneself." We need not rush to determine the correctness of the two views; instead, let us first expose the fact that commercial capital has indeed been on the decline. The commercial capital, in accordance with its own laws of movement, will, as we previously discussed, gradually reduce the scale of production in society, which will have a twofold effect on commercial capital itself. That is, the objects of its activities will be reduced, and the purchasing power of the general society will thus decrease. Wherever we go in that metropolis or town of abnormal prosperity, if we gaze a little, we will find that the number of industrial products being turned over by commercial capital is constantly decreasing, and the auction shops filling the streets and alleyways are obviously not trading newly produced products but rather adapting the old products to the market with lower purchasing power. It has become increasingly difficult to find buyers for slightly more expensive items. Aside from the wealthy, powerful individuals who continue to indulge in immediate consumption and entertainment and maintain a rather extravagant scene, including producers, civil servants, soldiers, and other large social groups, are constantly lowering their living standards and narrowing the circle of needs. Certainly, has commercial capital, guided by profits, not shifted the object of its activity toward the original products in rural areas and the land from which these products originate? Where there are profits, There are its destructive effects. As time goes on, the more commercial capital seeks to maintain and expand its own interests, the greater its destructive effects will be on the interests of the general production of society. When its profits are achieved at the expense of the general interests of society and the destruction of social production, it will ultimately realize that once the interests of the general production of society have been irretrievably sacrificed, its own interests and existence will soon be extinct. This so-called tragic phenomenon of "a louse will die if its host dies" has historically been described as "the destruction of social vitality and the disintegration of commercial relations from the root."

Perhaps, as the movement of commercial capital enters a downturn, the adoption of various coercive intervention methods may yield some effects. However, if the damage caused by such interventions of commercial capital can be compensated by society, then increasing pressure on commercial capital will correspondingly inflict equal or even greater destruction on the interests of production of the whole of society. In fact, the outcomes of previous controls over commercial capital activities in terms of transportation, monopolies, and finance in China have already illustrated the validity of this logic.

At this point, it seems we have drawn a very pessimistic conclusion: allowing commercial capital to operate itself is too dangerous, while arbitrary intervention may similarly accelerate its path to destruction. Since, as previously discussed, its destruction will inevitably lead to the collapse of the entire social economy, is the current socioeconomic structure in China destined to reach the so-called situation of "how can it do well? It is merely falling into the water together"?

However, the aforementioned pessimistic historical facts also point to a reasonable approach for managing commercial capital.

The existence and activities of commercial capital are contingent upon the existence of specific social conditions. The consequence of this is that society itself is the unfortunate victim of such actions, whether they result in the collapse of the system or are actively encouraged to do so. Furthermore, throughout Chinese history, commercial capital has repeatedly played a destructive role in the development of the overall economy. However, in recent times, the commercial capital of European and American countries has increasingly contributed to the growth of industrial capital. It would be erroneous, therefore, to regard the activities of commercial capital as universally treasonous and heretical. Even if the prohibition of commercial capital is confined to its illicit and irrational aspects, it is possible to achieve effective results without inadvertently leading to a situation in which all parties are adversely affected. It would be prudent to pursue the course of action recommended by modern economic science, with a view to discerning the manner in which the law of the movement of commercial capital manifests itself, and then guiding it in accordance with the circumstances. Subsequently, the terms "interfere," "control," and even "oppress" can only transform commercial capital from an unreasonable and illegal scope of activity to a scope conducive to general economic development under certain conditions and under the premise that certain historical prerequisites have been established. This so-called historical prerequisite is the elimination of the possibility of the transformation of commercial capital into land and consequently into usury.

History has taught us that the destruction of agricultural production by commercial capital in the past started from land. The predicament caused by the excessive production cost of the peasant masses on the land prices and land rents, in turn, opened up a paradise of sins for the usury industry. In recent years, with the reduction of the scope and objects of commerce, land and land products have become potential favorable outlets for commercial capital to break the stagnation situation. The implementation of various urban control policies, combined with the general public's hatred for capital owners, has "driven the fish into deep waters" and has led to frequent traces of wealthy merchants who have fled and sought profits in the vicinity of the large rear cities and even in remote areas. "The pressure is directed towards the areas where the resistance is weak," and the tightening of control has led to a loophole regarding land, and the tighter the control has become, the more significant the destructive effects on production in rural areas cannot be ignored.

Therefore, I conclude that, in order to control commerce during wartime and prevent destruction to the overall economy, it is necessary to recognize Chinese socioeconomic laws and sever the relationship between commercial capital and land capitalization. How to sever this relationship is a long story, but it should always be ensured that non-producers are not allowed to purchase land or own land above a certain limit, while producers should not be deprived of their land or allowed to retain land below a certain limit. Only then will the accumulation of commercial capital not accelerate the destruction in rural areas, and the activities of commercial capital owners regarding land products will be significantly restricted. Once this approach of grasping the law of the movement of commercial capital in China and taking fundamental treatments is put into practice, and with the various controls imposed on commercial capital—such as those related to transportation, finance, monopoly, and taxation—will not only avoid indirectly destroying the basic undertakings of production but will also, on the contrary, encourage the accumulation of commercial capital to be directed towards socially beneficial uses, namely, towards Industrial Capital. On that occasion, various methods and policies for rewarding industry are likely to be particularly effective.

In short, from the perspective of the general development of society, commercial capital is not necessarily a capital that remains in the sphere of circulation, nor is the merchant necessarily a man who cannot change his way of life. Moreover, under certain historical prerequisites that have been created, commercial capital is not only a capital that can be cursed, nor is the merchant a man that can be cursed. It or he can even perform social functions comparable to those of Industrial Capital and industrialists.

In modern times, the commercial capital has played a significant role in promoting industrial development in advanced countries. When the owners of commercial capital realize that they can no longer maintain their interests through the deception and plunder of buying cheap and selling dear, at least some of them quickly transformed from the circulation process to the production process, becoming producers and capitalists of production. It is also in this situation that Industrial Capital gradually comes to dominate commercial capital, leading to a corresponding change in the social function of commercial capital. It is no longer a destroyer of industry or production but rather a facilitator of it.

It is evident that the transformation of commercial capital into industrial capital, much like the commercialisation of industrial capital, is not achieved spontaneously by individual capital owners. Specific social and historical circumstances oblige commercial capital to gravitate towards more propitious conditions. The production of commercial capital, or the capitalisation of productive capital, is a significant issue that is inextricably linked to social and historical change and is undoubtedly a complex phenomenon. Among the numerous conditions that must be met in order to achieve this historical objective, one of the most fundamental and decisive is the reform of the relations of land ownership and use. It is a near-universal phenomenon that countries have first completed land reform and then embarked on the process of the industrial revolution based on the changed land relations. The specific content and procedural aspects of land reform have varied across countries, reflecting the influence of diverse natural and historical conditions. However, the liberation of peasants from feudal bondage, the establishment of a reasonable and legal basis for tenancy relationships, and the guarantee that land ownership does not fundamentally hinder its use of land were similar objectives across countries. On the surface, it would appear that the peasants in China today are not as constrained by the land as their counterparts in Western Europe and Japan were during their land reforms. Nevertheless, the objective circumstances resulting from the forms of land ownership and tenancy relationships render them no less dependent on the land than they are constrained by the regulations of pure feudalism. As they increasingly rely on the land as their sole source of income, the land itself becomes a more effective means of accumulating wealth, functioning as a primary territory for the expansion of commercial capital.

In recent years, in view of the increasingly serious financial and economic problems, both the government and the public have come to recognise the need to reassess and reconsider all the previous economic understandings and economic plans. Consequently, there has been a gradual shift in focus from the circulation process to the production process, from a technical perspective to a social perspective, and an increasing awareness of the interconnections between commercial and land issues. The issue of the law of the movement of commercial capital in China, which I have previously referenced, may be an issue that has been conceptualised by all of you but has not yet been systematised. My role is merely to articulate the intentions of the people in question. In the economy of the Principles of People's Livelihood, Dr. Sun Yat-sen placed particular emphasis on the issues of land and capital, identifying them as the cornerstones of national financial and economic policy. He was fully aware that in order to address the full range of economic challenges associated with modernisation, it was essential to consider the fundamental characteristics of

Chinese society and the distinctive dynamics of the various economic forms within the Chinese context.

Chapter 36
The Laws of Circulation and Conversion Between Commercial and Industrial Capital

36.1 Core of the Issue

Among the current economic issues in China, the circulation between commercial and industrial capital is of particular significance, representing a fundamental and essential aspect of the country's economic landscape. The practical understanding of this issue can be found in the unbalanced development between industry and commerce. This can be defined as the abnormal situation where industrial capital is too weak while commercial capital is excessively inflated. The objective of this book is to examine the means of transforming commercial capital into industrial capital, which necessitates an elucidation of the interrelationship between the natures of commercial and industrial capital.

Those preoccupied with the prevailing economic circumstances in China have initiated a process of addressing the long-neglected issue of the excessive expansion of commercial capital. It appears that this phenomenon first emerged during wartime, particularly in the second and third years of the Anti-Japanese War. It is unsurprising that the issue of commercial capital has attracted attention, given the circumstances. However, upon closer examination of its objective aspects, it becomes evident that the circumstances accompanying this issue in modern Chinese society are more indicative of normalcy than abnormality. Rather than representing the onset of something severe, they represent the continuation or development of severity.

Since the commencement of China's modernisation process, this issue has been of paramount importance. Nevertheless, it is only within the last decade that this issue has been acknowledged and brought to the attention of a limited number of individuals. It is a common human tendency to treat issues that have not previously been considered as if they were objectively non-existent. It is therefore unsurprising that our discussion of this issue today is of significant historical interest. Indeed, it is challenging to elucidate a significant social historical issue in a disjunctive and isolated manner.

Y. Wang, *The Basic Theory of Chinese Economy*,
https://doi.org/10.1007/978-981-95-6330-2_36

36.2 Basic Understandings of Circulation of Capital

If we understand commercial capital as distinct from industrial capital, we can identify a social watershed between the two. In a society where industry had developed and become the dominant force in society, commerce was continuously transformed to meet the needs of industry. In this context, the merchant played a role in the division of labor for the industrial capitalist, with the circulation process of commerce integrated into the overall production process. Commercial gains, or profits, are derived from total industrial profits. Commercial activities cannot exceed the limits permitted by industrial capital, which simultaneously urges them not to fall too far below these limits. The regulator there into is the law of equalization of profit. If the profits of industrial capital are lower than that of commercial capital, capital in society will flow from industry to commerce, leading to a decrease in the profits of commercial capital relative to the general profit level. Conversely, if there is a surplus of industrial capital over commercial capital, the same law of profit will compel capital to flow back. The circulation of capital in such a society is less likely to encounter issues. Even if issues do arise under specific circumstances, their nature will be entirely different from the circulation issues concerning commercial and industrial capital in China that we are currently discussing.

In a society with underdeveloped industry, that is to say, in a pre-capitalist society, the relationship between commerce and industry assumes a form that is markedly distinct from that observed in more developed economic systems. Not only has commerce never been integrated into the broader social process of production, but the disparate and autonomous industries within society continue to exist in a primitive state, rendering it implausible for them to form an organic social production process or to gain sufficient social advantage to dominate commerce. Conversely, commerce can leverage its relatively stable position to exert control over product pricing, thereby exerting dominance over the general industry of society from outside the production process. The greater the potential for commerce to exert control over industry, the more it can engage in its exploitative practices of purchasing goods at low prices and selling them at high prices. In this context, if it is asserted that there is still profit to be made in the industry (which is essentially a transformation of the wages of labor), it would be more accurate to use the term 'profit' to refer to the gain of the producer. However, this profit or gain will evidently be reversed as if it were distributed according to the principles of commercial profit. In broad-sense economics, a law is posited which states that in a capitalist society, industrial profit regulates commercial profit, while in pre-capitalist societies, commercial profit regulates industrial profit. It is not possible to establish the capitalist law of profit in any pre-capitalist society. Consequently, the circulation between commercial and industrial capital in a pre-capitalist society cannot be understood or addressed according to the principles of free competition.

However, the issue we are about to discuss requires a deeper understanding of its preconditions. When a society passes from a pre-capitalist form to a capitalist form, it is certain that one will encounter some confusing and ambiguous economic phenomena if one looks at them from the perspective of the circulation of capital. Industry in relation to trade, as well as industrial capital in relation to commercial capital, and the profits of industrial capital in relation to those of commercial capital, may in some cases have established the appearance of modernisation but not changed their past nature; in other cases, although some aspects of their past nature may have changed, such changes were not sufficient to establish all the relations of modernisation. In such situations, we need to use scientific analysis to grasp the essence of the problems by looking beyond the surface phenomena of the problems.

36.3 New Appearance of Chinese Commercial Capital in Classical Form

Before the beginning of the process of modernisation, commercial capital in China always had the peculiarity of being isolated from productive capital, and this peculiarity was largely based on the feudal system of the landlord economy in China. We do not need to explain here why our feudal system did not bring into play the basic factors of its landlord economy, but gradually developed the basic factors of its landlord economy, and we can only say that in the landlord economy the relationship between commercial capital and landed property is completely different from that in the landlord economy. For example, in Western European countries, merchants and seigneurs, i.e. commercial capital and landed property, have historically been in opposition to each other. Land was acquired through inheritance or enfeoffment, supported by systems such as the equal field system and primogeniture. But for those civilians without noble lineage and status, especially merchants, land ownership was excluded. For this reason, the capital accumulated by merchants in trade had a greater potential to be transformed into productive capital. On the contrary, Chinese commercial capital in the form of the landlord economy had a close relationship with land ownership because of the following facts: first, merchants could trade land freely (with only a few dynasties imposing restrictions on land trade for short periods), thus establishing a channel between commercial capital and land ownership. Second, most of the goods that merchants traded were the products of the land that peasants contributed to the imperial court in the form of taxes. These products typically entered the treasury in the form of currency through the process of circulation. This effectively created an indirect, circuitous bridge of convenience between trade and landed property. Thirdly, merchants could acquire land without restriction and use it as a stepping stone to get close to the officialdom and embark on an official career. This led to close links between officials and merchants within the social relations of production, thus strongly supporting the relationship between commercial capital and landed property. Of course, we cannot deny that China has historically pursued a policy of emphasising agriculture and restricting trade, just as we cannot overlook the fact that merchants in Western European countries also acquired a significant amount of land in the early modern period. This does not, however, undermine the basic thesis. On the contrary, it can be strengthened from this contrasting perspective. Unfortunately, space does not permit a more detailed explanation here.

In fact, the close link between Chinese trade and landed property was not only due to the difficulty of directly utilising the capital accumulated in trade for industrial purposes, but also because landed property absorbed too much social capital, preventing trade activities from expanding into foreign trade. On the one hand, this was clearly the result of the merchants' thirst for adventure and profit being drawn towards land ownership. On the other hand, the political power of merchants was decentralised by their division into landowners, leading to a lack of influence over national foreign trade policy. The interplay of these two factors contributed to the underdevelopment of foreign trade in China, which in turn had a fundamental impact on the underdevelopment of industry. Here we can also see how superficial and negligent it is for general economic historians of China to use geographical factors to explain China's underdeveloped foreign trade and industry.

When Chinese trade remained tied to the foundations of the landlord economy, helplessly repeating its historical patterns amid the rise and fall of successive dynasties. While the commercial capital of Western European countries, having been excluded from land ownership, had expanded outwards, gradually disintegrating and undermining the foundation of the landlord economy through continuous accumulation in foreign trade. In the process, a new method of production was established, and with it a new way of expanding foreign trade. As a result, China's foreign trade, unable to develop autonomously, was forced to develop passively.

In the period before and after the five-port trade, Chinese trade underwent a transformation akin to that of a mummy exposed to the air. This transformation, however, was not due to a fundamental change in the socioeconomic basis of Chinese society, but rather to a change in social relations with the outside world. As a result, although foreign trade had diluted or even transformed the interest of mercantile capital in land ownership, all mercantile capital accumulation, firstly, came from domestic sources, acquired through comprador foreign trade relations under less favourable and stricter conditions, rather than directly from abroad. Secondly, in order to secure this kind of comprador trade, foreign countries destroyed or undermined all the necessary conditions for Chinese industrial development through various kinds of unequal treaties. Thirdly, the original social and economic organisations in the coastal metropolises, where certain comprador traders and their comprador enterprises operate, and even in certain cities in the interior and their surroundings connected by new means of transport, have been transformed and given the appearance of capitalism; in the vast rural areas, only the natural link between handicraft and agriculture has been destroyed, while the other forms of land ownership and use, the basic part of feudal relations of production, still stubbornly persist. Consequently, in the context of increasing and widening commodity-money relations, although the importance of land has diminished and its attraction has been replaced by new profit-making enterprises, the most variable commercial capital, or the accumulation that commerce can earn, has remained unlikely to be redirected into industry. It is true that we have taken advantage of the conflicts and contradictions between the international imperialist countries during periods of their slackening pressure to achieve some small industrial successes. However, These achievements were not sufficient to change the social superiority of trade over industry and collapsed in a matter of moments under the intensification of this pressure.

Therefore, we know that in the past hundred years, Chinese commercial capital has undoubtedly taken on a new guise in its classical form. But this new face was more of a disguise. It did not establish modern relations with industry, and it did not serve Chinese industry, but rather served foreign industry at the expense of our domestic industry. Under these circumstances, it is clearly unrealistic for us to expect a normal flow of capital between our trade and industry.

36.4 Industrial Capitalization of Commercial Capital and Commercial Capitalization of Industrial Capital in Wartime

After the outbreak of the Anti-Japanese War, the situation was somewhat different. With the loss of the major foreign markets on the coast and the blockade of foreign trade, Chinese commercial capital had to temporarily shed its new appearance or disguise to serve Chinese domestic industries rather than foreign industries. Meanwhile, the shortage of common goods and military supplies caused by the blockade of foreign trade gave a great boost to national industry. At the same time, the unequal contracts that had always bound Chinese industry were invisibly abolished, and the government, in order to fulfil the tasks of the Anti-Japanese War and the founding of a new country, made greater efforts to facilitate and support industry. Under these circumstances, if there were still problems with Industrial Capital, it was due to the lack of funds in society as a whole rather than to the unbalanced development of commercial and Industrial Capital. However, contrary to expectations, it was precisely because of the overexpansion of commercial capital that our Industrial Capital was severely depressed at that time.

During the Anti-Japanese War, amidst rising inflation, Chinese commercial capital took advantage of supply shortages and soaring prices to accumulate a significant amount of assets in the form of currency. However, despite this accumulation, merchants were still reluctant to transform themselves into factory owners and their capital into Industrial Capital, as the commercial operators in early modern Western European countries did. Their assets—whether in the form of currency, commodities for sale, or the production of commercial equipment—remained trapped within the circulation process. Merchants expanded the object of commercial activities to the land, which seemingly restored the connection between commerce and land ownership. However, in today's highly developed commodity-money relationships, it is more commercial speculation. In other words, whether the capital accumulated in commerce is directly invested in commercial activities or indirectly funneled through land ownership back into commerce, it is primarily aimed at self-expansion, resulting in the phenomenon of a surplus of floating capital in commerce.

However, why is not this surplus floating capital directed towards industry? An obvious obstacle is that the industrial profit is significantly lower compared with commercial profit. It seems that for this reason, not only is it not easy for the commercial capital to be converted into Industrial Capital, but even a little bit of industrial that the government has painstakingly supported in many ways has a tendency to be commercialized. According to reports in the newspapers, many public and private factories regarded their factory sites as land and viewed their machines, tools, and raw materials as hoards.

The inverse relationship between commercial and Industrial Capital, which contradicted general expectations, could easily leave us with the impression that the social economy in China had created conditions favorable for the aforementioned law of average profit. In other words, it suggested that China had undergone a process of capitalism, with its social capital flowing into sectors that yielded higher profits in accordance with the laws of movement of capitalism. Therefore, many people accordingly inferred that if we could use financial policies to restrict the profits of commercial capital and simultaneously increase industrial profits in various ways, commercial capital would naturally flow into industry. In reality, the issue was far more complex.

The Chinese commercial capital refused to be transformed into an Industrial Capital and instead commercialised Industrial Capital. According to the laws of movement of capitalism, when capital is transferred to trade, industry should experience a shortage of capital, leading to the reduction of enterprises, the reduction of products and the reduction of supply, which will consequently increase profits. Conversely, in commerce, profits should fall as the absolute relative increase of its capital to the goods is reversed. However, our current reality is exactly the opposite. It seems that the more capital is concentrated and absorbed in commerce, the higher the profits generated by that commerce. It is true that we have to follow the usual explanation of ordinary people and even general economists, which is that we are at war and everything is inevitably abnormal, but even if the impact of war is significant, it is still not enough to explain this abnormality. At best, it can be seen as a "perversion" of Chinese society in wartime. We can imagine how many countries are involved in the war, but none of them have encountered the same problems between their commercial and Industrial Capital as we have in China. When the theories were developed to such an extent, our economists, who advocate capitalist financial policies to solve the current problems of capital, in turn generalised this situation as the "backwardness of the Chinese economy" in order to avoid the shortcomings of their own theories. But once they had got around this deficiency, they temporarily and unconsciously dropped the "backwardness of the Chinese economy" thesis without recognising any contradiction. Then they went back to characterising the war economy of China and the nature of the various economic problems arising from it with various labels of capitalism.

In fact, the "perverted" development of current commercial capital in China serves to illustrate a law of the Broad-sense Economics: the more commercial capital develops independently from the overall production process, the less industrial capital will develop; that is, the development of the former is inversely proportional to that of the latter. This law works under the economic conditions of pre-capitalist societies. We certainly cannot deny the existence of capitalist factors in the Chinese economy, but that existence, in terms of scale and proportion, has obviously not reached the level of preventing that law from working. When discussing the circulation between commercial and industrial capital in China, we should always keep this fundamental viewpoint in mind. On one hand, we might regard the high rate of profit in commerce as the reason for the expansion of the scale of its activities by absorbing capital. However, on the other hand, we must understand that this so-called high rate of commercial profit is neither in the sense of capitalism nor formed in isolation; it has the overall social economic basis for its existence.

36.5 Prerequisites for Solving the Problems of Industrial Capital

In the past six months, the government has indeed made considerable efforts to promote state-owned industries and subsidise nascent private industries. On the one hand, it has encouraged the industrialisation of commercial capital; on the other, it has tried to prevent the commercialisation of industrial capital. To this day, the difficulties continue to escalate. The reason for this is most easily explained by the fact that commerce can still maintain a high rate of profit. But doesn't the government impose restrictions and crack down on commerce through taxation, finance and various price control measures? This is the crux of the matter. The modern relationship between industry and commerce has been established in a country; industry itself has the function of regulating commercial capital. Although it may occasionally need the help of capital or fiscal policy to perform this function effectively. Chinese industry, for example, has always been subordinate to commerce because it has not yet built a solid foundation capable of restraining it. In addition, the existence of backward social relations of production that are adapted to this fact makes it difficult to effectively implement the government's laws and policies aimed at restricting commerce. As a result, many policies intended to restrain commercial activities have instead become excuses for merchants to further increase their already excessive profits. While the policies themselves may be well-intentioned, they have been distorted by the objective social conditions under which they are applied.

Moreover, if we look at the social economy as a whole, each part is essentially interdependent. The development of this unbalanced relationship between commercial and industrial capital in China should be adjusted by imitating the financial policies of modern countries. In fact, this is exactly what we have done. There is one point worth mentioning: our financial capital, in terms of social composition, has already become a complement to our commercial and industrial capital. It can even be said that the abnormal development of commercial and industrial capital has been greatly facilitated by our financial capital or banking capital. In the capitalist countries, so-called bank capital was originally created for the purpose of facilitating the financing of industry, thus creating an indissoluble link between banks and industry. In backward countries, on the other hand, there was only the usurious finance industry, which undermined production, and no bank capital to support industry. If there was nominally bank capital in backward countries, it was likely to retain the characteristics of usury. As a result, it could easily become closely associated with trade, and could even become trade through its associations and dependencies. Consequently, it seems difficult to achieve the desired effects by using such bank capital to implement the policy of supporting industry while restraining commerce. At this key point, the question arises of how to use bank capital to reduce commercial capital or to increase industrial capital, which in turn raises the question of how to change the nature of bank capital itself.

All measures related to the issues of circulation of commercial and industrial capital, if this line of reasoning is adopted, will ultimately lead to the conclusion that, while we need to resist the war while also establishing a new country and reforming Chinese society, so that Chinese society itself will not allow the existence of unreasonable phenomena related to current capital issues and other issues.

Under this understanding of the prerequisite, I would like to emphasize in particular the land policy highlighted by the Principles of People's Livelihood. The realistic social production relations that this land policy proposed served as the foundation for all backward economic relations, and they are also the most basic reason for the issues of the circulation of commercial and Industrial Capital that we are discussing here. On other occasions (see my articles such as *General Analysis of Current Economic Issues* and *Chinese Commercial Capital* in the second chapter of my book *Papers on Chinese economy*), I have pointed out the connection between current commercial capital activities and land investment. Furthermore, I have also pointed out that the accumulation of commercial capital should be freely invested in the land, thereby enhancing the momentum of commerce in various ways. First, it will commercialize the land and thus expand the scope of commercial activities. The individual who speculated on land in the metropolis before the war, while during wartime, he would show a fierce interest in purchasing land in the vicinity of these cities as well as in relatively remote areas. Second, the commercialization of land provides a shortcut for commercial capital to engage in the hoarding of land products and serves as a convenient means for it to evade regulations. Third, the substantial rents derived from exploiting backward ownership and usage relations of land can be reinvested to strengthen commercial capital. But there is another more essential effect, which is best added here, that the closer the relationship between commerce and land ownership, the more it may undermine backward social relations of production, thereby making it difficult to implement any tasks aimed at cracking down on commerce. Therefore, I believe that among all the imperfect policies aimed at restricting the activities of commercial capital, preventing the circulation of commercial capital on the land is still an effective method. However, This does not necessarily mean that commercial capital will be redirected to industrial sectors if this circulation is hindered. The transfer of social capital from trade to industry undoubtedly requires certain historical preconditions. However, if we do not understand the policy of preventing the arbitrary sale of land in isolation, we will certainly recognise that other revolutionary steps, coordinated with the implementation of this policy, will contribute significantly to the reform of the socioeconomic base caused by the current problems of the circulation of commercial and Industrial Capital.

36.6 Four Conclusions

So far, the above opinions can be summarised in the following four conclusions.

First, the problem of the unbalanced development of commercial and Industrial Capital in China has not arisen today; it was an important problem even before the outbreak of the Anti-Japanese War. However, it was only during the war that this problem, which had not attracted much attention, was brought to our minds by the pressing needs of reality. In this sense, the Anti-Japanese War has indeed provided us with a valuable social test for the study of Chinese social history.

Second, whether in the past or in the present, the formation of the problem of the circulation of Chinese commercial and Industrial Capital is based on the overall socioeconomic form of China. Solving such problems is not as easy as solving other problems of a mainly technical nature, where the government can simply build a few railways, steamships or canals and try to achieve results within the limits of financial and technical possibilities, without considering the general socioeconomic basis. But the problems of capital and land, which are closely related to capital, which we are discussing here, cannot be solved by technical efforts alone.

Thirdly, in order for commercial capital to regulate its circulation in accordance with the law of average profit, certain socioeconomic conditions must be created. However, prior to the creation of these fundamental conditions, we cannot passively allow commercial capital to ruthlessly devour all productive capital. If tax policies, financial policies, price limit policies, and other strategies that restrict commerce while supporting industry development can be fully implemented, considerable results may be achieved. But we should first clarify that in backward social relations of production, taxes, finance, and prices, etc. are factors by which these relations of production are manifested, and that there is a limit to the possibility of making them sound. Consequently, the utility of using them to regulate the issue of the circulation of capital is even more limited.

Fourthly, the current constant expansion of commercial capital casts an increasingly negative shadow over society in general, and the industrial sector in particular. It is also easy to foresee the negative effects of this expansion on commercial capital itself. The lack of industrial development is, of course, a prerequisite for the independent development of commerce. If, however, the products for the turnover of commerce are gradually reduced, both the object and the scope of commercial activity will be correspondingly narrowed. Moreover, as production declines, consumers will lose purchasing power, which will further affect commercial activities. At present, while a few particular merchants may still be intoxicated by their profits, measured in terms of the quantity of currency, it is clear to the whole commercial and merchant class that, as the scale of social production continues to shrink and the wealth of society diminishes, the capital they possess, measured in terms of currency, is nothing but virtual capital. It is like a castle in the air or a floating cloud of smoke that can be completely blown away by a strong wind. Therefore, for their own sake, they urgently need to change course and change the use of their capital. But the capital of individual merchants has already been transformed into a specific form of commercial capital. This specific form of commercial capital has already taken effect under certain socioeconomic conditions. As a result, individual merchants find it difficult to control their own funds, so they have to follow the dynamics of the overall commercial capital. Moreover, this dynamic of the whole of mercantile capital is not wholly constrained by the mercantile class as a whole. If we consider the frequent lament of the merchants that "there is nothing we can do", we will understand that not only the industrialists but also the merchants expect a reversal of the prevailing general trend through a democratic policy of land capital.

Chapter 37
The Nature and Evolutionary Process of the Chinese Public Economy

37.1 Introduction

First of all, I must point out that the Chinese public economy, as the subject of this research, refers primarily to the state-owned and provincially-owned enterprises run by the central and provincial governments. What are the advantages and disadvantages of this type of public economy? What are its management guidelines? What is its relationship with the general private economy? Readers can seek explanations from experts at the economic forums. What I would like to discuss in detail here are the basic questions that most experts do not pay much attention to, but which are actually the most important questions in this regard.

In order to discuss the public economy as a category of social enterprises, it is first necessary to change or correct many of the unsound methods of investigation typically used in relation to such enterprises.

For example, in all economic activities, it is common to measure the degree of success or failure of an activity by its profit or loss in monetary terms, or by the size of its profit. When this narrow concept of profit is applied to public enterprises, it not only overlooks the standpoint of the public economy, but also distorts its real social role. The real profits of the public economy should be measured not only by their monetary value, but also by the positive contributions they make to the general social economy. Therefore, if the activities of a public enterprise have negative or harmful effects on the general social economy, even if the monetary value of its capital increases significantly, this should not be considered a success, but rather a failure of that enterprise. On the contrary, if the activity effectively meets the urgent needs of society and contributes significantly to the success of other public and private economic activities, it can be considered a success even if the monetary value of its capital does not increase or even decreases. If we do not adopt this public and social view of the public economy and public enterprises, we will inevitably drive those involved in public enterprises to take wrong paths, seek quick success and immediate profits, and fundamentally lose their standpoint for building a sound public economy.

Y. Wang, *The Basic Theory of Chinese Economy*,
https://doi.org/10.1007/978-981-95-6330-2_37

Secondly, the views of the general public and those engaged in public economic activities on the public economy will certainly influence the prospects of the public economy; however, it is the historical and social conditions that underlie its establishment that truly limit its prospects. The public economy has existed in nearly all historical eras, but the public economy of any given era differs significantly from that of other eras in terms of content, scope, and nature. We are currently living in a great era of multiple transitions and transformations.where it is easy to observe various forms of the public economy while forgetting its social and historical foundation. We might come to believe that the achievements of the public economy are solely the result of human effort and technology, and we can create any ideal form at will. It is a clear example that many people tend to evaluate the success or failure of the public economy based solely on technical and human conditions. We used to place great emphasis on the importance of technical and human conditions in all public and private operations. However, even these conditions should be explained from the standpoint of society, as the level of technology and the progressiveness of individuals are not coincidental.

The two aforementioned points, the former is based on the social value of public economic activities, and the latter is based on the social prerequisites underlying the existence of the public economy itself. By grasping the key to these two understandings, we can avoid superficial or biased evaluations of the state-owned and provincial-owned public economy, ensuring that our emphasis on the public economy remains within realistic limits. While articulating these basic points of understanding are relatively straightforward, providing a scientific explanation for them, especially for the latter, and drawing conclusions about the possible prospects of the Chinese public economy is quite challenging. I hope that this part can achieve this task to some extent.

37.2 The Development Process of Modern Public Economy

The public economy that China currently has and is in the process of building clearly simulates or imitates to some extent, or at least has been influenced by, the public economic models of modern advanced countries. Therefore, it is essential to have a basic understanding of the reality and developmental limits of our public economy and to analyse the developmental dynamics of its economic forms.

The so-called modern economy generally refers to the capitalist private or national economy. From the end of the eighteenth century to the end of the nineteenth century, capitalist economic activity, whether consciously or unconsciously, adopted as its rules the economic principles laid down by Adam Smith. According to this principle, there are only three things that a state or government can do with regard to socioeconomic activities: firstly, national defence to protect economic activities; secondly, the work of the judiciary to maintain economic order; and thirdly, transport, education and other social work to facilitate economic facilities. All other matters are left to the people. This is the so-called laissez-faire policy of individualism. The economy that has developed under the influence of this policy clearly belongs to the category of private economy.

However, during the last quarter of the nineteenth century, this type of private economy, due to its inherent defects, inevitably embarked on the road of revising or gradually negating its economic form. As a result, the public economy, which had previously been confined to an extremely narrow range, was likely to gradually increase its share in the overall national economy. However, this possibility was not the result of any genius design but rather a consequence of the inevitable development of objective economic reality. The modern public economy generally takes the following realities of private economic society as the premise for its gradual expansion.

Firstly, the transition from a free economy to a controlled economy.

A free economy is an alternative term for an individualistic economy. Due to the anarchy resulting from the self-interested actions of individuals, each economic entity naturally perceived the adverse consequences of free competition. As a result, various combinations of economic forms have emerged to mitigate or eliminate internal competition. On the one hand, the rise of business forms such as cartels, trusts and syndicates increased the size and strength of each competing unit, transforming fragmented and disorganised competition into integrated and organised competition. On the other hand, through this kind of organisation and integration of aggregated parts into a whole, competition within these organisations or integrations was eliminated. In addition, the emergence of these various integrated economic forms provided the government with the pretext and convenience to intervene and regulate the individual free economy on many occasions. Firstly, after the emergence of such new vertically and horizontally integrated enterprises, those enterprises that did not participate or could not participate in these new integrations were in an extremely disadvantageous position, making them highly susceptible to bankruptcy and unemployment. Secondly, the internal organisation and advanced capital structure of the newly integrated companies would inevitably lead to a relative reduction in labor and employment opportunities for the relevant aspect. These factors, which contributed to social and economic crises, increased the demand for government relief and protection. Thirdly, the integration of various enterprises into their own provided a basis for government intervention and regulation. In fact, during the process of transition from a free economy to a controlled economy, we also observe another significant change:

Secondly, the transition from an industry-dominated to a finance-dominated economy.

According to the inherent laws of the development of capitalism, the scale of modern enterprise organizations is becoming increasingly concentrated and expanded. This concentration and expansion not only led to more government regulation and intervention, which has been mentioned previously, but also required increasingly larger amounts of capital due to the higher degree of organic composition of capital in the process of concentrated expansion. Moreover, the time required for capital to transfer its full value was lengthening, as the variable portion of capital became relatively smaller while the constant portion grew relatively larger. As a result, any industrialist with substantial assets had to gradually deepen their dependence on bank capital since the turnover of funds in their trade depended on banks. In order to adapt to the expanding scale, the joint-stock company adopted a method of general fundraising, which also had to be done through banks. Since banks controlled the financial lifeline of industries and had a common destiny with industries, they also had to further seek to supervise and intervene in the activities of these industries. As a result of the combination of bank capital and Industrial Capital, the original form of industry-dominated in the national economy had gradually transformed to the form of finance-dominated. This transition further strengthened and enlarged the integration among various enterprises, thereby establishing the foundation for the dominance of the so-called financial oligarchy. In the process of the transition from an industry-dominated to a finance-dominated economy, we inevitably encounter another change:

Thirdly, the transition from a national to a national defense economy.

The so-called national economy, in contrast to the national defense economy, refers to the routine and regular economic system, while the national defense economy refers to an extraordinary and responsive economic system. If a national economy requires the intervention and control of the government, and at the same time, the dominance of a financial oligarchy potentially makes it more possible to reinforce that intervention and control, then each national economic unit, whether the internal contradictions and inconsistencies may exist, gradually transforms into the form of a major trust in its external relations. That is to say, each national economic system has become a competitor against others. The various forms of protective tariffs and currency conflicts, along with tightened control over their respective colonies and fierce struggle for subcolonial territories, as well as the distinct formations of the Autarky Economy and Block Economy, had all contributed to the antagonism between nations. These economic situations extended into the political aspects, where the deterioration of international political relations further exacerbated tensions between countries, ultimately leading to a worsening of domestic economic situations within each nation. Under such circumstances, each country that was suffering from domestic economic crises and thus social crises needed to: firstly, divert the attention of its unemployed workforce from home to abroad; secondly, divert underutilized industrial institutions and reserves to the production of munitions. These two tendencies originally existed in every capitalist country; however, due to the varying strengths of their respective industrial foundations, the more vulnerable countries tended to more urgently require measures for war preparation or national defense. Once some countries adopted these measures, whether explicitly or implicitly, others had to follow in their footsteps. Eventually, The transition from a national economy to a national defense economy became a general phenomenon.

The current trends in the development of the modern economy include the transition from a free economy to a controlled economy, the transition from an industry-dominated economy to a finance-dominated economy, and the transition of a national economy into a national defense economy. They manifested the strengthening of private ownership. However, at the same time, in this process of strengthening of this nature, they had contributed to the consequences of the socialization of the private economy in a dialectical manner. The government had intervened in and regulated private economic activities, expanding the scope of public ownership by means of relief, subsidies, capital participation, and the increase of construction of public utilities. Furthermore, in order to establish a national defense economic system and meet urgent needs, it had to exercise further control over various heavy industries and transportation sectors related to munitions and military transportation. This may involve retaining ownership while temporarily acquiring the rights of use, as noted by Munk (refer to Xu Zongshi's translation of *The Economics of Force*). All of these are an inevitable process in the socialization of the modern private economy. In all capitalist countries, regardless of the proportion that the public economy component may occupy within the national economy as a whole and the impure specific or temporary nature it may possess in comparison to the public economy under state socialism, it clearly shows the following characteristics:

1. It represents the transformation of a highly developed private economy.
2. It is established on the technical basis of the society of the private economy.
3. It serves as a transitional or preliminary form towards more organized economic development.

37.3 Nature of Public Economy in Traditional Chinese Economic Forms

The so-called traditional economy in China here actually refers to the feudal economy in traditional China.

The general feudal economy is characterized by the form of isolation and self-sufficiency of each territory and manor. However, under the typical feudal system in China, this isolation was not only generally broken, but also various forms of public economy emerged quite early on. As far back as the Western Han Dynasty, in addition to the minting of coins, had been unified by the three officials, indicating that the public operation of the "Official Monetary Bureau" and the "Mint" had reached a considerable scale (during the reign of Emperor Ping of the Han Dynasty, the minting of coins of five baht amounted to over twenty- eight billion pieces). Additionally, there were a number of the following public undertakings.

Firstly, promoting the production of salt and iron. "Mountains and seas are the treasures of heaven and earth, and they should be managed by local government... It is hoped to recruit the public who can boil salt at their own expense, with the equipment of the government to boil salt, the government to provide salt boiling utensils and tools.... Those who dare to cast iron or boil salt without permission will have their toes of their left foot clamped, and their utensils and tools will be confiscated. In prefectures and counties where no iron is produced, small officials should be designated, and they shall be in charge of the iron affairs of the county." (*Historical Records: Essay on Price Stabilizing*).

Secondly, establishing the institutions of uniform purchase and transportation of goods and stabilizing prices. "...Establishing dozens of officials in the Agricultural

Department to oversee agricultural affairs in each county across the country. Designated officials at the county level manage the transportation, salt, and iron affairs. The government issues orders to these officials in remote areas to transport their local specialties as tributes, referring to the goods that local merchants sell to other regions when prices are high. These tributes can be viewed as taxes and are transported by the government. Institutions for price stabilization are established in the capitals to manage all goods transported from across the country. Craftsmen are summoned to manufacture vehicles and other utensils, with costs covered by the Agricultural Department. The various agencies within the Agricultural Department monopolize all major goods of the country, selling them at high prices and buying them at low prices, thus controlling and stabilizing the prices of all goods."

Thirdly, establishing the Ever-normal Granary. "It is ordered that all border counties build granaries. When prices are low, grains should be purchased at higher prices to stock up, benefiting agriculture; when prices are high, grains should be sold at lower prices to stabilize the market, which is the ultimate goal. These are called Ever-normal Granary."

In the reign of Emperor Wu of the Han Dynasty, in addition to the aforementioned institutions, a regulation on wine management was established. Even in the period of Wang Mang, a system was introduced for the national management of essential goods and credit, which not only allowed the state to monopolize key manufacturing sectors and control the market but also to provide credit. It stated that "if people are unable to afford sacrifices and funerals, they can borrow money from the government based on the tributes from their industries or commerce… Those wishing to start a business can also receive loans, with interest not exceeding one-tenth of their total annual profit." (*History of Han Dynasty: Economic History*).

Regarding the aforementioned public undertakings, subsequent dynasties largely continued these practices with some modifications of increase or decrease. However, the practice of operating foreign trade officially became a major source of national revenue until the Song and Ming Dynasties. In regard to this kind of public economy in China, foreigners perceived it as follows.

"The Chinese bureaucracy is not only linked to landlords but has also become an embodiment of them. It is not only connected to commercial capital but has itself transformed into the largest merchant, monopolizing the trade of iron and silk and controlling the operations of salt and iron. Until recently, before the onset of imperialist invasions, it maintained a monopoly over foreign trade and dominated the grain market. This bureaucracy is not only associated with loan capital but also acts as the largest usurer. It utilizes the warehouse system, local banking (money shops), and the pawn system to ensure that commerce, handicrafts, transportation, and all other economic activities are subject to its control." (Refer to pages 70–71, *Research on Chinese Agricultural Economy*, written by Madjar and translated by Peng Chen).

The aforementioned paragraph can be used to illustrate the nature of the economic undertakings of the Chinese government in the past, but it is far from sufficient. The reason why the feudal system in China could give rise to this form of public economy lies fundamentally in its economic foundation: the landlord economy rather than the seigneurial economy. Only on this basis of landlord economy could taxes from across the country be concentrated in the central government, and all local officials were dependent on the central authority. This is why a centralized bureaucratic feudal system could be established. Only the government could obtain a significant quantity of agricultural and industrial products through taxes and tributes, and with its power to dominate the whole country, it could engage in various large-scale public undertakings. Moreover, because any form of feudal system is closely dependent on agriculture and land, the feudal bureaucratic government in China, on the one hand, was connected to the commerce and usury industry; on the other hand, it remained concerned that the intense activities of commerce and usury industry could jeopardize the basis of the agricultural and land-based economy, and at least subjectively, it sought to use direct government economic activities to mitigate that trend. Objectively, however, this type of public economic activity further strengthened the links between officials and merchants and deepened the exploitation of direct producers, so that each dynasty inevitably followed the decline of its predecessor. In short, the public economy in traditional China shows us the following characteristics:

(1) It emerged as a special product of the centralized feudal system.
(2) As a special product of the centralized feudal system, it manifested as a national economic form.
(3) It was closely connected to the bureaucracy and often served as a "political sideline" for bureaucrats to benefit personally under the guise of public service.
(4) While it bears some resemblance to the restrictive economic measures adopted by various countries under the autocratic monarchies in early modern times, the latter is a transitional form toward the present individualistic economy, while the former is a "normal facility" attached to the special feudal system in China.

37.4 Achievements of the Chinese Public Economy in the Process of Modernisation

It is generally accepted that there was a period of state-owned or state-directed enterprises in the process of Chinese industrial modernisation, roughly covering the several decades from the end of the Taiping Rebellion in 1862 to the Sino-Japanese War in 1895. In 1862, Zeng Guofan and Li Hongzhang observed the significant impact of new-style weaponry during the campaigns against the Taiping Army, prompting them to establish machine repair and manufacturing industries in Anqing, Shanghai and other places. Later, the Jiangnan Shipyard and the Mawei Shipyard were established in Fujian. The famous China Merchants Bureau was founded in 1872. Although the largest company, Hanyeping, was officially founded in 1908, its preparations began in 1890. In the same year, Li Hongzhang established the Mechanical Textile Bureau and the New Spinning Bureau in Shanghai. Three years later, Zhang Zhidong established the Mechanical Textile Bureau in Wuchang. All these new-style state-owned or provincially-owned enterprises represent the specific content of this government-led stage in the process of Chinese industrial modernisation.

In fact, from the Sino-Japanese War in 1895 until the onset of the recent Anti-Japanese War, Chinese state-owned and provincial-owned enterprises continued to be established. However, compared with this current phase, the proportion of private enterprises has increasingly exceeded that of government-run enterprises. This was partly due to the loss of industrial rights under the Treaty of Shimonoseki and the growing number of factories set up by foreigners in China, which gave a great stimulus to Chinese private enterprises. At the same time, however, we should not neglect the lack of achievements from public or government-run enterprises.

The aforementioned government-run enterprises included those related to mechanical manufacturing, textiles, mining and metallurgy, and transportation; although their sectors varied, their failures shared common characteristics. We do not have enough space here for a detailed analysis of the reasons for these failures, but to facilitate an explanation of the nature of our public enterprises or public economy, we can refer to several reasons analyzed by Wu Jingchao regarding the failure of the Hanyeping Company (see *The Road of Chinese Economic Construction*, starting on page 15).

The first reason, he supposed, was poor planning. Zhang Zhidong, during his tenure as governor of Guangdong and Guangxi Provinces, ordered machine furnaces from abroad to establish an iron factory. However, by the time the furnaces arrived, he had been transferred to Hunan and Hubei, and his successor was unwilling to accept them. Consequently, the furnaces were transported to Hanyang, Hubei. Zhang then sought raw materials from the Daye Iron Mine and fuel from the Pingxiang Coal Mine, leading to an extremely hasty and makeshift start to the factory. Later, Sheng Xuanhuai took over the factory, and in his memorial to the throne, he stated, "Such a factory has never been seen in East Asia. The process of refining coke from coal, refining iron from coke, and refining steel from iron is extremely cumbersome and confusing. There are too many types of machine furnaces, and the work is exhausting and complicated, like a blind person searching for a needle, completely clueless. Once we begin, we cannot stop."

The second reason, he argued, was due to improper employment. "Most of the staff in the company are idle officials and gentry, drawn by the reputations of Zhang Zhidong and Sheng Xuanhuai, hoping to profit personally without any real interest in the development of the company." "Many employees and technicians lack professional knowledge and experience and grope in the dark. It is inevitable that a company will make many mistakes even if it operates on its own strength. Not to mention that there are some employees who deliberately muddled through their work and spent the funds of the company recklessly, resulting in various drawbacks that are difficult to list one by one."

The third reason, he thought, was mismanagement. There are two noteworthy points: one is the muddled personnel management, and the other is the disorganized accounts. "The company's losses have exceeded ten million yuan, yet none of the shareholders are aware of this." "when examining the accounts, revenues, and expenditures, there often appear to be a surplus instead of a deficit."

The fourth reason, he believed, was an adverse environment. The successive military operations in the provinces of Hunan, Jiangxi, and Hubei had caused the company to suffer losses in various aspects such as transportation, labor, and supply. The Ministry of Transportation ordered the rails but refused to pay the agreed price, while local governments imposed numerous restrictions and demanded donations.

These four reasons for the failure are the common defects of all public enterprises in China, not merely the Hanyeping Company. If we desire to further understand its basic nature, it is evident that our public economic form manifestsit clearly shows the following characteristics: it is evident that this public economic form demonstrates the following two features.

(1) It formally imitates the controlled or directly state-ownedrun mode adopted by advanced countries during the later stages of capitalism.
(2) It essentially follows the traditional methods of conducting public enterprises that have been practiced in China for thousands of years.

In other words, operating public enterprises that require the application of more advanced science and technology with a backward bureaucratic government. Implementing a controlled economy without having experienced a free economy; implementing a rationing economy without having gone through a commodity economy; and implementing a public economy without experiencing a private economy. Naturally, all of these are without foundation and without reliance. The person in charge openly admitted that he was "like a blind person searching for a needle, completely clueless," while the "employees and technicians" were left to "grope in the dark." Consequently, it is not surprising that everyone who "deliberately muddled through their work and spent the funds of the company recklessly" and perceived the company as a "yamen" for "idle officials and gentry." An economic researcher who attributed the failure of Chinese state-owned enterprises to political tradition once remarked, "After the Han Dynasty, the reason why the state ownership and regulation of industrial and mining undertakings failed to promote the progress of productive undertakings and organizations was that the government's primary focus on tax collection, especially those in charge, arbitrarily demanded resources, sought personal profits, and engaged in malpractices for selfish ends. Up to the present, despite the existence of strict inspection and accounting systems, monopoly enterprises and checkpoint revenue collection are still regarded as gravy trains. With such a prevailing social atmosphere, when it comes to state-owned enterprises with more complex tasks and heavier responsibilities, there are even more drawbacks, leading to an increasingly unmanageable situation.

The failure of the Westernization Movement initiated by Li Hongzhang and Zhang Zhidong in the late Qing Dynasty, as well as the losses suffered by the China Merchants Bureau, the New Textile Bureau, and the Hanyeping Company, were indeed closely related to the overall government administration and primarily influenced by entrenched traditional political customs that were difficult to change." (See Chen Zhenhan, *Chinese Political Tradition and Economic Construction Policy*, *Oriental Magazine*, Vol. 39, No. 13).

Explaining the failure of public enterprises in China from the perspective of traditional political customs can be considered a step forward compared to the four reasons proposed by Wu Jingchao. However, this should not be the end of the analysis. Any political tradition must take root in society. Therefore, we need to delve deeper into the issue.

37.5 Characteristics of Wartime Public Economic Measures

As mentioned above, from the First Sino-Japanese War to the Anti-Japanese War, there was a period of stagnation for Chinese state-owned enterprises. And after the outbreak of the July 7 Incident in 1937, the activities of state-owned enterprises were revived due to the urgent needs of the war. The excessive "prosperity" of the state and provincial financial enterprises was nothing to sneeze at. As for industry, at the end of 1931, "if we consider only the Resource Committee under the Ministry of Economy, it consisted of 78 units, and its capital was almost twice that of the existing private industry. The fastest-growing provincial enterprises, such as Guizhou Enterprise Company, Chuankang Xingye Company, Dianxi Enterprise Company, Guangxi Enterprise Company, Hubei Enterprise Company, Jiangxi Xingye Company, Wannan Industrial Company, Fujian Enterprise Company, Shaanxi Enterprise Company, Gansu Water Conservancy, Forestry and Animal Husbandry Company, etc., existed in almost all provinces. And the organizational form of these enterprises had a common nature of "branch of branch", that is, there were several subsidiaries under the parent company, and Guizhou Enterprise Company is a typical example." (See the reference series of *Ta Kung Pao: An Overview of Chinese Industry in Wartime*) This is the case in China's financial and industrial sectors, and as for the agricultural and transportation sectors, especially trade, institutions controlled or directly run by the state or province have been established almost every month. This phenomenon seems to indicate that China has embarked on the road of denying its private economy.

Of course, the number of these national and provincial enterprises that are flourishing in wartime is much greater than in the past, and they are much more popular. In terms of their nature, they are also better than those in the state and provincial stage. However, these kinds of improvements are not so much of a social nature as they are of a technical nature. The technical improvements are obviously due to the considerable progress in the level of Chinese science and technology in recent decades, but more fundamentally, they should be attributed to the tender foundation and small development of Chinese private enterprises. Since this kind of improvement is about technology rather than society, the extent of its improvement obviously depends on social conditions. In the newspapers and magazines in recent years, people have read this kind of criticism of the public or semi-public auditing departments as follows.

People can start with the semi-public auditing departments.

"Because of China's failure to eradicate corruption and other undesirable behaviors in politics, all the measures to balance prices have failed, and all the control measures have turned into opportunities for corrupt officials to make money by exploiting the national disaster!" (See *General Discussion on Wartime Economic and Fiscal Policy*, No. 3, Vol. 5, *Research on Construction*).

Some facts to justify this argument are that, due to the unified control of coal and salt control in Sichuan Province, and that of tung oil in Hunan Province, some malpractices arose. Take the former as an example: "As a result of the control of the salt water of the gravity wells and the fuel, the salt producers had to get permission before they could buy salt water and coal for their production, and the Jiuda Refined Salt Company had to reduce its production… As for those who ran the coal mines, they had to bribe and ask influential people for help because the Fuel Control Bureau would not sell them coal." (See *General Discussion on Wartime Economic and Fiscal Policy*, No. 3, Vol. 5, *Research on Construction*).

"After the implementation of tung oil control in Hunan Province, the affiliated company of the Trade Committee and the Provincial Trade Bureau have been restricting each other to compete for the right to collect tung oil in the province, so that 150,000 dan of tung oil could be exported in half a year through commercial operation, but now only 7,000 dan can be exported. For example, in the Jingshi area, at the end of the Chinese lunar year, the Trade Bureau stopped collecting oil, so the merchants had to ship their products themselves, and they were rejected and foiled everywhere. The oil merchants could not afford to buy them for lack of capital. The tung oil farmers needed money at the end of the year and were forced to sell their tung oil at an extremely low price to these hoarders. So they told their colleagues to cut down the tung trees and replant other trees." (See *Ta Kung Pao*, June 12, 1932).

In fact, the malpractices highlighted here exist in all controlling departments.

Then there is state-owned industry.

> If there is bureaucracy in state-owned enterprises, they will not succeed. It is no secret that there are many people who run state-owned enterprises as officials. As for those who are not so sophisticated, they will make decisions arbitrarily rather than according to practical needs because they are not familiar with industrial management. They may order a certain department to do a certain job within a certain time today, and then give another order for demolition or closure within a certain time tomorrow. This second-guessing only exhausts the workers and prevents them from getting anything done. For example, the construction of a factory or a boiler for casting iron and steel started two or three years ago, but it has not been completed yet. For the greedy people in charge, they meticulously use the enterprises to make money for themselves by taking commissions, falsifying accounts, and so on. In this way, they have become really rich before the factory officially 'produces' anything.
>
> Under China's special circumstances, people who run state-owned enterprises often have bureaucratic habits, such as breaking the law and becoming corrupt, engaging in malpractice and gaining private benefits, excluding people with different ideas, and gaining popularity by deceiving the public, and so on. The failure of modern enterprises is inevitable when such people are in charge. (See combined issue of No. 15 and No. 6, Volume III, *Contemporary Review*)

The above comment was made by Fan Hong, but Xu Baiyuan in the *Financial Review* (Issue 2, Volume 7) made a more general and moderate remark that "State-owned and large public enterprises are very likely to cause problems such as high costs, low efficiency, complicated personnel affairs and slack work, etc."

Thirdly, it is about finance.

> The financial policies formulated by state financial institutions have been in effect for a long time, the institutions themselves have become groups of commercial capital, so they can neither limit the abnormal development of social commercial capital, nor enable or induce private and local financial institutions to embark on the road of industrial finance....
>
> Because China's financial and fiscal policies have formed an abnormal combination, when financial policies need to be changed, fiscal policies also need to be changed.... (See Gao Shukang, *The Abnormal Development of Commercial Capital*, Issue 11, bimonthly *New Economy*)

At present, some of the above-mentioned shortcomings of the public economy have been improved, and others are still in the process of improvement. However, in order to have an explicit knowledge of the possible development prospects of China's public economy, it is necessary here to cite the criticisms of the above-mentioned public enterprises from various sources in order to better understand the core of their problems.

First, the bureaucratic style of operation is at the center of criticism.

Second, commercial activities are leading and dominating both public and private industries throughout the country, so that industries are gradually becoming captives or vassals of commerce.

Thirdly, all the public financial organs are associated with commerce instead of industry, thus becoming the so-called "commercial capital groups".

Fourth, there are mutual constraints and frictions between the central and provincial public organs and among the provincial public organs.

If we compare the situation in these aspects with the characteristics of public enterprises at the above-mentioned state stage, we can certainly see that the commercial and financial dynamism of the public economy is becoming stronger and stronger. Its share in the national economy is certainly increasing, but its nature does not seem to have changed significantly. At least, this must be the case logically and factually.

37.6 Possible Prospects of the Chinese Public Economy

From the above, we can see that the future of China's national and provincial enterprises, or the development of China's public economy, still seems to be fraught with difficulties. We also hope that the ailments of China's public economy are related to the general abnormalities of the war economy, and that these problems will also be solved after the war is over. But as we imagine:

(1) The public economy cannot grow in isolation; its growth must not only be in close and organic coordination with the overall national economy, but also be supported by general social conditions that allow and complement it.
(2) The public economy faces significant threats from bureaucratism, commercial dominance, and even regionalism, all of which have their roots in the social base. There seems to be no reason why this social foundation should automatically disappear with the end of the war.

If we add these two considerations to the question of the future development of the public economy in China, we will see that even if we subjectively want to catch up, in view of the disadvantages caused by the private economic system in the capitalist countries of the world, and in view of the fact that the free economy in these countries is constantly being dominated, and the private or individualistic economy is constantly being socialized and communalized, In order to carry out this as an important state policy, we must further study the realistic nature of the public economy in China, the realistic conditions for the socialization and public ownership of their economies, and the realistic social basis for our adoption of the public economy. Otherwise, we may not be able to prevent the anti-separation phenomenon of "falsifying public interests" or "turning public interests into private interests" from continuing despite our efforts to build a public economy.

In this connection, it may seem clear that the reason I have referred to the traditional Chinese public economy is that our public economy today has, at least in essence, a social origin with which it retains a considerable history. The bureaucracy may have changed some of its appearance over time, but the land tenure relations on which it depends and on which it operates have not yet been found to have changed in any essential way. I have said this on other occasions (see my book *Social Science Theses Fourth On China's Postwar Rural Industrialization*): Today's domestic experts and scholars talk about industrialization, all kinds of industrialization should pay attention to people's livelihood, but pay attention to national defense; emphasis should be placed on light industry rather than heavy industry, which should be concentrated in urban areas rather than rural areas. We should focus on technical issues such as private ownership and the restriction of public ownership, rather than first asking whether our present social conditions are suitable for any form of industrialization. There is no objection to the principle that industrialization in all its forms and content must be carried out on the basis of the principle of people's livelihood, but the first step of people's livelihood requires the implementation of equal land rights and the change of traditional land relations in order to fundamentally eliminate the bureaucracy that hinders industrialization and all the backward social causes that impede the growth of new or communal economic forms.

Ill-informed people think that the land problem and the problem of industrialization do not seem to have much to do with each other, and the more sophisticated old and young economists think only that the original land relations that hinder industrialization are the absorption of funds from the land that could be transferred to industry, but if the problem is so simple, the land problem can be solved by serious expropriation. In fact, all the backward relations, bad customs, outdated ideologies and many other social phenomena that go against the trend of the times are based on the old land relations as a parasitic foundation. What directly hinders the development of the general economy is that the old land relations help the comprador of traditional commercial capital. It promotes the control of international capital over Chinese finance and currency so that it cannot play the function of national capital; it hinders the introduction of new technical conditions in industry and agriculture; and it has hindered the accumulation of Chinese social capital and its transformation into production. (For a detailed explanation, see my book *Chinese Economic Treatise* page 1801 below).

Of course, all the traditional land ownership relations that hinder the development of the general national economy also hinder the growth of the public economy.
To change the argument from negative to positive, I have two personal views on China's public economy:
The first point is that China's public economy should start with public ownership of land.
The second point is that China's public economy can only succeed on the basis of public land ownership.

A brief explanation of the previous point is:

Our national policy, which emphasizes efforts to build a national and provincial public economy, undoubtedly takes into account the general trend of economic development in the world and the lessons of social transformation that these countries have taught us. We recognize that if China's modernization were to start from scratch-first fully developing the private economy and then sequentially moving to the public economy stage-it would not only be too circuitous and out of step with the times, but also probably not feasible given the rapidly changing global economic environment. Thus, today's focus on building the public economy has the dual intention of "mending the fence after the sheep have been lost" and "catching up with the times". To ensure that our new economic efforts do not deviate from the traditional path of the public economy as they have in the past, we must first fundamentally change our traditional land ownership relations. However, compared with the characteristics of pre-capitalist societies, China's traditional land tenure system has a certain degree of progressiveness and resilience. If we were to adopt the kind of land reform that other countries undertook in the early modern period, it might not only seem unnecessary-because the existing land tenure relations in their formal structure allow for the free transfer of land and labor, leading many to believe that China has no need for the kind of reforms that liberated serfs and land in other nations. This is one of the reasons why, even after a century of modernization, the importance of land reform has yet to be fully addressed. Moreover, such reforms would not easily eradicate all the backward social customs and institutions that persist because of our outdated land relations, nor would they effectively support the establishment of a new public economy.

A brief explanation of the latter point is as follows:

Our public enterprises do not resemble the form recently adopted by so-called state capitalist countries, where the publicization and socialization of the economy is built on the foundation of already developed and concentrated private capital. Obviously, we do not have such a foundation, so we have to rely on something else. Of course, we cannot pin all our hopes on foreigners to take responsibility for providing us with construction funds. If we are to rely on self-sufficiency, we must make greater efforts in the field of land. By establishing a rational system of land distribution that leads to a rational method of land use or management, we can both eliminate all the traditional practices that hinder current economic growth and enhance the vitality of our national economy as a whole. At the same time, this approach can effectively ensure the development of the general public economy.

At present, whether the national land equalization policy should be implemented through private ownership or state ownership remains a topic of debate among contemporary scholars and experts. From my perspective as a researcher focusing on the development of China's public economy, I offer my personal opinion in favor of state ownership of land. If this opinion is considered to have some merit, I intend to engage in a more extensive discussion of the matter.

Chapter 38
A Theoretical Analysis of the Formation and Essence of Bureaucratic Capital

38.1 How Should We Understand Bureaucratic Capital

In the period since the end of the War of Resistance Against Japanese Aggression, "bureaucratic capital" has become a buzzword. Although bureaucratic capital had existed for some time before that, when it was mentioned occasionally or when related terms such as "comprador capital" were discussed, the word "capital" was often censored, and sometimes even the word "capital" itself was replaced by "xx," or such terms were banned outright as being considered disrespectful and damaging to the reputation of officials. However, in a very short time, public opinion began to openly criticize and condemn bureaucratic capital without any reservations. Even the Party and government forums, which had previously avoided such terms, are now publicly targeting what they once considered to be defamatory terms, viewing them as objects to be eliminated. This significant change is partly due to the progress of the times, in which democratic ideals have become an unstoppable trend. In addition, the rampant activities of bureaucratic capital had reached a point where, if left unchecked, it would endanger not only the entire national economy but also the very survival of the Party and the government. In addition, internal conflicts within the bureaucratic capitalist groups, fueled by the law of uneven development, " also contributed to this change. Regardless of the reasons, we have now achieved a certain degree of "freedom" to discuss bureaucratic capital.

But perhaps because we have only recently gained this freedom of limited discussion, the general public cannot help but feel a certain "indifference" toward bureaucratic capital itself. The Guangzhou General Publishing House has compiled and printed a small series of books entitled On Bureaucratic Capital, which collects in one place recent articles on the subject by Di Chaobai, Ma Yinchu, Zhou Enlai, Wu Dakun, Zheng Senyu, Zheng Zhenduo, Jiang Qingxiang and Zhao Yuanhao, published in various magazines and newspapers. These words, because some of them are temporary speech records, some of them are included in other topics, so

Y. Wang, *The Basic Theory of Chinese Economy*,
https://doi.org/10.1007/978-981-95-6330-2_38

most of them cannot help being "vague." I think that for such an important topic, we should devote more time to elaborating its characteristics and functions.

At present, there seem to be two almost opposing views of bureaucratic capital. One view focuses on the static aspect of bureaucratic capital, treating it as a mere tautological expression, simply equating it with "capital owned by bureaucrats". This rigid interpretation naturally hinders a scientific analysis of bureaucratic capital. The other view emphasizes its dynamic aspect, exaggerating its fluidity, which ultimately makes bureaucratic capital something elusive and difficult to grasp.

In fact, bureaucratic capital is very vivid, but also very specific.

Bureaucratic capital manifests itself in three specific forms: the form of capital owned by bureaucrats, the form of capital used by bureaucrats, and the form of capital controlled by bureaucrats. The interdependence and fluidity among these three forms constitute the concrete content and conditions that shape bureaucratic capital. In some cases, these forms may exist independently, while in others they may overlap. However, understanding one form in isolation is not sufficient to fully understand the others.

Let's first clarify the characteristics of each form and then consider their collective functions. The form of bureaucrat-owned capital refers to enterprises and businesses that are directly established and managed by bureaucrats themselves. To the extent that private individuals are allowed to freely conduct business, their capital activities are not included in this form of ownership capital, regardless of whether the person in question is currently a bureaucrat or has ceased to be one (of course, we are well aware that a significant portion of actual bureaucratic capital is controlled by individuals who have already retired from the political stage, but the definitive end of one's political career often marks the beginning of the transformation of one's ownership capital into other forms). In the bureaucratic form of ownership, the owner must still be a bureaucrat who engages in political activities in his official capacity, while at the same time engaging in economic activities as a private individual. In such cases, regardless of whether these economic activities are prohibited or permitted, and regardless of whether the bureaucrat manages the business directly or delegates it to others, the capital used for these economic activities seems to acquire the attributes of bureaucratic capital. However, this notion is immediately challenged by the following facts. Modern society is often described as a bourgeois society dominated by industrial and commercial entrepreneurs. It is quite common for businessmen or industrialists to become bureaucrats. When a successful merchant, industrialist, or banker enters government service, does it mean that he must cease all his former business activities? Does it necessarily follow that when they enter the political arena, they must leave the economic sphere? Or, if they continue to engage in economic activities, does the capital they previously used for these activities automatically become bureaucratic capital simply because they have entered politics? If these questions cannot be answered with a definitive "yes," then we have reason to believe that bureaucratic capital, even in its ownership form, cannot be judged solely by the fact that it is owned by a bureaucrat. Instead, it must be judged on the basis of the specific circumstances under which the capital is owned by a bureaucrat. The reason why bureaucrats who manage their own capital are often condemned and criticized is that the source of their capital and their economic activities are closely related to their official positions. This leads us to understand that the form of bureaucratic-owned capital is only one of the various manifestations of bureaucratic capital. We call it the first form of bureaucratic capital.

Second, there is the form of capital **used** by bureaucrats: public enterprises owned by the state, provinces, cities, the army, or other public bodies, whose operations are in practice disposed of by officials.. All the enterprises that are run by the public, the main body of the operation, whether it is the state, the province, the city, another party, the government, the army, or even social and cultural organizations, the actual operators are all kinds of officials; bureaucrats do not own such capital enterprises, but they have the power to use them. In fact, all modern countries have public enterprises of this kind, large and small, and most of them are run by officials, but can their operating capital be classified as bureaucratic capital? If not, why not? In the first place, it can be said that their public capital is not inseparable from that of the government or the government itself; in the second place, it can be said that those who are managers of public enterprises, even if they are appointed by the government office, even if they are civil servants, once they arrive at these operating institutions, they do not act there in the capacity of civil servants, in the function of civil servants, but as entrepreneurs, experts or technicians. Precisely because of this second reason, the first reason is established. From this we also understand that it is not the capital used by the public and operated by the government that becomes bureaucratic capital, but the business operation of the public, which is in the hands of the bureaucrats and can be disposed of by the bureaucrats at will, and which makes its internal connection with all forms of capital of the above-mentioned bureaucrats, whether explicit or implicit, disgusting and cursed. This is what I call the second form of bureaucratic capital in this way is called the second form of bureaucratic capital.

Thirdly, we come to the form of capital dominated by bureaucrats. Originally, the capital owned by the bureaucrats and the public capital used by the bureaucrats can be said to be under their domination and control, but here we are referring to something different, that is, the capital of those private enterprises which are neither directly owned nor directly used by the bureaucrats, but which are obviously under the domination and control of the bureaucrats in many ways, and where there is a close connection between the economy and politics, and where there is no clear boundary of legal power to separate them, especially where private capital has to be supported by the government in various ways to maintain itself, almost all private enterprises or their capital are under the domination of the bureaucrats. On those occasions when private capital can only be maintained by obtaining various forms of government support, almost all private enterprises or their capital will inevitably become, to varying degrees and in various ways, the "captives" of the bureaucrats, the pools in which the bureaucrats fish and swim freely, and another source of expansion and pooling for the forms of all their capital. It becomes another source of expansion for all their forms of capital. Such a form of capital is what we call the third form of bureaucratic capital.

From the above separate explanations, we should have a general concept of bureaucratic capital, that is, bureaucratic capital should be the general term for the organic combination of all kinds of capital owned, used and controlled by bureaucrats under special social conditions. First, the three forms of bureaucratic capital, with officials as the hub of their interaction; without the authority of the government, this attribute of capital simply cannot exist.

Secondly, one pole of bureaucratic capital is the official or bureaucrat of human nature, while its opposite pole is the capital of material nature. It is possible for capital to bear the imprint of bureaucracy only under certain social and political conditions, so the emergence and development of bureaucratic capital should be understood from the specific social and political relations, which are at the same time the embodiment of specific social and political relations.

Thirdly, the above three forms of bureaucratic capital seem to be based in one respect, or in the summary of their activities, on the first form, the bureaucratic form of all capital, since the self-interested use of public capital and the self-interested control of private capital are intended only for the rapid expansion of all its forms of capital. But on the other hand, or in terms of its function of activity, the second and third forms of capital are not only equally important, but even more important, without which the first form of capital could not easily be produced at all, and even if it were, it would hardly be formed into bureaucratic capital.

At this point, you may still think that my general concept of bureaucratic capital is not comprehensive enough. That is, in reality, apart from the three forms of bureaucratic capital mentioned above, is it not clear that there is a form of capital jointly operated by government and business? From a detailed analysis, the so-called joint officials of government and business are not officials, but officials or civil servants, and the so-called businessmen are not businessmen, but officials or bureaucrats. In the process of its function, bureaucratic capital can have many ways of connection, and thus show many compound forms. Government and private capital are combined with public capital; officials combine with public capital, join the group with private capital; officials use the capital of the so-called government-business joint financial institutions to participate in private capital or public capital; officials use state-owned capital to participate in local government-business joint ventures or state-owned enterprises… All kinds of combination methods are just "convenient bridges" built by officials to expand and strengthen their capital activities. We must understand them as derivative forms of the three basic forms mentioned above, and as links or results of their action, the truth of which will be clearly revealed in the course of the activity of bureaucratic capital, which will be discussed later.

38.2 The Role of Bureaucratic Capital and its Consequences

In this regard, we can make the following two points.

(1) Bureaucratic capital operates in a way that is closely related to loan capital in all its activities. Historically, the original form of bureaucratic capital in China, which existed before the modern era, was accumulated through various forms of usurious practices. Pawnshops, installment lending, and myriad other traditional methods of lending, although generally dispersed among the populace, were primarily operated by officials awaiting appointment, current officials, or their close relatives and associates. Because these individuals held significant political power in society, their lending capital not only had a secure source and strong backing, but also became a highly coercive tool for land seizure. It is fair to say that usury or loan capital was an extension of the political power of the bureaucrats into the economic sphere.

In modern times, with the emergence of banking capital, our banking capital has essentially retained a strong usurious character (as I have analyzed in detail in the section on "Forms of Capital in China" in my book *The Basic Theory of the Chinese Economy*), or perhaps even more strongly retained its bureaucratic character. The lifestyle of Chinese bureaucrats and current social conditions are not conducive to productive activities, but rather to usurious speculative financial activities. Various other related factors have come together to make financial enterprises the natural starting point for the economic ventures of bureaucrats, both large and small.

In China's financial sector, there has long been a system known as the "Four Banks of the South and Four Banks of the North". In recent years, with the emergence of many new financial forces, the original system has undergone several overlapping changes. However, one thing has either remained the same or become more pronounced: no matter which bank's board of directors or supervisory board you examine, you will invariably find that they are filled with bureaucrats, quasi-bureaucrats, or their families. This is true not only of public banks, but also of so-called private banks, which are in fact "government-owned" banks. Even some genuinely private banks, in order to gain certain operational advantages, have had no choice but to bring in some political figures to enhance their image. Although these political figures often risk losing their official status for improper business dealings, they sometimes list fictitious merchants as "fake backers" to keep up appearances. In this scenario, it is not the people who are using "official power," but rather the officials who are using "people's names". I have often thought that the most complex situations in Chinese society are often orchestrated by these "resourceful" bureaucrats.

Bureaucrats are so enthusiastic about the financial industry because, after all, they are human (even if they sometimes act like "superhumans"). Where there is great profit, people are naturally drawn to it. The great benefits of the financial industry are not in the financial activities themselves. In the past, it was about using high-interest loans to expand trade, seize land, and secure political positions. In the modern era, however, it is clearly about using financial activities to get closer to and participate in all profitable public and private sectors of the economy. The ways in which they participate are numerous and more complex than the methods used by banking capital in modern advanced nations. Let me give a few examples to illustrate. The China Construction Industrial Development Company is closely related to the China Construction Bank. The capital of the China Construction Bank comes from the national treasury, the Chuan-Kang governments, and so-called commercial shares, which are essentially government shares. This composition determines its bureaucratic nature. In reality, these "commercial shares" are nothing but government shares. Through the China Construction Industrial Development Company, bureaucrats have monopolized all profitable enterprises. Similarly, the capital for the Guizhou Enterprises Company comes from the Guizhou provincial government, the China National Bank, the Ministry of Communications Bank, the Peasants' Bank and the Guizhou Provincial Bank, along with so-called commercial shares that are actually government shares. This company is known nationwide for its extensive involvement, managing virtually all modern enterprises in the province. During the war, other provinces established enterprise companies modeled on Guizhou Enterprises Company. Even though some of these were fully funded and operated by provincial banks or governments, They often carried the public banner while secretly functioning as special interest groups that engaged in side economic deals through various intricate methods. In essence, bureaucrats typically control banks and then use this control to participate in or dominate economic enterprises. The result is that bureaucratic financial activities become the focal point of the entire bureaucratic capital operation. Often, one person plays the roles of government official, financier, and entrepreneur. The concept of a political leader, bank director and hidden company boss as a "trinity" is already widely recognized.

Professor Laski of the United Kingdom once produced a comparative table of these three types of figures within the British Empire, as if to suggest that in this respect we had already caught up with the advanced nations and were worthy of "praise". The unfortunate reality, however, is not only the fundamental differences we've already pointed out, but also the highly dangerous consequences that flow from these essential differences.

(2) The consequences of the operation of bureaucratic capital under private ownership, especially in the context of modern private ownership, make it basically irrelevant whether social capital or wealth is accumulated in the hands of officials or non-officials. Bureaucratic capital becomes a target of public criticism because it inevitably leads to harmful effects on the country and the people, and hinders the development of the social economy. Looking at the whole process of the operation of bureaucratic capital, we can observe the following prominent tendencies:

a. Monopolization of Capital

On August 15, 1946, a journalist from the American New York Times, who was very sympathetic to the Chinese government, sent a telegram from Nanjing reporting that "the Chinese government, through various business organizations, has taken control of all the major domestic economic enterprises, managing the production of minerals, electricity, heavy industry, silk, cotton yarn, and sugar". In fact, it was not just production; almost all major commodities, such as tea, tung oil, cotton, and others, were monopolized or dominated by state enterprises or similar entities. The emergence and development of this monopolistic tendency is nothing but the inevitable result of the operation of bureaucratic capital. We understand that the tendency of bureaucratic capital to monopolize is mainly due to the fact that this form of capital not only facilitates the development of such tendencies, but also necessarily maintains them. The survival and expansion of bureaucratic capital depends on the extent to which it maintains its monopolistic control.

I have already pointed out the various forms of bureaucratic capital, its modes of operation and other intermediate forms. In a society in which the bourgeois class has not yet gained political influence, enterprises which operate wholly or mainly under public authority can determine their monopoly scope according to the whims of the rulers or the calculations of individual private interests. In times of war, this process is even more subject to the desires of those in power. Our society, by its very nature, lacks the inherent conditions for the implementation of a controlled economy. Nevertheless, during the war and even after the war, many so-called public or semi-public enterprises have relied on preferential financial treatment or special advantages in production, sales and procurement to maintain themselves. For example, in today's environment where bankruptcies and closures have become widespread, large enterprises such as the China Textile Construction Company still proclaim and expect substantial profits (in fact, among public enterprises, the China Textile Construction Company is perhaps the only one that dares to claim profitability, while the manager of the simultaneously established China Silk Company laments, "We are a loss-making enterprise"). Isn't this a refutation of previous criticism of public enterprises? On closer analysis, however, it becomes clear that this profitability is the result of enjoying special privileges in all aspects of its operations; in other words, it is due to its monopoly. Profits from monopolistic operations, when judged by general economic principles, are always at the expense of other similar enterprises that do not enjoy the same privileges. It grows by feeding on the sacrifices of its peers. Consider the unlimited credit facilities that the China Textile Construction Company receives from the central bank, the preferential access to foreign exchange and transportation for the purchase of raw materials and machinery, the rent-free use of public buildings, The distribution advantages it enjoys through its close ties with the yarn and fabric control system, the enormous size of its trust organization, and the tax benefits it receives-almost all of these are due to its monopoly status. From the case of the China Textile Construction Company, it is not difficult to infer the development patterns of other public or semi-public bureaucratic enterprises. Moreover, the monopoly itself often becomes a temptation to specialization and bureaucratization for other similar enterprises that have not enjoyed such advantages and have suffered fatal damage as a result. Private enterprises that do not enjoy monopoly advantages are left with two choices: watch themselves decline or allow those with political and economic power to participate in giving them a share of the monopoly advantages. In fact, any enterprise that involves bureaucrats is inevitably subject to nepotism, expediency and formalism, and gradually becomes inefficient. But it is precisely because of this inefficiency that the monopoly becomes even more necessary. Many naive people still call for the abolition of discrimination between public and semi-public enterprises, but this is essentially the same as calling for the abolition of bureaucratic capital itself. Is that even possible? The survival and development of a company does not depend on its management techniques or efficiency, but on its ability to secure monopoly rights. In this respect, the obstruction of bureaucratic capital to the improvement or increase of private capital and the general efficiency of enterprises is all too obvious. But the disadvantages do not stop there.

b. The Politicization of Capital

Bureaucratic elites can gain monopolistic advantages in three ways: first, by profiting from the operation of state-owned enterprises. Second, by participating in the so-called "commercial shares" within parastatal enterprises that enjoy monopoly rights. Third, by allowing private enterprises to obtain certain monopolies, thereby securing corresponding "special shares" in those private enterprises. Regardless of the method, monopolistic benefits are inextricably linked to political power; they cannot be secured without the backing of bureaucracy and political influence. The extent of these benefits is directly related to the level of political power and influence. As a result, the activities of bureaucratic capital inevitably manifest themselves as political struggles in which the acquisition of political power becomes a prerequisite for the acquisition of various benefits of bureaucratic capital. However, this is only one aspect of the problem; the other, more damaging aspect lies elsewhere. In order for an official, or a group of closely related officials, to maintain or expand their existing political power, they often need to control or manage significant amounts of bureaucratic capital. In this sense, bureaucratic capital becomes a prerequisite for gaining political power. From the smallest administrative unit, such as a county, to the provincial and central levels, the power struggles among various factions and regional interests, despite seemingly very different or seemingly reasonable justifications, can be easily understood by those familiar with the situation. In most cases, I dare say, these conflicts or struggles are essentially struggles over the distribution of monopoly rights within bureaucratic capital.

Viewing bureaucratic capital as a means of maintaining political power is inextricably linked to viewing political power as a means of acquiring bureaucratic capital. However, the damage caused by the former is significantly greater and more severe than the latter. In the former scenario, bureaucratic capital is likely to be transformed into political capital, and the activities of bureaucratic capital are likely to be diverted, away from the economic sphere itself. If a particular public enterprise is controlled by a political heavyweight, that enterprise will naturally become a "stronghold" for that heavyweight's faction. As a result, the likelihood that such enterprises will become bureaucratic and corrupt increases significantly, with corruption and bribery being further encouraged under the guise of "political activity expenses". Ultimately, the economic goals of bureaucratic capital are likely to be sacrificed to its political goals.

Because bureaucratic capital is so closely tied to politics and political power, any political upheaval or change in political power quickly affects all economic sectors under bureaucratic influence. Whether it's banks, corporations, or other business organizations, they tend to experience disruption or disintegration in response to such political shifts. The first economic "adjustment" of new political forces is often to fill in the "big gaps" left by their predecessors. While they may vigorously attack the targets they sought to overthrow when out of power, once in office they may show a surprising degree of tolerance for the corruption of their predecessors. This "protective" philosophy among officials has recently been clearly exposed as a scheme to muddle through and prepare for their own eventual departure from power. Consider the past decade: many state and municipal public enterprises have disintegrated in tandem with the decline of the relevant political forces. I am confident that despite the seemingly effective management and financial success of companies like the China Textile Construction Company, when someone familiar with the details examines it closely, it may not be as "satisfactory" as its predecessors claimed. Even if it really is, it may well face a fate similar to that of the once-prominent China Merchants Group after several more rounds of "transitional changes".

But the evils of bureaucratic capital activities do not end there.

c. The Capitalization of Comprador Capital

I must point out that the concentration of bureaucratic capital and its transformation into political capital are undoubtedly part of an inevitable process of development. As for the tendency to comprador capitalism, although in some cases it develops from political capitalism, in practice our bureaucratic capital has been inseparable from comprador capital from the very beginning of its activities and as a significant economic form. We can even say that comprador capital and bureaucratic capital initially appeared as twin brothers; both are inevitable products of China's social conditions under the influence of international capital. In order to supplement the previous explanation of the formation of bureaucratic capital, I would like to briefly touch upon the main point. International capital, in dominating or turning backward regions into its vital supply lines, must first destroy the existing methods of production in those regions in order to provide a market for manufactured goods and a source of raw materials. In order to achieve this, in areas already colonized, political domination allows for actions in line with its interests, while in countries not fully colonized, international capital must offer certain economic benefits to the political rulers of these countries. This leads to the establishment of various kinds of credit, procurement organizations and modern enterprises. The so-called government-run and government-business joint enterprises in early modern China were realized under such practical requirements. Political figures who are close to foreigners, whether borrowing or repaying debts, buying or selling on behalf of the state, are considered to have considerable advantages. This is an aspect of the initial accumulation of bureaucratic capital and reflects the deep-rooted connection between bureaucratic capital and comprador capital. Subsequently, almost all activities related to bureaucratic capital are associated with foreign investment and thus bear the "comprador" stamp. However, In the theoretical narrative logic, we must especially note that once the tendency of bureaucratic capital to transform into political capital takes shape, it will inevitably strengthen its tendency towards comprador capitalism. This can be explained by the following points:

First, when bureaucratic capital becomes a means to achieve political goals and turns into political capital, it inevitably takes on the characteristics of comprador capital, whether positive or negative. In order to use bureaucratic capital to maintain political power, it is essential for such capital activities to involve powerful foreign capital forces, which essentially provide strong external support. This is an observable fact. At the same time, from a negative perspective, in order to secure their bureaucratic capital in case their political power falters and thus preserve the possibility of regaining political power, the bureaucrats must also involve foreign capital forces in their capital activities. The recent plans and organizations often reported in the press as involving Sino-American companies are clearly related to the subjective calculations of individual bureaucrats. However, in the process of bureaucratic capital activities, this situation has actually created an even more dangerous scenario of comprador capitalism, which applies not only to bureaucratic capital but also to social capital in general. Specifically:

Second, as mentioned above, bureaucratic capital, by means of various monopolies, hinders the development of ordinary people's industries and the improvement of ordinary management techniques, and by transforming them into political means, will from time to time cause the destructive effects of chaos and dislocation on the whole economy. The accumulation of goods that can be used as capital is bound to have as its only possible outlet mainly the circulation economy of all external matters of finance, trade, communication and market speculation. The development of this tendency is the total external dependence of industry, that is, the total capitalization of the comprador. Of course, we do not deny that our political forces also have great intentions for the construction of China's economy, but it is equally difficult for us to deny that their "small attempts" to secure their own economic power and that of their faction often take precedence over these great efforts and are made to accommodate these great efforts. That is why, in the course of setting up a Sino-American shipping company and a Sino-American trading company, we have also set up a Sino-American agricultural mission… -Class advisers and leading organizations have come or will come from far away. These visitors may not have come entirely as volunteers, and they may not have had their own interests at heart, but judging from the reports of their findings (such as the recently published report of the Sino-American Agricultural Technology Mission), they were not too ignorant of the fundamental nature of Chinese society. If one is too disinterested in the construction of the Chinese economy, and if one examines their activities in relation to the dynamics of the comprador of our bureaucratic capital, one cannot help but fear the prospect of the colonization of the Chinese economy.

Chapter 39
The Dialectical Relationship Between National Capital and Bureaucratic Capital

39.1 Different Interpretations

In China today, there is a highly contradictory phenomenon: on the one hand, bureaucratic capital is incessantly condemned by everyone, both within the government and among the public; on the other hand, bureaucratic capital continues to expand, and many who criticize bureaucratic capital for harming the nation and its people are themselves eager to become bureaucratic capitalists and are making various efforts to join their ranks. Of course, if bureaucratic capital were not so rampant and competitively tempting, people might not pay so much attention to it or curse it so vigorously. Upon closer examination, however, one of the main reasons for this contradictory situation seems to be a general misunderstanding of the nature and scope of bureaucratic capital. People often confuse our bureaucratic capital with the so-called state capital that is prevalent in Western Europe today. As a result, state capital becomes a convenient excuse, and many of those who are most vocal in attacking bureaucratic capital are themselves desperately trying to become part of the bureaucratic capitalist camp. They believe, at least subjectively, that their economic activities contribute to state capital rather than bureaucratic capital. Conversely, they see their targets of criticism as problematic precisely because they are seen as contributing to bureaucratic capital rather than to state capital. It is therefore crucial to make a clear distinction between bureaucratic capital and state capital.

39.2 The Different Contents of State Capital in Different Societies

The concept of state capital in modern Western European society is generally expressed in two different forms of reality. This difference is not due to the type of capital, not to its natural characteristics, but to its social characteristics. In other

Y. Wang, *The Basic Theory of Chinese Economy*,
https://doi.org/10.1007/978-981-95-6330-2_39

words, the same national capital will have a different social character under different relations of production.

For example, in the socioeconomic attitude of the Soviet Union today, private movable property, or property limited to private use, is still allowed, but private capital, that is, private ownership of the means of production by which private individuals exploit the labor of others, is absolutely prohibited. In Soviet economics, therefore, the term "capital" has taken on a completely different meaning. We can, if we want to be a little more vague, call the assets that society as a whole uses to maintain and expand reproduction "social capital" in the strict sense (that is, social capital that belongs entirely to all the people of society, as opposed to the sense in which we usually conflate the individual private capital that exists in society with "social capital"); it can also be called "state capital" because of the limitation of its so-called "social capital" (which is considered only as the social capital of the Soviet society), that is, its social or national capital in relation to the union of the Soviet Union with other countries. From this we can see that in the social relations of production of the Soviet Union the state capital is absolute, it is capital in general, capital as a whole, and no other form of capital exists except this form of capital. Since no other form of capital is allowed to exist, there is no possibility for those who hold political power to use their power to expand their personal economic rights and interests.

But under the other social relations of production, that is, under capitalist social relations, it is quite different. We know that many modern states that respect private property have some degree of state property or state capital. For this reason, the budgets of many countries often include a special revenue for state enterprises. We do not need to analyze further the essential relationship between the state and political and economic power. Quantitatively, it is obvious that the state capital in such countries exists only in the pores of private capital; According to Adam Smith, an authoritative speaker on private economy or private capital, social enterprises, such as transportation, public services, are essential for the activity of private capital, and when it is not easy to raise money in private situations, it is borne by the state, and the result is that this kind of state capital coexists with private capital from the very beginning of the capitalist economy, that is, to facilitate or complement the development of private capital in general. From this we can clearly see that this form of state capital, compared to that of the Soviet Union, plays only a subsidiary role. In capitalist society, private capital, if not capital in general, is undoubtedly the main body of capital. Thus, there is a possible gap between private capital and state capital, which can be "communicated", "transformed" or "pretended to serve private interests". However, this "gap" has very different limits in the course of capitalist economic development.

In the early stages of capitalism, when private capital was just beginning to emerge, politics still manifested itself as a mixed form of despotism, bureaucratism and feudalism. As a result, it was possible to "seize temple property, fraudulently transfer state land, plunder communal land and seize feudal or clan land, transforming it into modern private property under unchecked terrorism". Similarly, in the field of movable property, "a big bank, decorated in the name of the nation, is essentially just a private speculative company from its inception. It is on the side of the government and uses the privileges granted by the government to acquire the status of lending money to the government", thus becoming a creditor of government bonds. "The creditor of government bonds has not actually contributed anything, because the amount it has lent has been converted into easily transferable government bonds. These bonds, in his possession, have the same function as hard currency of the same amount. The result was the creation of an idle rentier class". (All of the above can be found in the translated edition of Guo Wang's *Capital*).

In addition, private capital had gradually gained an advantage in society, and the class of owners of private capital, in order to secure their acquired right to capital, had already pressed for a political form more suited to their interests; although they had taken it by exploiting their political privilege, they did not want others to take it from them by exploiting their political privilege. "Hou's gate, benevolence and justice exist", the distinction between rights and duties, the distinction between the rule of law of the group was emphasised and adhered to. After the capitalist economy has been nurtured and developed under the care of a political system suitable for it, all the power of the state is regarded as something shared and exercised by the whole capitalist class. At a time when the prospects for the development of private capital seem very bright and the opportunities very abundant, on the one hand, operations in the name of the State have become relatively unimportant or very limited; on the other hand, the use of power by the politically powerful to expand their private capital becomes not only impossible but unnecessary. In typical capitalism, therefore, the term "bureaucracy", although it is still used from time to time to attack the government, is almost something different from its early form, and that is why "bureaucratic capital" is almost an unspoken term at this stage of the capitalist economy.

However, as this typical liberal-individualist economy evolves into a transformational stage, the state gradually expands its intervention and control. On the one hand, it seems that political figures are gradually gaining more say and control over the economy, but on the other hand, it means that economic figures are gradually gaining more say and control over politics.

A simple analysis of the situation is that the political form adapted to the free economy is called parliamentary or party politics because it is the product of capitalist society and because capitalism, from the very first stages of its existence, contains an internal contradiction, an antithesis, in which the working class is present and which develops as it progresses. Thus, parliamentary politics, which was originally intended to facilitate the capitalist economy, becomes something inappropriate or detrimental to the capitalist economic order with the increase of the power of the working class, with the increase of the power of the working class in parliament. As a result, the capitalist class, which is in opposition to the working class, demands a revision or repudiation of the political form it had promoted in the previous stage of development. If so, why do some countries reject this form of policy altogether, while others are content to modify it? It is not really a question of whether the attitude of their political and economic forces is fierce or moderate, but rather of the different economic conditions in which the relationship affects or shapes their attitude. In the industrial organization of the capitalist state, it is necessary and possible from the outset to adopt a more concentrated, more highly organic form. It is necessary because it is not like that, it is not enough to compete with the advanced capitalist countries in the commodity market; it is possible because it draws on the experience and technical conditions of the advanced capitalist countries. However, in response to this industrial organization, their banking capital soon took the form of financial capital, which combined with industry and dominated it. Once the oligarchic domination of finance capital was established, the state intervention in this period had a different nature and content from the initial state intervention. The state or the government has to be transformed into an institution that directly executes the will and orders of the finance capitalists, and parliamentary politics, which involves the forces of different social classes, becomes an obstacle to the free expression of the will of the monopolistic finance capitalists, and a crisis of self-annihilation of parliamentary politics is implicit in this situation.

What we need to understand here is what kind of new content so-called "state capital" actually has in this form of state-capitalist economy. This requires a detailed explanation.

39.3 What Is National Capitalism?

Many people think that under a state-capitalist economy, "state capital" will naturally develop, which is a literal statement. The main reason for this confusion may be that the essential difference between state capitalism and state socialism has not been made very clear.

Using the state as a pretext to impose capitalist dictatorship is a succinct explanation of state capitalism. (When the Soviet Union adopted the term "state capitalism" during the implementation of its New Economic Policy, it was, in my view, a strategic slogan. This is very different from Hitler's use of state socialism to impose state capitalism—details of which can be found in my forthcoming work, *State Capitalist and State Socialist Economic Forms*). Capitalist forms are inherently contradictory. Apart from the class struggle of the working class, the interests of individual capitalists often clash with those of the capitalist class as a whole. The "state" in state capitalism essentially seeks to defuse internal conflicts within the capitalist class and to mitigate crises caused by the unchecked expansion of the interests of individual capitalists that threaten the existence of the capitalist class as a whole. This is the context of Bukharin's theory of "organized capitalism". However, each capitalist country entrusts the task of "containment" to state bodies, government officials or political figures, which paradoxically deepens the contradictions and conflicts between the nationalist economic entities of different countries. Thus, state capitalism is not only a nationalist economic system, but also a war economic system.

This situation has developed gradually. In order to maintain the existence of the capitalist class as a whole, many individual capitalists, especially those of the lower and middle ranks, must inevitably sacrifice their existence to a certain extent in certain situations. In order to fulfil or improve the wartime economic system, even the big capitalist class must temporarily relinquish some direct control over capital in order to retain ownership of it. It is in this context that Munk's "theory of the revolution of usufruct" (as discussed in *The Economics of Force*) emerges. Banks, big factories and other large enterprises were restructured accordingly; for example, the wartime Göring factory in Germany, which employed some one million workers, was restructured in this way. After the restructuring, although the capitalists retained ownership and profits according to Nazi economic laws, these industries and capital were branded with the "state" label. In fact, in this context, the state, the government or the political rulers effectively became the "managers" of capitalist enterprises. Despite the "disgust" of some big capitalists for this form of capital, as Munk described it, it was a form dictated by the economic conditions of their capitalist society. In this form, the state increasingly becomes the owner of big capital, while social capital also appears to be increasingly state-owned.

We can call this capital "state capital", then this state capital is the special form in which capitalism has developed to the highest classes.

39.4 Can Chinese Society Allow National Capital to Exist?

According to the above statement, we have seen two "forms of state capital" which are absolutely different in nature:

One is the state capital of the Soviet Union, the other is the state capital of capitalist society. Any omnipotent mental plagiarist, I am afraid, would be ashamed to say that the bureaucratic capital in question today happens to be a state capital of the Soviet type, and that what we have to consider is the resemblance of our bureaucratic capital to that form in the various stages of capitalist development; or something more than a superficial resemblance.

In any case, at the height of capitalism, the liberal economy, the "state capital" of that time, combined with parliamentary politics, could not exist for us. Because not only do we not have that kind of economic conditions, we also do not have that kind of political conditions, in particular, politicians are not allowed to arbitrarily invade the fishing industry and private industry and mix public and private capital, which is nothing like what we call bureaucratic capital.

If we still acknowledge that China has not completely left the transitional social form of its early stages, and if we cannot deny that private capital in China is still in the early stages of formation, with political practices still showing a mixture of authoritarianism, bureaucracy and feudalism, then in areas such as land, circulating capital and other modern industries, any business conducted in the name of the state, and even a large part of private business, inevitably involves relationships with official privileges. I have previously analyzed Chinese bureaucratic capital in a different context by dividing it into three forms (see my paper *Theoretical Analysis of Chinese Bureaucratic Capital*). These are capital acquired mainly by bureaucrats themselves through official authority; capital used directly by officials in their official capacity; and capital in which officials use public capital to indirectly control private enterprises. Among these, the form of capital used by bureaucrats is what is called "state capital" in official rhetoric. This capital, adorned with the name of the state, has clearly been and will continue to be a major source of bureaucratic capital under the current political form.

But reality is always richer than theory. Leaving aside the historical conditions of traditional China, we cannot say that our bureaucratic capital has the same nature and content as the general state capitalism of the early modern period. Our society is in a transitional phase, while most countries in the world are in another transitional phase. For China as an isolated entity, we are in the early stage of capitalism. However, as part of the global context, we cannot escape the political and economic influences of the late stage of capitalism. We have experimented with Soviet-style state operations such as state farms and state trade during the war, and have continued to work on industrial organization under state capitalism. Although donning Napoleon's clothes does not make one Napoleon, it undeniably changes the appearance of the wearer. This adds to the complexity of our understanding.

If we still allow and even encourage private capital under certain conditions, and if Chinese bureaucratic capital can become a driving force in the formation of Chinese capitalism, we need not harbor excessive suspicion or resentment towards bureaucratic capital. This is a historical path that we have all experienced, and one that could lead to a better future. What we find regrettable, however, is that our bureaucratic capital is neither willing nor able to carry out this historical task for us. As I pointed out in my paper, Theoretical Analysis of Chinese Bureaucratic Capital, the role of our bureaucratic capital, following the logical progression of monopoly capital, political capital and comprador capital, will lead to the rapid withering and decline of our national capital.

In short, what I want to say in this article is: (1) All the bureaucratic capital that we now decorate in the name of the state or the people not only has nothing to do with the "state capital" of the Soviet Union, nor can it be "state capital" under the advanced economic form of state capitalism, land rights and property rights dominated by the rulers are similar, but because of the special conditions of our traditional history and the surrounding international capital relations, its content and appearance will become an important subject for future historians of the new Asian method of production. (2) I believe that anyone with a modicum of national and modern thought would want the bureaucratic capital that China condemns today, especially that part of it that operates in the name of the public or the state, to become "state capital" as it is; but according to our analysis above, state capital does not exist in a vacuum; it must have some social basis. We want it to be Soviet when our social relations of production are already Soviet; we want it to be typically capitalist when our social relations of production are already typically capitalist. Is it possible for us to maintain our social relations of production in the initial stage of capital and yet "demand" that our state and even our private enterprises not be bureaucratically capitalized? Therefore, (3) I do not unconditionally commend the government for auctioning off many public enterprises piecemeal to the private sector, even though this is the view of both old and new economists in China. If our backward social relations of production could be substantially reformed, if the economic autocracy, bureaucracy and feudalism that exist today could be substantially curtailed, the cause of any form of socialization and nationalization would rather be promoted.

In a word, social production organizations that allow bureaucratic capital to develop cannot allow state capital to develop at the same time. In one socioeconomic system, state capital can be transformed into bureaucratic capital, and in the other, bureaucratic capital can be transformed into state capital.

This is what economics tells us: bureaucratic capital and state capital cannot coexist.

Chapter 40
The Methodology and Sinicization of Political Economy

40.1 Political Economy Input as an Import

40.1.1 No Environment for the Birth of Political Economy in China

As far as the social sciences in general are concerned, political economy is the science that best reflects reality and must be most grounded in reality, and within the limits of its study of the modern capitalist economy, such as in China, an economically backward semi-feudal country, where to this day there are still quite a few people who advocate the transfer of the European and American capitalist system as an ideal, there is of course no possibility of political economy. The economics or political economy that we are now studying has been imported as a finished import from the advanced capitalist countries, following the goods or machinery of these advanced capitalist countries.

It should be noted, however, that when this cultural import is traced back to its origin, it is mostly a kind of re-export of goods, first passing through Japan and then exported to China. The translation of political economy is still used in Japan. For example, Yan Youling, who first translated Western European economic classics from Yuan Fu, originally translated political economy or economics as planning. However, with the evolution of China's social and economic development and the corresponding improvement of China's cultural level, economics and even all other modern social and natural sciences, which had been entirely or mainly imported from Japan, were gradually able to import themselves directly. But whether imported through Japan or directly from Europe and the United States, we have not yet left the stage of political economy. Is the fantasy of "all the old" nationalist (remember the May Fourth Movement, a people from a certain country magazine published a big article on Confucius, which said "the Analects" "all the people born, the few people who eat, for it also disease, use it also comfortable, then wealth constant

Y. Wang, *The Basic Theory of Chinese Economy*,
https://doi.org/10.1007/978-981-95-6330-2_40

enough" these words, is the economic principle of Confucius, so Confucius is a "great economist". This kind of talk has been silenced recently, but a doctor of economics said in a Shanghai magazine a few years ago that the various measures in the king's economic policy was the source of the modern controlled economy, and finally there is a coincidence. I am afraid it is impossible to deny this fact!

Speaking on this subject, it seems that we should not "forget our roots" by not mentioning the following piece of "research". More than ten years ago, a Japanese economist called Seiichi Takimoto wrote a book called *The History of European Economics*. In the appendix of this book there is a section entitled "The Origins of the Fundamental Ideas of the Physiocrats". The main point of this appendix is to repeatedly emphasise that the ideas of the physiocrats originated entirely from the ancient Chinese "Four Books" and "Five Classics". He concludes this revisionist essay by saying: "In short, the basic ideas which form the basis of Quesnay's doctrine are entirely in accord with the ancient Chinese system of kingship as expressed in the Book of Documents and other classics. There is no difference in intent or spirit. I believe that this statement is not unfounded. However, people today generally believe that modern economics originated in France or Scotland, completely ignoring its important maternal source, China. This is truly a great pity for us in the East!".

When we come across this passage, we are naturally delighted, as if economics had become "a treasure in its own right". On closer inspection, however, it becomes clear that this legendary explanation does not correspond to the facts. Quesnay, the doctor in question, once wrote a work entitled *Le Despotisme de la Chine* ("The Despotism of China") to express his admiration for enlightened despotism. Observing the decline of the French countryside, he hoped for an ideal political system to address the agrarian crisis of the time. However, as Louis XV's physician, it was not appropriate for him to openly criticize France's corrupt political system and its devastating effects on the countryside. So he adopted the strategy used by ancient Chinese scholars of "referring to antiquity to reform the present", and depicted the autocratic rule of ancient Chinese monarchs according to his idealized vision, as a way of subtly admonishing and advising the current ruler. The type of agriculture he hoped to achieve under such a political system was characterized by large-scale farming, wealthy farmers, or a form of capitalist agriculture. His agrarian ideas bore no resemblance to the agrarian policies or measures of ancient China, except that both emphasized the importance of agriculture. Therefore, it is very far-fetched to claim that his physiocratic ideas originated in China simply because he praised the Chinese autocratic system. We do not deny that the birthplace of modern economics was in France and Scotland, and it may be added that the Scottish Adam Smith did indeed "seek advice" from the physiocrats before writing his monumental work, The Wealth of Nations. But the economic theories that earned the Physiocrats the title of "the first systematic spokesmen of modern capitalism" have nothing to do with the agrarian ideas of ancient China.

40.1.2 Comparison with Germany

Indeed, the fact that economic backwardness inevitably leads to backward economic thinking is something that all economically less developed countries have experienced. For example, Germany in the 1770s, despite its remarkable achievements in philosophy and other academic fields, had to humble itself and learn from the more advanced countries of England and France when it came to political economy. This was because Germany's economic development was hampered by historical and social obstacles. This situation was frankly acknowledged by one of Germany's great thinkers.

> Even today - in 1873 - economics is still considered a foreign science in Germany. ... The development of the capitalist mode of production in Germany, and with it the establishment of a modern bourgeois society, was hindered by certain historical events. The ground for the development of economics in Germany remains undeveloped. This science is still imported as a finished product from England and France. The professors of economics in Germany are still students. (From the preface to the second edition of Volume I of *Das Kapital*, translated by Guo Dali and Wang Yanan)

We are not here to compare whether China is in the same position today as Germany was 70 years ago. But there is one problem that is worth worrying about: our economic environment does not allow us to have our own economy, and our same economic environment does not allow us to properly understand the economy imported from abroad. Under the objective conditions of pre-capitalism, it would be very difficult for us to express our views or to elaborate on the problems of the capitalist economy, with which we are very unfamiliar, except in our efforts to improve and catch up with the real economy. This was also the case in Germany seventy years ago, where the great German thinker, immediately after the passage quoted above, expressed the following opinion:

> The economics professors in Germany are still students. In their hands, the representation of foreign realities and theories has become a compilation of doctrines. The world around them is a petty-bourgeois world. The interpretation of these various theories based on this world has led to misunderstandings. They feel that they lack significant strength in science. They are also uncomfortably aware that the problems they are studying are not really familiar to them. Most of them rely on the polished veneer of erudition in the history of doctrine, or patch together unrelated materials... to cover it up". (From the same book mentioned above)

The last two sentences were addressed to the German Historical School. We often mistakenly and unconsciously compare the German Historical School with the British Orthodox or Classical School, as if Germany had produced a new science of economics distinct from British economics. In reality, the achievements of the Historical School in economics were, at best, a minor methodological shift. The reason for this shift was simply that Germany at the time could not compete with the more advanced British in free economic competition. A few economists, starting with Friedrich List, modified and supplemented Germany's traditional mercantilist-oriented cameralism (Kamer-alwissenschaft) to create a protectionist economic policy theory disguised as historical economic thought. From the perspective of capitalist economics, this not only failed to introduce any significant new ideas, but also distorted the science.

However, we must return to the point that classical economics reached its zenith with Riccato in England and Sismondi in France, and that we cannot expect any new contribution from the German economists within the same capitalist horizon. The formation of this fragmented historical economic theory is the result of the rapid development of the German capitalist economy before and after the Franco-Prussian War in 1871.

Let's look at our own country. Looking back from the present to the period around the First Sino-Japanese War (1,894–1,895), it cannot be denied that the components of China's capitalist economy have experienced a considerable degree of development. However, due to various historical and political obstacles, China's economy remained stuck in a transitional phase between feudalism and capitalism. Within the global economic order of the capitalist world, this backward economic condition inevitably manifested itself as a semi-colonial economic form characterized by considerable subordination. This was manifested in specific facts such as the dominance of comprador trade and finance, feudal land tenure, and the loss of tariff rights, industrial rights and navigation rights on inland rivers. In this economic environment, Chinese researchers naturally felt deeply the constraints and obstacles that traditional feudal systems imposed on the development of national capitalism. Although some researchers later, influenced by the progress of the national revolutionary movement, gradually recognized the inherent connection between anti-feudalism and anti-imperialism, they believed that for China to free itself from the oppression of feudalism and imperialism, it had to become a capitalist state itself. In other words, while the advanced capitalist nations might be detested, capitalism itself was considered desirable, and the theoretical expressions of the real economies of these advanced capitalist nations were highly valued. As a result, the blessing of capitalism and the praise of capitalist economic doctrines became the dominant fact in the study of political economy in China. Given the present economic situation in China alone, this reflection in consciousness was not only an inevitable result, but also should not be overly criticized. Compared with the past feudal socioeconomic structure and its consciousness, The admiration for capitalist institutions and their theoretical expressions could even be seen as a sign of progress.

However, during the difficult transition period of China's economy to capitalism, the flaws in the global dominance of capitalism were being exposed day by day. The rapid development of the Soviet economic model further highlighted the bleak future of capitalist economies. As a result, over the past decade, the consciousness originally rooted in China's feudal socioeconomic structure has inevitably been influenced by the changing global economic environment and the shifting economic consciousness worldwide. This has led to a growing demand for re-evaluation and selective reconsideration of the capitalist economic doctrines that were once unconditionally accepted. In other words, our study of political economy not only needs to be, but can now be, critical.

However, precisely because this 'possibility' is not the result of improvements within China's own socioeconomic structure, but rather a consequence of changes in the global economic environment, the result is that while some within the study of political economy focus on the broader dynamics of the world economy, there are still others—perhaps even a majority—who remain entangled in China's pre-capitalist economic conditions. They see capitalist economics as the necessary and enlightened path that China must follow, and thus see capitalist economics, or political economy, as our salvation. In today's Chinese economic community, the latter tendency is particularly pronounced. The majority of Chinese economists have returned after "learning the way" at institutions in advanced capitalist countries. If we may be so bold as to say that scholars often carry certain biases with them, then the prominence of this latter tendency in current economic discourse is hardly surprising.

Therefore, conducting a more detailed review of the study of political economy over the years, including the current situation, might be quite beneficial.

40.2 How Do We Study Political Economy?

The question of how we study political economy might seem to focus on the technical aspects of research, such as translating, writing, organizing study groups, publishing papers and so on. However, I do not intend to go into these details. Rather, I want to explore how they see political economy as a particular kind of discipline in their studies.

Broadly speaking, those who study political economy in China tend to have two different views of the discipline. If we were to make a somewhat imprecise distinction, one could be described as an overly empirical view, while the other could be described as an overly metaphysical view. Let me explain each in turn.

40.2.1 Physical Views

In the beginning, when political economy was first introduced to China, and for a long time afterwards, the field was viewed in a very straightforward or literal way, as a highly empirical discipline—a study of how to get rich, or how to make both individuals and the nation wealthy. This is not surprising. Many economists of the past, especially those from the early stages of capitalism, were constrained by the basic economic concepts of their time and wanted to make their theories credible to rulers and citizens alike. As a result, they often titled their economic writings in relation to wealth. For example, the major work of the physiocrat Turgot was entitled *Reflections on the Formation and Distribution of Wealth* (Réflexions sur la formation et la distribution des richesses). Even Adam Smith, who is credited with founding political economy, titled his seminal work *The Wealth of Nations*, with the full title *An Inquiry into the Nature and Causes of the Wealth of Nations*. In this work, he explicitly stated that "the purpose of political economy is to enrich both the people and their ruler" (see Guo Dali and Wang Yanan's translation of *The Wealth of Nations*, first paragraph of the fourth book). After Smith, however, economics developed into a full-fledged science, no longer just a guide to getting rich. Moreover, later economists looked not only at the causes of wealth but also at the causes of poverty. As capitalist economies developed, on the one hand, society became richer, but on the other it also seemed to become poorer. The majority of the rich in a nation saw their wealth limited by the poverty of the majority, and even the rich began to feel insecure. Both wealth and poverty became the subject of economic study, leading to the conclusion that economics could no longer be seen as a shortcut to wealth.

However, in the advanced countries, which both enjoyed the benefits of capitalism and suffered from its drawbacks, it was well understood that economics, as a study focused on capitalist economies, could not provide a method for getting rich. But when economics began to be introduced into less developed countries—or rather, when less developed countries sought to introduce this discipline—this was clearly the intention. For example, Yan Youling's selection and translation of Smith's *The Wealth of Nations*, along with the numerous notes he added to the book, illustrates this point perfectly.

However, the development of real economic conditions has gradually taught Chinese economists that studying economics with the intention of getting rich is utterly futile. At this point, I would like to add a few remarks that are neither entirely humorous nor entirely off-topic: If someone really wants to get rich by studying economics, he might actually find a shortcut and an example in an anti-capitalist economics book. The first volume of *Capital*, in its section on the accumulation of capital (Part VII), provides many vivid examples of how modern capitalists were formed. It also provides clear examples of how small capitalists became big capitalists (as detailed in Parts III, IV, V and VI of the same volume). What may be somewhat discouraging, however, is that in the same process of non-capitalists becoming small capitalists and small capitalists becoming large capitalists, it also shows from the other side how independent producers became wage laborers and fell into poverty.

In short, political economy, whether from the perspective of defending capitalism or criticizing it, offers neither the smell of money nor the sound of its clinking. Although a small number of economists still cling to their traditional prejudices, the majority have awakened from the illusion of getting rich. With this awakening, however, the nature of economics in their hands immediately changed; it swung from one extreme to the other. Initially, they viewed economics in an overly empirical, materialistic way, but now they have shifted to an overly abstract, metaphysical perspective.

40.2.2 Metaphysical Views

Political economy is not, as the early economists proclaimed, "enriching the people and enriching the monarch", so what kind of science is it? As far as we Chinese economists who have introduced this knowledge are concerned, what is the need for us to introduce this knowledge here? The fact that economics has long been established as a science and has long been studied as a science justifies the use of the formula "learning for learning's sake". However, their understanding is not entirely consistent, or in other words, the degree of "transcendence" of political economy is different from each other, and if it is hardly distinguishable, there are three types:

(1) To regard economics as a purely abstract and irrelevant field may be an extreme view, but it is not particularly rare. Political economy originally emerged as a product of British socioeconomic conditions. The economic laws established by British economists were generally regarded as universal truths, both by those economists themselves and by economists in other countries who propagated their theories as doctrines. Adam Smith, in his seminal work The Wealth of Nations, often used the phrase "all times and all places". David Ricardo's great work, On the *Principles of Political Economy and Taxation*, was hailed by contemporary economists as a true science based on eternal laws (De Quincey, in *The Freedom of A Opium-Eater*, praised Ricardo's economics as "a true science based on eternal laws" that brought clarity to previously chaotic material). The mediocre economist Nassau Senior wanted to make economics an "abstract deductive science". With this approach, economic explanations seemed as straightforward as arithmetic operations, and the following two facts reinforced this belief: First, within the continued dominance of capitalism, the laws governing capitalist economic movement naturally retained considerable validity. Second, defending the capitalist system inevitably required affirming the validity of economic theories from an ideological and conceptual point of view. Thus, economics, presented as a complete and well-organized body of knowledge—from introduction to conclusion—was regarded by Chinese economists as an absolute doctrine, universally applicable over time. Unable to critically evaluate these theories because they were unfamiliar with or completely detached from the foreign economic realities reflected in them, Chinese economists had no choice but to accept them as irrelevant knowledge. Moreover, the spread of the Austrian School of Economics to continental European universities and other institutions quickly influenced academic circles in China. This school of economics is known for its generalism and absolutism in methodology. For example, Jevons described the "first principle of economics"—the law of marginal utility—as universally applicable, suggesting that such principles are general truths related to human nature. He also said: "The theory of this science is so simple, and so deeply founded on universal laws of human organization and of the external world, that it remains unchanged in all the periods we study" (see Keynes's Introduction to Economics, translated by Wang Yanan, Chapter Nine, notes). The notion of "general truths" that are "invariant over all periods" clearly lacks specific temporal and spatial relevance, much like the formula "two plus two equals four". Yet this view of economics as purely abstract and super-real is promoted by many Chinese economists as a new insight and discovery.

(2) It is good to treat economics as a subject that has nothing to do with the economic changes in the capitalist countries, but there are still many economists who

> understand that economics is a product of the real economy and that it cannot have a surreal existence. They are indifferent to what kind of modifications have been made to the principles of economics as a result of the economic changes in the capitalist countries or in the capitalist world as a whole, and how these principles cannot be applied to the new economic problems that have arisen. In fact, free economic competition was the backbone of the capitalist economic system, and this kind of economic form has been replaced by the unified economy of block economy in the capitalist countries or in the whole capitalist world, and has been dissolved by the economic form of cartel, trust, etc. However, the original economic theoretical system, which has the free economy as the core of its study, is still treated as a doctrine in Chinese economic circles to be presented superficially as if it were in the economy of the capitalist countries, as if it were in the economy of the capitalist countries, as if it were in the economy of the capitalist countries. The economy of the capitalist countries, that is, their economic theory, there is no change, this is how the 'calm' ah!

Indeed, our economists have not lagged behind in discussing these recent economic developments in our economic community and in our publications. However, the theories they expound and interpret on these issues—how discontinuous or fundamentally contradictory they are to the original economic doctrines—may not have been entirely lost on them, but they mostly treat them as completely different or unrelated matters. In other words, when discussing new economic changes and defending the old economic structure, they adopt a "dual approach". A brief survey of recent economic publications or statements by economists reveals many such examples. Moreover, the changes within capitalist economies, within the limits mentioned, are still changes within capitalism—from one stage to another. It may be understandable from a capitalist point of view to see these changes as having no significant connection with capitalist economic doctrines. But isn't it the case that one sixth of the world's territory has already "slipped" into another world? The implications of this for traditional economic theories should be significant and not to be taken lightly. Yet our economists remain remarkably "calm", even suggesting that the great dawn of economics is just around the corner. Let us consider the high opinion of one economist:

> Economics has long since become a science, but due to the criticism of scientific socialism and the historical school, the remaining achievements of the orthodox school have become almost lifeless. However, as a science dedicated to solving the problems of human life, economics occupies an extremely high position and bears a heavy responsibility. How could it lose heart because of a minor setback? ... The day when economics becomes a science that studies human behavior is near. (Zhu Tongjiu, *The Development of Economics After the War*)

From this passage we learn how "lofty the position and heavy the responsibility" of economics really is! It seems that this exalted position has been elevated by economists themselves! Leaving aside the wording, which needs further refinement, I would like to point out that his claim that economics will become a science that studies human behavior, although largely based on established sources (as the author of the above book states in a footnote that "much of the material in this book is translated from W.C. Mitchell's *The Prospects of Economics*", hence it is "largely based on established sources"), is vague and ambiguous if taken as the future content of economics. Moreover, the "science" to which he refers, the economics of the utility school (as he later explains), is already being promoted as established doctrine and does not need to wait for the future. However, he acknowledges that the remaining achievements of the orthodox school have almost lost their vitality. To see the revival of orthodox economics in the form of the utility school, and to believe that the "lifelessness" of economics is due solely to the critiques of scientific socialism and the historical school, while ignoring the loss of a significant part of the capitalist world's territory, shows how much he regards economics as a discipline unrelated to the economic changes in capitalist countries.

(3) Treating Economics as Unrelated to China's Socioeconomic Issues

Since political economy is an imported discipline, a science that focuses on the study of foreign capitalist economies, it seems almost natural for Chinese economists to see it as having little to do with China's socioeconomic problems. Whether the study of political economy is closely related to understanding and dealing with China's socioeconomic problems is something I intend to address in the final section. For now, I would like to point out this fact: many economists do not pay much attention to these issues, such as the economic category in which political economy places China's economic structure within its overall framework. How does our study and understanding of economics contribute to solving China's socioeconomic problems? Is the economic doctrine we support and promote, when applied in practice, significantly detrimental to the transformation of China's economy?

In fact, Chinese economists who raise the issue of economic reform in China, while vehemently condemning imperialism and advocating the liberation of national capital from constraints, base their proposed reform plans on the same set of political economy doctrines. However, this same set of doctrines essentially dictates that Chinese national capital "submit" to the broader capitalist system and function fully as part of a colonial economic structure. Yet they have failed to recognize this glaring contradiction. This is because they have never approached the study of political economy as a discipline related to China's socioeconomic problems.

The purpose of these three different ways of studying economics is nothing more than to separate theory from reality, but to different degrees.

40.3 What Kind of Political Economy Have We Studied?

The description of the method or way in which we have studied political economy in the previous section gives an idea of the content of the economics we have studied. But in order to supplement the previous statement, we shall here point out more specifically, in relation to the political economy we are studying, its fundamental defects.

In order to examine the economics we are studying, it is essential to pay attention to the currently popular books on economics, especially those on the principles of economics, or those entitled "principles" or "introductions" to economics. From university lecture halls to general economic publications, all should be the subject of our investigation. However, to focus the discussion and highlight general trends, it is best to look at the economic theories that our economists treat as doctrine and as unassailable standards. Alternatively, we can examine the most commonly used introductory economics books that every beginner must study, and point out the common, recurring themes and approaches they share as a basis for further critique and analysis.

Of course, the economics reading I am critiquing here is not limited to books by our own economists. It also includes the works of foreign economists on which our economists base their writings or use directly in teaching, as well as those recommended to beginners. In reality, Chinese economists cannot be held responsible for the shortcomings of modern economic doctrines; it seems unnecessary for them to take the blame for the mistakes of others. At most, they have done some work of transmission or reinterpretation. The most striking common feature of all these economic readings is very clearly reflected in their narrative style or structure. The so-called four-part division and the trinity approach to economics are almost universally used to construct the content of these works. If you open any of these books, after first defining economics and explaining its nature, tasks and methods, you will find a sequential deduction of the four main sections: production, distribution, exchange and consumption. Within each of these sections, the content is organized almost entirely around capital, labor and land, and further around capitalists, workers and landlords, and finally around profit, wages and rent—these major elements and units—forming a neatly arranged system of economics. This formal order symbolizes the apparent order of capitalist society, but the anarchy of production and the inequalities of distribution within capitalist society also symbolize the internal disorder of this seemingly ordered economy. I believe that by analyzing these formal structures or styles in economics, we can understand the true nature of the political economy we are studying. At the same time, it becomes easier to understand why many political economists often create a gulf between theory and reality. Let us now consider the four-part division and the trinity approach separately.

40.3.1 Review of the Four Division Theory

The emergence of the four-part division in economics is a result of the vulgarization of the discipline. The works of the great classical economists lack such a structure. Adam Smith's seminal work, *The Wealth of Nations*, begins with the theory of the division of labor, while David Ricardo's *On the Principles of Political Economy and Taxation* begins with the theory of value. Both authors explained the concepts of production, distribution, exchange and consumption as they arose naturally within the broader economic process, without adhering to a strict formal structure. In 1821, however, James Mill published his *Elements of Political Economy*, which he divided into four chapters: the first on production, the second on distribution, the third on exchange, and the fourth on consumption. This introduced what is known as the four-part division of economics. Mill wrote this book partly because of his friendship with Ricardo, who had published his great work *On the Principles of Political Economy and Taxation* at Mill's encouragement. However, Mill found Ricardo's work too complex and inaccessible for beginners. Therefore, during walks with his son John Stuart Mill, he would explain the main ideas of Ricardo's theory and John would take notes. These notes were later organized and refined into the book. To make Ricardo's complex theories more accessible and systematically clear, Mill adopted the four-part division. Although this approach somewhat obscured Ricardo's theoretical framework, it proved highly suitable for the subsequent trend of economics becoming increasingly superficial, widespread and popular. As a result, the four-part structure became the most common format for economic writing in the years that followed.

Observing the economic phenomena of capitalist society, it seems that the process of economic activity is as follows: first, goods are produced in the productive sector; then they are distributed among the various entities directly or indirectly involved in the production process, such as capitalists, workers and landowners. Each party uses its share for exchange, and finally the results of this exchange are consumed. At first sight, the division of the economy into four sectors according to this sequence—production, distribution, exchange and consumption—seems clear and natural. On closer inspection, however, it becomes clear that this division is highly unreasonable. There are two major errors to be highlighted:

(1) The Fragmentation of the Theoretical System

An organized theoretical system should have a focal point, a central hub that unifies the whole framework. The 'fourfold' division of economics, like a 'four-headed' political system, does not provide this central hub. The way in which the total production of a society is distributed among its members, the way in which they exchange, and the general conditions and proportions of consumption are all determined by the current production structure. Each type of social production structure corresponds to a compatible distribution structure. The relations of exchange shown in the general circulation function as a component of the entire production process, while consumption, within the limits of the means of production, is already an element of production; outside of this, as the consumption of living materials, it is merely an additional matter mentioned as necessary in economics. Of course, the general level of the capacity to consume, the volume of exchange and the fluctuations in the distribution proportions have a feedback effect on the scale and structure of production. However, this effect only operates within the limits allowed by a given production structure. The central role of production in overall economic activity is not adequately represented by simply placing it in the first chair of the fourfold division. To equate the peripheral with the central, to treat the masses and the leaders as indistinguishable, may easily appear disorganized to our economists, but they fail to perceive the chaotic nature of this approach and instead regard it as a well-ordered theoretical system. I should also point out that while the "classical" style of fourfold division in economics has generally been adopted in writings after the mid-nineteenth century, economists with some understanding and insight usually recognize that it is a format that hinders theoretical development. This can be seen in their writings.

(2) Disordered Explanation Procedure

It may be said that the special emphasis on production and the subordination of distribution, especially exchange and consumption, is the claim of a certain part of the people or a certain school of economics, not the "public opinion" that is unanimously agreed upon by all; it may also be said that the theoretical system of economics does not necessarily need to have a different view of production in order to be established, as in the case of the great economist Ricardo's masterpiece, *Principles of Economics and Taxation*, which focuses on the issue of distribution (Ricardo says in the preface of the book: "This distribution is governed by certain laws, and the distribution is not a matter of law, but is a matter of law, and the distribution is a matter of law". Ricardo's famous book "economics and the principle of taxation", is to focus on the distribution of the problem (Ricardo in the preface to the book said: "...... this distribution is governed by a certain law, to determine this law, is the main problem of economics.") The economists of the Austrian school, who advocate the theory of limited utility, put special emphasis on the problem of consumption; in addition, several economists of the historical school, who take exchange as the pivot of the stage of socioeconomic development, have accomplished a certain system of economic theories. Here, because of space, I cannot answer these questions in depth, but I have to point out that Ricardo puts the center of gravity of his research on distribution, which is related to the tetrarchy that has become a problem here, and he only limits the scope of his research, which is equivalent to the writing of a part of the matching theory.

Historical economists and Austrian school economists take exchange and consumption respectively as the starting point of their theories. Although their theories are fragmented, and we will have the opportunity to discuss them in detail later, they are not necessarily adherents to the theory of the four-part division. Even if we take a step back and say that the construction of economic theory does not necessarily have to focus on the mode of social production, explaining the whole of economic theory in terms of the four-part division or the theory of four-part division will certainly appear disorganized. Firstly, actual economic activities are not clearly segmented, with production followed by distribution, then exchange and finally consumption. If we consider the production process as a process of reproduction, the means of production are the results of exchange and distribution, while production itself is continuously supported by consumption. The consumption of tools, labor and even the consumption of living materials by workers are all explained as part of production. Conceptually, the forced separation of these processes into distinct stages is already fragmented enough, not to mention that in explaining them sequentially we also have to

> deal with their overlapping nature. Consumption takes place mainly in the field of production, and its completion is largely to be explained under production, then shifts again to be explained under consumption. The main agents of distribution operate mainly in the field of production, and in fact distribution is constantly taking place within production. Products re-enter the production process as factors of production, and products also leave the field of production as finished goods to enter the market, with an inseparable link between these stages and exchange. The buying and selling of labor power between workers and capitalists is a fundamental fact in the capitalist's production diary, but this question, which must be dealt with under production, is left to be dealt with under the category of exchange in the fourfold division. In short, the various economic facts which are forcibly separated under the quadripartite division are inevitably repeated over and over again.

Let us now proceed to discuss the economic trinity theory, which 'complements' the quadripartite division.

40.3.2 The Trinity Theory

The trinity theory in economics, or the economic trinity theory, is expressed by the following formula:

Land-Rent
Capital-Profit
Labor-Wages

This formula has been revered by economists since Adam Smith. But its application varies. In the first book of Smith's great work, *The Wealth of Nations*, entitled "On the Causes of Improvement in the Productive Powers of Labor" and "On the Natural Order of Distribution of the Produce of Labor to different Classes of Society", he explains the latter part of the title as follows:

> Whoever derives his income from his sources must derive it from these three sources: labor, capital or land. Income from labor is called wages; income from capital is called profit; ...... income derived exclusively from land is usually called "rent". (*The Wealth of Nations, Chinese Translation*, Volume 1, page 6) "The full price of the annual production of the labor of the land is naturally divided into three parts: wages of labor, profits of capital, and rent of land. To the three different classes of men - those who live by rent, those who live by profit, and those who live by wages - these constitute different incomes. (ibid., p. 60).

At the time when Smith put forward this view of distribution, the difficult problem was that production was not free, and so as regards distribution he thought that the interests of the classes would become equal if they were allowed to compete freely. He was very optimistic, but half a century later the difficult problems of English economics gradually shifted to distribution, so that Ricart's great contemporary work, *The Principles of Economics and Taxation*, made distribution the center of his research, and he explained it in the preface of the same book:

> The common use of labor, machinery and capital on the land, and all the land produce produced, is divided among the three classes of society, i.e. the landlords, capitalists and

> laborers. ...... All the land produce, under the name of land rent, profit and wages, is divided among the classes... ... (*Preface to Principles of Economics and Taxation*, translated by Guo Dali and Wang Yanan)

In these brief words we see no difference between Ricarto and Adam Smith's earlier statement. Smith's optimistic view of distribution, however, became very dim in Ricarto's hands. He has made a clear distinction between these three forms of distribution, rent and profit and wages, which reflects the actual situation. In other words, he lumps them together precisely because he wants to establish their essential differences, their opposition to each other. The post-Ricarto economists, in a situation where the problem of distribution was becoming more serious and had to be defended in economic terms, took advantage of the mystery of this formula and tried to use it to hide the distinction between the three and to eliminate their antagonism in concept.

Let us now analyze the irrationality of this formula in terms of the individual aspects of each group and its integrated whole.

(1) The irrationality of the individual examination

The so-called individual examination here is an examination of the organization of the three groups of the formula.

Let's look first at
Land—land rent

To regard land as the source of rent, as the cause of the formation of rent, and rent as the result of land, is not an untenable proposition in common sense, and in practice this proposition has become very obvious and stereotyped in the general conception of people. But this proposition, expressed in such a formula, is not intended to show that land is the source of rent, but mainly to show that land naturally demands rent, and that rent is a natural consequence of land. In the end, in a certain particular society, land—land rent, which is based on landed property, i.e. The private ownership of a part of the earth—manifests itself as a transcendental historical existence, and manifests itself as the most natural and reasonable truth. But this fact, which exists as a "truth", will be exposed as an unreasonable "inside story" once the secret it contains in the formula of land and rent is revealed. Land is a natural thing, and although it is used as a factor of production in every social form, it is not natural to create land rent and a social relation understood as a thing as soon as it is used as a factor of production. It can be seen that the view of land as a natural object as a means of extracting rent is a product of a particular society and is supported by a particular man-made law. Generally speaking, the formula of land—land rent cannot be established at all; as far as a particular society is concerned, it can only reflect an unnatural and irrational relationship.

Secondly
capital-profit

Economists sometimes refer to this grouping in a formula as capital-interest. This is more mysterious than the term capital gain. For in capital-interest the medium in all this disappears, and interest-bearing capital returns to the owner, separated from the cycle of the medium (that is, the cycle in which capital, in its real movement, is transformed first from money-capital into a means of production and then, through the process of production, into commodities which are sold and returned to the capitalist). It takes the form of money which produces its own money. So this expression, capital-interest, is the most meaningless, but perhaps because it is the most meaningless, it is the most mysterious. The expression capital-profit is undoubtedly closer to reality and more capable of showing the relationship between reality. But the common economist's view of this expression is that capital naturally produces profit, just as land naturally produces rent. Profit is produced as a result of capital. Here, for reasons of space, we cannot explain in detail that "capital is the social relationship between people and things as a medium", so the expression capital-profit is not appropriate at all. But the economists who advocate this expression sometimes unconsciously reject it, that is, they find it difficult to admit with confidence that profits arise directly from capital, whether they consider capital as a body of value (in terms of money) or as a material body (in terms of the use value of the conditions of production of labor: machines, raw materials, etc.).) In a twist of explanation, profit is the result of a reward for the work of the owner of capital, the capitalist, or of the capitalist's "forbearance" not to waste (the great discovery of the typical vulgar economist, Senior). In any case, the expression of capital—profit—is negated. Although economists themselves reject this expression, capital-profit remains a natural arrangement in their minds.

Finally, we look at labor—wages

This is the expression of wages as the price of labor. According to the previous explanation, here labor is regarded as the source of wages, and wages are naturally the result of labor; if you do not work, you do not get wages, and if you work, you cannot be denied wages. This is more like a natural and impartial jurisprudence. But first of all, we must understand, labor on its own, it does not exist, is an abstraction; on the social aspect of the study, it refers to human and natural material metabolism function of human production activities on the basis of, no matter on the interpretation of this point, we obviously cannot be said to pay the price of it, to be an abstraction, to pay the price of a kind of activity function, is how not to make sense. It is true that before the term "labor" (Arbeitskraf) was introduced, economists were not aware of the ambiguity of using "labor" as a substitute for "work". But this does not absolve them of their error. Labor—wages—has been interpreted as a transcendental historical expression. It is as if wage-labor, labor-wage, is a common form in all societies, and our present society, the capitalist society, has inherited this form as a traditional fact of history. Moreover, in societies where capital exercises domination, this form of expression is used to determine labor's claim to wages, as well as land's claim to rent and capital's claim to profit. Such "disinterested" and non-discriminatory expression can be said to be motivated by the "justice" and "generosity" of economists. But if we look at the various sub-groups of the whole formula in an integrated way, we can only see the "machinations" embedded in this kind of expression.

(2) The Unreasonableness Revealed by a Comprehensive Examination

This entire formula, namely the triadic combination of land-rent, capital-profit and labor-wages, seems to have only one thing in common: the way in which each category is represented is a general form that has eliminated all exceptions, apart from historical limitations. This leads to another common feature: each category is seen as a natural relationship, arranged by nature. However, when we examine the actual situation, we find that these two common features exist only in the minds of economists, or rather, economists have constructed this formula with these two points in mind. Let's look at the antecedents of these three categories, namely land, capital and labor. We already know that land is a natural entity; capital, whether in terms of its value relationship or its material form or its use-value relationship, represents a social relationship between people mediated by objects; and labor is a social function considered as a productive activity, which is in itself an abstraction. There is nothing in common in the nature of these three elements. The only thing that can be said to be common between rent, profit and wages, each of which is derived from these three categories, is that they constitute the incomes or earnings of different social classes. But here the question arises. Why is it that some incomes, such as the worker's, are obtained through his own productive activity; others, such as the capitalist's, are obtained without personal labor or only through the exercise of supervisory duties; and finally, some incomes, such as the landlord's, are obtained not only without direct productive activity, but also without the burden of supervision? The landlord only needs a legal claim to a piece of land to consume the fruits produced by others on that land, even if he is far away enjoying himself. These three different types of income should not be treated in the same way. Moreover, it is unfortunate that although economists have clearly defined the sources of these three types of income, Their ultimate origin is in fact none other than a certain amount of labor, driven by a certain amount of capital, producing value on a certain piece of land. This product value is first divided into wages and surplus value; the surplus value is then divided into profit and rent. The division of the same product of value, or, we might say, of a given quantity of product of value, into the sources of rent, profit and wages, and the proportionality of their distribution—in which the gain of one necessarily entails the loss of the others—clearly manifests itself as a relationship of mutual opposition, which undoubtedly constitutes a fatal contradiction of this triadic formula. This contradiction, though unflinchingly exposed by classical economists like Ricardo, is deliberately concealed by later vulgar economists, who use this very formula to conceal and gloss over the real contradictions. Moreover, these economists at least recognize that it is not only necessary but also perfectly reasonable for workers to receive wages sufficient to maintain their existence and enable them to continue working. Since this category within the formula is considered reasonable (still in the minds of these economists), the integration of the other two categories within the same formula naturally leads to the rationalization of the whole formula. However, this is only done consciously by a few of the more insightful economists; the rest merely mechanically imitate it, treating it as an unassailable doctrine.

Broadly speaking, the popularity of this Trinitarian formula was greatly influenced by the quadripartite view, and it could even be said that the two reinforced each other's irrationality. Within the framework of the quadripartite view, rent, wages and profit are categorized proportionally in the distribution section (as mentioned above, James Mill, the founder of the quadripartite view, explained these three items in separate sections in the chapter on distribution), while their sources—land, labor and capital—are categorized proportionally in the production section. In this way, the formula appears more rational on the surface. Since the factors involved in production each receive a share of the distribution, the formal arrangement of this formula also conveniently supports the adoption of the quadripartite view.

They complement each other perfectly, as if by coincidence.

This serves as a typical example and model of the general content of modern economics. Chinese economists, influenced by this tradition of economics, naturally reflect it in a repetitive and unoriginal manner within the Chinese economics community. However, a casual review of current economics literature seems to show some signs of "reform". It is said that because Austrian school economists place special emphasis on consumption, some recent Chinese economic writings have forcibly "promoted" the theory of consumption to a position before the theory of production (as seen in the works of Zhao Lanping, Wu Shirui, and others), making consumption the primary focus within the quadripartite framework. Additionally, in the production category, besides land, labor, and capital, a new production factor called "organization" has been added. However, this "reform" makes it difficult to identify who should receive the income derived from organization as a source in the distribution category. The likely outcome is that it will still be attributed to the capitalists, who bear the responsibility for organizing production. But this change seems to undermine the integrity of the trinity formula.

In summary, the political economy writings of the Chinese economic community are largely modelled on the quadripartite framework and the Trinitarian formula. Given this form, structure and nature of political economy, it is not surprising that scholars have come to see it as a discipline that has nothing to do with the realities of the economy, the economic changes in capitalist countries, and especially the issues of social and economic reform in China.

But should we study such a political economy?

40.4 We Should Study Political Economy from the Perspective of the Chinese People

As far as the Chinese economic community is concerned, the previous two sections have critiqued the approach traditionally used to study political economy, as well as the content considered to be the typical model of political economy. In this critique, I have always kept one point in mind: given China's current socioeconomic position, it is inevitable and undeniable that the Chinese economic community will show certain signs of backwardness. This is because political economy is inherently a product of modern capitalist society, and our own economic environment cannot produce a distinct political economy. Moreover, the current economic environment limits the extent of our expertise in political economy, making our tendency to imitate or echo the imported political economy an almost inevitable trend. Furthermore, as the capitalist economy declines, there is an increasing need for an economics that hides the true state of affairs, which has led to the proliferation of the kind of economics that is irrelevant to or distorts reality. This in turn reinforces the inevitable trend within our economic community.

However, the demands made on our understanding of political economy by China's real socioeconomic conditions are precisely the opposite of this trend. This clearly leads us to consider the purpose of studying political economy. From the perspective of the global capitalist system, China suffers from two capitalist hardships: one is the difficulty of developing Chinese capitalism, and the other is the burden of being surrounded by an overdeveloped world capitalist economy. These two factors are interrelated and have created China's current semi-colonial economic status. If we say that the nature of political economy is fundamentally different from purely metaphysical concepts that have no connection with real society—that it is, and should be, a theoretical representation of real economic conditions—then we cannot approach the study of this discipline with indifference or detachment. To do so would not be research, but a mere play with abstract ideas. Moreover, if our goal in studying political economy is to contribute to China's socioeconomic transformation, it is even more important for us to clearly understand the true nature of modern political economy. In short, when we study political economy, we must always remember that we are doing so from the perspective of the Chinese people. The starting point and demands of Chinese scholars engaged in this research are different from those of most economists in Europe, America, and even Japan. The conclusions they have drawn, or the conclusions they have contrived, based on their respective social conditions and needs, not only cannot be applied to our real economic situation but also hinder our understanding of the characteristics of both the world economy and the Chinese economy. The performance of our economic community over the years has truthfully illustrated this crucial point.

40.4.1 Three Preliminary Understandings

I think that before our political economy scholars start their studies, they should have some preliminary understanding.

First, as long as political economy is considered to focus on capitalist economies, when we reflect on China's subordinate position within the capitalist economic system, we can see what kind of perspective and motivation such an economic theory uses to discuss "semi-colonial" or "quasi-colonial" economies. While we may not be willing to categorize ourselves as part of a "colonial" economy, capitalist economists, especially after the last world war, have not forgotten China when discussing colonial economies, especially in the context of economic issues such as bloc economies. At the very least, a large part of their theories on colonial economies can be applied to China. Thus, to accept their theories of political economy as doctrine is tantamount to admitting that we are their spokesmen. For example, the current theory of an "agrarian economy" that has emerged in Chinese economic discussions unconsciously echoes the theory of an "agrarian China" within the East Asian Co-Prosperity Sphere.

Secondly, as capitalism has entered the stage of imperialism, its dangers have increased, but correspondingly its vigilance has also increased. It tries to mobilize all available forces to defend the domination of the capitalist world. Although the unique economic system of the Soviet Union suddenly appeared in the midst of internal contradictions, this only increased the vigilance of capitalism and forced it to engage in defense and confrontation in the political, economic, military and cultural fields. In the cultural sphere, the most realistic political economy is naturally given special attention. The establishment of economic research institutes in various countries, the creation of special chairs of political economy in universities, and the popularity of economic journals focusing on economic trends all seem to create an "economic boom" in the field of economics—both to mitigate domestic anti-capitalist sentiment and to stabilize the pessimism and despair caused by real economic crises. Naturally, when these ideas are spread in backward nations, especially in China, which is highly valued and is currently experiencing a surge in anti-imperialist sentiment, they will not miss the opportunity. The result is that in the eyes of many Chinese economists, who pride themselves on importing and promoting Western economics, the "bright future" of economics seems to shine, leading to the conclusion that we should not fear capitalism.

Third, because of the inherent contradictions and flaws in the operation of the capitalist economy, despite the efforts of the economists who defend it to cover up the cracks, many critical economic theories emerged around the mid-nineteenth century, during the heyday of capitalism. (Theoretical disputes between the historical schools, the Austrian school and the so-called new orthodox school—referring to a group of economists led by A. Marshall—should not be categorized as non-critical economic theories. On the contrary, they are a collection of defensive theories). Among these, the critical theory of the German socialist school, which still analyzed the capitalist economy but was born out of the study of British economic conditions and economic history, became increasingly influential in the field of political economy as it highlighted the growing flaws in the capitalist economy. The emergence of the Soviet economy, based on this economic theory, further strengthened its position in the field of political economy. Therefore, although the economic community in various countries has, as we have said, been repeating old doctrines and fabricating new bright futures, it is not difficult to see the growth and spread of opposing theories. Professor Theodor Gregory of Great Britain, in an article entitled "The Future of Capitalism" in 1932, began by stating that "hope for the survival of the present system is now at its weakest; there has never been such a phenomenon in the history of modern economic development; the two years of economic depression have shaken the foundations of the whole international economic structure…". This reality has led to criticism of the capitalist system in various countries. He first discussed how certain American schools have questioned the capitalist system and then mentioned the situation in universities worldwide: "As for the academic atmosphere in universities, the situation is no better; on the European continent, universities are the centers of opposition to the existing system". (See the translated article in the first issue of Prospect magazine.) Although his remarks did not distinguish between fascist theories that seek to "block" the decline of capitalism in other ways, they generally reflect how modern capitalism and the political economy that relies on it have reached a fragmented stage.

From the above three points we know, firstly, that traditional political economy is not conducive to the socioeconomic transformation of a country like China; secondly, that this political economy is still being used as a weapon of cultural aggression to prevent us from reforming our socio-economy; and secondly, that even if political economy has no imperial purpose in its existence, it is already devastated and cannot help us much, either practically or theoretically, if we do not study it from a critical point of view. If we do not study it from a critical point of view, it will not help us much, either practically or theoretically.

40.4.2 Three Main Research Objectives

The preliminary ideas discussed above already indicate the purpose of our political economy research. Broadly speaking, there are three main points: First, the aim is to provide a basic understanding of all social sciences and to serve as a practical guide for engaging in social activities through the study of economics. We know that the material process of life, or the economic process, which is the subject of political economy, forms the basis of real society. Therefore, whether one is engaged in general social science research or in any practical social activities, it is necessary to understand this real social foundation through economics. Bogdanov once remarked: "Whether one considers the whole of history or the development of social meaning, whether one studies diplomatic or religious issues, one cannot ignore the economic links within society (the structure of social foundations) and one cannot avoid using economic conclusions". Economics can therefore be seen as a fundamental science in the system of social sciences, just as physics and chemistry are in the study of organic and inorganic processes. A botanist, zoologist, astronomer or agricultural scientist who does not understand the conclusions of physics and chemistry is like an unarmed soldier. Similarly, sociologists, historians and jurists who lack economic understanding are in the same predicament. Moreover, individuals involved in social struggle and social enterprise who do not understand economics are similar to unarmed soldiers (See Zhou's translation of Bogdanov's *Introduction to Economics*, page 4). In today's world, as economic affairs become increasingly complex and various forms of social struggle and interaction with nature directly or indirectly involve economic causality, every human being is inevitably involved. Whether we are engaged in social science research or participating in social enterprises, we are also subject to various economic laws in our daily lives. In this sense, The study of economics or the acquisition of economic knowledge is not limited to the needs of a particular group of people.

Second, through the study of political economy, the aim is to thoroughly understand the laws governing the movement of modern capitalist economies. This involves determining the inevitable outcomes of capitalism and providing reasonable explanations or interpretations of the defects, contradictions, conflicts and desperate struggles that manifest themselves during its inevitable development. This requirement is a common concern among economists in different types of countries (whether socialist, capitalist or colonial). But it is particularly crucial for China. China is still struggling with the transition from feudalism to capitalism, and is uncertain whether to move towards capitalism or towards a form of socialism that focuses on people's livelihoods. If theory, combined with reality, points to the harm and decline of capitalism, even if we do not fear capitalism, there is no reason for us to "embrace" it. Third, the purpose is to clear away all conceptual obstructions that hinder the socioeconomic transformation of China through the study of political economy. These obstructions are not only related to political economy itself but also pertain to all social sciences and even natural sciences beyond economics. Political economy is a highly practical and real science (considering it as irrelevant to reality, as mentioned earlier, is not because political economy itself lacks relevance, but rather because there is an attempt to avoid its reality). By grasping the correct theoretical core in economics, various prejudices and illusions held in political science, sociology, philosophy, and even natural sciences can be clarified. In fact, under the influence of imperialist forces, the entire social consciousness in China is permeated with the toxins of imperialist cultural invasion. Every reform in China's socioeconomic sphere encounters these toxins as obstacles. Therefore, if China is to transform, Political economy must become a "cultural weapon" against backward feudal consciousness and imperialist cultural invasion. It is the responsibility of Chinese political economy researchers to determine how to use and refine this weapon effectively.

In addition, I would like to emphasize the following requirement to strengthen the responsibility of our researchers: we must gradually create a political economy through our studies that is specifically tailored to Chinese readers. Some may question this: First, science has no national boundaries, so it is unnecessary for each country to have its own specific science; second, political economy is a theoretical representation of real economic processes, and a backward economy like China's, as mentioned in the first section, cannot produce its own unique economy. If, on the other hand, we interpret the political economy we are trying to build as an economic theory tutorial that is particularly advantageous for Chinese readers, one that can specifically engage Chinese interests and point out ways for the transformation of Chinese society and economy, then it is a different matter. Such a theoretical system would pay special attention to how its conclusions or assertions apply to socioeconomic conditions in China, and would use Chinese economic realities as much as possible as material for examples and quotations. So far, we have not found such a type of political economy in terms of both form and content. Although there are many advanced political economy texts available for reference, and some foreign economists have made significant contributions to theories on Chinese socioeconomic issues, they do not fully meet our specific needs. Of course, the content of the political economy I am referring to, designed for Chinese study, is essentially a more practical political economy textbook. The reason why I emphasize this effort as a goal for Chinese political economy researchers is that establishing a political economy with a distinct nature and content, aimed at transforming Chinese society and freeing it from intellectual constraints, is quite different from compiling a textbook based on existing materials. This requires us, as political economy researchers, to make considerable efforts to elucidate the correct theoretical system for both the world and Chinese economies.

Chapter 41
A Critical Analysis of the Austrian School and Its Dissemination in China

41.1 Explanation of the Topic

Over the past five years, my research has focused somewhat vaguely on the topic of "Chinese economics". The term "Chinese economics" has been mentioned more than once, but I have not given it a specific definition. Theoretically, such a term is not very appropriate and can easily lead to many unnecessary misunderstandings. As a science, economics should not be compromised in its general adequacy and systemic nature by using such a term; there is only one economics.

Indeed, readers may have encountered terms such as 'British economics' or 'German economics' in the works of the Italian economic historian Gossa and the British economic historian Ingram. The main drawback of this method of national classification in the history of economic thought is that it establishes national boundaries within the field of economic ideas, disrupting the connections and affiliations of different schools across countries. This approach equates important economic theories with less important ones, leading to a fragmented view of modern economics. However, since they mainly collect past economic ideas or theories from different countries as historical material, these problems are somewhat mitigated when viewed as historical records. Indeed, the histories of economic thought by figures such as Gossa and Ingram remain within the realm of historical material. In their view, economics does not pose general or scientific systemic problems. In contrast, I am a proponent of the general principles of economic science. I believe that the economic laws formed under certain social production relations, production conditions, and exchange conditions can be applied to all societies with similar social production relations or similar production and exchange conditions. Of course, no society's natural or historical conditions will perfectly match those of another society. Within these limits, the economic laws of one society should not be fully applicable to others. However, we must be clear about two facts: First, all economic laws are derived from the commonalities observed in the economic phenomena of different societies at the same stage of social development, despite their unique characteristics.

Y. Wang, *The Basic Theory of Chinese Economy*,
https://doi.org/10.1007/978-981-95-6330-2_41

Second, although modern economics was established primarily on the basis of the specific environment of the British economy, the general trends, the main content and even the evolution of British economics can also be seen in countries such as France, the United States and Germany. Not only were British economic theories confirmed by other, later developing capitalist countries, but, in fact, when British economists began their scientific research, economists from other countries, especially French economists, had already partially deduced or illustrated the fundamental laws of modern economics (as can be seen in the economic tables of the French physiocrats, such as those of Quesnay). This gave British economists a considerable advantage in their research.

From the above summary, we can derive the following basic concepts regarding the development and application of economics:

(1) The general and global nature of economics: The general and global nature of economics is based on the universal aspects of economic reality. Economics as a science is based on the general and global characteristics of economic processes.
(2) Abstraction and generalization of specific economic conditions: The general or global nature of economics does not negate the specific economic conditions of particular societies. Rather, it means abstracting and generalizing from these specific conditions. Positively, this means that economic laws reflect a synthesis of individual special conditions into a general framework. Negatively, it means the exclusion of special conditions that cannot be generalized.
(3) Application of economic theories: The economics derived from this research process may differ in application, even when applied to economic realities at the same stage of development as the one in which the theory was formulated. For example, if the economics we are discussing relates to capitalist economies, its applicability to economies that have reached the capitalist stage may be limited by differences in developmental maturity and unique developmental conditions. As a result, existing formulas and theories may not fit perfectly. Moreover, the application of such theories to economies that are transitioning beyond the capitalist stage or have not yet reached it would be even less appropriate, as the theories may not be adaptable to different development contexts.

This point about the application of economics is particularly emphasized here. Theoretically, there is only one economics, but in application, economics is not the same for every country. On this premise, I propose the term "Chinese economics". The most compelling reason for introducing this term is the acute sense that economics has been, and continues to be, misapplied in China. Economics, as a finished import from abroad, has been in China for several decades. However, our understanding of how economics as a science should be applied to support China's economic transformation remains at odds. This disconnect exists not only among the general public, but especially among economists, including those who see themselves as realists or guides to China's economic reality.

It may seem surprising to some that economists don't fully understand what economics is, but it is as common as a monk not understanding what Buddhist scriptures are, even though he recites or promotes them daily. Indeed, when we economists focus on metaphysical economic theories, our understanding is as far removed from practical economics as a monk's knowledge of scripture is from practical Buddhist teachings.

The "metaphysical economic theory" to which I refer here is primarily the Austrian school of economics. In the following sections, I will explain what this school of thought entails, how it has been introduced into China, how it has spread particularly aggressively there, and how it conflicts with our national economic policies and hinders our economic transformation.

41.2 The Essence of Austrian School Economics

There are many scholars who belong to the Austrian School, and their theories are not entirely consistent. However, it is generally accepted that Carl Menger, Eugen von Böhm-Bawerk and Friedrich von Wieser are the leading figures of this school and their theories are considered to be the core of Austrian economics.

We cannot give a full discussion of their theoretical system here, but we can outline some of their key points. They are critical of the classical school, but adopt its logical framework from an opposing perspective. They place particular emphasis on economic methodology, value theory and distribution theory. They base their understanding of distribution theory on value theory and place the basic propositions of value theory within the framework of methodology. This approach is essentially a reinterpretation of the ideas of the classical school, and the so-called "renaissance of economics" or "reformation of economics" by the Austrian school in particular, especially in the USA, could be seen as reflecting this "reinterpretation", although they emphasize different viewpoints in this reinterpretation.

Let's start with a brief comment on their methodology.

In their view, national economic phenomena can be studied from historical, theoretical and practical perspectives. Theoretical economics, as a "science of being", should be separated from practical economics, such as public finance and economic policy, which the classical school combined. Statistical and historical studies originally provided practical examples and materials for theoretical economics, but the Historical School used them to replace theoretical understanding. Because of this relationship, the Austrian School emerged with a 'crusading' attitude to the reconstruction of theoretical economics. They believe that the study of theoretical economics should adopt the so-called "exact method", making real economic phenomena the simplest and most precise elements for analysis. The forms of phenomena considered in economic studies, such as individuals pursuing only economic goals and their psychological states during economic activities, are considered the most universal and significant. Isolating and studying these economic psychological states is the starting point of economics. As Carl Menger put it, real economic theory must first "explore the main arteries of human activity - pleasures and pains". According to William Stanley Jevons, the scope of economic research is the relationship between the pleasures and pains resulting from the satisfaction of desires and the inevitable sacrifices endured. In this sense, economics is almost a form of "hedonics". The naturalness of human instinctive needs (hedonism) means that economic laws are not in conflict with the natural sciences and psychology. As Böhm-Bawerk stated, "Discussions of economic issues must be based on the principles of science and psychology".

But how can general economic theories be derived from psychological studies? The Austrian School systematically treats value theory as the central lynchpin of economics. If value theory can be established on the basis of psychology, then their whole system of thought is based on it. The theory of marginal utility is seen as the nerve center of their entire economic theory. For them, value is the degree of importance that individuals attach to goods in satisfying their desires, i.e. value arises from subjective evaluation. This subjective evaluation does include the objective value of goods (such as the nutritional value of meat or the calorific value of coal), but it is not the subject of economic value research; it is subjective value.

Thus, although all goods have objective value and utility in satisfying desires, not all useful things have value (i.e. subjective value). The value of goods is only manifested when there is a certain demand relationship in the satisfaction of desires. For example, the same good may have value or no value depending on the supply and demand situation; water is generally useless, but has value to a traveler in the desert. In this understanding, the emergence of value is necessarily related to the scarcity and utility of goods. Utility is the source of value, and scarcity is a condition that makes goods valuable in certain situations. From this perspective, it is not accurate to describe the Austrian School as merely a school of utility. Although they acknowledge that utility is the source of value, they do not claim that the existence or extent of the value of a good depends solely on the existence or extent of utility. If they did, they would be advocates of an objective theory of value rather than a subjective theory of value.

At the heart of the Austrian School's entire theory of value is the theory of marginal utility. But what exactly is marginal utility? To answer this question, it is important to understand the following: "The magnitude of the utility of a good depends on its importance in satisfying our desires. Our desires are of many kinds, and each kind has different degrees of intensity. By considering both the types of desires and their intensities, we can determine the order of utility, which leads to an understanding of marginal utility. That is, the same good can satisfy different desires of different importance, or the same desire with different degrees of urgency. If the current stock of a particular good is sufficient to satisfy our desires to the point of saturation, then there is no economic problem with that good. However, if some of this stock is lost due to some circumstance, leaving at least one desire unsatisfied among the various desires or degrees of urgency, our instinct to avoid pain and seek pleasure will lead us to leave unsatisfied the least significant desire that causes the least inconvenience or pain. This least important desire is the marginal desire, and the utility felt in relation to this marginal desire is the marginal utility. The value we place on a good to satisfy this marginal desire is called its marginal utility. The greater the degree of lack or urgency we feel in satisfying our desires, the greater the marginal utility and the corresponding marginal value".

In moving from value to price, the Austrian school cleverly borrowed from the classical school by considering value as the essence and price as the phenomenon. They argue that when individuals engage in exchange, they base the feasibility of the exchange on their self-interest and their subjective valuation of the goods they need. Since each person has a different subjective valuation based on their marginal utility and different calculations of self-interest, exchange takes place in such a way that each party benefits according to their valuation.

But if everyone's valuation is different, how can a specific market price be formed? This is where competition plays a crucial role. The Austrian School logically describes the process, starting with isolated exchanges, then moving to situations of unilateral competition (including unilateral competition by both buyers and sellers), and finally describing scenarios of mutual competition. The last scenario reflects the modern market situation where many buyers and sellers compete for the same product. As competition among buyers increases, prices rise; as competition among sellers decreases, prices fall. The result of mutual competition is an equilibrium between the number of buyers and sellers. The market price is set within a range defined by the subjective valuations of the last buyer and the least competitive seller as the upper limit, and the subjective valuations of the last seller and the least competitive buyer as the lower limit. These pairs of buyers and sellers are called the "marginal pair", and the price determined by this marginal pair is called the "marginal price". Although this marginal price may not correspond exactly to each individual's marginal utility, it can determine the general range of variation and maintain a substantial link with the marginal utility or individual subjective valuation.

Since the price of goods is related to subjective marginal utility, the goods traded as commodities have no direct relationship with the costs incurred in their production. In other words, the value of a good is not determined by the cost of production, but by the importance and urgency that consumers feel in satisfying their desires with that good. To "complete" their argument, the Austrian School distinguishes between consumer goods and production goods. The former directly satisfy our desires, such as bread, while the latter indirectly satisfy our desires, such as the flour and ovens used to make bread, and even the wheat and mills used to produce flour, down to the land, tools and agricultural labor used to grow the wheat. They classify goods that directly satisfy desires as first-order goods, while the others are sequentially classified as second-order goods, third-order goods, and so on.

The value of first-order goods is undoubtedly determined by the marginal utility of these goods to the immediate consumer. But how is the value of second-order and lower-order goods determined? In particular, how is the value of production goods determined? The Austrian school holds that production goods and consumption activities form a continuous process. The value of first-order goods, such as bread, is determined by the marginal utility of directly consuming these goods; the value of second-order goods, such as flour and ovens, is measured by the marginal utility of first-order goods; and the value of third-order goods, such as wheat mills, is measured by the marginal utility of second-order goods. Thus, the value of all lower-order goods is ultimately determined by the marginal utility of the first-order goods they help to produce. Accordingly, Wieser claims that the value of production goods is determined by the value of the goods they produce. Within this framework, the cost of production is related to value, and hence to price, through various "bridges of convenience".

The Austrian School's elaborate theory of value is undoubtedly aimed at applying it to the theory of distribution. Among the various aspects of distribution, the theory of interest stands out as the most ambitious application of their theory of marginal utility. However, within the entire body of Austrian economic thought, the credit for this particular innovation belongs exclusively to Böhm-Bawerk, whose "patent" it essentially is. Indeed, without this innovation, the economic theory of the Austrian School would lose much of its practical significance.

Böhm-Bawerk distinguishes between present and future goods based on the concept of time. The significance of this distinction lies in the idea that "present goods, for technical reasons, serve as a more complete means of satisfying our desires and thus have a higher marginal utility for us than future goods". To elaborate, the argument is that, for technical reasons, bringing production goods into the production process earlier rather than later yields more output. Furthermore, if we currently have sufficient consumption goods, we would not need to increase the marginal utility of desired goods due to a lack of or insufficient satisfaction of desires, nor would we need to engage in less profitable production activities.

Given the above advantages of present goods over future goods, a lender who provides present goods in exchange for future goods will naturally demand compensation beyond the principal. Similarly, a borrower who receives present goods and repays with future goods is willing to offer such compensation. Both parties to a loan transaction are aware of this time difference in the value of the goods, which is the psychological basis for the existence of interest. According to this principle, when a capitalist uses current consumer goods, which could satisfy current desires, to purchase raw materials, machinery and labor (i.e. higher-order production goods), this is analogous to exchanging current goods for future goods. Naturally, the capitalist has reason to expect an additional return when these future goods are realized, known as profit or capital income. This additional return comes from the fact that the total value of the goods produced is always less than the value of the goods produced, so there is a surplus when the value of production exceeds the cost.

Böhm-Bawerk was particularly concerned that his theory might be misunderstood, especially the idea that merely storing goods over time would increase their value. He insisted that "to transform future goods into present goods, they must first be invested in the production process, after which they can be transformed into finished consumer goods". Without this production process, capital remains dead capital, and the value of the means of production would never be equal to the value of present goods. As a result, there would be no profit or interest. The merit of capitalists, therefore, lies in their willingness to save current consumption, to use the saved goods as capital and to invest them in the production process. The more they save and invest, the more goods are transformed into finished consumer goods, and the greater the resulting profit and interest.

This difference between time and value, derived from psychological experience, not only explains interest and profit, but also provides a framework for understanding wages.

Böhm-Bawerk generously claimed that workers have the right to demand the full value of what their labor produces. But he argued that this claim was only partial. He said: "Everyone can demand, in the present, the full value of the present goods he sells. But no one can demand, in the present, the full value of goods to be sold in the future". When workers sell their labor to capitalists, producing goods that will only have value in the future, they are effectively transferring future goods to the capitalists. In return, they receive payment earlier—essentially in the present. Therefore, the capitalist is exchanging future goods for present goods, and because future goods are worth less than present goods, the capitalist is justified in paying workers less than the full value of the future products. According to Böhm-Bawerk, this arrangement is not only fair, it is the very definition of fairness.

The core theories of the Austrian School have been fully set out here. At first glance, they appear to form a well-organized system of thought, but closer examination reveals that the system, much like the capitalist system it represents, has numerous flaws and inconsistencies. A major criticism is the reliance on the concept of time to explain the origin of profit and to justify why workers should accept less than the full value of their labor. This explanation seems almost preposterous. Moreover, the whole theoretical framework is unsound. The basic propositions of distributional theory are based on the theory of value, but they introduce the concept of time to measure value based on the distance between the present and the future. This time-based approach is then used to determine how much profit capitalists should make and how much workers should be paid. The Austrian School attempts to bridge this gap by suggesting that future goods have lower marginal utility than present goods, but there is little logical connection between the marginal utility of satisfying desires and the length of time involved. If time is measured by actual intervals—such as a year or a month—rather than by subjective experience, then objective factors have been inadvertently introduced into what should be a purely subjective evaluation.

In the real market, the Austrian School's distinction between present and future goods is often unnecessary (although crucial to Austrian theorists). Similarly, their classification of goods into first-order, second-order and so on has little practical relevance. In a market where suppliers are also consumers, especially if they act as capitalists, their transactions are at least indirectly related to consumption. However, the necessity of exchange, especially the necessity of "buying to sell", tends to eliminate subjective evaluations and force them to conform to objective standards. Moreover, individual subjective evaluations are based on objective standards from the outset.

It is clear that the fragmented value theory of the Austrian School is flawed, rooted in its methodological approach. They took the classical concept of "economic man" and made it even more abstract and universal. The classical economists focused on individual self-interest, first emphasizing production and later distribution, which still met the general needs of their time. In contrast, the Austrian School emphasized consumption, claiming that "production is for consumption". They treated this self-evident truth as a groundbreaking discovery and believed that their economics rested on an unshakable foundation. But the key issue is not the truth of the starting proposition, but the validity of the conclusions drawn from it. In other words, it is crucial to assess whether their research is grounded in current economic reality and whether it can adequately explain that reality. In a capitalist society of commodity production, neither the capitalist nor the worker produces for their own consumption. They both produce exchange value, not use value. If production were really driven by the desire to consume, the phenomenon of overproduction and the resulting crises of under-consumption would be inexplicable.

In summary, the Austrian School's methodological focus on the individual is problematic because it isolates the individual from his or her social context, presenting him or her as a superhuman agent outside of specific social relations of production. The psychological state of such an individual is obviously disconnected from the realities of society. Consequently, an economics that focuses solely on the psychology of this individual, especially his or her consumer desires, is inherently metaphysical in nature.

41.3 The Spread of Austrian School Economics to the World

The metaphysical turn in economics can be seen as a denial of the discipline itself. In the twentieth century, however, the economics community seemed to accept this metaphysical form of economics, which denies its own existence, as a matter of course as the standard form of economics. In short, Austrian School economics and its various offshoots or sub-branches spread throughout the world's economic academia (with the notable exception of the Soviet Union). This phenomenon was arrogantly claimed by its German follower, Schumpeter, who declared: "In recent times, the only economics that can and should be universally accepted in all countries is the theory of marginal utility. Nine-tenths of all recent theoretical economic writings revolve within the intellectual circle of the psychological school". If we think the proponents' claims are exaggerated, let's consider the argument of their American opponent, Veblen. Veblen said that Austrian School economics and its variants "lead people into metaphysics. It will undoubtedly flourish in the future, but it has not and cannot explain real problems". Given that this economics cannot explain real economic problems, why has it already flourished and why will it continue to flourish? We need to explore the reasons for this.

First, it should be noted that Austrian School economics is fundamentally based on a naturalistic perspective. Theories that start from a natural point of view can easily give the impression of being irrefutable. For example, Malthus' theory of population starts from two undeniable human needs: the desire for food and the desire for sex.

One of the main reasons why population theory has been so highly praised and misleading for so long is that it starts from these undeniable premises. But scientific truth does not lie in explaining self-evident facts. The more self-evident a fact is, the less it needs scientific explanation. Although the Austrian School emphasizes the desire to consume, which is an undeniable fact, economics does not need to spend much effort explaining it or the psychological state of people when they satisfy this desire. What economics needs to explain are the material conditions under which some people can fully satisfy their consumption desires while others cannot, and the inevitable causal relationships between these conditions. The Austrian School, however, avoids such explanations and instead uses self-evident facts to avoid the issues that should be explained.

The second reason for the widespread dissemination of Austrian School economics is that its entire theoretical content is mixed with various economic principles already well established by the Classical School. Concepts such as free competition, supply and demand, and the laws governing the movement of economic forms such as profit are all incorporated into their theory in roundabout, indirect and sometimes even the most cunning ways. In particular, the subjective theory of value, which they regard as the "key to their whole theory", is in fact a disguised plagiarism of the labor theory of value of the classical school, which they vehemently reject. A clear example of this is how the Classical School distinguishes between value and price, interpreting it as a distinction between essence and phenomenon, with the fluctuations of the latter centered around the former. The Austrian School's emphasis on the relationship between marginal utility and marginal value follows this model, giving its theory a scientific veneer. Furthermore, whereas the Classical School sees the labor expended in producing commodities as the source of their value, with their utility or use value being the condition for achieving exchange value, the Austrian School replaces this with the notion that the utility of a commodity in satisfying human desires is the source of its value, with its scarcity being the condition for achieving exchange value. Moreover, whereas the classical school includes surplus value above capital value in commodity value, the Austrian school emphasizes that the value of productive goods is always less than the value of their products. All these points show the "plagiarism techniques" of Austrian School scholars. However, the value of economics is not in its logical procedures, but in the accuracy of the facts that these procedures seek to explain.

If the second reason for the spread of Austrian School economics is its covert plagiarism of scientific research methods, the third is that it incorporates many superficial ideas that appeal directly to common sense to enrich its theoretical content. For example, the starting point of their research, the desire to consume, and their explanations of the nature and level of satisfaction of these desires, are practically below the level of common sense. When it comes to explaining the origin of capital interest and profit in terms of the difference in value caused by the perceived difference in time—i.e. the "great discovery" that present goods are more valuable than future goods—it not only appeals to common sense, it "manufactures" common sense. Other concepts, such as the values of first-order goods, second-order goods, third-order goods, and so on up to infinite levels of goods, where the marginal utility of each level determines the value of the next, and the value of first-order goods is determined by the immediate importance perceived by the consumer in satisfying his desires, may not be found in common sense, but they are clearly meant to be understood by common sense. Anyone with even the slightest scientific background can easily see them as unanalyzable ramblings. Finally, concepts such as "substitute goods" and "complementary goods", which are highly prized by followers of the Austrian School but which we have not yet mentioned, seem to be derived from very basic common sense.

The Austrian School emphasizes pure economic theory. To compensate for the shortcomings of this common sense approach, they consciously or unconsciously combine their theory with mathematics, using the generality and irrefutability of mathematics to strongly support their convoluted economic theories. This can be seen as the fourth reason for the global spread of this school. In fact, the scholars considered to be the forerunners of the Austrian School, such as the Frenchman Cournot, the Swiss Walras, the British Jevons and the German Gossen, all used mathematical analysis as their basic research method. Later, scholars who accepted the basic propositions of the Austrian School, such as Marshall, its German follower Liefmann, and especially those in the United States, such as Clark, Carver and Fisher, used mathematical analysis to explain economic phenomena. Even Cassel, who was highly critical of the Austrian School's value theory, leaned towards mathematical methods in his research approach. This mathematical style of economic research made it easier for Austrian economics to spread, while at the same time, the so-called pure and abstract research of the Austrian School made it more suitable for mathematical methods. The mathematical approach can and should be applied, but there are limits to its use in explaining economic phenomena. If it is used to further clarify economic laws established by other methods, its use is permissible. However, when mathematical concepts are used from the outset and all economic propositions are constrained within equations, the result is that economic phenomena are adjusted to fit mathematical methods rather than mathematics being used to clarify economic phenomena. In such cases, mathematical methods exclude the use of all other research methods.

However, all the above reasons for the spread of the Austrian School of Economics only gain practical significance under the conditions of the last reason we are about to discuss. This reason is that the development of capitalist economics in the last decades of the nineteenth century and the beginning of the twentieth century had exposed its internal contradictions and inevitable fate to such an extent that critical economic theories could no longer ignore them. To counter this "crisis" in economic consciousness, the Austrian School emerged as the heroic defender of capitalism. The objective approach, handed down from the classical school to the critical schools, forced people to face reality and expose the roots of the capitalist crisis. The Austrian School, given its "special" mission, had no choice but to adopt a subjective approach. The metaphysical turn in economic thought, although incapable of explaining real economic problems, was generally welcomed by the world of capitalists, especially those who were completely detached from production and focused solely on pleasure, such as finance capitalists. This is the most fundamental reason for the spread of Austrian School economics.

41.4 Introduction of the Austrian School of Economics to China

The Austrian School of Economics has also spread to China and seems to have taken root. But China is not a capitalist country, so why do we need this type of economics? Do the reasons that have facilitated the spread of Austrian School economics in capitalist countries also apply to China? The purpose of this article is to explain the actual situation of how the Austrian School was introduced to China, which is why the previous section discussed its spread to various countries around the world. The various ideologies of modern capitalism came to China with the influx of capitalist goods. The import of goods is closely linked to the import of commodity ideologies (economics). When a country independently imports goods, it can also independently import the ideologies that go with them; but when the import of goods is imposed on a country by external forces, the import of the ideologies that go with them becomes an auxiliary method imposed by the same forces. Under such circumstances, the imported goods are likely to be harmful to the receiving country, and the economic ideologies or economics that accompany them may also be harmful.

Indeed, since the beginning of the twentieth century, China has gradually gained the ability to independently choose what to import in terms of commodity ideologies, much as it does with physical goods. However, the restrictions on importing economic ideologies or economics are much greater than those on goods. Although we send a large number of students abroad every year, including many who study political economy, to autonomously import the economic science we need, this effort is first of all hindered by the general level of knowledge in our society. In other countries, many economic theories have become common knowledge through practical experience and application, but in China we still have to make great efforts to learn them.

Second, the economics we import from abroad is the economics of capitalism. Since we have not yet developed the economic conditions of capitalism in China, studying such economics not only increases the difficulty of understanding and comprehension, but also makes it impossible to verify whether the principles studied are correct or applicable to our reality.

Thirdly, as capitalism developed in the twentieth century, the implementation of cultural policies by imperialist powers became increasingly necessary. In the past, advanced nations boasted of their mission to develop and spread economic and cultural progress to underdeveloped regions. However, as they entered the imperialist phase, they began to hesitate to develop industries in these regions and instead adopted strategies to "preserve" or "restrain" these areas from advancing beyond a pre-capitalist socioeconomic system. In response to these strategies, they could not help but impose stricter limits on the "export" of basic political economy theories than in the laissez-faire era. In this respect, it might be more accurate to say that these powers focused more on controlling the 'import' process in the recipient regions than on their own 'export' efforts, a privilege they did indeed have in these underdeveloped areas.

However, what we have pointed out above is only one side of the issue—only the reasons why the Austrian School of Economics has been readily imported. The fact is that the economic circles of capitalist countries are, as we have said, heavily influenced by the atmosphere of Austrian School economics. From public forums to university lectures to various economic research institutes set up by governments and private bodies, so-called subjective economics has almost always played a leading role, either directly or indirectly. This trend has only become more pronounced over time. In this context, the economic theories that the capitalist countries introduce and promote in the underdeveloped regions are, of course, those that they themselves advocate and practice. In fact, they seem to be acting out of "selflessness" and "integrity". In regions like China, where the local population either sends people abroad to study or invites foreign experts to help with research, we lack both the ability to choose freely and the social conditions to test these theories. Therefore, everything is passively accepted. Moreover, many of the features that make Austrian School economics particularly transferable are particularly suited to being taught to researchers in underdeveloped countries. For example, the emphasis on the causal relationships of common phenomena is easily accepted by minds that are either immature or less scientifically trained. The emphasis on the theory of consumption, the theory of desire, the explanation of interest and profit based on time differences, and various formulae and numerical explanations "invented" on the basis of market economic phenomena may be questionable, but they are most palatable to beginners or those with a shallow understanding of economics. The tendency to popularize economics inevitably leads to another characteristic of the spread of the Austrian School: the belief that business practices, market trends, changes in supply and demand, and technical economic knowledge, which play only a supporting, secondary or peripheral role in economic theory, constitute the essence of economics. This is something that economists need to be particularly careful about, and yet some of our economists seem to have fallen into this trap. Moreover, there is another feature of Austrian School economics that superficially seems to contradict its tendency towards popularization and technicalization, but is actually related to it—a deeply fundamental feature. This is perhaps the most damaging aspect for Chinese economists: the view that economics is metaphysics, a purely theoretical discipline. It may be that because the Austrian School treats economics as metaphysics, they have had no choice but to rely on technology and common sense to ground their theories in reality. Or perhaps it is because they see economics as an abstract, deductive discipline—one without historical context—that they are more easily driven by economic common sense and technology. Whatever the case, the popularization, technicalization and simultaneous metaphysical approach to economics create multiple layers of confusion and obstacles for Chinese scholars engaged in economic research. Despite these contradictions, they seem to reconcile these differences by categorizing the popularized and technical aspects as practical economics, which is easy to understand and quickly grasped, and the metaphysical aspects as pure theoretical economics, which is difficult to comprehend and requires only a vague understanding. In conclusion, these three factors are important reasons why Austrian School economics has so easily "taken root" in China's economic academia.

41.5 The Prevalence of Austrian School Economic Thought in Chinese Economics and Its Reflection in Economic Practice

So far, we have outlined the key aspects of Austrian School economics. To understand why this school of thought is so prevalent in Chinese economics, it seems sufficient for readers to make a comparative analysis for themselves, without further explanation. For example, if one examines the university economics textbooks published by major bookstores, it is guaranteed that ninety per cent of them are derived from American university economics textbooks. As for the "model" textbooks, they are usually based on the works of economists such as Carver, Taussig, Ely and Seligman. It is not necessary to go into detail about which books or ideas are specific promoters of Austrian School economics; a more general criterion will suffice. The most fundamental premise of Austrian School economics is based on a superhistorical perspective. Whether in academic textbooks or general publications on economic theory, any work that neglects the social nature of the subjects studied—such as commodities, money, capital, value, wages, and even production and consumption—while abstracting from these concepts, is likely to be a product of Austrian School economics. We are indeed tired of and familiar with such works.

At this point, it is easy to recall the criticism of a German economist from the mid-nineteenth century who said of the German economic community at that time: "Economic writers or professors are obsessed with the cosmopolitan school and regard all protective tariffs as 'theoretical abominations'. They have British interests to support them, so they are always victorious. What is even more deplorable is that the British Cabinet skillfully uses the power of money to suppress foreign opinion, and spends it lavishly and unreservedly for its commercial interests. Many correspondents, leading writers… have been wandering about in various places, for the sole purpose of attacking the 'unreasonable' 'wishes' of German industrialists for protective tariffs… The prevailing doctrines and the views of German scholars are all in their favor, which makes the task of defending British interests particularly easy" (from Wang's translation of List's "National Economics"). Although this was written over a century ago, it still seems relevant today. While List criticized the British for using cosmopolitan economics to obstruct German economic reform, here we are pointing out how capitalist countries are using Austrian School economics to obstruct China's economic transformation. Indeed, while Germany's obstruction was limited to protective tariffs, in China the harmful effects go beyond tariffs to the entire process of social and economic transformation and modernization.

Of course, given China's international position, it is impossible to fully control the input and distribution of raw materials and economic thought (i.e. economics). However, it must also be recognized that there is still a range of autonomous and proactive options in these areas. Foreign economic advisers and experts assisting China's economic "revival" do not attribute the obstacles to this revival to imperialist policies, which is undoubtedly natural. However, many "authoritative" works on "China's economic transformation" also refuse to address the imperialist policies according to the superficial logic of foreign scholars. Although discussions criticizing imperialist policies have increased in the past decade or so, they mostly remain at a superficial level and fail to explore how imperialist policies negatively affect China's economy and the theories they impose. Consequently, while there has been some erosion of the dominance of Austrian School economics in general social forums, it still prevails in university lectures and influential economic research institutions, where metaphysical economic theories remain widespread. Even when confronted with pressing economic issues, these institutions tend to approach them from a commonsense, technical perspective. From an academic point of view, the economic theories of the Austrian School are undoubtedly an area of study that we should engage with. However, our study of these theories must be critical, recognizing that they are part of a defense system created or nurtured by capitalist countries to stabilize their financial or global dominance. This approach will help us to understand global economic trends and, in particular, the economic policies imposed on less developed areas. We must avoid designing China's economic transformation plans based on an awareness of such theories, which could be detrimental to our economic reform efforts.

Unfortunately, in recent times, Chinese economists building or speaking for China's economic infrastructure have often ignored China's existing economic fundamentals. They fail to consider whether their plans are consistent with or permitted by China's current economic conditions. They naively equate the basic categories of China's overall economic form—such as commodities, value, profit, wages, money and capital—with the eponymous basic concepts learnt from economics textbooks and Austrian School economics. When their plans encounter obstacles in implementation, they complain about China's technical conditions, without reflecting on the fact that their plans or arrangements did not take into account China's social and technical levels. This was the case in the past and is still the case today.

41.6 The Divergence of Austrian School Economics from Principles of People's Livelihood in Theory and Practice

In fact, more than twenty years ago, when the Chinese economy was still in a state of confusion, Mr. Sun Yat-sen had already accurately proposed the necessary path for China's economic transformation. The land and capital policy advocated in principles of people's livelihood not only addressed the fundamental economic realities of Chinese society and recognized the shortcomings of capitalism, but also theoretically established that no modern economic transformation could be carried out smoothly without land reform to eliminate the remnants of feudal society. This is an ironclad fact that every modern country has experienced, and is also clearly demonstrated by classical and critical economists through historical economic laws. The Austrian School, however, is particularly averse to the theory of historical stages. In order to defend the "eternity" of the stage of finance capital, they abstract and disregard the unique economic characteristics or conditions of different societies. In their view, there is no essential difference between the primitive tools used by early man and the modern methods of production controlled by capitalists. Thus, the products made by primitive man with stone tools were for consumption, just as the products made by capitalists with modern means of production are also for consumption. Extending this to other forms of economy, they believe that all economic systems, past and present, differ only in their complexity. Under this understanding, the basic concepts of economics become abstract concepts of time and space, devoid of historical reality, leaving mathematics to perform its deductive functions. The origins and development of capitalist economies cannot be traced in such economics. At a time when the capitalist system is threatened by recurrent economic crises, the prevalence of this denial of historical economic laws in capitalist countries has at least a negative significance.

For China, which is struggling with the setbacks of modernization, the uncritical adoption of such economics is tantamount to neglecting the nature of the economy of Chinese society and obscuring the economic theory of the principles of people's livelihood. Thus, despite the increasing activity and prosperity of economic research and introduction over the past two decades, the basic economic theory of the people's livelihood principle proposed by Mr. Sun Yat-sen—that modern economic infrastructure should be discussed only after the feudal forces have been eradicated from land ownership—has been relegated to the sidelines. In the more than twenty years of the national revolution, the most basic and preliminary land reform policy of the people's livelihood principle has not been implemented. While there are various objective obstacles related to China's national conditions, a significant part of the blame for the lack of subjective effort should be attributed to the influence of the Austrian School in our economic community. Economists with a say in economic construction rarely touch on the essential changes needed in Chinese society. When they encounter practical obstacles to economic development, they may occasionally mention China's backwardness, using it to hide the gap between their proposals and reality. But what is the social meaning of "economic backwardness"? On academic and forum platforms, they have never given us any clear, specific guidance. It is quite astonishing that a country guided by the principles of people's livelihood should have its economic community and economists adhering to economic theories that are completely contrary to this guiding principle. What is even more surprising is that this long-standing fact has not been pointed out until today.

41.7 The Responsibility of Economists

I would like to conclude my discussion with the following summarized points:

(1) Respect for academic freedom: I fully respect the spirit of academic freedom in research. Studying any school of economics, including the Austrian School, not only broadens our understanding of modern thought, but also enhances our understanding of global economic realities. In this sense, Austrian School economics is as worthy of study and attention as classical economics, historical economics and Marxist economics.
(2) Contextual understanding of the Austrian School: It is important to understand that the Austrian School of Economics emerged in response to the realities of the decline of capitalism. Historically, it is not the "revival" or "reinvention" of economics, as its proponents often claim. If we accept that economics reflects real economic conditions, then there can be no "new" theoretical discoveries from a capitalist perspective in times of capitalist crisis. Even if we are subjectively influenced by this school, we must recognize that the Austrian School is only one current within modern economic thought. Its importance should be recognized, but it should not be confused with the whole of economics.
(3) China's situation with Austrian economics: It is naive to assume that China has its own Austrian school of economics simply because of the backwardness of its economic structure and ideological environment. China's inability to produce its own goods and its difficulty in distinguishing the authenticity of foreign goods, as well as its difficulty in developing and evaluating economic theories, contribute to this situation. While it is true that China's economic and ideological environment has been influenced by comprador commercial and financial elites, as well as imperialist cultural policies, this does not necessarily mean that Austrian economics has a distinct presence in China. In reality, the adoption of Austrian economics in China is more passive and reflective of external influences than an active, conscious choice.
(4) The way forward: Just as our economy is struggling against the constraints of historical capitalism to achieve liberation, our foreign-influenced economic consciousness must also be addressed through our efforts and expanded research perspectives. Mr. Sun Yat-sen has already shown the way to economic liberation, and the objective dynamics of global economic development are sufficient to enlighten us. If Chinese economists are willing to break out of the "ivory tower"

of Austrian School economics, the Chinese economic community will undoubtedly experience a transformation. This, at least, is the conscious responsibility that economists should bear.

Academic Chronology of Wang Ya'nan

1901

(27th year of the reign of Guangxu in the Qing Dynasty).

On October 15th, he was born in Wangjiafang, Tuanfeng, Huanggang, Hubei, known as Zhihuai, with the style name Yucun, pseudonyms Wang Zhen and Bihui.

1907

(33rd year of the reign of Guangxu in the Qing Dynasty).

He went to a private school and received a traditional cultural education, and read *The Analects, Zuo Tradition, Discourses of the States, Records of the Grand Historian*, etc.

1916

He graduated from Huangzhou Higher Primary School, and was admitted to Wuchang No. 1 Middle School with honors.

1922

In the autumn, he was accepted into the School of Education at Wuhan Zhonghua University, while working as a middle school English teacher to support himself.

1926

That year, he graduated from university and taught at Wuchang Private Chengcheng Middle School. After the autumn, when Chengcheng Middle School was closed, he was introduced by his friend Wang Zhongyou to travel to Changsha, where he joined the Northern Expedition Army and served as a political instructor in the Student Army Teaching Corps.

1927

After the failure of the Great Revolution, he left Changsha and returned to Wuchang, then failed to get a job there and in Shanghai.

1928

After travelling from Shanghai to Hangzhou, he stayed at the Great Buddha Temple and met Guo Dali. The two hit it off and agreed to do economic research and were determined to translate *Das Kapital* together.

At the end of the year, he was financed by his friend Fang Dagong and travelled east to Japan.

Y. Wang, *The Basic Theory of Chinese Economy*,
https://doi.org/10.1007/978-981-95-6330-2

1929

In Tokyo, he studied Marxist economics and wrote and translated classical economics.

1930

That year he continued to study Marxist economics, learning Japanese and German, and began to translate works such as *The History of Human Marriage* by Finnish author Edward Westermarck, *The Principles of Political Economy and Taxation* by British economist David Ricardo, and *The History of Rent Thought* by Japanese scholar Takasu. In July, his translation of Edward Westermarck's *The History of Human Marriage* was published by Shen Zhou Guo Guang Press in Shanghai.

1931

In January, his co-translation with Guo Dali of Adam Smith's *The Wealth of Nations (Volume I)* was first published by Shanghai Shenzhou Guoguang Press. His co-translation with Guo Dali of David Ricardo's *Principles of Economics and Taxation* was first published by Shanghai Shenzhou Guoguang Press (the book was originally published by Beijing Commercial Press in September 1962, renamed *The Principles of Political Economy and Taxation*).

In June, his translation of *Thought History of Land Rent* by Takabatake Motoyuki of Japan was published by Shanghai Shenzhou Guoguang Press.

In the same year, his article *Lectures on World Famous Economic Books* was published in the special issue of the first volume of *Reading Magazine*. His article *Famous Books of Orthodox Economics (I, II, III)* was successively published in the 2nd, 3rd and 9th issues of the magazine. His article *On the Feudal System* was published in the 4th and 5th issues of the magazine. His article *On the Basis of Economics and Answers to Xin Rujun* was published in the 6th issue of the magazine.

At the end of the year, he returned to Shanghai from Japan, took up translation and writing, and worked as a professor at Ji'nan University.

1932

His book *The History of Economics (Volume I)* was published by Shanghai Minzhi Press. His article *On Economic Debate in the Soviet Union* was published in the 1st issue of *Culture Magazine*.

From May to June, his two articles *Economics Classics of the Historical School* and *On Interpretation of Several Aliases of Economics* were published in the 5th and 6th issues of the 2nd volume of *Reading Magazine*.

In August, his co-translation with Guo Dali of Adam Smith's *The Wealth of Nations (Volume II)*, first published by Shanghai Shenzhou Guoguang Press (Volume I was published by Beijing Commercial Press in October 1972 and Volume II in June 1974), was renamed *Research on the Nature and Causes of National Wealth*, in accordance with the full title of the original work.)

1933

In March, his translation of *The Scope and Method of Political Economy* by British Klais was published by Shanghai Minzhi Press.

In April, his article *Military Reduction Conference and Arms Competition* was published in Issue 7, Volume 1, *New China*.

In May, his two articles *On the Crisis of Modern Thought* and *The Old Washington Conference and the Washington Conference* were published in the 5th and 10th issues of the 3rd volume of *Reading Magazine.*

In August his article *Chinese Industrial Control Theory* was published in Issue 15, Volume 1, *New China.* His article *Rejuvenation of American Industry in Telecommunications* was published in Issue 16, Volume 1, *New China.*

In September, his article *Surrender to Japan and Rescue the League of Nations* was published in Issue 17, Volume 1, *New China.*

In October, his book *Modern Diplomacy and International Relations* was published by Shanghai Zhonghua Press. His article *The Fate of Chinese Intellectuals* was published in Issue 19, Volume 1, *New China.*

In November, Li Jishen, together with Jiang Guangding, Cai Tingcuo and other generals of the 19th Route Army, launched the "Fujian Revolution" in Fuzhou and set up the Fujian People's Government. Wang became the government's commissioner for culture and education and editor of *The People's Daily* (the government's official newspaper). His article *The Big Break in 1936* was published in Issue 22, Volume 1, *New China.*

1934

In January, his article *Production Economics* was published in the *People's Daily* on the 10th.

"Fujian Revolution" failed, so he was wanted and travelled to Hong Kong and then to Shanghai.

In the summer, with the financial support of friends, he went to Europe. Before leaving, he gave the remaining four chapters of the German F. H. Knight's *Economic History of Europe* to Guo Dali for further translation.

In the same year, he lived in Germany and England, studied German and the capitalist system in Western Europe in depth, and continued to work on economic translation and writing. He completed *The Past, Present and Future of Germany.*

1935

In January, the articles *Where is Japan Headed?* and *The Monetary Problem in Economic Panic and the Weight of Labor Issues* were published consecutively in *New China*, Vol. 3, Issues 1 and 2.

In February, *The Struggle Between Gold and Silver* (Japan Correspondence) was published in *The Eastern Miscellany*, Vol. 32, No. 3.

In March, the co-translation of Knight's *The Economic History of Europe* with Guo Dali was published by Shanghai World Book Company. The article *The Past and Future of Chinese Industry* was published in *Culture*, Issue 13. In the autumn he travelled from London to Japan.

At the end of the year, he moved from Japan to Shanghai, where he was reunited with Guo Dali. The two decided to start translating *The Capital.* During this time, he served as an executive member of the Shanghai Authors' Association and participated in anti-Japanese propaganda activities.

1936

In January, his books *Economic Policy* and *Germany's Past, Present and Future* were published by Shanghai Zhonghua Book Company. The article *A Panorama of Tokyo* was published in *New China*, Vol. 4, Issue 1.

In February, the article *Japanese Elections and the Future of the Okada Cabinet* was published in *New China*, Vol. 4, Issue 4.

In March, the articles *The Fascist Forces and Finance Capital in Japan* and *The International Situation After the Tokyo Coup* were published in *New China*, Vol. 4, Issues 5 and 6, respectively.

In April, his book *An Introduction to the Modern World Economy* was published by Shanghai Zhonghua Book Company.

In June, the article *Babata's Financial Theory in Japan* was published in *New China*, Vol. 4, Issue 11.

In July, his book *Outline of China's Social and Economic History* was first published by Shanghai Life Bookstore, and the article *The Colonialization of the Northeast Economy* was published in *New China*, Vol. 4, Issue 13.

In August, the article *The Harmony and Conflict Between the Japanese and Manchurian Economies* was published in *New China*, Vol. 4, No. 15.

In September, the article *The Struggles of the Hirota Cabinet Under Attack from the Military and Political Parties* was published in *New China*, Vol. 4, No. 18.

His book *China's Economic Reader* was also published in the same year (publisher unknown).

1937

In January his article *To Study the Chinese Economy* was published in No.1, Series 1, Volume 1, Self-study University. His two articles *Fascist State in 1936* and *On the Reform of Japanese Political Institutions* were published successively in No.1 and 2, Volume 5, *New China.*

In February his article *From the Collapse of the Hirota Cabinet to the Establishment of the Lin Cabinet* was published in Issue 4, Volume 5, *New China.*

In March, his article *On the Change of Japanese Diplomacy to China* was published in Issue 6, Volume 5, *New China.*

In December, his book *Economic Issues and Economic Policy in Wartime* was published by Shanghai Guangming Press.

1938

At the beginning of the year he left Hong Kong for Wuhan, where he was a member of the Design Committee of the Political Department of the Military Commission of the Kuomintang government. The head of the committee was Zhou Enlai.

In June, his article *Readings on Wartime Economy* was published in Issue 2, Volume 1, *Wartime Culture.*

From August to September, his co-translation of Karl Marx's *Das Kapital: A Critique of Political Economy* with Guo Dali, Volumes I, II and III were published by Shanghai Reading Life Press.

1939

In August, his co-translation with Wang Bojin of British Cole's *System of World Economic Institutions (Volumes I and II)* was published by Shanghai Zhonghua Press.

1940

In February, his article *Life and War* was published in No. 2, Vol. 2, *Chinese Youth.*

Xu Chongqing, President of Sun Yat-sen University in Guangdong, personally went to Chongqing to invite him to teach at the university.

In September, he left Chongqing and arrived in Pingshi, Guangdong, where he worked as a professor and dean of the School of Economics at Sun Yat-Sen University, and founded and served as editor-in-chief of the journal Economic Science.

1941

In October, his article *Political Economy in China* was published in Issue 10, Volume 2, *New Construction.*

1942

In March, his article *Signs of the Ideological Evolution of Modern Economy* was published in Issue 4 of Zhongshan Journal.

In April, his article *People in Political Economy—An Economic Note* was published in Issue 2 of *Economic Science.*

In June, his article *Philosophy and Economics* was published in Issue 6, Volume 5, *Times China.*

In July, his article *World War and World Economy* was published in Issue 7 and 8, Volume 8, *New Construction.*

In October, *Song* was published in Issue 5 and 6, Volume 6, *Times China.*

In December, his article *Chinese Business Capital* was published in Issue 4, Volume 2, *Guangdong Provincial Bank Quarterly.*

1943

In January, his article *General Introduction to Chinese Currency* was published in Issue 1, Volume 3, *Guangdong Provincial Bank Quarterly.*

In April, his article *The Present Stage of Chinese Economic Research* was published in Issue 5, *Economic Science.*

In May, his article *Current Issues of Price and Price Control* was published in Issues 3 and 4, Volume 4, *New Construction.* His article *The Laws of Political Economy* was published in No. 4, Vol. 3, *Journal of Culture.*

In the summer, the famous British scholar Dr. Joseph Needham visited Pingshi, Guangdong, and the two had two long conversations. Needham talked about the pertinent issues of Chinese bureaucracy, which later became the motivation for Wang to write *Research on Chinese Bureaucracy.*

In August his article *The Importance of Economy and Chinese Economic Policy in Wartime* was published in Issue 7, Volume 4, *New Construction.*

In September, his article *General Introduction to Chinese Capital* was published in Issues 2 and 3, Volume 3, *Guangdong Provincial Bank Quarterly.*

In October, his book *Collected Essays of Economic Science* was published by Zhonghua Zhengqi Publishing House in Ganxian County, Jiangxi Province. His article *Austrian Economics in Chinese Economic Circles* was published in Issue 3, Volume 1, *Zhongshan Cultural Quarterly.*

1944

In March, his article *General Introduction to Chinese Pattern of Economic Panic* was published in Issue 1, Volume 4, *Guangdong Provincial Bank Quarterly*. His article *On Research Guidance of Economic Sciences* was published in the 6th issue of *Economic Sciences*. His article *On East–West Culture and East–West Economy* was published in Issue 3, Volume 5, *New Construction*.

In October, his article *Basic Understandings of Social Science Research* was published in Issue 2, Volume 10, *Improvement*.

In December, his article *On the Research Objectives and Research Methods of Chinese Economics* was published in Issue 4, Volume 10, *Improvement*.

In the same year, the Japanese army attacked northern Guangdong and Sun Yat-sen University was forced to relocate. So Wang left the university and went to Yong'an, Fujian, where he served as director of the Institute of Social Sciences of the Fujian Academy and founded the journal Social Sciences and the Economic Science Press.

He arranged for people to go to western Fujian to investigate land reform in the Red Army base area, and served as a visiting professor at the Economics Department of Xiamen University, which had moved to Changting, teaching "Advanced Economics", "Issues of China Land" and other special subjects.

1945

In January, his article *Social Science and Natural Science* was published in Issue 1, Volume 1, *Social Sciences*.

In the spring, in protest at the death of progressive journalist Yang Zao (formerly known as Yang Chao) at the hands of the Kuomintang, he resigned from his post as director of the Institute of Social Sciences of the Fujian Academy.

In April, his article *General Introduction to Fujian Economy* was published in Issue 1 of the *Fujian Provincial Bank Quarterly*. His article *On Culture and Economy* was published in Issue 2, Volume 11, *Improvement*.

In June, his book *The Outline of Social Sciences* was published by Southeast Publishing House, Yongan, Fujian.

In autumn, he became the Dean of the School of Economics and the Dean of the Law School of Xiamen University.

In August, his article *Feelings at the End of the Anti-Japanese War* was published in Issues 5 and 6, Volume 11, *Improvement*.

In September, his article *Criticism of the Mixed Economic System* was published in Issues 2 and 3, Volume 1, *Social Sciences*.

In the same year, at the invitation of President Zhuang Chang-gong of National Taiwan University, he spent a month lecturing at the Law School of National Taiwan University.

In December, the revised edition of *Outline of Social Sciences* was published by Fuzhou Economic Science Press and renamed *New Theory of Social Sciences*. His article *Research on Chinese Public Economy* was published in Issue 1, *Research Report of the Institute of Social Sciences*, Fujian Academy. His article *Legal Issues in Chinese Socioeconomic History* was published in Issue 4, Volume 1, *Social Sciences*.

1946

In January, his book *The Basic Theory of Chinese Economy* was published by Fuzhou Economic Science Press (the Japanese translation of the book was published in 1955 by Aoki Shoten and Japan China Economic Research Association, and the book was renamed *On Semi-colonial Economy* when the latter was published. The Russian translation was published in 1958, the revised edition of the book was published by Beijing People's Press in January 1957, and the book was renamed *Research on the Form of Chinese Semi-feudal and Semi-colonial Economy* when it was reprinted in December 1980).

From April to June, his article *On the Status of Technology in Production and Construction* was published in Issue 8, Yu Min.

In May, his article *Corrigendum of Capital* was published in Issue 20, Volume 2, *Economic Weekly*.

In November, his article *An Open Letter to the Students of the Department of Economics of Sun Yat-sen University* was published in Daily Forum (this article was later included in the book Wang Ya'nan and Education, renamed *How to Give Full Play to the Spirit of Self-study*).

In December, his article *We are in a Great Era* was published in Combined Issues 3 and 4, Volume 2, Social Sciences.

1947

On January 1st, the article *A Look at China's Economic and Economic Academia in the Year 36 of the Republic* was published in *Jiang Sheng Daily*. That same month, the article *On Finance* was published in *Guangdong Provincial Bank Quarterly*, Vol. 3, Issue 1.

On March 25th, the article *A Theoretical Analysis of Chinese Bureaucratic Capitalism* was published in *Wenhui Daily*.

In April, the articles *Chinese Bureaucratic Capitalism and State Capital* was published in *Time and Literature*, Vol. 1, Issue 4, and *How Should We Understand Bureaucratic Capitalism* was published in *Modern Economic Digest*, Vol. 1, Issue 4.

In May, the article *The Forms of Chinese Economic Phenomena in Political Economy—A Brief Discussion on Several Understandings of China's Economic Form* was published in the *Fujian Provincial Academy of Social Sciences Research Report*, Issue 2.

In June, the article *On the socioeconomic Relations Between Chinese Cities and Rural Areas* was published in *Time and Literature*, Vol. 1, Issue 15, and the article *How Bureaucratic Capitalism Was Formed* was published in *Modern Economic Digest*, Issue 6.

In September, the articles *On So-Called Bureaucratic Politics*, *Bureaucratic Politics in Various Countries*, and *The Special Manifestations of Chinese Bureaucratic Politics* were successively published in *Time and Literature*, Vol. 2, Issues 1, 2, and 3.

In October, the articles *The socioeconomic Foundations of Chinese Bureaucratic Politics*, *The Internal Interests of Bureaucratic and Bureaucratic Classes and the Spirit of the General Bureaucratic System*, and *Bureaucratic Politics and Confucian*

Thought were successively published in *Time and Literature*, Vol. 2, Issues 4, 5, and 6.

In November, the articles *Bureaucratic Aristocracy and Family Clans* and *The First Major Lever Supporting the High Development of Bureaucratic Politics—The Two-Tax System* were successively published in *Time and Literature*, Vol. 2, Issues 10 and 11.

In December, the article *The Political and Economic Life of Scholar-Officials* was published in *Time and Literature*, Vol. 2, Issue 12.

1948

On 1 January, the article *Welcoming 1948* was published in *Jiang Sheng Daily*. In the same month, the article *The Path of China's Economy* was published in *Economic Review*, Vol. 2, No. 15, followed by the article *The Path of Chinese Economic Research* in *Economic Review*, Vol. 2, No. 17. The article *The Social and Economic Life of Peasants Under Bureaucratic Politics* was also published in *Time and Literature*, Vol. 2, No. 17.

In February, the article' *On the Relationship Between China's National Economy and National Income'* was published in *New China*, Vol. 6, No. 4, and the article *The Impact of Bureaucratic Politics on China's Long-Term Social Stagnation* was published in *Time and Literature*, Vol. 2, No. 19.

In March, the articles *The Transformation of Chinese Bureaucratic Politics in Modern Times* and *The Collapse of Traditional Old Bureaucratic Politics* were published consecutively in *Time and Literature*, Vol. 2, Issues 21 and 24, while the article *What Kind of New Economic Doctrine System Do We Need* was published in *Social Science*, Vol. 4, Issue 1.

On 11–12 April, the article *Research on China's Land Reform Problem* was published in the *Jiang Sheng Daily*. In the same month and in May, the article *On the Economic Form of State Capitalism and the Formation of State Socialism (Parts I and II)* was published successively in *China Construction*, Vol. 6, Issues 1 and 2.

In May, the articles *The Transition and Transformation of Old and New Bureaucratic Politics* and *The Growth of New Bureaucratic Politics* were successively published in *Time and Literature*, Vol. 3, Issues 6 and 7. The article *The Outlook of Chinese Economic Research in the World* was published in *Economic Weekly*, Vol. 6, Issue 21. On 30 May, the article *Opposing American Imperialism's Support of Japan-Professors' Discussions*, co-signed with scholars Lu Jiaxi, Lin Li and Xiong Deji, was published in *Starlight Daily*.

In June, the article *Research on China's Land Reform Problem* was published in *Social Science*, Vol. 4, Issue 2, and the article *The Future of Chinese Bureaucratic Politics* was published in *Time and Literature*, Vol. 3, Issue 8. The article *On the Problem of the Acquisition and Loss of Traditional Chinese Thought* was published in *New China*, Vol. 6, Issue 11.

In July, the article *On China's Lectern Socialists* was published in *China Construction*, Vol. 6, Issue 4. On 8–9 August, the article *Further Discussion on China's Land Reform Problem* was published in *Jiang Sheng Daily*. In September, the article *(Research on Chinese Bureaucratic Politics) Preface* was published in the last issue of *Time and Literature*.

In October, 17 special articles published in *Time and Literature* were collected in a book entitled *Research on Chinese Bureaucratic Politics*, published by Shanghai Times Culture Press. The article *Recent Trends in Popular Economic Research (Parts I and II)* was published in the combined issue of *New China*, Vol. 6, Issues 19 and 20.

In December, the article *The Natural Conditions for Social and Economic Transformation in China* was published in *Social Science*, Vol. 4, Issue 4.

1949

In January he left Xiamen for Hong Kong, where he taught economics at Dade College, run by the underground Chinese Communist Party, and wrote articles for Ta Kung Pao and Wenhui Daily. His two articles *The Current Situation of China's Economy, Its Characteristics and Problems* and *Capital in China's Socioeconomic Transformation* were published in Issues 1 and 2, Volume 12, *New China.*

In February, his article *On the Guiding Principles of China's Current Socioeconomic Reconstruction* was published in Issue 4, Volume 12, *New China.*

On 6 March, his article *On Scientific Researchers in Social Transformation* was published in *Ta Kung Pao (Hong Kong).*

On 5 April, his article *On Businessmen in Social Transformation* was published in Issue 115 of *China Economic Herald (Hong Kong).* In the same month his article *History of Political Economy and New Historiography* was published in Issue 7, Volume 12, *New China.*

In May, he left Hong Kong for Peiping to teach political economy at Tsinghua University. His two articles, *Research on China's socioeconomic Transformation* and *Research on the Interrelationship of Law, Politics and Economy* were published consecutively in Issue 9 and 10, Volume 12, *New China.*

In July, his book *Outline of the History of Political Economy* was published by Shanghai Zhonghua Book Company. His article *America and the Soviet Union* was published in Issue 13, Volume 12, *New China.*

In August, his article *From Semi-Feudal & Semi-Colonial Economy to New Democratic Economy* was published in Issue 15, Volume 12, *New China.*

In September his article *Lenin's On the State* appeared in Issue 1, Volume 1, *Learning.*

In October, his two articles *Old Social Production Relationships and the Laws Revealed in the Land Reform Process* and *Three Economic Guiding Principles and the Liberation and Development of Social Productive Forces* were published in Issues 19 and 20, Volume 12, New China. His article *The Origin of Family, Property and State (Commentary on the Famous Book)* was published in Issue 2, Volume 1, *Learning.*

1950

In January, his article *Categories and Laws of the New Economy in the People's Power* was published in Issue 12, Volume 13, *New China.* His article *On the Bureaucratic Class in Social Transformation* was published in Issue 11, Volume 1, *New Construction.* His article *On the Unification of Revolution and Science* was published in Issue 5, Volume 6, *Observation.*

In March, his article *Marxist-Leninism and the socioeconomic Form of the New Democracy* was published in Issue 6, Volume 13, *New China.*

On 10 May he became president of Xiamen University.

In June, he left Beijing for Xiamen to take up his post. During his tenure, he built Xiamen University with his unique educational philosophy, educational thinking and school management ideas, and initiated educational reform.

In September, his article *The Significance of Land Reform and Its Influence on Industry and Commerce* was published in Issue 18, Volume 13, *New China.*

In November, his book *Research on Thought of China's Socioeconomic Transformation* was published by Shanghai Zhonghua Book Company. His article *Socioeconomic Systems of the Soviet Union and the United States and Their Global Policies* was published in Issue 2, Volume 3, *New Construction.*

On 21 December, his article *Stalin and the People* was published in the *Xiamen Daily.*

In the same year, he founded the Institute of Economic Research of Xiamen University and served as its director. He enrolled the first 8 graduate students of economics with a 2–3 year school system, and served as a personal tutor.

1951

In the same year, he reformed the finance department of Xiamen University. The Economics Department was separated from the Law School and merged with the Business School to form the School of Economics.

In January, his article *Purpose and Method of Political Learning* was published in Issue 1, Volume 14, *New China.*

In March, his article *Introduction to General Political Economy (Part I and II)* was published in the combined issue of 5 and 6, Volume 14, *New China.* His article *Understanding the Theory of Practice* was published in Issue 6, Volume 3, *New Construction.* His two articles *New Tasks of Political Economy* and *Research Directions in the New Economics Field* were published in *New Economics Essays*, Beijing October Publishing House.

From May to June, his article *Basic Principles Implemented in General Political Economy (Part I and II)* was published in Issue 10 and 11, Volume 14, *New China.*

In August, his article *The Communist Party of China and Marxism* was published in Issue 5, Volume 4, *New Construction.*

On 15 October, his article *The Significance of Land Reform and Its Impact on Industry and Commerce* was published in New Xiamen University.

1952

In July, Xiamen University established a research department under his auspices, of which he was the director. The original *Journal of Xiamen University* (called the *Xiamen University Quarterly* when it was first published in April 1926, renamed the *Xiamen University Journal* in 1931) resumed publication (the first university journal in the country to resume publication after the founding of the PRC), and he personally participated in its design, writing, reviewing and editing.

In September, his two articles *Marxist Political Economy and Bourgeois Political Economy* and *Editor's Postscript* were published in the first issue of the *Journal of Xiamen University (Finance & Economics).*

On 7 November, his article *The October Revolution and the Truth of Marxism* was published in the *Xiamen Daily*. In the same month, his article *Marxist Political Economy and Bourgeois Political Economy* was published in Issue 11, Vol 4, *New Construction*. It was renamed *How to Identify the Different Natures of Marxist Political Economy and Bourgeois Political Economy from Position, Viewpoint and Method* and collected in *Selected Works of Political Economy and Essays of History of Economic Thought* by Wang Ya'nan. His article *Relationships between Political Economy and General Sciences* was published in Issue 6 of *Journal of Literature, History & Philosophy*.

1953

In March, his article *Marx and Capital* was published in Issue 3, Volume 5, *New Construction*.

In May, his article *From the Introduction of Feudal Lordship Economy and Landlord Economy to Issues in the History of Chinese Social Development (Part I)* was published in Issue 3, Journal of *Literature, History & Philosophy*.

On 10 June, his article *Some Understandings of Studying Das Kapital* was published in the *Guangming Daily*.

On 15 July, the Faculty and Department Adjustment Committee of Xiamen University was established, with Wang as chairman.

On 29 November his article *Marxist Agricultural Theory and Policy and Agricultural Collectivisation in the Transitional Period* was published in *Jiefang Daily*.

1954

In February, his article *Literature & Art and Economic Basis (Part I)—Marxism-Leninist View on Literature & Art* was published in the first issue of the *Journal of Xiamen University (Literature & History)*. His article *From the Introduction to Lord Economy and Landlord Economy to the Issues in the History of Chinese Social Development (II)* was published in the second issue of *Journal of Literature, History & Philosophy*.

On 19 June, his article *Marxist-Leninist Views on State Legal Rights and the Draft Constitution of the People's Republic of China* was published in the New Xiamen University.

In July, his article *From the Introduction to Lord Economy and Landlord Economy to the Issues in the History of Chinese Social Development (Part III)* was published in Issue 7, *Journal of Literature, History & Philosophy. The Development and New Stage of Marxist Political Economy—Some Understandings in Studying Soviet Socialist Economy* was published in Issue 2, *Journal of Xiamen University (Finance & Economics)*.

In September, he was elected as a delegate to the First National People's Congress and also served as Vice-Chairman of the Fujian Provincial Political Consultative Conference, Chairman of the Fujian Provincial Federation of Teachers and Chairman of the Fujian Provincial Federation of Philosophical and Social Sciences.

In November, his book *The Outline of China's Feudal System of Landlord Economy* was published by the Shanghai East China People's Publishing House.

1955

From this year, the four departments of Statistics, Accounting, Finance and Commerce at the University were ordered to cease operations. The former School of Economics was abolished and the Department of Economics was established. It consists of five departments: Political Economy, Statistics, Accounting, Money and Credit, and Trade. With a stable team of teachers, it has accumulated strength for the revival and development of economics at Xiamen University in the future.

In February, his article *The Social Basis of Realism in A Dream of Red Mansions: Understanding the Social and Historical Origin of Realism in A Dream of Red Mansions from the Characteristics of China's Feudalism of Landlord Economy* was published in Issue 1, *Journal of Xiamen University (Social Sciences).*

In April, his article *The Publication of A Textbook of Political Economy is A New Era in the Study of Marxist Political Economy* was published in the second issue of *Journal of Xiamen University (Social Sciences).* His article *What Role Do the Basic Economic Laws of Socialism Play in the General Economic Movement in the Chinese Transition Period* was published in the second issue of *Journal of Xiamen University (Social Sciences)* (this article was later included in *Selected Papers on Political Economy*, renamed *How to Apply the Principles and Laws of Political Economy to Chinese Economic Reality in the Transition Period*).

In May, his article *Outstanding Contribution of A Textbook of Political Economy* was published in Issue 5, *New Construction* (later included in *Selected Papers on Political Economy* and renamed *How to Distinguish the Different Natures of Socialist Economic Form and Capitalist Economic Form by Category and Law*).

In June, the Institute of Philosophy and Social Sciences of the Chinese Academy of Sciences was established, and Wang was elected a member of the Institute and its Standing Committee.

1956

Wang led a delegation from Xiamen University and visited India.

In February, his article *China's First Five-Year Plan for the Development of the National Economy and the Economic Laws in the Transition Period* was published in Issue 1 of the *Economic Research Journal.*

On 8 March, his article *Talking About Some Fundamental Experience of Scientific Research with Comrades* was published in New Xiamen University.

In April his article T*he Origin, Nature, Structure and Research Methods of Capital* was published in Issue 2, *Journal of Xiamen University (Social Sciences).*

On 29 August, his article *On the Unification of Chinese Guiding Ideology and the Principles of Contention of a Hundred Schools of Thought* was published in *People's Daily.*

On 4 December, his article *Is the Driving Force for the Development of the Productive Forces the Contradiction within the Productive Forces? The relations of production? Or Something Else?* was published in the *Fujian Daily.* In the same month, his book *Marxist Theory of Population and Chinese Population was published by*

Beijing Science Press. His article *Theory Linking Practice of Political Economy* was published in the December issue of *Learning.*

1957

In January, his article *To Learn Lessons from the Study of Bourgeois Economics* was published in Issue 1, *New Construction.*

In February, Academic Forum was founded by him, and his article *Forward to the Periodical* was published in Issue 1, *Academic Forum.*

In May, his article *On Marxist Theory of Population and Chinese Population* was published in Issue 5, *New Construction.*

In July, his article *On Bureaucracy and Bureaucratism* was published in No. 7, *Academic Monthly.*

In October, his article *On the so-called bourgeois social sciences* was published in No. 10, *Academic Monthly.*

In November his work *Selected Papers on Political Economy* was published by Fujian People's Publishing House.

In the winter, he led a Chinese group of education experts and worked in Myanmar for 3 months.

1958

He returned from Myanmar in early January.

In May, his article *The Revolutionary and Scientific Tasks of the Critique of Keynesian Theory* was published in Issue 5, *New Construction.*

In September, he founded the Collection of Economic Survey and Research, which published its first issue in October of that year.

In October, his two articles *The Orientation and Practice of Chinese Economic Research—Forward to Collection of Economic Survey and Research* and *Self-criticism of Theory Linking Practice of Political Economy in Teaching* were published in *Collection of Economic Survey and Research (Episode 1).* His article *On Some Key Issues in the History of Chinese Social Development—Preface to the Russian Translation of the Book The Status of China's Semi-Feudal and Semi-Colonial Economy* was published in Issue 3, *Academic Forum.*

In the same year, the Fujian Provincial Party Committee made preparations for the establishment of Fuzhou University, and he gave it his full support, allocating almost half of the Faculty of Science (including experts and scholars he personally invited) to Fuzhou University.

1959

In January, with the approval of the Central Propaganda Department of the Chinese Communist Party, the *Economic Survey Research Journal* was renamed *China Economic Issues* and officially published.

In April, he was elected as a delegate to the Second National People's Congress. The article *On the Question of Commodity Production and the Role of the Law of Value in the Socialist Stage of Our Country from the Perspective of Developing Social Production* (with an appendix on the role of the law of value in the socialist economy of our country) was published in *China Economic Issues*, No. 4.

On 15 May, the article *Fully Utilizing the Positive Role of the Law of Value in Our Country's Socialist Economy* was published in the *People's Daily.* In the same month, the article *Learning Insights from the National Economic Conference* was published in *China Economic Issues*, Issue 5.

In June, the article *On Ma Yinchu's New Philosophy and New Economics* was published in *Journal of Xiamen University (Social Sciences Edition)*, Issue 1.

In July, the article *Calling on Cadres from the Working Class and Peasants to Study Political Economy* was published in *China Economic Issues*, No. 7.

In August, the article *Let's all study political economy* was published in *China Economic Issues*, Issue 8, and the article *Why should we study political economy* was published in *Red and Expert*, Issue 14. On 31 August, the article *The Strong Economic Contrast Between Two Social Systems* was published in *People's Daily*.

In October, the book *On the Different Economic Phenomena and Market Issues Under Two Social Systems* was published by Shanghai People's Publishing House.

In November, the article *On Capital and the Purpose and Method of Its Study (Part 1)* was published in *China Economic Issues*, Issue 11.

In December, the article *On Capital and the Purpose and Method of Its Study (Part 2)* was published in *China Economic Issues*, No. 12, and the article *What Makes Capital a Great Work Related to the Destiny of Mankind* was published in *Academic Monthly*, No. 12.

1960

In January, his article *How to Study Capital-On Capital and the Purpose and Method of Research (3)* was published in Issue 1, *China Economic Studies*. His article *Talking About Some Premise Recognitions in the Contention of a Hundred Schools of Thought* was published in Issue 1, *Academic Monthly*.

From February to March, his article *Re-discussion on the New Philosophy and New Economics of Ma Yinchu* was published in Issue 2, *New Construction*. *A Systematic Understanding of the General Structure of Capital (Parts 1 and 2): The Influence of the General Structure, Dialectics and System of Capital on the Study of Political Economy (Part 1 and Part 2)* were published in Issue 2 and 5, *China Economic Studies*.

In April, his article *Vigorously Carrying Out Economic Research Work and Accelerating Social Construction* was published in Issue 4, *China Economic Studies*.

From June to July, his articles *Dialectics Embodied in Capital (Part I, Part II)—On the Influence of the General Structure, Dialectics and its System on the Study of Political Economy, Part III and IV* were published successively in Issue 6 and 7, *China Economic Studies*.

In September, his article *The Influence of the Structure of the System of Capital on the Study of Political Economy—On the Influence of the General Structure, Dialectics and Its System on the Study of Political Economy, Part IV* was published in Issue 9, *China Economic Studies*.

On 9 November, his article *A Preliminary Investigation of the Theory of Taking Agriculture as the Foundation of the National Economy* was published in *Fujian Daily*.

1961

From April to May, his article *The Study and Application of Das Kapital* was published in Issue 1 and 2, *China Economic Studies*.

In September his article *On the Application of the System of Das Kapital to the Study of the Socialist Part of Political Economy* was published in Issue 2, *Journal of Xiamen University (Social Science).*

On 19 October, his article *On the Basic Knowledge and Basic Theory of Political Economy* was published in *Wenhui Daily.*

In November his article *The Popular Lecture on Capital—Preface to The Popular Lecture on Capital* was published in Issue 8, *China Economic Studies.*

On 5 December, his article *Keynesianism: Theory and Policy of State Monopoly Capitalism* was published in *Wenhui Daily.* In the same month, his article *The Systematic Understanding of Volume 1 of Capital* was published in Issue 3, *Journal of Xiamen University (Social Science).*

1962

On January 9–10, the article *Three Hundred Years of William Petty's Treatise of Taxes* was published successively in *Guangming Daily.* On the 13th, the article *The Practical Significance of Studying Classical Economics* was published in *People's Daily.* On the 19th, the article *Marx's Attitude and Method in Criticizing Bourgeois Political Economy* was published in *Jiefang Daily.*

In May, the article *A Comprehensive and Systematic Understanding of Capital* was published in *Academic Monthly*, Issue 5. On May 31, *Analysis and Critique of the Manifesto of the Capitalists (Summary of a Report)* was published in *Wenhui Daily.*

On July 26, the article *Some Theoretical Issues in Social and Economic Development* was published in *Wenhui Daily.*

In October, the article *Classical Political Economy and Its Development* was published in *New Construction*, Issue 10.

In November, the article *Marxist Political Economy and Classical Bourgeois Economics* was published in *Economic Research.*

In December, the article *Historical Materialism and the Methodology of Marxist Political Economy* was published in *China Economic Issues*, Issue 12. The article *The Method of Capital* was published in *Economic Research*, Issue 12.

1963

In March, his article *The Time Background of and the Class Historical Task of the Generation of Das Kapital—Commemorating the 80th Anniversary of Marx's Death* was published in issues 2 and 3 of *China Economic Studies.*

On 14 April, his article *Marx's Basic Principles on the Transformation of Capitalism from Free Form to Monopoly Form* was published in *Wenhui Daily.*

In May his article *Re-discussion on the Method of Das Kapital* was published in Issue 3, *Philosophical Research.*

In September, his article *Objects and Methods of Research on Das Kapital* was published in Issue 9, *China Economic Studies.*

In December, *Lectures on Capital* (Volume 1, co-edited with Yuan Zhenyue) was published by Shanghai People's Publishing House.

1964

In January his article *The Structure and System of Capital* was published in Issue 1, *China Economic Studies.* His article *Critique of Keynesian Economic Theory* was published in Issue 1, *New Construction.*

In March, his article *Study Summary and Issues of Volume I of Capital* was published in Issue 2 and 3, *China Economic Studies.*

In April, his article *Bourgeois Vulgar Economics is the Source and Foundation of Economic Theories of Various Vulgar Societies* was published in Issue 2, *Zhejiang Academic Journal.*

In May, his article *Capital is a Model of Political Economy and Class* was published in Issue 5, *Academic Monthly.*

From June to August, his article *Study Summary and Issues of Volume II of Capital* was published in issues 6, 7 and 8, *China Economic Studies.*

In October, his article *Several Issues Notable for Studying the Volume III of Das Kapital* was published in Issue 10, *China Economic Studies.*

In November, his article *The Theoretical Struggle Between the So-called Production Price Faction and the Value Faction on the Current Front of Political Economy* was published in Issue 11, *China Economic Issues.*

In December, he was elected as a delegate to the Third National People's Congress.

1965

In May, his article *Comrade Mao Zedong's Teaching on Research on the Theory of Marxism-Leninism with Purpose and Study of Das Kapital* was published in Issue 5, *China Economic Studies.*

In September, his article *Overview of the Main Content of Volume 5 of Das Kapital* was published in Issue 1, *Journal of Xiamen University (Social Science).*

In November, his article *The Theoretical Basis That Profit Is the Purpose of Social Production Can Never Be Found in Das Kapital* was published in Issue 5, *China Economic Studies.*

In December, his book S*elected Collection of Classical Political Economy of the Bourgeoisie* was published by Beijing Commercial Press.

1966

In January, his article *A Brief Description of the Last Passage of Volume III of Capital, Various Incomes and Their Sources* was published in Issue 1 of the *Journal of Xiamen University (Social Science).*

1967

The "red storm" swept through the campus of Xiamen University, and he was labelled a "reactionary academic authority", and thus criticized and put under house arrest.

1968

He was unable to do academic research and could only take the time to learn French on his own.

1969

In the spring he felt unwell.

In the summer, his condition worsened and he was paralyzed below the chest.

On 13 November, he died in Shanghai East China Hospital at the age of 68.

A Successful Model of the Sinicization of Political Economy

Hu Peizhao

This book is one of Wang Yanan's most important works from the 1940s. Conceived at Sun Yat-sen University and completed at Xiamen University, it has had a lasting impact both in China and abroad, becoming an immortal masterpiece.

A Strenuous Academic Career

Wang Yanan's academic career can be roughly divided into two phases: before 1938, he concentrated mainly on translation. In addition to collaborating with Guo Dali in translating classic British economic works such as Adam Smith's *The Wealth of Nations* (also known as *An Inquiry into the Nature and Causes of the Wealth of Nations*), David Ricardo's *Principles of Political Economy and Taxation*, and the Marxist classic *Das Kapital*, he also translated other works himself, such as the Finnish scholar Edward Westermarck's *History of Human Marriage*, the Japanese scholar Takamichi Koso's *History of Rent Thought*, the British economist C. A. Christ's *Introduction to Economics* and the British scholar Knight's *European Economic History*. After 1938, his focus shifted to research. He believed that "economics is a practical science" (Essays on Economic Science) and that without practice, true economics would be impossible.

At that time, mainstream economics in Chinese universities and society was largely imported from abroad, often filtered through countries such as Japan. University professors, as Marx criticized in *Das Kapital*, were like "little students, blind followers and echoers" of foreign teachings, parroting imported ideas with little innovation or adaptation to Chinese realities. The dominant economic discourse centered on the same old theories, often based on the four-part division of the economy (production, distribution, exchange, consumption) and the trinity formula (land-rent, capital-profit, labor-wages). This was criticized by Professor Xia Yande of Fudan University in 1937, who lamented the lack of an economic theory that took into account China's national conditions and needs. He noted that even after four or five decades of the introduction of economics in China, no original economic system based on the country's realities had been developed.

In response to this situation, Wang Yanan sought a different path by focusing on the actual conditions of Chinese society and its economy. In his article *Political*

Y. Wang, *The Basic Theory of Chinese Economy*,
https://doi.org/10.1007/978-981-95-6330-2

Economy in China published in *New Construction* in 1941, he advocated the establishment of *Chinese economics*. In 1942, he further argued that "we should study political economy from the standpoint of the Chinese people", and that through research we should gradually build a political economy specifically for Chinese scholars to study (*Essays on Economic Science*). He argued that in order to conduct meaningful research, we must first and foremost understand the nature of Chinese society. Without a clear understanding of the real characteristics of society, research would be futile.

His book *Outline of Chinese Economics* embodies these ideals and presents a successful model of Sinicizing political economy. The work creatively applies Marxist principles, views and methods to analyze the Chinese economy from the perspective of a Chinese scholar. In the preface, the author writes: "I have introduced the term 'Chinese economics'. If anyone, today or in the future, touches upon the Sinicisation of science, especially the Sinicisation of political economy, this book may offer some insights into the difficult process of exploration and trial and error involved.

The Great Debate on the Nature of Chinese Society

Before the founding of the People's Republic of China, the question of the nature of Chinese society sparked intense debate among various economists. Almost all academic groups and prominent scholars participated, each presenting their own perspective. Eventually, two clearly opposing camps emerged. One camp argued that after the Opium War, China became a semi-colonial, semi-feudal society in which feudal relations played a dominant role. The other camp argued that Chinese society had already fully transitioned to capitalism and that the feudal economy no longer existed. This debate, which began during Wang Yanan's student years, continued after he became a university lecturer and lasted until the founding of the new China.

Between these two perspectives, Wang Yanan sided with the view that pre-1949 China was a semi-feudal, semi-colonial society. In 1936 he remarked: "Under the present circumstances, where the capitalist forces have penetrated to the very base of society, the feudal organization, once supported by the exploitation of land, has naturally been eroded. However, due to the stranglehold of various imperialist powers, which want to turn China into a market for their manufactured goods and a supplier of raw materials, China has absolutely no chance of becoming a capitalist country. This state of stagnation is precisely the socioeconomic profile of the "semi-colonial society in transition" that we face today.

Although his phrasing differed slightly from the standard "semi-colonial, semi-feudal society" used by others, Wang Yanan often described it more specifically as a "semi-feudal, subordinate colonial" or "semi-feudal, semi-colonial" society. He also called it a "transitional society". However, he always felt the need to comprehensively and systematically provide economic evidence to scientifically determine the true nature of Chinese society, making it indisputable that China was indeed a semi-feudal, semi-colonial society. Wang Yanan devoted about four years to this investigation.

Finally, in 1946, he completed the work and published *The Basic Theory of Chinese Economy*. Creatively building on the structure, system and categories of the first volume of *Das Kapital* and applying its basic principles, Wang thoroughly and systematically examined, analyzed and clarified the economic form of ancient China. He convincingly demonstrated that, whether one looks at the categories of commodities, currency, markets, capital, wage relations, land relations or economic crises, or examines urban and rural areas, industry, agriculture or trade, the Chinese economy was not a purely capitalist or feudal economy. Instead, it was a unique mixture of feudal, capitalist, national and comprador economic relations. Each economic category bore the deep imprint of a semi-feudal, semi-colonial nature, showing that China's economic structure at that time was undoubtedly a semi-feudal, semi-colonial economy.

The Basic Theory of Chinese Economy was first published by the China Economic Science Press in Fujian in January 1946. In July 1947 it was reprinted by the Shanghai Life Bookstore, and in May 1950 it was published by the Sanlian Bookstore as part of the New China University series (*Life, Reading and New Knowledge*). In the post-liberation preface, Wang noted that although the 1947 edition had some additions and deletions, "its subject of study remained limited to the semi-feudal, semi-colonial economic form". He explained that since "China's economy is now in transition from a semi-feudal, semi-colonial state to a new democratic society", understanding this process requires a clear and scientific analysis of the semi-feudal, semi-colonial nature of the old Chinese economy.

China is Semi-Feudal, Semi-Colonial Economic Structure

We can get an idea of how the author shows that China's economy during this period was clearly a semi-feudal, semi-colonial structure by examining his analysis of several key economic categories.

1. Commodity and Monetary Forms Bear Feudal Characteristics and the Marks of Colonial Exploitation, Stagnating in a Backward State

Under capitalism, commodity production is highly developed and widespread, with labor itself becoming a commodity. More than 90% of people depend on selling their labor power for their livelihood, and the relationship between wage labor and capital becomes the axis around which society revolves. However, the commodity economy of pre-modern China had not yet reached this level, and was primarily characterized by the simple form of "selling to buy", indicating a pre-capitalist nature. For example, China's industrial sector consisted mainly of light textile industries and was largely based on handicrafts, with only a small proportion of products provided by modern industries. Manufacturing or processing industries were quantitatively "an extension of handicrafts" and qualitatively "a link between small-scale production and large-scale industry", still relying on the surplus labor of direct producers under old production methods. As a result, manufacturing became "a typical form of industrial production in a transitional society". This transitional form of industry, which acted as a link between small-scale production and large-scale industry, naturally produced goods of a dual nature—partly capitalist, partly pre-capitalist—and was controlled by both international and national commercial capital. All industrial and agricultural products entered the market in an irregular way. Many producers were supplied with raw materials, tools and funds by merchants, leading to a form of "predetermined production" for the merchants, where prices were set by the merchants before the products were even sold. The conditions of labor and the means of production were rooted in pre-capitalist methods of production, making it difficult to conclude that these products were entirely capitalist in nature.

In terms of labor as a commodity, feudal relations still prevailed and labor was not freely exchanged in the capitalist sense. Most of the labor that migrated from rural areas was not employed in factories or on farms, but remained untransformed into a commodity. Even for those who did enter the labor market, their labor was not fully commodified. China did not have a labor market where labor could be freely sold under capitalist conditions. Labor, "even if it has the appearance of a 'commodity", still retains the essence of a 'tribute'". Factories commonly used the exploitative "putting-out system", where workers were hired to produce goods at home, and the "contract labor system", where contractors hired workers for production, often including child apprentices and indentured laborers. Other forms of employment, such as apprenticeship, were also widespread, all closely linked to feudal relations and subject to extra-legal forms of exploitation, coercion and extortion. In foreign-owned factories, Chinese workers were treated with utter contempt. Agricultural workers were mostly serfs, working seasonally, as tenant laborers, or in mutual labor arrangements, with various bizarre forms of labor coexisting. The price of labor was unstable, allowing capitalists to arbitrarily depress wages and extract more surplus value. As a symbol of capitalism, therefore, labor as a commodity had only just begun to sprout in Chinese society. The theory that China was already a fully capitalist society was fundamentally at odds with reality.

With the underdevelopment of raw materials, the form of money was similarly backward. Before 1935, China was on the silver standard, a century behind Europe and eight years behind India. China, Mexico and Spain were the last three countries in the world to maintain the silver standard. The monetary system was also highly complex, with both coins and paper money in circulation. Coins included silver dollars, foreign coins and copper coins, while paper money came in many varieties, issued by the government, banks and private companies, and even foreign currencies circulated freely in China. The monetary form bore the marks of a simple, feudal and colonial system. After the currency reform of 1935, while the chaotic monetary system was unified, it took on a fiscal and commercial character and became a tool for exploiting the people. When the government faced financial difficulties, it resorted to printing paper money to fill the gap. This reckless issuing of money intensified commercial speculation. The form of commodity money in ancient China clearly bore feudal characteristics and the marks of imperialist exploitation, and it remained stuck in a backward state.

2. The Backwardness and Diversity of Capital Forms

The underdevelopment and complexity of commodities and currency determined the backwardness and diversity of capital forms. In any developed capitalist society, the economy is not purely homogeneous, and some relatively backward sectors and pre-capitalist forms of capital remain, albeit on a small scale and with little influence. But China was different. Pre-capitalist forms of capital not only existed, but also played a decisive role in hindering the development of modern capital. Ranking the forms of capital by their size and influence, commercial capital had an absolute advantage, followed by usury capital and banking capital, with industrial capital being the weakest.

The Chinese commercial capital was built on the foundation of the landlord economy, where land could be freely bought and sold. As a result, commercial capital flowed easily into land, with merchants using their profits to buy land and become landlords. Merchants and landlords were therefore closely linked. Through land ownership, they also established political ties, often forming alliances with government officials. Historically, prominent merchants were able to interact with the government, with some even rising to high positions. With the invasion of imperialism, commercial capital followed foreign capital and served as compradors, catering to foreign powers by "collecting local products and managing global goods" for them. Commercial capital grew ruthlessly, "like a tiger with wings", creating insurmountable difficulties for Industrial Capital caught between commercial and foreign capital and hindering its development.

Firstly, Industrial Capital had no guarantee of profit. What little profit it could make was what was left over after commercial capital had already taken its share, making it difficult to accumulate capital and expand production.

Second, the unstable social environment made industrial capitalists reluctant to increase fixed assets or adopt advanced technology. Instead, they opted for flexible and mobile forms of capital, choosing methods that were "easy to assemble and disassemble" and "stop whenever necessary". In times of crisis, they could simply lay off workers to minimize losses, thus avoiding significant depreciation of fixed assets. As a result, China's Industrial Capital had an extremely low organic composition, with obsolete tools everywhere as cheap labor displaced machines.

Third, while mercantile capital rarely turned into industrial capital, industrial capital easily turned back into mercantile capital, especially under the threat of growing inflation. Inflation only made matters worse, exacerbating the difficulties of industrial capital. It was common for industrialists to resort to 'commercialization of industry' or 'commercialization of industry' as a survival strategy, as it became the most effective way to escape financial ruin. These challenges made "industrial production an intimidating path for Chinese entrepreneurs".

During and after the anti-Japanese war, industrial capital faced even more difficulties. Bureaucratic capital took advantage of the situation, amassing wealth by nationalizing private property, transforming private wealth into "public" wealth under the guise of state ownership, and rapidly expanding its influence. Meanwhile, some of China's capital was absorbed by foreign capital, becoming "foreign capital operating under Chinese names". Wang Yanan sharply criticized this, saying: "Many of the new enterprises built on the foundations of enemy and puppet industries, as well as the social wealth preserved by various means, have been directly or indirectly siphoned off abroad, facilitated by the collusion between bureaucrats and compradors." Feudal comprador commercial capital, combined with foreign capital, dominated and exploited industrial capital (national capital), making it impossible for industrial capital to flourish or for capitalism to develop fully in China.

3. The Coexistence of Feudal Economic Crises of Production Shortage and Capitalist Economic Crises of Overproduction

Wang Yanan believed that China's economy, influenced by both feudalism and capitalism, experienced economic crises of a dual nature. These crises had the characteristics of both traditional feudal economic crises and capitalist economic crises, exposing Chinese society to the double pains of economic instability. The first type of crisis was the feudal production shortage crisis caused by natural disasters and man-made calamities. The second type was the capitalist crisis of overproduction, which was transferred to China and aggravated its own unique economic crisis. When global capitalist economic crises hit, raw materials produced specifically for the international market could not be sold, while foreign goods flooded in. Overproduction and shortages thus coexisted. In 1932, for example, agricultural production boomed in various provinces, causing grain prices to fall by 30%. However, 14.4 million dan (a traditional unit of weight) of rice was imported into Guangdong from overseas, while 10 million dan of wheat was piling up on railway lines in northern China, yet Shanghai continued to import large quantities of wheat every year. Similarly, the domestic market was oversupplied with tea, while tea from Ceylon, India and Java continued to flood the market; raw silk was overproduced, but Japan and India continued to export large quantities of artificial silk and silk fabrics; sugar production in Guangdong and Jiangxi exceeded demand, while sugar from Southeast Asia and Japan saturated the market. This double economic crisis severely damaged China's industrial and agricultural production, making recovery long and difficult.

Although the economic crisis had two dimensions, it cannot be explained by a simplistic binary theory. Instead, it requires a unified analysis of the production process, since the two dimensions are interrelated, one being primary and the other secondary. The primary crisis was "rural, characterized by a chronic and persistent shortage of production". The secondary crisis arose from the global capitalist economic crisis, which exacerbated the inherent domestic crisis. In other words, the impact of foreign capitalist economic crises on China was mediated by its internal, pre-existing economic crisis. Therefore, the ultimate cause of China's economic crisis was the transition of its economy from a natural economy to a more commercialized one, with the increasing commodification of production. However, this commercialization was based on small-scale production, which was relatively underdeveloped in terms of both type and scale.

Small-scale production societies are generally agricultural, where land is more productive than industry. The surplus products that serve as the basis for reproduction, such as rent, come primarily from agriculture. With the development of foreign trade, commercial capital, subordinated to foreign capital, came to dominate both agricultural and industrial production, extracting most of the surplus products or surplus value. In unequal foreign trade relations, a significant part of this surplus value was exported abroad through comprador trade. The prosperity of the cities and the luxury of the state depended directly on the surplus value of agriculture, which was extracted through taxes, land rents, usury and commercial activities that further burdened agriculture. The more agriculture was taxed, the less capital remained to invest in agricultural production. As a result, the productivity of the land gradually declined, and agricultural production, especially grain, steadily declined.

"Our agrarian, production-deficient, chronic economic crisis," Wang argued, "is the result of this series of interrelated economic activities—small-scale commodity production, the transformation of products into commodities by commerce, the dominance of commerce over industry, the higher profitability of commerce compared to industry, the regulation of profits by interest rates, various forms of unequal exchange, the flow of capital to the cities and abroad, the interaction of primitive forms of capital in the countryside and the circulation of capital among them, the displacement of machinery and even animals by labor—all these factors have combined to produce this systemic problem." This inherent problem made China vulnerable to capitalist economic crises, turning a single-layer crisis into a double-layer crisis.

Wang Yanan's analysis was deeply insightful and vividly revealed the nature of China's semi-feudal and semi-colonial society. The book had a wide and lasting impact and was reprinted several times. In 1957, after revision and expansion, it was republished by the People's Publishing House as *A Study of China's Semi-Feudal and Semi-Colonial Economic Structure*, and translated into Japanese and Russian, among other languages. Just as Guo Moruo's *A Study of Ancient Chinese Society* was seen as the Chinese version of Engels' *The Origin of the Family, Private Property and the State*, Wang Yanan's work has been seen as the Chinese version of *The Capital*. While it may not be on a par with *Das Kapital* in terms of scope and influence, Wang's work, which used the economic categories and basic principles of the first volume of *Das Kapital* to analyze China's economic structure, was undeniably groundbreaking and unparalleled in Chinese economic discourse at the time.

Conclusion

After 1949, the prevailing view of Chinese society before 1949 was generally described as a "semi-colonial, semi-feudal society". However, there were also those who described it as a "semi-feudal, semi-colonial society". It seemed that the two terms could be used interchangeably, and few questioned the differences between the two. In reality, the order of "semi-colonial" and "semi-feudal" carries considerable weight. Placing "semi-colonial" first implies that colonialism was the primary determinant of China's social structure, suggesting that China lacked feudal characteristics before the Opium Wars and that feudalism emerged as a by-product of colonialism. Such a view would imply that China's transition from a feudal to a semi-feudal, semi-capitalist system was driven by the invasion of the Western powers, which is a false interpretation.

Although the China of the late Qing dynasty was corrupt and inefficient, it was still an independent state before the Opium Wars, not a semi-colony or a colony. From the perspective of feudal development, China may not have embarked on a capitalist path as early as Europe in the sixteenth century, but it was not stagnant either. There was already a degree of commodity economy, particularly in the Ming and Qing dynasties, when it grew rapidly. Before the Opium Wars, industries such as cotton spinning, silk weaving, ceramics, metallurgy, salt production and lacquerware were all supported by the wage labor characteristic of capitalist workshops. These industries were scattered throughout the south-eastern coastal areas and inland river towns, where trade and commerce flourished. Phrases such as "the bustling crowds pursue profit, the ebb and flow of people seek wealth" and "business thrives throughout the world, wealth flows to the three rivers" were not just poetic expressions, but historical descriptions of the vibrant marketplace of the time.

This shows that within the broad framework of China's feudal system there were already nascent capitalist economic relations, although they had not yet become dominant. Nevertheless, these nascent forces should not be underestimated. Even if the division between semi-feudal and semi-capitalist is not a strict 50/50 split, it could still be said that China had developed a predominantly feudal but partly capitalist economic structure before the Opium Wars. Without this structure, the British Empire would not have been able to establish trading ports such as the "Five Ports" immediately after the Opium Wars. Cities such as Shanghai, which already had a population of two or three hundred thousand at the time, and Xiamen, which opened up to British trade as early as 1670 (the tenth year of Emperor Kangxi's reign), bear this out.

There is also a consensus: "Even without foreign capitalist influence, China would have slowly developed into a capitalist society". This further illustrates that the seeds of capitalism were already germinating in China before the Opium Wars, and that "semi-feudalism" did not arise solely as a result of colonialism. In other words, the nature of Chinese society before 1949 was characterized by the "semi-feudalism" that existed before the Opium Wars, which was then compounded by "semi-colonialism" after the Opium Wars to form the "semi-feudal, semi-colonial society". Clearly, "semi-feudalism" preceded "semi-colonialism", not the other way around. The deleterious effect of the Opium Wars was that the Western powers stunted the development of the capitalist elements that had already begun to emerge in China, locking them into the semi-feudal, semi-colonial structure that suited their interests.

Wang Yanan's conclusion in *The Basic Theory of Chinese Economy* that ancient China was a "semi-feudal, semi-colonial society" is credible. Scholarship demands precision, not ambiguity. Among the many writings that survive from the great debates of the time, Wang Yanan's work stands out as a rare, comprehensive and systematic study of the economic structure of China's semi-feudal, semi-colonial society.

MIX
Papier aus verantwortungsvollen Quellen
Paper from responsible sources
FSC® C105338
FSC
www.fsc.org

If you have any concerns about our products,
you can contact us on
ProductSafety@springernature.com

In case Publisher is established outside the EU,
the EU authorized representative is:
Springer Nature Customer Service Center GmbH
Europaplatz 3, 69115 Heidelberg, Germany

Printed by Libri Plureos GmbH
in Hamburg, Germany